Algorithms and
Data Structures in C++

Algorithms and Data Structures in C++

Leendert Ammeraal
Hogeschool van Utrecht, The Netherlands

JOHN WILEY & SONS
Chichester • New York • Brisbane • Toronto • Singapore

Other Wiley Editorial Offices

John Wiley & Sons, Inc., 605 Third Avenue,
New York, NY 10158-0012, USA

Jacaranda Wiley Ltd, 33 Park Road, Milton,
Queensland 4064, Australia

John Wiley & Sons (Canada) Ltd, 22 Worcester Road,
Rexdale, Ontario M9W 1L1, Canada

John Wiley & Sons (Asia) Pte Ltd, 2 Clementi Loop #02-01,
Jin Xing Distripark, Singapore 0512

British Library Cataloguing in Publication Data

A catalogue record for this book is available from the British Library

ISBN   0 471 96355 0

Produced from camera-ready copy supplied by the author using MS Word for Windows version 6.0
Printed and bound in Great Britain by Bookcraft (Bath) Ltd
This book is printed on acid-free paper responsibly manufactured from sustainable forestation,
for which at least two trees are planted for each one used for paper production.

Contents

Preface

This book is related to *Programs and Data Structures in C* (or *Programs*, for short), the first edition of which was published in 1987 and the second in 1992. The latter book was published at a time when the C language was rather unusual for textbooks, so I motivated this choice of language in a considerable portion of its preface, especially for those who were using Pascal and had to be persuaded to switch to C. These days the situation is different. Although not everyone has made the move from C to C++, it seems to me that this step requires less persuasion. Since the present book is *not* intended to explain this language, you may also need a book on C++, such as *C++ for Programmers*, Second Edition, also from Wiley.

Although C++ can very well be used simply as 'a better C', I have benefited from the class concept in this book more than I did in previous ones. In comparison with *Programs*, you will also find many more algorithms. Each algorithm is implemented as a ready-to-run program, and I have done my best to make these programs as efficient and as portable as possible.

When writing a book about algorithms and programming, it is always a point of serious deliberation in what degree program readability should be sacrificed to improve efficiency, generality, portability and robustness. I often had to compromise, hopefully making programs readable enough for you (and myself) to understand them, but I am aware that I could have improved readability if I had completely ignored the other aspects. On the other hand, many programs in this book would have been less readable if I had written them only for *users*, who do not see any source code and who judge programs only by the way they execute. For example, if a number is read from the keyboard in a commercial program, there should be a check to see if the user has really entered numeric data in an acceptable format. Most textbooks omit such checks because they tend to deflect the reader's attention from the subject under discussion. My book is not an exception in this regard. When speaking about readability, efficiency and so on, I did not mention *correctness* because it goes without saying that any program should be correct. I hope you will not find any of mine that are not, but if so please let me know.

When discussing an algorithm, I frequently referred to other places in the book that may be helpful, but I tried to avoid a habit that sometimes irritates me in other books, namely that of using a complicated example as an extension of a previous one, which in turn is based on a previous one, and so on, in such a way that skipping one example makes many others that follow incomprehensible. I always prefer simple examples to possibly more impressive and realistic ones.

In Chapter 1 you will find some material that is closely related to the C++ language itself. You may skip the sections about templates and exception handling if you already have a thorough knowledge of these subjects, but it would surprise me if this applied to most readers.

The 'arithmetic algorithms' of Chapter 2 include not only some traditional ones, such as radix conversion and exponentiation, also found in my *Programs* book, but also the exciting subject of multi-precision arithmetic. For this purpose, a C++ class, *large*, is briefly discussed here, along with some application programs, such as one to compute π in, say, a thousand decimals. The implementation of this class can be found in Appendix A.

Chapter 3 discusses more than ten sorting algorithms, among which is one for external sorting, known as *balanced multiway merging*. The C++ template concept enabled me to present these sorting algorithms in the form of generally applicable, reusable and nevertheless readable code. Because of its relation to sorting, there is also a section about finding the nth largest element of a sequence, which, for example, can be used to compute the *median* efficiently.

In Chapter 4, the traditional subjects of linked lists, stacks and queues are supplemented by a section about the use of a stack for recursion removal.

The subjects of binary search and hashing can be found in Section 5, along with the Boyer–Moore text-searching algorithm.

Most of Chapters 6, 7 and 8 is about trees. At the end of Chapter 8 you will find the Huffman algorithm for file compression.

Chapter 9, an introduction to graph algorithms, includes programs for topological sorting, CPM project planning and route planning based on Dijkstra's shortest-path algorithm.

Chapter 10 deals with the generation of permutations and combinations as well as two classical subjects of Operations Research: the knapsack problem and dynamic programming.

Finally, Chapter 11 is about interpreting and translating simple arithmetic expressions. It uses the *recursive descent* method to develop both an interpreter and a compiler for a tiny language.

At the moment, the source code listed in this book can be downloaded (as a single file, *algdscpp.zip*) via anonymous FTP, directory pub/ammeraal, from ftp.expa.fnt.hvu.nl or pitel_lnx.ibk.fnt.hvu.nl. We will do our best to continue this facility. My email address is ammeraal@ibk.fnt.hvu.nl.

I am grateful to Frans den Heijer and Jan Zuurbier for their comments on the manuscript and to Wim van der Poel for useful discussions about multi-precision arithmetic.

Leendert Ammeraal
January 1996

1

Some Aspects of Programming in C++

1.1 Introduction

Although there are many simple programming problems for which the C++ class concept is not really essential, it is a good idea to group data and related operations together into a class. Even if we hardly benefit from this, the experience gained by this approach may come in very handy later, when we will be dealing with more complex applications. Let us illustrate this use of a class by converting a positive integer into a Roman numeral. To understand the way this is programmed, we must first get familiar with the rules of the game. Here are the Roman digits we will be using:

M	*D*	*C*	*L*	*X*	*V*	*I*
1000	500	100	50	10	5	1

Things are simple as long as the values of the digits do not increase. For example, we can read *MDXXIII* as the nonincreasing value sequence 1000, 500, 10, 10, 1, 1, 1, forming together 1523. The following 2-character pairs have special meanings; in each pair, the lower value, placed before the higher one, is to be subtracted from it, as the given values indicate:

CM	*CD*	*XC*	*XL*	*IX*	*IV*
900	400	90	40	9	4

For example, the value of *CM* is $1000 - 100 = 900$. One way to convert a number to Roman is by trying to subtract the largest of the above values, 1000, as often from the

1

number as possible, each time placing the character *M* in the Roman numeral we are constructing. If this is no longer possible, we try 900, the second largest of the above numbers, adding the Roman equivalent *CM* to the string if subtracting 900 succeeds, and so on. The following program is based on this principle:

```
// roman1: From decimal to Roman.
#include <iostream.h>
#include <stdlib.h>

class Roman {
private:
   enum {L=100};
public:
   Roman(unsigned n);
   char a[L];
};

Roman::Roman(unsigned n)
{  int v[] = {1000, 900, 500, 400, 100, 90, 50,
        40, 10, 9, 5, 4, 1}, len = sizeof(v)/sizeof(*v);
   char *r[] = {"M", "CM", "D", "CD", "C", "XC", "L",
        "XL", "X", "IX", "V", "IV", "I"};
   int pos = 0;
   for (int i=0; i<len; i++)
   {  while (v[i] <= n)
        {  if (pos + 3 > L)
           {  cout << " Number too large.\n"; exit(1);
           }
           a[pos++] = r[i][0];
           if (r[i][1]) a[pos++] = r[i][1];
           n -= v[i];
        }
   }
   a[pos] = '\0';
}

int main()
{  unsigned n;
   cout << "Enter a decimal number: ";
   cin >> n;
   cout << "Roman: " << Roman(n).a << endl;
   return 0;
}
```

Here is a demonstration of this program:

```
Enter a decimal number: 1999
Roman: MCMXCIX
```

This Roman numeral is composed of *M* (= 1000), *CM* (= 900), *XC* (= 90) and *IX* (= 9).

A program to do the conversion in the opposite direction, converting a given Roman numeral into a normal integer value, will be given at the end of Section 1.4.

Readability, correctness and efficiency

The *Roman* constructor, which does almost all the work, could be made more readable in two rather dubious ways:

1. We could have omitted the test on overflow for the result array *a*.
2. We could have used the standard library functions *strlen* and *strcat*.

As for the first point, array overflow is a very nasty error. Since the user may enter very large numbers (especially if *int* values take 4 bytes), it is doubtful whether we can call the program correct if we omitted this test. We could use the second above point, replacing the fragment after the declarations and initialization of the two arrays with:

```
number = n; strcpy(a, "");
for (int i=0; i<len; i++)
{  while (v[i] <= n)
   {  if (strlen(a) + strlen(r[i]) >= L)
      {  cout << "Number too large.\n"; exit(1);
      }
      strcat(a, r[i]);
      n -= v[i];
   }
}
}
```

Although we would not notice the difference, this would take substantially more computing time because each execution of the *strlen* function results in a loop that looks for the terminating null character. Consequently, there are three nested loops in this latest fragment, while there were only two in the corresponding original form.

Big-oh notation

Unlike program *roman*1, many algorithms that contain nested loops tend to take more computer time than we like. Besides simply measuring a program's running time, using either a watch or the computer's internal clock, we can approach the subject of efficiency from an analytic angle. In many cases, running time $T(n)$ is a function of the input size n. For example, a certain program that sorts an array of n numbers may have running time

$$T(n) = cn^2$$

where c is a constant. Although the value of c is not irrelevant, the fact that running time is a quadratic function of the input size n is far more important. We therefore use the so-called '*big-oh*' notation, and say that, in our example, running time $T(n)$ is $O(n^2)$. In general, we say that $T(n)$ is $O(f(n))$ if there are nonnegative constants c and n_0 such that $T(n) \leq cf(n)$ whenever $n \geq n_0$. According to this definition, the fact that '$T(n)$ is $O(n^2)$' implies that '$T(n)$ is $O(n^3)$', but the latter is a weaker statement than the former, and in cases like this it is customary to ignore such weaker statements. We also use the terms *growth rate* and *time complexity* for the function $f(n)$ used in the notation $O(f(n))$. In

Chapter 3 we will see that there are sorting algorithms with time complexity $n \log n$ instead of n^2. It will be clear that this is an enormous improvement, provided that the length n of the sequence to be sorted is large. With present-day computers we can more easily accommodate such large sequences than we could, say, 20 years ago, so considerations of efficiency (or *complexity*, as computer scientists would rather say) are at least as important with fast modern computers as they used to be with slower computers of the past.

1.2 References and Reference Counting

There are normally several reasonable solutions to a C++ programming problem, even if this problem is very elementary. Suppose that we want a function to exchange (or 'swap') two *int* variables, say, *i* and *j*. One way to do this is by using pointer parameters, as any C programmer would do:

```
void swap1(int *p, int *q)
{   int w = *p; *p = *q; *q = w;
}
```

Usage:

```
swap1(&i, &j);
```

In C++ we can do this also in the following way, using reference parameters:

```
void swap2(int &x, int &y)
{   int t = x; x = y; y = t;
}
```

Usage:

```
swap2(i, j);
```

Actually, these two solutions will probably result in the same compiled code. In general, the style of *swap2* may lead to slightly simpler function code, but it has the drawback that a call to this function alone does not reveal the fact that the arguments can be changed, as the ampersands indicate in the above call to *swap1*.

Using *const* for reference and pointer parameters

C programmers will be familiar with the use of the *const* keywords in function definitions or declarations. For example, if we write

```
int fun(const char *p);
```

then this usage of *const* indicates that *fun* will not modify the character string argument. In fact, it makes such modifications impossible. The same principle applies to reference arguments, as the following example illustrates:

```
#include <string.h>
struct stype {char a[10]; int n;};

int slen(const stype &s)
{   return fun(s.a);
}
```

This use of *const* makes it impossible for *slen* to change either the array member *a* or the *int* member *n* of the argument. Using *fun* here is possible only because this function also has a *const* argument, as we have just seen. In other words, the above function *slen* would not be correct if the declaration of *fun* had been written as follows:

```
int fun(char *p);
```

If this had been allowed, it would have been possible for *fun* to modify the characters pointed to by *p*, that is, the array *s.a*, which would imply that *const* in function *slen* is ineffective. In reality, this *const* keyword guarantees that *slen* can modify *s* neither directly nor indirectly by means of another function.

The relationship between a (formal) parameter and an argument is similar to the left-hand and right-hand sides of an assignment. For two (compatible) pointers *p* and *q*, the assignment

```
p = q;
```

may or may not be allowed, depending on *p* or *q* being *const* pointers. As the following fragment shows, there are four cases to consider:

```
char *p, *q;            // Assignment p = q allowed
const char *p, *q;      // Assignment p = q allowed
const char *p; char *q; // Assignment p = q allowed
char *p; const char *q; // Assignment p = q not allowed
```

As the last comment indicates, assigning a *const* pointer to a non-*const* pointer is not allowed. If *p = q* were allowed in this last case, a subsequent assignment such as **p = 'a'* would be a sneaky way of modifying the character string pointed to by the *const* pointer *q*. Fortunately, such confusing code has been made impossible.

Classes and *const*

In connection with classes we can use the *const* keyword in two ways that may require clarification. Consider this example:

```
class num {
public:
    num(int k): j(k){i = k;}
    int ivalue() const {return i;}
private:
    int i;
    const int j;
};
```

Since *const* has been used for *j*, we cannot give *j* its initial value in the *num* constructor by means of an assignment $j = k$. Instead, initialization of the form $j(k)$ is required here. This is different for *i*, as this example shows. If we like, we can also initialize *i* instead of assigning a value to this variable. We then write

```
num(int k): i(k), j(k){}
```

The *const* keyword also occurs in the *ivalue* member function. Here it indicates that this function will not modify any data members of the class. For example, we cannot change the data member *i*, as in

```
int ivalue() const {return i++;}   // Error
```

because of the *const* keyword. It is highly recommended to use *const* in this way wherever possible because this makes the function clearer to the reader, it prevents possible unintended changes in data members, and it may lead to more efficient code.

Reference counting

Straightforward implementations of classes with dynamically allocated memory will sometimes suffer from inefficiency due to copying activities that can be avoided. For example, consider the following application of a class *ints*:

```
// intsapp: Application of class ints: dynamic arrays.

#include "ints0.h"
// ints0.h is a preliminary version;
// it is to be replaced with ints.h, see below.

int main()
{   int u[3] = {10, 15, 8},
        v[5] = {7, 12, 5, 40, 19};
    ints A(u, 3), B = A;
    cout << A.len() << endl;            // Output: 3
    cout << B.len() << endl;            // Output: 3
    B = ints(v, 5);
    cout << A.len() << endl;            // Output: 3
    cout << B.len() << endl;            // Output: 5
    return 0;
}
```

As this program illustrates, *ints* objects can contain *int* arrays of any length. (Some other aspects of such *dynamic arrays* will be discussed in Section 1.5.) Although this example seems to be very simple, it requires both a copy constructor and an assignment operator to make deep copies. After all, we want *B* to be independent from *A*: although initially these two objects are identical, this must no longer be the case after assigning a new value to *B*. The following header file, *ints0.h*, shows the declarations of the constructors, the destructor and the assignment operator:

```
// ints0.h: Dynamic arrays without reference counting.
#include <iostream.h>

class ints {
public:
    ints(){p = NULL; length=0;}
    ints(int *a, int n);
    ints(const ints &r);
    ~ints(){delete[]p;}
    ints &operator=(const ints &r);
    int len()const {return length;}
private:
    int *p;
    int length;
};
```

This implementation of class *ints* is straightforward and not particularly efficient, as we will see in a moment. Here is the corresponding implementation file:

```
// ints0.cpp: Implementation of class ints
//       (preliminary version: no reference counting).

#include "ints0.h"

ints::ints(int *a, int n)
{   p = new int[n];
    for (int i=0; i<n; i++)
        p[i] = a[i];
    length = n;
}

ints::ints(const ints &r)
{   length = r.length;
    p = new int[length];
    for (int i=0; i<length; i++)
        p[i] = r.p[i];
}

ints &ints::operator=(const ints &r)
{   if (&r != this)
    {   delete[] p;
        length = r.length;
        p = new int[length];
        for (int i=0; i<length; i++)
            p[i] = r.p[i];
    }
    return *this;
}
```

To increase readability, many member functions are defined inside their class in this book. They are defined outside their class if they contain loops. The Borland C++ compiler gives the warning *Functions containing* ***for*** *are not expanded inline* if a member function containing a for-statement is defined inside a class.

Figure 1.1 shows that the integers 10, 15 and 8 are stored separately for *A* and for *B*.

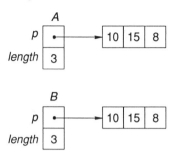

Figure 1.1 *Situation after **ints** A(u, 3), B = A; (straightforward solution)*

In this way there is no problem when we assign a new value to *B* by executing

```
B = ints(v, 5);
```

Yet duplicating these integers seems a waste of memory. It looks attractive to change our solution in such a way that we could replace Figure 1.1 with Figure 1.2:

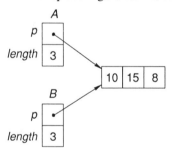

Figure 1.2 *Failed attempt to save memory space*

Unfortunately, we now have a problem when the above new assignment to *B* is to take place, since neither *B* nor the memory pointed to by *B* contains any information about *A* referring to the same memory area. In other words, it is not clear whether or not this area can be released.

There is a rather sophisticated solution to this problem. It is based on keeping track of the number of pointers that refer to the area in question. This *reference-counting* solution is also known as *lazy copying*, and clarified by Figures 1.3 and 1.4.

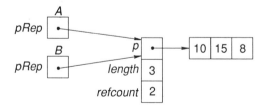

Figure 1.3 *Situation after **ints** A(u, 3), B = A; (with reference counting)*

Allocating memory for *B* is done only when this is really necessary. This is the case when a different value is assigned to *B*. The situation changes then as shown in Figure 1.4.

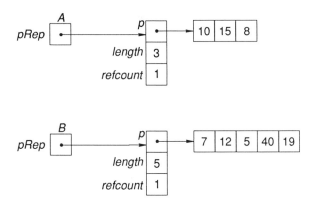

Figure 1.4 *Situation after B = ints(v, 5); (with reference counting)*

This solution with reference counting is more complex in that there is a separate structure associated with the memory area that contains the actual data. Besides a pointer to this area, we store the array length and a reference count in this structure, as the following header file shows:

```
// ints.h: Dynamic arrays based on reference counting.

#include <iostream.h>

class ints {
public:
   ints()
   {  pRep = new intsrep;
      pRep->p = NULL;
      pRep->length = pRep->refcount = 1;
   }

   ints(int *a, int n);   // Defined in ints.cpp

   ints(const ints &r)
   {  r.pRep->refcount++;
      pRep = r.pRep;
   }

   ~ints()
   {  if (--pRep->refcount == 0)
      {  delete[] pRep->p;
         delete pRep;
      }
   }
```

```
    ints &operator=(const ints &r)
    {   r.pRep->refcount++;
        if (--pRep->refcount == 0)
        {   delete[] pRep->p;
            delete pRep;
        }
        pRep = r.pRep;
        return *this;
    }
    int len()const {return pRep->length;}
private:
    struct intsrep{int *p, length, refcount;} *pRep;
};
```

'Copying an object' does not imply that the actual data is immediately copied; instead, the reference count is increased by 1. Similarly, a destructor decreases this reference count, and both this additional structure and the area pointed to are actually released only when this reference count becomes zero. The implementation file is a very small one because we have adopted the convention of defining member functions inside their class unless they contain loops:

```
// ints.cpp: Implementation of class ints.
#include "ints.h"

ints::ints(int *a, int n)
{   pRep = new intsrep;
    pRep->p = new int[n];
    for (int i=0; i<n; i++) pRep->p[i] = a[i];
    pRep->length = n;
    pRep->refcount = 1;
}
```

Although reference counting makes the implementation more complex, this does not affect the application program. Program *intsapp* needs no modifications other than replacing the file name *ints0.h* with *ints.h* in a *#include* line almost at the top.

1.3 Function Templates

To demonstrate a general principle, it is often desirable to start with a special case and generalize this later. Working the other way round, starting with a general form and ending with special cases, may seem more logical but is usually hard to understand. This is why programming textbooks frequently deal with integers, where in practice other data types may be more useful. This book is not an exception. However, the C++ language offers a new concept to make programs, and in particular, functions, more general than we are used to in other languages. We will discuss this here, so from now on you may benefit from this new language concept, known as *function templates*.

Suppose that we often want to exchange two objects. Instead of starting with the most general solution, we begin with three special cases. First, we exchange the values of two variables of type *int*:

```
void swap(int &x, int &y)
{  int w = x; x = y; y = w;
}
...
int i = 5, j = 8;
swap(i, j);  // i = 8 and j = 5
```

Second, we swap two pointers to characters:

```
void swap(char* &p, char * &q)
{  char *w = p; p = q; q = w;
}

char *month1 = "April", *month4 = "January";
swap(month1, month4); // month1 = "January", month4 = "April"
```

As a third special case, we swap two objects of type *point*:

```
struct point{float x, y;} P = {3, 4}, Q = {8, 2};
...
void swap(point &x, point &y)
{  point w = x; x = y; y = w;
}
...
swap(P, Q);   // P = (8, 2) and Q = (3, 4)
```

Thanks to the principle of function *overloading*, we can use two functions *swap* in the same program file. The compiler can tell them apart because of their parameter types. Since these two functions are almost identical, it is desirable to write only one *function template* instead of these two functions. The following complete program demonstrates how this can be done:

```
// swap: Demonstration of a swap template.
#include <iostream.h>
struct point{float x, y;};

template <class T>
void swap(T &x, T &y)
{  T w = x; x = y; y = w;
}
int main()
{  int i = 5, j = 8;
   char *month1 = "April", *month4 = "January";
   point P = {3, 4}, Q = {8, 2};
   swap(i, j); // Two integers swapped
   swap(month1, month4); // Two pointers swapped
   swap(P, Q); // Two points swapped
   cout << "i=" << i << "  j=" << j << endl;
   cout << month1 << endl << month4 << endl;
   cout << "P: (" << P.x << ", " << P.y << ")\n";
   cout << "Q: (" << Q.x << ", " << Q.y << ")\n";
   return 0;
}
```

The output of this program is shown below:

```
i=8   j=5
January
April
P:  (8,  2)
Q:  (3,  4)
```

There are books that use the term *template function* rather than *function template*. The latter term, used in this book, is also used by Stroustrup. It indicates that what we write is not really a function, but rather a template for a function. However, it would make sense to refer to the generated functions as *template functions*, to distinguish them from normal functions, written by ourselves. Note that besides *function templates*, there are also *class templates*, to be discussed in Section 1.5.

1.4 Recursive Functions

Suppose we want to know how many times a given character *ch* occurs in a given string *s*. The function we want for this purpose should have the following prototype:

```
int countch(const char *s, char ch);
```

For example, the value of

```
countch("programming", 'r')
```

should be 2 because the character 'r' occurs twice in the string "*programming*". One way to tackle this problem is by inductive reasoning:

If *s* has length 0, *ch* occurs zero times in *s*. Otherwise, we split *s* into its first character, to be called its *head*, and the remaining part, its *tail*; then the number of times *ch* occurs in *s* is equal to the number of times it occurs in its tail, unless its head is equal to *ch*. In the latter case this number is to be increased by 1.

We could use this idea to write either of the following recursive functions:

```
int countch(const char *s, char ch) // Very inefficient
{   int k;
    if (strlen(s) == 0) return 0; else
    {   if (s[0] == ch) k = 1; else k = 0;
        return countch(s + 1, ch) + k;
    }
}

int countch(const char *s, char ch) // Improved version
{   return *s ? (*s == ch) + countch(s + 1, ch) : 0;
}
```

Using *strlen* in the first of the above two functions is very inefficient: this function is called many times (depending on the string length). To determine if *s* is the empty string, all we need to do is test to see if **s* (that is, *s*[0]) is zero.

Although our second, improved version does not suffer from unnecessary calls to *strlen*, we may want to replace it with an iterative version because recursion might cause stack overflow. In this case, this is unlikely to occur unless string *s* is a very long one, but it is a good principle to replace recursion with iteration. Such a nonrecursive version may also be more efficient, because fewer function calls will be executed.

Since in either function the execution of the recursive call to *countch* occurs only as the last action we can easily write an iterative version instead:

```
int countch(const char *s, char ch)
{   int n = 0;
    while (*s) if (*s++ == ch) n++;
    return n;
}
```

This is a general rule which we should bear in mind: if only one recursive call is executed and this is the final action of the function, we can easily replace recursion with iteration. Here is about the simplest example to illustrate this rule:

```
void f(int n)
{   if (n > 0)
    {   cout << n << " ";
        f(n - 1);
    }
}
```

Since at most one recursive call is executed and since this is the very last action, we refer to this type of recursion as *tail recursion*. We can replace this function with the following iterative one:

```
void f(int n)
{   while (n > 0)
        cout << n-- << " ";
}
```

The following function shows a different situation: although there is only one recursive call, placed at the very end of the function, this is not a case of tail recursion because this call is executed more than once:

```
void h(int n)
{   int j;
    cout << n << " ";
    for (j=n-1; j>0; j--) h(j);
}
```

Recursion removal is more difficult in this case than it was previously. We will solve this problem in Section 4.10.

Roman numerals revisited

Recursion frequently enables us to provide elegant, compact solutions to problems that at first look complicated. Let us illustrate this by doing the opposite of what we did in Section 1.1. Given a (correct) Roman numeral, we now want to compute its value. For example, if we have to evaluate

CMXCIX

we can proceed as follows. In a function, say, *StringValue*, starting at the beginning of the given string, we search this string for the character that has the highest value in the sense of Roman numerals. In our example, this is $M = 1000$. We can then use this maximum value, subtracting the preceding portion ($C = 100$) from it and adding the portion ($XCIX = 99$) that follows to it. For both these portions we can recursively call the very function *StringValue* that we are dealing with. This recursive function requires both a start address and the string length as arguments:

```
int StringValue(const char *s, int n)
{   int max = 0, imax, v;
    if (n > 0)
    {   for (int i=0; i<n; i++)
            if ((v = val(s[i])) > max){max = v; imax = i;}
        max -= StringValue(s, imax);
        max += StringValue(s + imax + 1, n - imax - 1);
    }
    return max;
}
```

The function *val*, used in *StringValue*, simply returns the values of one-character Roman numerals. For example, $val(L) = 50$.

In many cases, recursion is a good way to find a solution quickly, but not good enough for the final version. In this example, the first recursive call deals with a string length *imax* = 0 or 1, so that we can easily eliminate it. The remaining recursive call, executed almost at the end of the function, is then not difficult to get rid of either. Instead of replacing this recursive function *StringValue* with an equivalent iterative one, we may as well do all the work in the constructor of a class, *FromRoman*, as program *roman2* shows. Both the above function *StringValue* and the *Roman* constructor in the program below also accept strings that are incorrect Roman numerals, and they may return different results for such incorrect strings. However, if we use them for correct Roman numerals, such as those generated by program *roman1* from Section 1.1, the resulting values will be identical.

```
// roman2: Evaluating a Roman numeral.

#include <iostream.h>
#include <iomanip.h>
#include <stdlib.h>
#include <ctype.h>
```

```
class FromRoman {
public:
   FromRoman(const char *s);
   int number;
private:
   int val(char ch);
};

FromRoman::FromRoman(const char *s)
{  number = 0;
   int i = 0, si, si1;
   while (s[i])
   {  si = val(s[i]);
      if (s[i+1] && (si1 = val(s[i+1])) > si)
      {  number += si1 - si;
         i += 2;
      } else
      {  number += si;
         i++;
      }
   }
}

int FromRoman::val(char ch)
{  switch(toupper(ch))
   {  case 'M': return 1000;
      case 'D': return 500;
      case 'C': return 100;
      case 'L': return 50;
      case 'X': return 10;
      case 'V': return 5;
      case 'I': return 1;
   }
   cout << "Illegal character.\n"; exit(1);
   return 0;
}

int main()
{  char str[100];
   cout << "Enter a Roman numeral: ";
   cin >> setw(100) >> str;
   cout << "Value: " << FromRoman(str).number << endl;
   return 0;
}
```

Here are two demonstrations of this program (the second referring to Knuth's famous MIX computer, the name of which is related to the average value 1009 of some historic computer type numbers):

```
Enter a Roman number: MCMXCIX
Value: 1999

Enter a Roman number: MIX
Value: 1009
```

1.5 Dynamic Arrays, Chunks and Class Templates

If a variable number of objects are to be stored in memory, we have to choose the most appropriate data structure for that application. If we know in advance an upper limit of the number of objects to be stored, we can dynamically create an array, as we did in Section 1.2. For example, the following fragment allocates room for *n* objects of type *float*.

```
float *a;
a = new float[n];
for (int i=0; i<n; i++) a[n] = 1.5 * i;
...
delete[] a;
```

Although *a* is technically a *pointer*, we can use it as an array, and we will therefore sometimes use the term *array* for it. If we do not know in advance how many objects there will be, we can reallocate enlarged space, but for reasons of efficiency it is not normally wise to increase the number of allocated objects by 1. Instead, we prefer increasing by 'chunks' that are somewhat larger. Here is a complete program that demonstrates this principle:

```
// chunk: Variable number of float numbers stored.

#include <iostream.h>
#include <stdlib.h>

int ChunkSize = 4; // May be larger in practice

class list {
public:
   list(){LEN = ChunkSize; a = new float[LEN]; len = 0;}
   ~list() {delete[] a;}
   void AddItem(float x); // Defined below
   float &operator[](unsigned i)
   {  if (i >= len){cout << "Out of bounds.\n"; exit(1);}
      return a[i];
   }
   int GetLen()const {return len;}
private:
   int len, LEN; // Logical and physical lengths
   float *a;
};

void list::AddItem(float x)
{  if (len == LEN)
   {  float *aOld = a;
      a = new float[LEN += ChunkSize];
      for (int i=0; i<len; i++) a[i] = aOld[i];
      delete[] aOld;
   }
   a[len++] = x;
}
```

```
int main()
{  list L;
   float x;
   int n;
   cout << "Enter nonzero numbers, the last one\n"
           "followed by 0:\n";
   while (cin >> x, x != 0) L.AddItem(x);
   n = L.GetLen();
   cout << "The following " << n <<
           " nonzero numbers have been read:\n";
   for (int i=0; i<n; i++) cout << L[i] << " ";
   cout << endl;
   return 0;
}
```

Since we have chosen a chunk size of 4, allocation of physical memory takes place after reading the 1st, 5th, 9th, etc., number, and at most three array elements are allocated but not used. The larger the chunk size, the more possibly unused positions there are but the less frequently reallocation will take place. The latter is important with regard to computing time because all previously stored data has to be copied to the enlarged array. Here is a demonstration of this program:

```
Enter nonzero numbers, the last one
followed by 0:
1 2 3 4 5 6 7 8 9 10 20 30 40
The following 13 nonzero numbers have been read:
1 2 3 4 5 6 7 8 9 10 20 30 40
```

Since dynamic arrays are not available in some other languages, programming problems such as this one are more often solved by using linked lists, as we will discuss in Chapter 4. These linked lists are more flexible with regard to inserting and deleting elements at positions other than at the end and they do not require the reallocation and copying process that we have seen here. On the other hand, the links also may take a considerable amount of memory space. More importantly, arrays have the advantage of random access. Program *chunk* demonstrates this very clearly by overloading the subscripting operator. Although variable *L* is of type *chunk*, which is not an array, we can write *L*[*i*] instead of *L.a*[*i*].

Class templates

In program *chunk* we have used a *float* array. If we need other array types in programs that are equally simple, we could easily change the program text, replacing *float* with some other type. However, there is a C++ facility, *class templates*, to generalize classes, much in the same way as we can write function templates to generalize functions (see Section 1.2). To do this in program *chunk*, we have to take the following actions:

1. We insert the text *template <class T>* in front of both the class declaration and the member functions defined outside the class.
2. In the class and in the class member functions, we replace *float* with *T*.
3. The generalized type is denoted by either *list<T>* or *list<float>*; we use the former form in the definitions of the member functions and the latter in the *main* function.

The template version obtained in this way is shown below. It behaves exactly in the same way as program *chunk*, but it is very easy to use the template also for *int* arrays, for example.

```
// tplchunk: Variable number of float numbers stored,
//           using a class template.

#include <iostream.h>
#include <stdlib.h>

int ChunkSize = 4; // May be larger in practice

template <class T>
class list {
public:
   list(){LEN = ChunkSize; a = new T[LEN]; len = 0;}
   ~list() {delete[] a;}
   void AddItem(T x); // Defined below
   T &operator[](unsigned i)
   {  if (i >= len){cout << "Out of bounds.\n"; exit(1);}
      return a[i];
   }
   int GetLen()const {return len;}
private:
   int len, LEN; // Logical and physical lengths
   T *a;
};

template <class T>
void list<T>::AddItem(T x)
{  if (len == LEN)
   {  T *aOld = a;
      a = new T[LEN += ChunkSize];
      for (int i=0; i<len; i++)
         a[i] = aOld[i];
      delete[] aOld;
   }
   a[len++] = x;
}

int main()
{  list<float> L;
   float x;
   int n;
   cout << "Enter nonzero numbers, the last one\n"
           "followed by 0:\n";
   while (cin >> x, x != 0) L.AddItem(x);
   n = L.GetLen();
   cout << "The following " << n <<
           " nonzero numbers have been read:\n";
   for (int i=0; i<n; i++) cout << L[i] << " ";
   cout << endl;
   return 0;
}
```

1.6 Exception Handling

Most programs in books like this require that their users behave reasonably. For example, if we discuss a program that, among other things, is to read ten integers and to place them in the array *a*, we normally write

```
for (i=0; i<10; i++) cin >> a[i];
```

However, this will not work if the user enters any nonnumerical character before having entered ten integers. The above program line was deliberately written down in a simple, unrealistic form. In a real, practical program, checking the validity of input data is highly recommended. In this particular case, we could write, for example,

```
for (i=0; i<10; i++)
{ cin >> a[i];
  if (cin.fail())
  { cout << "Incorrect input data. Program terminated\n";
    exit(1);
  }
}
```

Suppose that an irregular situation such as this occurs in some low-level function (other than *main*), while we want to deal with this error at a higher level, say, in the *main* function. The C++ exception-handling mechanism provides an excellent means to realize this. It is based on the keywords *try*, *catch* and *throw*. Here is a complete program to explain how this works:

```
// except: Program demonstrating exception handling.
#include <iostream.h>

float ReadIntArray(int *p, int n)
{ float sum = 0;
  cout << "Enter " << n << " integers:\n";
  for (int i=0; i<n; i++)
  { cin >> p[i];
    if (cin.fail()) throw i;
    sum += p[i];
  }
  return sum/n;
}

int main()
{ float avg;
  int a[10], b[12];
  cout << "See what happens if, somewhere in the input,\n"
          "you type some incorrect character.\n";
  try
  { avg = ReadIntArray(a, 10);
    cout << "10 integers read. Average: " << avg << endl;
    avg = ReadIntArray(b, 12);
    cout << "12 integers read. Average: " << avg << endl;
  }
```

```
    catch (int k)
    {  cout <<  "Only " << k << " integers read "
          "due to incorrect input.\n";
    }
    cout << "End of program.\n";
    return 0;
}
```

This example illustrates that it may be desirable to react to an error at the higher level: the final message *End of program* is displayed whether or not the 'exception is thrown'. The latter phrase implies that the statement *throw i;* in function *ReadIntArray* is executed. Because this happens via function calls placed in

```
try
{  ...
}
```

control is transferred to the statements placed in the subsequent fragment

```
catch (int k)
{  ...
}
```

This fragment is skipped if the throw statement is not executed, that is, in the case of correct input. Here is a demonstration of this program:

```
See what happens if, somewhere in the input,
you type some incorrect character.
Enter 10 integers:
0 9 8 7 6 5 4 3 2 1
10 integers read. Average: 4.5
Enter 12 integers:
1 2 3 x
Only 3 integers read due to incorrect input.
End of program.
```

If there is an input error in the first ten integers, the second call to *ReadIntArray* will not be executed.

Memory allocation errors

Since testing for memory allocation failure depends on the compiler we are using and on future developments, we will simply omit such tests in this book. Although C++ is an exciting language and usually very pleasant to work with, we sometimes feel nostalgia for the C language because of its standardization and portability. For example, it is very usual for a C program to contain a fragment like this:

```
int *a, n;
...
a = (int *) malloc(n * sizeof(int));
if (a == NULL) {puts("Memory allocation fails."); exit(1);}
```

Actually, now that we are using C++ we can still use this way of memory allocation, but we will frequently prefer the typical C++ operators *new* and *delete* to the C standard library functions *malloc* and *free*. Unfortunately, the C++ language has been subject to several minor changes, and the way to check the success of memory allocation is one of them. For a good many years we had to do this check in the same way as with *malloc*, so that we could write the following lines instead of two similar lines shown above:

```
a = new int[n];
if (a == NULL) {cout << "Memory allocation fails."; exit(1);}
```

However, you can no longer be sure that this works. There are now, in principle, three ways of performing the test in question:

1. Testing whether new returns *NULL*

With many compilers the *new* operator still returns *NULL* if memory allocation fails, so that we can test for memory allocation failure as shown in the above fragment. With Borland C++ 4.5, the call *set_new_handler*(0) is required for this. We perform this call only once, before the first use of *new*. With many other compilers, including Microsoft Visual C++ 4.0, we simply omit this call to *set_new_handler*.

2. Supplying our own 'new-handler'

Instead of 0, we can use the name of a function of our own, known as a *new-handler*, in the above call to the function *set_new_handler*. This new-handler is called if and when memory allocation fails. With Borland C++ 4.5, a new-handler is a *void* function without parameters; with Microsoft Visual C++ 4.0 it is an *int* function with a *size_t* parameter. Besides, this compiler requires a slightly different spelling, *_set_new_handler*, with an underscore at the very beginning.

3. Using a system exception

By default, Borland C++ 4.5 throws the *xalloc* exception if the *new* operator fails. If we do not catch this exception ourselves, program termination follows when it is thrown. With Microsoft Visual C++ 4.0, the call *_set_new_handler*(_standard_new_handler), executed once, before the use of *new*, is required for such behavior. The name *xalloc* may change in the future.

Conclusion

Since the way to deal with memory allocation failure depends on the compiler we are using and on future developments, we will simply omit such tests in this book. Although C++ is an exciting language and usually very pleasant to work with, we sometimes feel nostalgia for the C language because of its standardization and portability.

Exercises

1.1 Write a class *charstring* for string manipulations, based on reference counting to avoid duplication of identical strings. Your class should at least provide the facilities required to run the following application program:

```
// Application, to be linked with charstring.cpp.
#include "charstring.h"

int main()
{   charstring s = "Smith ", t = s, u = t + s;
    s = t + "Johnson " + u;
    cout << t << endl << u << endl << s << endl;
    return 0;
}
```

Immediately after the above initialization of *t*, the variables *s* and *t* should refer to the same memory area containing the string "*Smith*". This program should produce the following output:

```
Smith
Smith Smith
Smith Johnson Smith Smith
```

1.2 Write a program that reads *n*, followed by a sequence of positive integers $a_1, a_2, ..., a_n$, followed by zero, and prints these positive integers in reverse order, $a_n, a_{n-1}, ..., a_1$. Your program must not impose a limit on *n*. Show that, with the help of a recursive function, it is possible to do this without using an array.

1.3 Improve program *roman2* so that invalid strings, such as *VIXLMVV*, are rejected.

1.4 Demonstrate exception handling, using the keywords *try*, *throw* and *catch*, in a program of your own. For example, you can write a function in which a division occurs, throwing an exception in case of division by zero.

2

Arithmetic

2.1 Euclid's Algorithm for the GCD

Programmers should be familiar with some well-known algorithms. Let us begin with one published by the old Greek mathematician Euclid, but nevertheless very suitable for present-day computers.

The greatest common divisor $gcd(x, y)$ of two nonnegative integers x and y, not both zero, is defined as the largest integer which evenly divides both x and y. For example, the greatest common divisor of 1260 and 350 is 70 because the two numbers 1260 and 350 are both multiples of 70, and there is no integer greater than 70 of which both 1260 and 350 are multiples. If we did not know better, we would probably compute this by factoring 1260 and 350:

$$1260 = \underline{2} \times 2 \times 3 \times 3 \times \underline{5} \times \underline{7}$$
$$350 = \underline{2} \times \underline{5} \times 5 \times \underline{7}$$

The common factors are underlined; although 1260 contains two factors 2 we cannot underline them both because there is only one factor 2 in 350, and so on. In this way we find the greatest common divisor

$$2 \times 5 \times 7 = 70$$

Instead of using this method, we had better use an entirely different and very elegant method, known as *Euclid's algorithm*. It is based on the idea that we can simplify the problem by subtracting the smaller number from the greater: all divisors of 1260 and 350 are also divisors of (1260 − 350 =) 910 and 350. Repeating this process, we find that we can replace 1260 with the remainder from 1260 ÷ 350, denoted by 1260 % 350 and equal to 210. We now interchange the two numbers, and so on, which gives

$$gcd(1260, 350) = gcd(350, 210) = gcd(210, 140) = gcd(140, 70) = gcd(70, 0) = 70$$

In general, we have

$gcd(x, y) = gcd(y, x \% y)$ if $y \neq 0$, and
$gcd(x, 0) = x$

Here is a recursive implementation of Euclid's algorithm:

```
int gcd(int x, int y)
{   return y ? gcd(y, x % y) : x;
}
```

Instead of using recursion, we can easily write an iterative version:

```
int gcd(int x, int y)
{   int y0;
    while (y)
    {   y0 = y;
        y = x % y;
        x = y0;
    }
    return x;
}
```

2.2 Horner's Rule

Suppose that we are given the seven numbers

$x, a_5, a_4, a_3, a_2, a_1, a_0$

and that we want to compute the polynomial

$$P_5(x) = a_5x^5 + a_4x^4 + a_3x^3 + a_2x^2 + a_1x + a_0$$

We do this preferably in the following efficient way, known as *Horner's rule*:

$$P_5(x) = ((((a_5x + a_4)x + a_3)x + a_2)x + a_1)x + a_0$$

In this way, only five multiplications and five additions are needed in this example. In general, we have to perform only n multiplications and n additions to compute a polynomial of degree n. Besides speed, Horner's rule also offers elegance and simplicity, and it may increase numerical accuracy. Here is a C(++) function to compute $P_n(x)$, based on Horner's rule, and on coefficients $a_0, ..., a_n$ being given as the $n + 1$ array elements $a[0]$, ..., $a[n]$:

```
double P(double x, const double *a, int n)
{   double s = a[n];
    while (--n >= 0) s = s * x + a[n];
    return s;
}
```

2.3 Radix Conversion for Input Operations

Horner's rule is used in input routines for numbers. For example, if we are reading the integer 5482, the following four characters are actually read at a lower level:

'5', '4', '8', '2'

With these characters, followed by a nondigit character, entered on the keyboard, and the fragment

```
int n;
cin >> n
```

being executed, the standard library routine for input will compute the following polynomial:

$$P_3(10) = 5 \times 10^3 + 4 \times 10^2 + 8 \times 10 + 2 = 5482$$

but instead of using powers of 10, such as 10^3, it will actually use Horner's rule, computing the equivalent form

$$P_3(10) = ((5 \times 10 + 4) \times 10 + 8) \times 10 + 2 = 5482$$

The number 10 is called the *radix* or *base* of our (decimal) number system. Since numbers are stored in computer memory as binary numbers, we sometimes say that input routines convert the radix, normally from 10 to 2. We can now write our own radix conversion function for integers, with digits stored in a character array. The null-character or any other nonnumeric character will terminate the string. As usual, the most significant digit will be the first, so the string "5482" is to be converted to the integer 5482. We may as well admit any radix greater than 1 and not greater than 10, using 10 as a default argument:

```
int iNumIn(const char *a, int radix=10)
{   int s=0, i=0, d;
    while ((d = a[i++] - '0') >= 0 && d < radix)
        s = radix * s + d;
    return s;
}
```

For example, we now have

iNumIn("5482")	=	5482	(first argument of *iNumIn* is decimal)
iNumIn("5482", 10)	=	5482	(first argument of *iNumIn* is decimal)
iNumIn("111", 2)	=	7	(first argument of *iNumIn* is binary)
iNumIn("17", 8)	=	15	(first argument of *iNumIn* is octal)

The function *iNumIn* does not perform any checks on the correctness of its arguments: such checks take time and are superfluous if this function is used correctly. For example, the result will make no sense if integer overflow occurs or if the second argument is greater than 10. Possible extensions, so as to admit negative numbers or 16 as a radix, are left as an exercise.

If there is any danger of integer overflow, we can use the function *fNumIn* in the following demonstration program. This function is similar to *iNumIn* (also demonstrated in this program), but it recognizes a decimal period and digits that follow it:

```
// buildnum: Building numbers out of characters.
#include <iostream.h>

int iNumIn(const char *a, int radix=10)
{   int s=0, i=0, d;
    while ((d = a[i++] - '0') >= 0 && d < radix)
        s = radix * s + d;
    return s;
}

double fNumIn(const char *a, int radix=10)
{   int i=0, d;
    double s=0, PowerOfRadix=1;
    while ((d = a[i++] - '0') >= 0 && d < radix)
        s = radix * s + d;
    if (a[i-1] == '.')
    while ((d = a[i++] - '0') >= 0 && d < radix)
    {   PowerOfRadix *= radix;
        s += d/PowerOfRadix;
    }
    return s;
}

int main()
{   cout << iNumIn("5482")     << "       " << iNumIn("5482", 10)
        << endl;
    cout << iNumIn("111", 2) << "          " << iNumIn("17", 8)
        << endl;
    cout << fNumIn("123.4567") << " " << fNumIn(".111", 2)
        << endl;
    cout << fNumIn("123.") << "       " << fNumIn("123")
        << endl;
    return 0;
}
```

The output of this program is as follows:

```
5482     5482
7        15
123.457  0.875
123      123
```

To understand the second and third lines, remember:

$$(111)_{\text{binary}} = 1 \times 2^2 + 1 \times 2 + 1 = 7$$
$$(17)_{\text{octal}} = 1 \times 8 + 7 = 15$$
$$(.111)_{\text{binary}} = 1 \times 2^{-1} + 1 \times 2^{-2} + 1 \times 2^{-3} = 0.5 + 0.25 + 0.125 = 0.875$$

Note that we can easily transform the functions *iNumIn* and *fNumIn* into input functions. We would then let the functions read characters from the keyboard or a file instead of from an array *a* supplied as an argument.

2.4 Radix Conversion for Output Operations

Output routines for numbers do the reverse from what we have just seen. They are supplied with a number which is to be decomposed into its digits. Instead of doing real output, we will place these digits in an array *a* of characters. By repeatedly dividing by the radix (10, for example) and taking the remainder, we obtain the digits from right to left. This idea is also related to Horner's rule. For example, if we divide

$$5482 = ((5 \times 10 + 4) \times 10 + 8) \times 10 + 2$$

by 10, we obviously obtain 2 as the remainder and

$$548 = (5 \times 10 + 4) \times 10 + 8$$

as the quotient. Dividing this by 10 again, we obtain the second last digit, 8, and so on. The function *innumout* in the following program is based on this principle. This is in turn the basis for its floating-point counterpart *fNumOut*, also demonstrated by this program:

```cpp
// num2char: Converting numbers to character strings.
#include <iostream.h>
#include <math.h>

int iNumOut(char *a, int x, int width, int radix=10)
{  // This function places the digits of x (possibly preceded
   // by blanks and/or a minus sign) in
   // a[0], a[1], ..., a[width - 1], and
   // '\0' in a[width] (so at least width + 1 positions
   // should be available in a).
   // Return value: 0 (= OK), or 1 (= width too small).
   int i=0, r, neg = x < 0;
   for (i=0; i<width; i++) a[i] = ' ';
   a[width] = '\0';
```

```
      if (neg) x = -x; else
      if (x == 0 && width > 0) {a[width-1] = '0'; return 0;}
      // i == width
      do
      {  r = x % radix;
         if (--i < 0) return 1;
         a[i] = '0' + r;
         x /= radix;
      }  while (x);
      if (neg)
      {  if (--i < 0) return 1; else a[i] = '-';
      }
      return 0;
   }

   int fNumOut(char *a, double x, int width, int precision,
      int radix=10)
   {  int i, PeriodDone = 0, neg = x < 0;
      double radixpower = 1, q;
      if (neg) x = -x;
      for (i=0; i<precision; i++) radixpower *= radix;
      for (i=0; i<width; i++) a[i] = ' ';
      a[width] = '\0';
      x = x * radixpower + 0.5;
      i = width;
      do
      {  if (i == width - precision)
         {  if (i > 0) a[--i] = '.'; else return 1;
            PeriodDone = 1;
         }
         q = floor(x/radix);
         if (i > 0) a[--i] = '0' + int(x - radix * q);
            else return 0;
         x = q;
      }  while (x > 0 || !PeriodDone);
      if (neg)
      {  if (i > 0) a[--i] = '-'; else return 1;
      }
      return 0;
   }

   int main()
   {  char s[20];
      if (iNumOut(s, 12345, 5) == 0)
         cout << s << " iNumOut(s, 12345, 5)\n";
      if (iNumOut(s, -234, 5) == 0)
         cout << s << " iNumOut(s, -234, 5)\n";
      if (iNumOut(s, -456, 3) == 0)    // Width insufficient:
         cout << s << " iNumOut(s, -456, 3)\n"; // no output.
      if (fNumOut(s, 3.45678, 5, 2) == 0)
         cout << s << " fNumOut(s, 3.45678, 5, 2)\n";
      if (fNumOut(s, 0, 5, 2) == 0)
         cout << s << " fNumOut(s, 0, 5, 2)\n";
      if (iNumOut(s, 12, 5, 2) == 0)
         cout << s << " iNumOut(s, 12, 5, 2)\n";
```

```
      if (fNumOut(s, -3, 5, 0, 2) == 0)
         cout << s << " fNumOut(s, -3, 5, 0, 2)\n";
      if (fNumOut(s, 0.75, 5, 2, 2) == 0)
         cout << s << " fNumOut(s, 0.75, 5, 2, 2)\n";
      if (fNumOut(s, 0.99999, 5, 2, 2) == 0)
         cout << s << " fNumOut(s, 0.99999, 5, 2, 2)\n";
      return 0;
   }
```

The output of this program is shown below:

```
12345 iNumOut(s, 12345, 5)
 -234 iNumOut(s, -234, 5)
 3.46 fNumOut(s, 3.45678, 5, 2)
 0.00 fNumOut(s, 0, 5, 2)
 1100 iNumOut(s, 12, 5, 2)
 -11. fNumOut(s, -3, 5, 0, 2)
 0.11 fNumOut(s, 0.75, 5, 2, 2)
 1.00 fNumOut(s, 0.99999, 5, 2, 2)
```

2.5 Powers with Integer Exponents

We will now develop a function *Pow* to compute the power x^n where x is a real number and n is an integer. Here is a straightforward version:

```
double Pow(double x, int n)
{   double y=1;
    int neg = n < 0;
    if (neg) n = -n;
    while (n--) y *= x;
    return neg ? 1.0/y : y;
}
```

For rather small values of (the absolute value of) n, this version works fine. However, it wastes computing time if n is large. For example, since there are 19 occurrences of $\times$ in

$$x^{20} = x \times x \times x \times x \times x \times x \times x \times x \times x \times x \times x \times x \times x \times x \times x \times x \times x \times x \times x \times x$$

the above version would perform 19 multiplications. If we had to compute x^{20} by hand, we would be more efficient. For example, using

$$x^2 = x \times x$$
$$x^4 = x^2 \times x^2$$
$$x^8 = x^4 \times x^4$$
$$x^{16} = x^8 \times x^8$$
$$x^{20} = x^{16} \times x^4$$

we find that no more than five multiplications are required. The following version of *Pow* is almost as efficient as the above method. Instead of five, it performs six multiplications, because it starts with $y = 1$ to keep the function simple:

```
double Pow(double x, int n)
{   int neg = n < 0;
    if (neg) n = -n;
    double y=1;
    while (n)
    {   if (n & 1) y *= x;
        x *= x;
        n >>= 1;
    }
    return neg ? 1.0/y : y;
}
```

To see how this works, let us use the symbols X and N for the (constant) argument values, while the program variables x, y and n change during the computation. Let us assume that $N > 0$. Immediately after entering the while-loop, we have $x = X$, $n = N$ and $y = 1$, so that clearly

$$y \times x^n = X^N \tag{1}$$

Inside the loop, if n is an even number, squaring x and halving n at the same time does not change the value of x^n, so that these combined actions do not affect the validity of (1). If n is an odd number, a simple integer division of n by 2 would make us miss one factor x. For example, if $n = 9$, halving n by shifting it one bit to the right gives the same result as if n were 8. The if-statement in the loop compensates for this error by multiplying y by x. As a result, (1) remains valid in the loop for both even and odd values of n. When the loop ends, (1) will still be valid, but by then n is zero, so that $x^n = 1$. Consequently, the equality (1) then implies $y = X^N$. Once you are convinced of the correctness of function *Pow* for positive values of N, you will have no difficulty in verifying this function also for $N \leq 0$.

2.6 Double-precision Unsigned Integers

With x and y of type *unsigned int*, the expression

```
x + y
```

will produce the desired value only if the mathematically correct sum fits into a memory location reserved for type *unsigned int*, that is, if this sum is not greater than the symbolic constant *UINT_MAX*, defined in *limits.h*. To make this discussion as simple as possible, let us assume that we have 16-bit machine words, so that

$$UINT\_MAX = (1111\ 1111\ 1111\ 1111)_2 = 0xFFFF = 2^{16} - 1 = 65535$$

Let us define

$$B = UINT\_MAX + 1 = 2^{16}$$

Then addition will be done modulo B. In other words, instead of $x + y$, the computer will actually produce the value

$$(x + y) \bmod B$$

which is the remainder we obtain when dividing $x + y$ by B. For example, we have

```
UINT_MAX + 1 = 0
UINT_MAX + 2 = 1
UINT_MAX + 3 = 2
       ...
UINT_MAX + UINT_MAX = UINT_MAX - 1
```

If we write

```
unsigned int x, y, s;
...
s = x + y;
```

then the mathematically correct sum $x + y$ is equal to either s or $s + B$. We can tell these two cases apart in a surprisingly simple way, based on this rule:

a. if the correct sum is s, we have $s \geq x$ and $s \geq y$;
b. otherwise, it is equal to $s + B$ and we have $s < x$ and $s < y$.

We will now regard B as the radix of a number system, so instead of having ten digits 0, 1, ..., 9, we now have the digits 0, 1, ..., *UINT_MAX*. Then our correct sum $x + y$ can be written in two digits $d_1 d_0$ of the new number system, where d_1 is either 0 or 1 and d_0 is equal to s. The following function computes the double-precision sum of x and y in this way:

```
#typedef unsigned int uint;
...
void dpSum(uint x, uint y, uint &d1, uint &d0)
{   d0 = x + y;
    d1 = d0 < x;
}
```

Recall that expressions such as $d0 < x$ return 1 or 0 for 'true' or 'false', respectively. You may therefore read the last, rather cryptic statement in this function as follows:

Assign 1 to $d1$ in the strange case that the computed sum of two nonnegative integers x and y is less than x, and 0 in the normal case, with the computed sum greater than or equal to x.

The value 0 or 1 assigned to $d1$ is called a *carry*. It may be instructive to compare all this with adding two one-digit numbers in the decimal system, giving a two-digit result:

Case a: $2 + 5 = 7$ $(carry = d_1 = 0, d_0 = 7; 7 \geq 2)$
Case b: $8 + 6 = 14$ $(carry = d_1 = 1, d_0 = 4; 4 < 8)$

Let us finish this section with a complete program to show how we can write a class for this type of double-precision arithmetic. It is very limited in that it can only add two numbers:

```
// dblulong: Double-precision unsigned long arithmetic.
#include <iostream.h>
#include <iomanip.h>
#include <limits.h>
typedef unsigned long ulong;

class ULONG {
public:
    friend ULONG operator+(const ULONG &x, const ULONG &y);
    ULONG(ulong u = 0){d[1] = 0; d[0]=u;}
    ulong d[2];
    friend ostream &operator<<(ostream &os, ULONG &u);
};

ULONG operator+(const ULONG &x, const ULONG &y)
{   ULONG s;
    s.d[0] = x.d[0] + y.d[0];
    s.d[1] = x.d[1] + y.d[1] + (s.d[0] < x.d[0]);
    return s;
}

ostream &operator<<(ostream &os, ULONG &u)
{   for (int i=1; i>=0; i--)
        os << hex << setw(2*sizeof(ulong)) << setfill('0')
           << u.d[i] << " ";
    return os;
}

int main()
{   ULONG u1 = ULONG_MAX, u2, u4, u8;
    cout << "1 * ULONG_MAX: " << u1 << endl;
    cout << "2 * ULONG_MAX: " << (u2 = u1 + u1) << endl;
    cout << "4 * ULONG_MAX: " << (u4 = u2 + u2) << endl;
    cout << "8 * ULONG_MAX: " << (u8 = u4 + u4) << endl;
    return 0;
}
```

This program produces the following output:

```
1 * ULONG_MAX: 00000000 ffffffff
2 * ULONG_MAX: 00000001 fffffffe
4 * ULONG_MAX: 00000003 fffffffc
8 * ULONG_MAX: 00000007 fffffff8
```

2.7 Multi-precision Arithmetic

Standard data types represent numbers in finite precision. For example, we normally have:

type long: 4 bytes   about 9 decimal digits
type double: 8 bytes   about 15 decimal digits

Although these numbers of digits are sufficient for most applications, it would be unsatisfactory if we were not able to use the computer for calculations that even a child can do by hand. An example is shown below:

```
12345678912345678912
11111111122222222233
──────────────────── +
23456790034567901145
```

We will use and briefly discuss a class for this kind of calculation with integers. Besides addition (+), we will also provide facilities for the other arithmetical operations: subtraction (−), multiplication (*), division (/) and taking the remainder (%). There will also be the three 'standard functions' *power*, *sqrt* and *abs*, for exponentiation (to raise a *large* number to an *unsigned int* power), the square root and the absolute value, respectively. Finally, it will be possible to use the operators << and >> both for shift and for I/O operations. Since our class can deal with very large integers, we will call it *large*. Here is a simple application module that shows some possibilities of this class:

```cpp
// lapp: A simple application of class 'large' for
//    arithmetical operations on very large integers
//    (to be linked with large.cpp, listed in Appendix A).
#include <iostream.h>
#include "large.h"

int main()
{  large a = "987654321012345",
        b =          "55544433", sum, dif, prod,
        quot, rem;
   sum = a + b;
   dif = a - b;
   prod = a * b;
   quot = a / b;
   rem = a % b;
   cout << a << " + " << b << " = " << sum << endl;
   cout << a << " - " << b << " = " << dif << endl;
   cout << a << " * " << b << " = " << prod << endl;
   cout << a << " / " << b << " = " << quot << endl;
   cout << a << " % " << b << " = " << rem << endl;
   return 0;
}
```

Using also the files *large.h* and *large.cpp*, we obtain the following output from the above program:

```
987654321012345 + 55544433 = 987654376556778
987654321012345 - 55544433 = 987654265467912
987654321012345 * 55544433 = 54858699260630689025385
987654321012345 / 55544433 = 17781337
987654321012345 % 55544433 = 39365424
```

Our class *large* is quite general in that there is no limit to the number of decimals, other than that imposed by the amount of memory that is available. The public part of the interface *large.h* is listed below:

```
// large.h: Multi-precision integer arithmetic.
#include <iostream.h>
typedef unsigned int uint;

class large {
public:
    large(const char *str);
    large(int i);
    large(uint i=0);
    large(long i);
    large(const large &v);
    ~large(){delete[]p;}
    friend large operator+(large x, const large &y);
    friend large operator-(large x, const large &y);
    friend large operator*(large x, const large &y);
    friend large operator/(large x, const large &y);
    friend large operator%(large x, const large &y);
    friend large operator<<(large u, uint k);
    friend large operator>>(large u, uint k);
    large operator-()const;
    large &operator=(const large &y);
    large &operator+=(const large &y);
    large &operator-=(const large &y);
    large &operator*=(int y);
    large &operator*=(large y);
    large &operator/=(const large &divisor);
    large &operator%=(const large &divisor);
    large &operator<<=(uint k);
    large &operator>>=(uint k);
    friend int operator==(const large &x, const large &y)
       {return x.compare(y)==0;}
    friend int operator!=(const large &x, const large &y)
       {return x.compare(y)!=0;}
    friend int operator<(const large &x, const large &y)
       {return x.compare(y) < 0;}
    friend int operator>(const large &x, const large &y)
       {return x.compare(y) > 0;}
    friend int operator<=(const large &x, const large &y)
       {return x.compare(y)<=0;}
    friend int operator>=(const large &x, const large &y)
       {return x.compare(y)>=0;}
    friend ostream &operator<<(ostream &os, const large &v);
    friend istream &operator>>(istream &os, large &v);
```

```
    friend large power(large x, uint n);
    friend large sqrt(const large &x);
    friend large abs(const large &x);
private:
    ...
};
```

A complete discussion of this class is beyond the scope of this book. You can nevertheless use it; it is quite normal for software tools to be used successfully without every statement of the source text being explained in full detail. In most cases the source code is not available at all. In this case it is: you can find it in Appendix A.

The above public functions are listed below once again, along with some notes about how to use them:

`large(const char *str);`
> Usage: x = "123456789"; or $y = x +$ "123456789";
> These string literals must contain digits only, no minus sign. The first digit must be nonzero, unless the string has length 1.

`large(int i);`
> Usage: x = 123; or $y = x +$ 123;

`large(uint i=0);`
> Usage: $large\ x$; or $y = x + 50000U$;

`large(long i);`
> Usage: $x = 1234567L$; or $y = x + 1234567L$;

`large(const large &x);`
> Copy constructor, for value parameter passing, for example.

`~large();`
> Destructor, to release memory space allocated by constructor.

`friend large operator+(large x, const large &y);`
> Usage: $x + y$, or $x +$ 123, or 123 $+ x$

`friend large operator-(large x, const large &y);`
> Negative numbers allowed: $large(12) - large(18) == large(-6)$

`friend large operator*(large x, const large &y);`
> Usage: a * b (no danger of 'integer overflow').

`friend large operator/(large x, const large &y);`
> Integer division: large(37)/large(5) == large(7)

`friend large operator%(large x, const large &y);`
> Remainder of division: large(37)%large(5) == large(2)

`friend large operator<<(large u, uint k);`
`friend large operator>>(large u, uint k);`
> These shift operators have their usual meaning. For example, $x = large(1) << 90$ assigns the value 2^{90} to the variable x.

`large operator-() const;`
> Unary minus operator, used, for example, in $y = -x + 1$;

```
large &operator=(const large &x);
```
   Assignment operator, used in *s* = *x* + *y*;

```
large &operator+=(const large &y);
```
   Usage: *x* += *y*, or *x* += 123
   (The operators –=, *=, /=, %=, <<=, and >>=, similar to +=, are also available.)

```
friend int operator==(const large &x, const large &y);
friend int operator!=(const large &x, const large &y);
friend int operator<(const large &x, const large &y);
friend int operator>(const large &x, const large &y);
friend int operator<=(const large &x, const large &y);
friend int operator>=(const large &x, const large &y);
```
   Six equality and relational operators with their usual meaning.

```
ostream &operator<<(ostream &os, const large &x);
```
   Usage: *cout* << *x* << *endl* << *y* << *endl*;
   Or: *MyOutputStream* << *x* << *endl* << *y* << *endl*;

```
istream &operator>>(istream &is, large &x);
```
   Usage: *cin* >> *x* >> *y*;
   Or: *MyInputStream* >> *x* >> *y*;

```
friend large power(large x, uint n);
```
   Usage: *y* = *power(10, 1000)*; to compute *y* = 10^{1000}.

```
friend large sqrt(const large &x);
```
   Usage: *y* = *sqrt(x)*; to compute *y* = $\sqrt{x}$.

```
friend large abs(const large &x);
```
   Usage: *abs(x)* is the absolute value of *x*.

We can now apply type *large* to some functions discussed in the previous sections. For example, we can write

```
#include "large.h"
...
large gcd(large x, large y)
{   large y0;
    while (y){y0 = y; y = x % y; x = y0;}
    return x;
}
```

to compute the greatest common divisor of very large integers. This function is similar to the one listed at the end of Section 2.1. Here is the function for exponentiation, declared in the above header file *large.h* and defined in the file *large.cpp* (in Appendix A):

```
large power(large x, uint n)
{   large y=1;
    while (n)
    {   if (n & 1) y *= x;
        x *= x;
        n >>= 1;
    }
    return y;
}
```

This version is slightly simpler than the function *Pow* in Section 2.5, because it restricted to the important special case of nonnegative integer exponents (*uint* being defined as *unsigned int* in *large.h*).

The *sqrt* function (listed in Appendix A) is based on the well-known Newton–Raphson algorithm, solving the equation $x^2 - a = 0$. We begin by shifting *a* to the right by about half its length to find an initial approximation of $\sqrt{a}$, used as a start value for the iteration process. This principle is explained in *C++ for Programmers* in the section about function overloading.

2.8 Binomial Coefficients

The expression

$$C(n, k) = \binom{n}{k} = \frac{n!}{k!(n-k)!} = \frac{n(n-1) \cdots (n-k+2)(n-k+1)}{k(k-1) \cdots 2 \times 1}$$

is called a binomial coefficient. As we will see in Section 10.3, a set of *n* elements has $C(n, k)$ subsets of *k* elements. Binomial coefficients are used for many purposes in mathematics. For example, we have

$$(a+b)^n = \sum_{k=0}^{n} \binom{n}{k} a^n b^{n-k}$$

If we use the built-in types *int* or *long* for binomial coefficients, we will soon be in trouble because of integer overflow. By contrast, our new type *large* is very suitable for this purpose. The following program computes a desired binomial coefficient in two ways: the first is based on the above definition of $C(n, k)$, the second on Pascal's triangle, as we will see shortly:

```
// binom: Binomials based on class large
//    (to be linked with large.cpp, listed in Appendix A).

#include "large.h"

large binom1(int n, int k)
{   if (k < 0 || n < k) return 0;
    if (k > n/2) k = n - k;
    int idenom = 1, inum = n - k + 1;
    large num = inum, denom = idenom;
    while (idenom < k)
    {   num *= ++inum;
        denom *= ++idenom;
    }
    return num/denom;
}
```

```
large binom2(int n, int k)
{   if (k < 0 || k > n) return 0;
    if (k > n/2) k = n - k;
    large *a = new large[k + 1];
    int limit;
    a[0] = 1;
    for (int i=1; i<=n; i++)
    {   limit = k - (n - i) - 1;
        if (limit < 0) limit = 0;
        for (int j=k; j>limit; j--)
            a[j] += a[j-1];
    }
    large result = a[k];
    delete[] a;
    return result;
}

int main()
{   int n, k;
    do
    {   cout << "Enter the integers (n >= 0) and k: ";
        cin >> n >> k;
    }   while (n < 0);
    cout << binom1(n, k) << endl;
    cout << binom2(n, k) << endl;
    return 0;
}
```

The value of $C(250, 200)$ is computed twice in the following demonstration:

```
Enter the integers (n >= 0) and k: 250 200
13477920270588432609101285414688840655869986372501254 5
13477920270588432609101285414688840655869986372501254 5
```

Program *binom* simply displays each large number as a single line of text. We will see in the next section how we can improve this format by inserting line breaks and blank spaces.

According to our definition, computing binomial coefficients requires many multiplications and one division. However, it is also possible to use only additions. This method is based on these equalities:

$$\binom{n}{k} = \binom{n-1}{k-1} + \binom{n-1}{k} \qquad (n > 0, 0 < k \le n)$$

$$\binom{n}{0} = 1$$

We could write a recursive function based on these equations, but that would be extremely inefficient because the same binomial coefficients would be computed many times. It is far better to build successive lines of Pascal's triangle, shown below for $n = 0, 1, ..., 4$:

```
                    1
                1       1
            1       2       1
        1       3       3       1
    1       4       6       4       1
```

The position on a line indicates k. For example, the number 6 occurs on the line corresponding to $n = 4$. Since the numbers 1, 4, 6, 4, 1 on this line are in the positions 0, 1, 2, 3, 4, the number 6 corresponds with $k = 2$, so we have

$$\binom{4}{2} = 6$$

Note that Pascal's triangle illustrates the above additive equation. Function *binom2* in program *binom* computes binomial coefficients by partially computing this triangle.

2.9 Decimal Expansion of π

Although class *large* is intended for large integers, we can also use it to approximate real numbers, provided we are prepared to do a little bookkeeping, also known as *scaling*. Let us demonstrate this by computing the mathematical constant π to an arbitrary number of decimals. This computation will be based on this equation:

$$\pi = 48 \arctan\frac{1}{18} + 32 \arctan\frac{1}{57} - 20 \arctan\frac{1}{239}$$

Some other formulas to compute π are given in Exercise 2.5. Advanced mathematicians who are interested in the calculation of π should consult *Pi and the AGM*, by Borwein and Borwein. Since we are focusing on programming, we will simply use the above equation, without proving it. The same applies to the way we can approximate the *arctan* function by using only the algebraic operations +, −, *, / in the following series:

$$\arctan x = x - \frac{x^3}{3} + \frac{x^5}{5} - \frac{x^7}{7} + \ldots$$

The user of our program will specify n, the desired number of decimal digits that follow the period. For example, π will be represented in the output as

```
3.
1415
```

if n is equal to 4. Since we are approximating real numbers by integers, we should be careful with the last one or two digits, avoiding errors related to the way we approximate the *arctan* function. We will therefore actually use the scale factor

TenPower $= 10^{n+3}$

and omit the final three digits when displaying the result. It follows from the above formulas that $TenPower \times \pi$ is approximately equal to the very large integer

$$Atan(18, 48 \times TenPower) + Atan(57, 32 \times TenPower) - Atan(239, 20 \times TenPower)$$

where

$$Atan(k, N) = N/k - N/(3k^3) + N/(5k^5) - N/(7k^7) + \ldots \qquad (\approx N \arctan k^{-1})$$

In the latter equation, N is a very large integer and the division operator / denotes integer division (as it does in $39/5 = 7$). The following program uses this *Atan* function:

```
// largepi: Large integers used to compute pi
//   (to be linked with large.cpp, listed in Appendix A).

#include <strstrea.h>
// This filename strstrea.h is in accordance
// with the draft C++ standard. If your compiler
// does not accept it, use strstream.h instead.

#include <fstream.h>
#include <time.h>
#include <stdlib.h>
#include "large.h"

// For the computation of pi:
large Atan(uint k, const large &N)
{   // Computes N * atan(1.0/k) as a large integer
    large a = 0,
        w = N * k,
        zero = 0,
        k2 = k * k,
        i = -1,
        two = 2;
    cout << "k = " << k << endl;
    while (w != zero)
    {   a += (w /= k2)/(i += two);
        a -= (w /= k2)/(i += two);
    }
    return a;
}

int main()
{   int n, m, FileOutput;
    cout << "Computation of pi. Number of decimals: ";
    cin >> n; m = n + 3;
    cout << "Copy of output to file pi.txt desired (y/n)? ";
    char answer;
    cin >> answer;
    FileOutput = (answer == 'Y' || answer == 'y');
    ofstream ofile;
    if (FileOutput) ofile.open("pi.txt");
    char *buf = new char[n + 5];
```

```
    ostrstream oo(buf, n + 5);
    large TenPower, Pi;
    clock_t tStart, tEnd;
    tStart = clock();

    TenPower = power(5, m); TenPower <<= m;
        // Faster than TenPower = power(10, m);
    Pi = (Atan(18, TenPower * 48) + Atan(57, TenPower * 32)
            - Atan(239, TenPower * 20))/1000;
    cout << "Digits of pi:" << endl;
    oo << Pi;    // The result is now available in array buf.
    tEnd = clock();

    cout << buf[0] << '.';
    if (FileOutput) ofile << buf[0] << '.';
    for (int i=1; i<=n; i++)
    {   if (i % 50 == 1)
        {   cout << endl;
            if (FileOutput) ofile << endl;
        }   else
        if (i % 10 == 1)
        {   cout << " ";
            if (FileOutput) ofile << " ";
        }
        cout << buf[i];
        if (FileOutput) ofile << buf[i];
    }
    cout << "\nTime: " << (tEnd - tStart) << " ticks\n";
    return 0;
}
```

To display the result in lines of 50 digits, as shown below, in-memory format conversion is used, based on the header-file *strstream.h*. Microsoft C++ requires this file name to be written as *strstrea.h*, hence the use of conditional compilation at the beginning of the program. Using a buffer of $n + 5$ bytes to accommodate

- the leading digit 3 that precedes the decimal period,
- $n + 3$ digits that follow the decimal period,
- a terminating null character,

we write

```
char *buf = new char[n + 5];
ostrstream oo(buf, n + 5);
```

After these preparations, the statement

```
oo << Pi;
```

writes the output into the character array *buf*, rather than directly to our screen. Once we have the digits available in this array, we can display them in any format we like.

With n much larger than 1000, you will notice that the program takes some time; to show progress, it is then desirable to display some intermediate output for each of the following steps:

1. Computing *TenPower* $= 10^m$, where $m = n + 3$.
2. Computing *Atan*(239, *TenPower* * 20);
3. Computing *Atan*(57, *TenPower* * 32);
4. Computing *Atan*(18, *TenPower* * 48);
5. Converting the *large* variable *Pi* to the n-digit character string for output.

In step 1, we can benefit from the shift-left operation, realizing that 10^m is equal to $5^m \times 2^m$ so that we can compute 5^m and shift the result m binary positions to the left. Remember, computing time required for multiplying *large* numbers depends on their length, so we can compute 5^m faster than 10^m.

The steps 2, 3 and 4 are not necessarily taken in this order. If an expression $f() - g()$ is to be evaluated, the C++ language does not specify the order in which the calls to f and g take place. In this demonstration call g happens to precede call f.

After the user has entered the desired number of decimals, he or she can indicate whether or not a copy of the output is to be written to a textfile, *pi.txt*, Then, when starting each of the above steps 2, 3 and 4, the program shows this by displaying some text, as this output demonstrates:

```
Computation of pi. Number of decimals: 1000
Copy of output to file pi.txt desired (y/n)? n
k = 239
k = 57
k = 18
Digits of pi:
3.
1415926535 8979323846 2643383279 5028841971 6939937510
5820974944 5923078164 0628620899 8628034825 3421170679
8214808651 3282306647 0938446095 5058223172 5359408128
4811174502 8410270193 8521105559 6446229489 5493038196
4428810975 6659334461 2847564823 3786783165 2712019091
4564856692 3460348610 4543266482 1339360726 0249141273
7245870066 0631558817 4881520920 9628292540 9171536436
7892590360 0113305305 4882046652 1384146951 9415116094
3305727036 5759591953 0921861173 8193261179 3105118548
0744623799 6274956735 1885752724 8912279381 8301194912
9833673362 4406566430 8602139494 6395224737 1907021798
6094370277 0539217176 2931767523 8467481846 7669405132
0005681271 4526356082 7785771342 7577896091 7363717872
1468440901 2249534301 4654958537 1050792279 6892589235
4201995611 2129021960 8640344181 5981362977 4771309960
5187072113 4999999837 2978049951 0597317328 1609631859
5024459455 3469083026 4252230825 3344685035 2619311881
7101000313 7838752886 5875332083 8142061717 7669147303
5982534904 2875546873 1159562863 8823537875 9375195778
1857780532 1712268066 1300192787 6611195909 2164201989
Time: 1480 ticks
```

This demonstration was done with a 486 DX2 computer and Microsoft Visual C++ 4.0, running in a DOS box under Windows 95. Since a tick is equivalent to 1 ms, this computation of π to a thousand decimal digits, including the conversion to a character string, took about 1.5 s. Program *largepi*, running on the same machine, computed 100 000 decimals of π in about an hour and 50 minutes. According to Borwein and Borwein, computation of π to the same number of decimals by Shanks and Wrench on an IBM 7090 in 1961 took about 9 hours. Our computation is much faster (and less expensive), but it is not really of scientific interest, since many more digits of π have been computed by others, such as Yasumasa Kanada from Tokyo, who computed as many as 10^9 decimals.

Exercises

2.1 Write the function *IsPrime*, which has a positive integer argument n. This function returns 1 if n is a prime number (2, 3, 5, 7, 11, ...) and 0 if it is not.

2.2 Write a program which reads a positive integer and writes this as a product of prime numbers. For example,

$$120 = 2 \times 2 \times 2 \times 3 \times 5$$

2.3 Write the function *trunc* with a floating-point argument x and a positive integer argument n. This function returns a floating-point value equal to x except for all fractional decimal positions after the nth, which are zero. For example,

$$trunc(-3.14159, 3) = -3.141$$

2.4 Write a program to compute the first n decimal values of e^x, where n is specified by the user. Use class *large* and

$$e^x = 1 + x + \frac{x^2}{2!} + \frac{x^3}{3!} + \frac{x^4}{4!} \cdots$$

You can scale e^x by a power of 10, as we did with π in Section 2.9.

2.5 Compute π by using one or more of the following formulas instead of the one used in Section 2.9. Which will be the slowest? Remember, the series used to compute the *arctan* function converges only reasonably quickly for small arguments of this function, which explains the comparatively good performance of program *largepi*. A proof of formula (1) can be found in many books on mathematics. It was derived by John Machin (1680–1752), who used it to calculate π to 100 digits in 1706. You can find these formulas, along with some historical details, in Section 11.1 (entitled *On the History of the Calculation of* π), of *Pi and the AGM* by Borwein and Borwein. As long as you are computing at most a thousand digits, you can check the correctness of your results by using the listing at the end of Section 2.9. If you compute more digits, it is a good idea to verify them by using several of these (or other) formulas:

$$\pi = 16 \arctan\frac{1}{5} - 4 \arctan\frac{1}{139} \qquad (1)$$

$$\pi = 20 \arctan\frac{1}{7} + 8 \arctan\frac{3}{79} \qquad (2)$$

$$\pi = 4\left(\arctan\frac{1}{2} + \arctan\frac{1}{5} + \arctan\frac{1}{8}\right) \qquad (3)$$

$$\pi = 12\left(\arctan\frac{1}{4} + 4 \arctan\frac{1}{20} + 4 \arctan\frac{1}{1985}\right) \qquad (4)$$

$$\pi = 24 \arctan\frac{1}{8} + 8 \arctan\frac{1}{57} + 4 \arctan\frac{1}{239} \qquad (5)$$

$$\pi = 4 \arctan 1 \qquad (6)$$

2.6   Write a class, *fraction*, for rational numbers, based on class *large* of Section 2.7. For example, after

```
fraction a(1, 10000), b(1, 9999), c;
        // a = 1/10000, b = 1/9999
c = a * a + b;
```

the value of *c* should be represented internally by the numerator 100 009 999 and the denominator 999 900 000 000, both of type *large*.

3

Sorting Arrays and Files

3.1 Sorting Very Short Lists

Sorting pairs

We will now use a function template to swap the objects x and y of a given type only if $x > y$ holds; in other words, we will *sort* the ordered pair (x, y), so that $x \leq y$ holds after the completion of this operation. Obviously, this makes sense only if relational operators, such as $>$ and $\leq$, are defined for the type just mentioned. Since we can define our own operators in C++, this need not be a problem in this language. For example, suppose R and S are records containing a name and a number, and we want to use the number as a key, as shown below:

	name	number
R	John	1234

	name	number
S	Mary	987

Comparing 1234 with 987, we see that the key of R is greater than that of S, so we want to swap R and S. Unlike C, the C++ language makes it easy to define the relation $R > S$ as $R.number > S.number$, as the following class declaration shows:

```
class record {
public:
   char name[30];
   int number;
   ...
   int operator>(record &s){return number > s.number;}
};
```

Using *R* and *S* of type *record* and a *swap* function that takes reference arguments, we can now write

```
if (R > S) swap(R, S);
```

Obviously, we should replace the above *operator>* function with the following one if we want to use the *name* rather than the *number* member as a key:

```
int operator>(record &s){return strcmp(name, s.name) > 0;}
```

Let us also have a look at another example. Suppose we are dealing with *point* objects given by their *x* and *y* coordinates, and for any two points P and Q we will say that P > Q if the distance between P and the origin O(0, 0) is greater than that between Q and O, as Figure 3.1 shows.

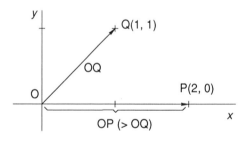

Figure 3.1 OP > OQ

The following program demonstrates templates to sort pairs of *record* objects, pairs of *point* objects and pairs of *int* array elements:

```
// sort2: Sorting lists of two objects.

#include <iostream.h>
#include <string.h>

template <class T>
void swap(T &x, T &y)
{  T w = x; x = y; y = w;
}
```

```
template <class T>
void sort2(T &x, T &y)
{  if (x > y) swap(x, y);
}

class record {
public:
    char name[30];
    int number;
    record(const char *s, int i): number(i)
    {  strcpy(name, s);
    }
    int operator>(record &s){return number > s.number;}
    friend ostream &operator<<(ostream &os, record &r)
    {  return os << r.name << " " << r.number;
    }
};

class point {
public:
    float x, y;
    point(float xx, float yy): x(xx), y(yy){}
    int operator>(const point &Q) const
    {  return x * x + y * y > Q.x * Q.x + Q.y * Q.y;
    }
    friend ostream &operator<<(ostream &os, point &P)
    {  return os << P.x << " " << P.y;
    }
};

int main()
{  record R("John", 1234), S("Mary", 987);
    point P(2, 0), Q(1, 1);
    int a[3] = {6, 3, 7};
    sort2(R, S);
    sort2(P, Q);
    sort2(a[0], a[1]);
    sort2(a[1], a[2]);
    sort2(a[0], a[1]);
    cout << "P: " << P << "    Q: " << Q << endl;
    cout << "R: " << R << "    S: " << S << endl;
    cout << "a: ";
    for (int i=0; i<3; i++) cout << a[i] << " ";
    cout << endl;
    return 0;
}
```

The output of this program shows that sorting takes place:

```
P: 1 1    Q: 2 0
R: Mary 987    S: John 1234
a: 3 6 7
```

Sorting a list of three objects

In program *sort2*, the program line that calls *sort2* for elements of array *a* shows that we can sort a list of three objects by sorting a list of two objects three times. Using simple variables *x*, *y* and *z*, we could write

```
sort2(x, y);
sort2(y, z);
sort2(x, y);
```

to sort these three variables, so $x \leq y \leq z$ holds after this process. However, execution of the third statement is not always required. It is required only if in the second statement *y* and *z* are really swapped. For example, with initial values $x = 6$, $y = 3$, $z = 7$, the list is already ordered after the first statement. We obviously have to compare *y* and *z* to detect this, so we cannot miss the second statement, but on finding that *z* is not less than *y* we need not perform the last statement. The following, slightly more complicated fragment will therefore be more efficient than the above one:

```
sort2(x, y);
if (y > z)
{  swap(y, z);
   sort2(x, y);
}
```

Both versions are based on the principle that we can only swap two elements at a time. It is also possible to perform a cyclic permutation of three elements *x*, *y* and *z*. Applying this to type *int*, we can use the following function:

```
void swap3int(int &x, int &y, int &z)
{  int w = x; x = y; y = z; z = w;
}
```

For example, if we have

$x = 3, y = 1, z = 2$

we could perform the call

```
swap3int(x, y, z);
```

which means:

- *x* is given the old value of *y*
- *y* is given the old value of *z*
- *z* is given the old value of *x*

Consequently, the call to *swap3int* in the above example assigns 1, 2 and 3 to *x*, *y* and *z*, respectively. We should also note that only one swap (of *x* and *z*) is required if $x > y > z$, while the two algorithms discussed so far perform three in this case. We can in fact place three different objects in increasing order by swapping only once, using either a function similar to *swap3int* or the *swap* function that simply exchanges two objects. This leads to the following function templates:

```
template <class T>
void swap(T &x, T &y)
{   T w = x; x = y; y = w;
}


template <class T>
void swap3(T &x, T &y, T &z)
{   T w = x; x = y; y = z; z = w;
}


template <class T>
void sort3(T &x, T &y, T &z)
{   if (x > y)
    {   if (x > z)
        {   if (y > z) swap(x, z);      // 3 2 1
            else swap3(x, y, z);        // 3 1 2
        } else swap(x, y);              // 2 1 3
    }
    else
    if (x > z) swap3(x, z, y);          // 2 3 1
    else
    if (y > z) swap(y, z);              // 1 3 2
    // else do nothing                  // 1 2 3
}
```

With three different objects, there are six essentially different cases, as the above comments show. Because of its efficiency, template *sort3* is very useful, as we will see in Section 3.7.

Sorting four objects

The idea of placing all objects immediately in their correct positions, as used in our *sort3* template, would lead to very complex algorithms with lists longer than 3. The following template sorts four objects, using only simple swaps. Based on the *sort2* template used before, it looks remarkably simple and it performs at most five swaps and is therefore reasonably efficient:

```
template <class T>
void sort4(T &a, T &b, T &c, T &d)
{   sort2(a, b);
    sort2(c, d);
    sort2(a, c);  // Least element in a
    sort2(b, d);  // Greatest element in c
    sort2(b, c);  // a <= b <= c <= d
}
```

Stability

Program *sort2* sorts objects of three types: *record*, *point* and *int*. Only in type *record* do the items to be sorted contain data other than the keys. In type *point*, the entire item is used to compute the key and the *int* elements of array *a* are at the same time the keys. In data processing applications, we normally sort records with keys that are only part of them. In such applications there may be distinct records with identical keys. If the only requirement is that the keys be placed in ascending order, there is nothing wrong with the situation after sorting below:

	name	number
R	John	1234
S	Victor	1234
T	Mary	987

Before sorting

	name	number
R	Mary	987
S	Victor	1234
T	John	1234

After unstable sorting, using *number* as the key

If you carefully compare the situation before and after sorting, you will notice that the order of the two records with identical keys 1234 is not preserved. The sorting process is said to be *unstable* if this can happen. In the above case the names *John* and *Victor* were in alphabetical order before sorting, which is no longer the case after sorting. Since this may be undesirable, sorting may be required to be stable. Obviously, we need not bother about a sorting process being stable or unstable if

a. the whole item acts as the key, or
b. the keys are unique, that is, with any two distinct items having different keys.

We will refer to these two cases and to the distinction between stable and unstable sorting in the next sections.

3.2 Selection Sort

Let us use an example to discuss a simple sorting method. If the sequence

      109   75   200   25   38   19   150   11   20

is to be sorted, it is a good idea to exchange the smallest item, 11, with the first, 109. We
then obtain the new sequence

<u>11</u> 75   200   25   38   19   150   109   20
OK

The first element of the sequence is now the smallest, so after this we can restrict ourselves
to the remaining elements. We now apply the same procedure to the subsequence that
starts at the second item, 75. Thus we select its smallest element, 19, and exchange it with
75, which gives:

<u>11   19</u> 200   25   38   75   150   109   20
     OK

We then proceed with the subsequence starting at the third element, 200, and so on, until
we have dealt with a subsequence of only two elements. This sorting method is called
straight selection. Here is a function template that sorts an array a of n items in this way:

```
template <class T>
void SelSort(T *a, int n)
{  int i, j, k;
   T min;
   for (i=0; i<n-1; i++)
   {  k = i; min = a[k];
      for (j=i+1; j<n; j++)
      if (a[j] < min) {k = j; min = a[k];}
      // Swap a[k] (= min) and a[i]:
      a[k] = a[i]; a[i] = min;
   }
}
```

For example, this template can be used as follows:

```
int a[5] = {30, 60, 10, 15, 25};
double b[4] = {1.2, 8.5, 0.3, 0.1};
SelSort(a, 5);
SelSort(b, 4);
```

The straight-selection algorithm (in the form of the above function *SelSort*) is *not* a stable
sorting method, as the following example demonstrates. In this example, to which we will
also apply other sorting methods, there are twelve records, each containing a numeric key
and an alphabetic data item. In the first line, the situation before sorting, record *5a*
precedes record *5b*, but this is no longer the case in the sorted situation on the second line.

```
5a 1a 5b 1b 5c 1c 2a 1d 5d 1e 2b 2c
1a 1b 1c 1d 1e 2a 2b 2c 5d 5c 5b 5a
```

You can easily verify that records with equal keys will not necessarily preserve their relative order with this method. Initially, the first record, 5*a*, is swapped with 1*a*, which has the least key of the remaining records. This gives the following sequence, in which the first item is now where it belongs:

```
1a  5a  5b  1b  5c  1c  2a  1d  5d  1e  2b  2c
```

Then the second item, 5*a*, is swapped with 1*c*, so we see that 5*a* is now placed after 5*b*. This shows that the order of items with equal keys is not preserved.

With this method, running time is proportional to the square of n, the number of array elements. If we made n twice as large, computing time would be approximately four times as much. This is because there are two nested loops in *SelSort*. If we doubled the value of n, the range of the controlled variable i, in the outer loop, would approximately be doubled. (Actually, this range would increase by a factor $(2n-1)/(n-1)$ instead of 2, hence the word 'approximately', which we usually omit.) As for the inner loop, with controlled variable j, the average range would also be doubled, so as a result of increasing n by a factor 2, the total running time would increase by a factor 4, and, in general, increasing n by a factor k implies an increase in running time by a factor k^2. This is expressed very briefly by saying that the running time is $O(n^2)$, or equivalently, that the algorithm has time complexity n^2.

Since the function *SelSort* has running time $O(n^2)$, it is suitable only for relatively small sequences. Besides straight selection, there are many other simple sorting methods which usually also have time complexity n^2. Collectively, we call them *straight methods*.

3.3 Bubblesort and Shakersort

With selection sort, the number of comparisons does not depend on the initial order of the elements to be sorted. This is different in some other sorting methods. We will now discuss two (related) sorting algorithms that are very fast if only a few elements are in a wrong position and all the others are in ascending order. Consider, for example, the following sequence:

```
10   21   92   35   50   69   80   83   90   95   100   120
```

The length of this sequence is $n = 12$. As usual in C and C++, we number the positions of the elements 0, 1, ..., $n-1$. Only the underlined element, 92, is in a wrong position. If, starting at the left, we compare each two neighboring elements, and exchange them if the left one is greater than the right one, then 92 is exchanged with 35, then with 50, and so on, until it is in its correct position, between 90 and 95. In this example, all elements are then in ascending order. If we proceed from left to right, and if after exchanging the elements in the positions k and $k+1$ no other exchanges are carried out during this scan, then all elements in the positions $k+1$, ..., $n-1$ are in their correct places, so only elements in the positions 0, 1, ..., k may still be wrong. We can now deal with these, again starting at the left. This way of sorting is called *bubblesort*: if we regard item $a[0]$ as being at the bottom and $a[n-1]$ at the top, then the way an element moves to the top until it is at its final position is reminiscent of water in which a bubble of air moves to the surface.

```
template <class T>
void swap(T &x, T &y)
{   T w = x; x = y; y = w;
}

template <class T>
void BubbleSort(T *a, int n)
{   int i, k, right = n - 1;
    while (right > 0)
    {   k = 0;
        for (i=0; i<right; i++)
            if (a[i+1] < a[i]){swap(a[i], a[i+1]); k = i;}
        right = k;
    }
}
```

This bubblesort function works fine for elements that have to move a long way to the right, as in this example:

```
10   20   1000 30   40   50   2000 60   70   80   90   100 110
```

Its behavior is not so good if some elements have to move a long way to the left, as in

```
10   20   30   40   50   60   70   15   80   90   25   100
```

This asymmetric behavior is avoided if we alternately move items to the left and to the right, retaining the principle of bubblesort that only neighboring items are swapped. This variation of bubblesort is known as *shakersort*:

```
// Shakersort, a variation of bubblesort.
template <class T>
void ShakerSort(T *a, int n)
{   int left = 0, right = n-1, k, i;
    while (left < right)
    {   k = 0;
        for (i=left; i<right; i++)
            if (a[i+1] < a[i]){swap(a[i], a[i+1]); k = i;}
        right = k; k = n - 1;
        for (i=right; i > left; i--)
            if (a[i-1] > a[i]) {swap(a[i-1], a[i]); k = i;}
        left = k;
    }
}
```

Both bubblesort and shakersort are stable sorting methods, as the following situations before and after sorting (with the digits acting as keys) illustrate:

```
5a 1a 5b 1b 5c 1c 2a 1d 5d 1e 2b 2c
1a 1b 1c 1d 1e 2a 2b 2c 5a 5b 5c 5d
```

3.4 Insertion Sort

Suppose that we have a number of items in ascending order, and a new item is to be inserted in its proper place. We would then find this place, shift all items with larger keys one position to the right to make room for the new item, and then put this item there. Obviously, the number of items increases by one, so we should distinguish between a large physical array size and a smaller number, n, indicating the number of array elements actually in use before insertion takes place:

```
template <class T>
void insert(T *a, int n, T x)
{   int j;
    for (j=n-1; j>=0; j--)
        if (x < a[j]) a[j+1] = a[j]; else break;
    a[j+1] = x;
}
```

This function also works correctly if we start with an empty array, or with an array of only one element. There is no problem if x, the item to be inserted, is less than the least item, $a[0]$, or greater than the greatest, $a[n-1]$. At first sight, we may be inclined to program two loops, one to find the position where x belongs and the other to make room for x by shifting array elements to the right. However, by starting from the right rather than from the left, we were able to combine these two actions in a single loop.

The function *insert* is useful for many purposes. One of these is a sorting algorithm, called *insertion sort*, as the following function shows:

```
template <class T>
void InsertSort(T *a, int n)
{   for (int i=0; i<n; i++) insert(a, i, a[i]);
}
```

This very compact function repeatedly inserts the original value of $a[i]$ in the (sub-)array consisting of the first i elements of array a. For example, the situation may be as follows when this happens with $i = 5$:

```
 0    1    2    3    4    5    6    7
12   18   23   24   38   20   11   15
```

The item 20 (= $a[5]$) is inserted in the array consisting of its first five elements, that is in the array

```
12   18   23   24   38
```

This means that the items 23, 24 and 38 are shifted one position to the right.

Insertion sort is rather inefficient. However, studying it is a good preparation for a much more efficient algorithm, to be discussed in the next section. It is also a stable sorting method, which could be illustrated by the final two lines at the end of the previous section.

3.5 Shellsort

The insertion sort discussed in the previous section is a good starting point for developing a much faster algorithm, known as *Shellsort*. It was published by D. L. Shell in 1959. We repeatedly sort all items that are h positions apart, starting with a large value of h and decreasing h gradually. Sorting all items that are h positions apart is called an h-sort. This principle is shown below for $h = 4$:

Situation before a 4-sort:

```
 0    1    2    3    4    5    6    7    8    9   10   11   12   13   14
90   55   15   32   64   20   32   16   63   24   27   83   25   48   91
```

Situation after this 4-sort:

```
 0    1    2    3    4    5    6    7    8    9   10   11   12   13   14
25   20   15   16   63   24   27   32   64   48   32   83   90   55   91
```

Note that the underlined items 25, 63, 64 and 90, which are four positions apart, are now in ascending order. The same applies to the items 20, 24, 48 and 55, printed in *italic*, and so on.

This method is based on the idea that initially, when h is large, each list to be sorted is small, while later, with smaller h values, the items will frequently be well ordered already, so that relatively few arrangements are required when the lists to be sorted grow larger. Since h gradually decreases, this method is also called insertion sort by *diminishing increment*.

So far we have not been very specific about the successive values of h. As suggested by D. E. Knuth and in accordance with common usage, we will use, in decreasing order, all values of the sequence 1, 4, 13, 40, 121, 364, ... that are less than some limit related to n. As you can see, the first element of this sequence is 1 and every other element h_i can be computed from its predecessor h_{i-1} as

$$h_i = 3h_{i-1} + 1$$

As for the limit just mentioned, we will start with the largest h (found in this sequence) such that all sequences to be sorted contain at least two elements. In other words, out of the sequence 1, 4, 13, 40, ... we take the element h that satisfies

$$2h \leq n \quad \text{and} \quad 2(3h + 1) > n$$

This value of h can be determined by the following loop, which starts with $h = 0$:

```
while (2 * (3 * h + 1) <= n) h = 3 * h + 1;
```

Written in a more efficient form, this loop occurs in the following template:

```
template <class T>
void ShellSort(T *a, int n)
{   int h = 0, i, j, next;
    T x;
    while (2 * (next = 3 * h + 1) <= n) h = next;
    for ( ; h > 0; h /= 3)
       for (i=h; i<n; i++)
       {   x = a[i];
           for (j=i-h; j>=0; j-=h)
              if (x < a[j]) a[j+h] = a[j]; else break;
           a[j+h] = x;
       }
}
```

Note the similarity between the inner loop of this function and the loop in the function *insert* discussed in the previous section.

The performance of (this implementation of) the Shellsort algorithm is significantly better than that of most other elementary sorting algorithms. It can be shown that it never does more than $n\sqrt{n}$ comparisons. The proof of this property is beyond the scope of this book. Unfortunately, the Shellsort algorithm is not a stable sorting method, as the following situations before and after sorting (with numeric keys) demonstrate:

```
5a 1a 5b 1b 5c 1c 2a 1d 5d 1e 2b 2c
1a 1b 1c 1d 1e 2a 2b 2c 5a 5c 5d 5b
```

3.6 Distribution Counting

If it is known that all keys lie in a limited range and some additional memory is available, we can sort extremely quickly. Let us begin with a very simple case: we are to sort *int* array elements $a[i]$, $i = 0, ..., n-1$, all satisfying

$$0 \le a[i] < m.$$

If allocating an *int* array of m elements is acceptable, the following function can be used for this purpose (and should in fact be recommended because of its speed):

```
void DistrSort0(int *a, int n)
{   int m=0, i, j;
    for (i=0; i<n; i++)
       if (a[i] < 0) return; else
       if (a[i] > m) m = a[i];
    m++;
    int *freq = new int[m];
    for (j=0; j<m; j++) freq[j] = 0;
    for (i=0; i<n; i++) freq[a[i]]++;
    i = 0;
    for (j=0; j<m; j++)
       while (freq[j]--) a[i++] = j;
    delete[] freq;
}
```

Let us use the following array as an example, with $n = 10$ and $m = 3$:

```
i:     0  1  2  3  4  5  6  7  8  9
a[i]:  2  1  1  0  1  1  2  0  2  1
```

This will lead to the following contents of the frequency-count array *freq*:

```
j:     0  1  2
freq:  2  5  3
```

It follows from these contents that array *a* is to be filled with two items 0, followed by five items 1, followed by three items 2, which gives the sorted array:

```
i:     0  1  2  3  4  5  6  7  8  9
a[i]:  0  0  1  1  1  1  1  2  2  2
```

With a fixed value of m, computing time is $O(n)$, which is even better than that of quicksort, to be discussed in the next section.

The problem is more complicated if we want to sort records, which also contain data other than the keys. In this case the frequency count alone will not be sufficient to construct the final situation because it provides us only with information about the keys, not about any additional data. Yet this problem too can be solved very efficiently, although it requires memory not only for the frequency array but also for a copy of the array to be sorted. In the following function template, the record type is denoted by T, while the keys will again be nonnegative integers less than m; the record type in question should have a member named *key*, which will be used as the sorting key:

```
template <class T>
void DistrSort(T *a, int n)
{   int m=0, i, j;
    for (i=0; i<n; i++)
        if (a[i].key < 0) return; else
        if (a[i].key > m) m = a[i].key;
    m++;
    int *freq = new int[m];
    T *b = new T[n];
    for (j=0; j<m; j++)
        freq[j] = 0;
    for (i=0; i<n; i++)
        freq[a[i].key]++;
    for (j=1; j<m; j++)
        freq[j] += freq[j-1];
    for (i=n-1; i>=0; i--)
        b[--freq[a[i].key]] = a[i];
    for (i=0; i<n; i++)
        a[i] = b[i];
    delete[] b;
    delete[] freq;
}
```

Here is a program fragment to show how *DistrSort* can be used:

```
struct rec {int key; char ch;};
rec a[8] = {{2, 'a'},
            {4, 'b'},
            {2, 'c'},
            {2, 'd'},
            {1, 'e'},
            {4, 'f'},
            {2, 'g'},
            {1, 'h'}};
DistrSort(a, 8);
for (i=0; i<8; i++) cout << a[i].key << a[i].ch << "   ";
```

The output produced by this is shown below:

```
1e   1h   2a   2c   2d   2g   4b   4f
```

With this example, the array *freq* is first given the following contents:

```
j:     0  1  2  3  4
freq:  0  2  4  0  2
```

These simple count values are then replaced with cumulative frequencies:

```
j:     0  1  2  3  4
freq:  0  2  6  6  8
```

For example, $freq[2] = 6$ now means that there are six keys that are not greater than 2. This information is used in the very complicated statement

```
for (i=n-1; i>=0; i--) b[--freq[a[i].key]] = a[i];
```

Initially, it takes $a[7]$, that is, $1h$, as the right-hand side of this assignment statement. This record is assigned to $b[--freq[1]]$, that is, to $b[1]$, which is the place where it belongs. When the key value 1 is used later, $freq[1]$ will again be decreased by one, so that $b[0]$ then occurs as the left-hand side of the assignment. Like the function *DistrSort0*, this template *DistrSort* is very fast, but it requires more memory. Distribution sort is stable, so the two lines at the end of Section 3.3 apply here as well.

3.7 The Quicksort Algorithm

We will now discuss a sorting method which is very efficient for large sequences of objects. This method, called *quicksort* (C. A. R. Hoare, *Computer Journal*, April 1962), is based on partitioning the given sequence into two subsequences. For some rather arbitrarily chosen element *x*, called a *pivot*, all elements of the first resulting subsequence are not greater than *x*, and all elements of the second are not less than *x*. Then the same method is applied to both subsequences, and so on. Here is a recursive quicksort function based on this principle:

```
// Quicksort; first version, two recursive calls.
template <class T>
void qsort1(T *a, int n)
{   int i = 0, j = n - 1;
    T x = a[j/2], w;
    do
    {   while (a[i] < x) i++;
        while (a[j] > x) j--;
        if (i < j) {w = a[i]; a[i] = a[j]; a[j] = w;} else
        {   if (i == j){i++; j--;}
            break;
        }
    }   while (++i <= --j);
    if (j > 0) qsort1(a, j+1);      //  a[0], ..., a[j]
    if (i < n-1) qsort1(a+i, n-i); //  a[i], ..., a[n-1]
}
```

If, for example, we have defined

```
int a[8] = {23, 398, 34, 100, 57, 67, 55, 320};
```

then we can use *qsort*1 as follows:

```
qsort1(a, 8);
```

In this example, we have $x = 100$, since $j = 7$ and $a[j/2] = a[3] = 100$. The integer variable i, starting at 0, is then incremented until $a[i] \geq x$, so in this example the first while-loop ends when $i = 1$, because then $a[i] = 398 \geq 100$. Also, j is initially given the value n − 1 = 7, and is decremented until it has such a value that $a[j] \leq x$. This is the case when $j = 6$, since $a[6] = 55 \leq 100$. The two elements 398 and 55 are then exchanged, and, in the comparison

```
++i <= --j
```

the i and j are updated once again, which gives $i = 2$ and $j = 5$. The new situation is as follows:

		i			j		
0	1	2	3	4	5	6	7
23	55	34	100	57	67	398	320

$x = 100$

The first while-loop is executed again, so i is incremented until we have $a[i] = a[3] = 100$. In the second while-loop, j is not decremented this time, since 67 is not greater than x. So the elements 100 and 67 are now exchanged, and i and j are updated once again, which gives $i = j = 4$, as shown below:

				i j			
0	1	2	3	4	5	6	7
23	55	34	67	57	100	398	320

$x = 100$

Since i is now equal to j, the test for continuation of the do-while-loop succeeds, and the first of the two inner while-loops is executed again; as 57 is less than x, the variable i is incremented. Then $a[i] = 100$, so this while-loop stops with $i = 5$. In the second while-loop, j is not decremented, since, with $j = 4$, element $a[j]$ is not greater than x. The do-while-loop now ends with $i = 5$ and $j = 4$:

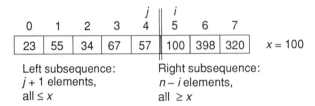

This completes the partitioning process. No element to the left of the double vertical line is greater than x, and no element to the right of this line is less. It is interesting that this method always works properly, even if x is unfortunately chosen. It would be ideal if x were the *median*, that is, if there were as many array elements less than x as there are elements greater than x. (We will discuss an efficient algorithm to compute the median in Section 3.12.) In less fortunate cases, the resulting subsequences have unequal lengths, as in the above example, where these lengths are 5 and 3. After partitioning the given sequence, it seems that we still have a long way to go before all elements are in ascending order. However, the only thing that remains to be done is to apply the same process to both the left and the right partitions, which have start addresses a and $a + i$, and lengths $j + 1$ and $n - i$, respectively. In *qsort*1 this is done recursively for both partitions, which is a very simple and elegant solution.

Because of the test at its end, the do-while-loop always ends with $i > j$. In our example, it ends with $i = j + 1$. The loop can also end with $i = j + 2$. This will occur, for example, if the sequence 50, 40, 30, 20, 10 is sorted. In this case, we have $i = 3$ and $j = 1$ after the do-while-loop, and the element $a[j+1] = x = 30$ lies between $a[i]$ and $a[j]$, and is already in its correct position. As above, the left and right subsequences are $a[0]$, ..., $a[j]$ and $a[i]$, ..., $a[n-1]$, with $a[j+1]$ in between.

You may want to see an example in which, immediately after the execution of the two while-loops, i is greater than j. If this situation had been impossible, the part *if* $(i == j)$ would have been superfluous. The case we are looking for occurs if we have $n = 5$ with the initial array contents 10, 20, 50, 30, 40. After executing the two while-loops, we have $x = 50$, $i = 2$, $j = 4$. Then 50 and 40 are exchanged, which gives 10, 20, 40, 30, 50 as the new array contents, with pivot x still equal to 50. Then after execution of the test $++i <= --j$ we have $i = j = 3$. Now the two while-loops are executed again, resulting in $i = 4$, $j = 3$, which is the case we were looking for. It would now not be correct if i were incremented and j decremented because that would result in a left partition of three elements (10, 20, 40) and an empty right partition, so that 40 and 30 would remain in that order and the array would not be properly sorted. This shows that we cannot omit the part *if* $(i == j)$. The two cases mentioned here illustrate that the quicksort algorithm is trickier than it looks.

Except for the worst-case situation, which in practice is extremely unlikely to occur, the running time of quicksort is $O(n \cdot \log n)$, so it will be approximately equal to $cn \cdot \log n$, where c is some constant. Note that the base of the logarithm only influences the value of

c, and, since we leave the latter unspecified, that base is irrelevant in our discussion. Remember that for large arguments, logarithmic functions increase extremely slowly. For example, using base 10, we have

$$\log 1000 \quad = 3$$
$$\log 10\,000 \ = 4$$

so if we switch from problem size $n_1 = 1000$ to problem size $n_2 = 10\,000$, the running time will increase by a factor

$$\frac{n_2 \cdot \log n_2}{n_1 \cdot \log n_1} = \frac{10\,000 \times 4}{1000 \times 3} \approx 13.3$$

whereas with a straight sorting method, with running time $O(n^2)$, that factor would be

$$\frac{n_2{}^2}{n_1{}^2} = \frac{10\,000^2}{1000^2} = 100$$

This example illustrates the significance of the concept of time complexity, as introduced in Section 1.1. For any algorithm with running time $O(n \cdot \log n)$ and any other algorithm with running time $O(n^2)$, there is a value of n beyond which the former algorithm will be faster than the latter. In practice we may work with values of n that will not exceed some limit, and we should be aware that we have not really shown that quicksort is faster than straight sorting methods, for, let us say, $n = 1000$, although we will probably expect that to be the case. Both analytic and experimental investigations have confirmed such expectations, that is, they have shown that quicksort is really a very fast sorting algorithm, even for rather small values of n, such as, say, 100.

It is not difficult to eliminate one of the two recursive calls in *qsort*1. As we will see in Section 4.10, recursion is associated with the use of a stack, so it is reasonable to ask whether function *qsort*1 might cause stack overflow if large arrays are to be sorted. In practice stack overflow is most unlikely to happen, but such a vague answer is not completely satisfactory. If each recursive call is applied to a subsequence that is almost as long as the current sequence, then, indeed, the recursion depth can be considerable and may even cause stack overflow. Although very improbable, this is not impossible. It would be nice if each recursive call were applied to a subsequence of at most half the size of the sequence under consideration. Fortunately, we can achieve this. In *qsort*1, one recursive call is at the very end of this function. As with *tail recursion* (where there is only one recursive call, as discussed in Section 1.4), that call at the end can be replaced with iteration. Instead of simply eliminating the second recursive call in *qsort*1, we actually want to eliminate the one that deals with the *longer subsequence*. That recursive call would always be the very last action in *qsort*1 if the two program lines

```
if (j > 0) qsort1(a, j+1);      //  a[0], ..., a[j]
if (i < n-1) qsort1(a+i, n-i); //  a[i], ..., a[n-1]
```

were replaced with

```
if (j + 1 < n - i)
{ if (j > 0) qsort1(a, j+1);      // The shorter sequence
  if (i < n-1) qsort1(a+i, n-i); // The longer sequence
}
else
{ if (i < n-1) qsort1(a+i, n-i); // The shorter sequence
  if (j > 0) qsort1(a, j+1);      // The longer sequence
}
```

With this modification, the shorter subsequence is dealt with first, and the recursive call
applied to the longer subsequence is executed as the final statement of the function. Then,
in the if and the else branches, we can easily eliminate the final recursive calls, as function
q_sort shows:

```
// Quicksort with limited recursion depth.

template <class T>
void q_sort(T *a, int n)
{ int i, j;
  T x, w;
  do
  { i=0;
    j=n-1;
    x = a[j/2];
    do
    { while (a[i] < x) i++;
      while (a[j] > x) j--;
      if (i < j)
      { w = a[i]; a[i] = a[j]; a[j] = w;
      } else
      { if (i == j){i++; j--;}
        break;
      }
    } while (++i <= --j);
    if (j+1 < n-i)
    { if (j > 0) q_sort(a, j+1);
      a += i; n -= i;
    } else
    { if (i < n-1) q_sort(a+i, n-i);
      n = j + 1;
    }
  } while (n > 1);
}
```

Since in each recursive call the sequence length is reduced by at least a factor 2, the
recursion depth is not greater than the logarithm (to the base 2) of the original sequence
length. This will be quite acceptable in practice. For example, when we sort an array of 10
000 elements, the recursion depth will be less than 14 because $\log_2 10\,000 \approx 13.3$. We will
therefore not remove this single recursive call in this section. If you are nevertheless
interested in how this could be done, you may be pleased to know that we will discuss a
nonrecursive version of quicksort in Section 4.11.

An improved version

So far, we have used *x*, computed as

```
j = n - 1;
x = a[j/2];
```

as a pivot for partitioning. Ideally, this pivot should be the median, that is, there should be about as many items less than the pivot as there are greater ones. Instead of just taking the item in the middle, we can find a better pivot by using the median of three items: the first, the one in the middle and the last. When finding this item, we may as well sort the three items just mentioned. Besides finding a better pivot value, this also has two other advantages: first, the first and the last items are then in the partitions in which they belong, so we need not compare them once again, and second, the sequence we are currently dealing with is immediately sorted if its length happens to be 3. Here is a version that is longer than the previous ones, but also slightly faster; it uses the *swap*, *swap3* and *sort3* templates (prefixed by *inline*) that we discussed at the beginning of this chapter:

```
// quicksrt.h: A quicksort template.
template <class T>
inline void swap(T &x, T &y)
{   T w = x; x = y; y = w;
}

template <class T>
inline void swap3(T &x, T &y, T &z)
{   T w = x; x = y; y = z; z = w;
}

template <class T>
inline void sort3(T &x, T &y, T &z)
{   if (x > y)
    {   if (x > z)
        {   if (y > z) swap(x, z);    // 3 2 1
            else swap3(x, y, z);      // 3 1 2
        } else swap(x, y);            // 2 1 3
    } else
    if (x > z) swap3(x, z, y);        // 2 3 1
    else
    if (y > z) swap(y, z);            // 1 3 2
    // else do nothing                // 1 2 3
}

template <class T>
void QuickSort(T *a, int n)
{   int i, j, nleft, nright;
    T x;
    while (n >= 3)
    {   j = n - 1; i = j/2;
        sort3(a[0], a[i], a[j]);
        if (n == 3) return;
        x = a[i];
        i = 1; j--;
```

```
       do
       {   while (a[i] < x) i++;
           while (a[j] > x) j--;
           if (i < j) swap(a[i], a[j]); else
           {   if (i == j){i++; j--;}
               break;
           }
       } while (++i <= --j);
       nleft = j + 1;
       nright = n - i;
       if (nleft < nright)
       {   if (j > 0)
               QuickSort(a, nleft);
           a += i;
           n = nright;
       } else
       {   if (nright > 1)
               QuickSort(a + i, nright);
           n = nleft;
       }
   }
   if (n == 2 && a[0] > a[1])
       swap(a[0], a[1]);
}
```

Here is a program that shows how the *QuickSort* template can be used:

```
// qsrtapp: An application of the QuickSort template.
#include <iostream.h>
#include <iomanip.h>
#include "quicksrt.h"

int main()
{   double a[] = {15, 1, 20, 3, 18, 7, 4, 1, 1, 2};
    int n = sizeof(a)/sizeof(*a), i;
    cout << "Before sorting:\n";
    for (i=0; i<n; i++)
       cout << setw(3) << a[i];
    cout << endl;
    QuickSort(a, n);
    cout << "After sorting:\n";
    for (i=0; i<n; i++)
       cout << setw(3) << a[i];
    cout << endl;
    return 0;
}
```

Quicksort is not a stable sorting method, as the following situations before and after sorting (with *QuickSort* and numeric keys) illustrate:

```
5a 1a 5b 1b 5c 1c 2a 1d 5d 1e 2b 2c
1a 1e 1d 1c 1b 2c 2b 2a 5c 5b 5a 5d
```

3.8 The *qsort* Library Function

As every C and C++ programmer should know, there is a library function *qsort*, which can sort any array. For example, we can sort the array *a* with *n* elements of type *T* by writing

```
#include <stdlib.h>
...
qsort(a, n, sizeof(T), compare);
```

where *compare* is a function of our own, indicating how two array elements *a*[*i*] and *a*[*j*] are to be compared. This function is similar to the well-known string function *strcmp* in that it returns zero in case of equality, any negative integer for 'less than' and any positive integer for 'greater than'. For example, if *a* is a *float* array (so that we replace *T* by *float* in the above call to *qsort*), we can write this function as follows:

```
int compare(const void *p, const void *q)
{   return *(float *)p < *(float *)q ? -1 :
            *(float *)p > *(float *)q;
}
```

On the other hand, if type *T* is declared (in a C++ program) as

```
struct T{char *name; int num;};
```

and we want to use the *num* member as a key, we can write

```
int compare(const void *p, const void *q)
{   return ((T *)p)->num - ((T *)q)->num;
}
```

By contrast, if the *name* member of *struct T* is to be used as a key, we write

```
int compare(const void *p, const void *q)
{   return strcmp(((T *)p)->name, ((T *)q)->name);
}
```

Finally, let us use yet another example to show how versatile *qsort* is. It sorts the program arguments and displays them in alphabetic order:

```
// progarg: Program arguments sorted by qsort.

#include <iostream.h>
#include <stdlib.h>
#include <string.h>

int compare(const void *p, const void *q)
{   return strcmp(*(char **)p, *(char **)q);
}
```

```
int main(int argc, char *argv[])
{  qsort(argv + 1, argc - 1, sizeof(char *), compare);
   for (int i=1; i<argc; i++) cout << argv[i] << endl;
   return 0;
}
```

Notice that each element of array *argv* is of type 'pointer to char'. Since the parameters *p* and *q* contain the *addresses* of such array elements, we should convert their type to 'pointer to pointer to char', hence the cast (*char* **) used here. Then the dereferencing operator * is also to be used here because we should supply the *strcpy* function with the start addresses of the character strings, not the addresses of the (pointer) array elements.

For example, if we start this program as

```
progarg Mary John Arthur Jim Cathy James Gaynor Clare Helen
```

its output will be as follows:

```
Arthur
Cathy
Clare
Gaynor
Helen
James
Jim
John
Mary
```

So much for *using* the *qsort* library function. It would be unsatisfactory if we omitted a discussion about the way we can write a *qsort* function ourselves. To declare our own quicksort function, *qsorta*, we use the following header file:

```
// qsorta.h: Header file for our own qsort version.
void qsorta(void *base, size_t n, size_t width,
   int (*fcmp)(const void *, const void *));
```

This function is defined at the end of the following file, which, after compilation, is to be linked with an application program. The performance of *qsorta* compares well with some *qsort* versions that come with commercial compilers:

```
// qsorta: Function compatible with the qsort library function.
#include <stdlib.h>

static void swap(void *p, void *q, size_t width)
{  char w, *pp=(char*)p, *qq=(char*)q;
   while (width--)
   {  w = *pp;
      *pp++ = *qq;
      *qq++ = w;
   }
}
```

```
static void swapint(void *p, void *q, size_t width)
{  register int w, *pp=(int*)p, *qq=(int*)q;
   while (width--)
   {  w = *pp;
      *pp++ = *qq;
      *qq++ = w;
   }
}

static void swap3(void *p, void *q, void *r, size_t width)
{  char w, *pp=(char*)p, *qq=(char*)q, *rr=(char*)r;
   while (width--)
   {  w = *pp;
      *pp++ = *qq;
      *qq++ = *rr;
      *rr++ = w;
   }
}

static void swap3int(void *p, void *q, void *r, size_t width)
{  register int w, *pp=(int*)p, *qq=(int*)q, *rr=(int*)r;
   while (width--)
   {  w = *pp;
      *pp++ = *qq;
      *qq++ = *rr;
      *rr++ = w;
   }
}

static void (*swp)(void *p, void *q, size_t width);
static void (*swp3)(void *p, void *q, void *r, size_t width);
static size_t width1;
static int (*fcmp)(const void *, const void *);

static void qsort1(char *a, size_t n, size_t width)
{  int ci, cj;
   size_t nleft, nright;
   char *pi, *pj, *ph, *plast;
   while (n >= 3)
   {  plast = a + (n - 1) * width;
      ph = a + ((n-1)/2) * width;
      if (fcmp(a, ph) > 0)
      {  if (fcmp(a, plast) > 0)
         {  if (fcmp(ph, plast) > 0) swp(a, plast, width1);//321
            else swp3(a, ph, plast, width1);                //312
         }  else swp(a, ph, width1);                        //213
      }  else
      if (fcmp(a, plast) > 0) swp3(a, plast, ph, width1);   //231
      else
      if (fcmp(ph, plast) > 0) swp(ph, plast, width1);      //132
      // else do nothing                                    //123

      if (n == 3) return;
      pi = a + width; pj = plast - width;
      // Pivot a[ph] is median of three elements
```

```
        do
        {   while ((ci = fcmp(pi, ph)) < 0) pi += width;
            while ((cj = fcmp(pj, ph)) > 0) pj -= width;
            if (pi < pj)
            {   swp(pi, pj, width1);
                if (ph == pi) ph = pj; else
                if (ph == pj) ph = pi;
            } else
            {   if (pi == pj) {pi += width; pj -= width;} else
                {   if (ci == 0) pi += width;
                    if (cj == 0) pj -= width;
                }
                break;
            }
        } while ((pi += width) <= (pj -= width));
        nleft = (pj + width - a)/width;
        nright = (plast + width - pi)/width;
        if (nleft < nright)
        {   if (nleft > 1)
                qsort1(a, nleft, width);
            a = pi; n = nright;
        } else
        {   if (nright > 1)
                qsort1(pi, nright, width);
            n = nleft;
        }
    }
    if (n == 2 && fcmp(a, a + width) > 0)
        swp(a, a + width, width1);
}

void qsorta(void *base, size_t n, size_t width,
    int (*cmp)(const void *, const void *))
{   if (width % sizeof(int) == 0)
    {   swp = swapint; swp3 = swap3int;
        width1 = width/sizeof(int);
    } else
    {   swp = swap; swp3 = swap3; width1 = width;
    }
    fcmp = cmp;
    qsort1((char *)base, n, width);
}
```

Our *qsorta* function has no information about the types of the data items other than their size, provided as the third argument, *width*. If *width* is a multiple of *sizeof(int)*, two array elements are swapped by swapping *width/sizeof(int)* pairs of integers; if not, we swap *width* pairs of characters. We therefore have two swap functions, *swapint* for integers and *swap* for characters. The function *qsorta* decides which of these will be used for the given array. It places the address of the chosen swap function in the pointer *swp*, which is then used in the function *qsort*1. This is a recursive function that does the actual work, while *qsorta* is nonrecursive. Similarly, there is a pointer *swp*3, in which *qsorta* places the address of either *swap3int* or *swap*3.

The following demonstration program shows that our own function *qsorta* is used in the same way as the standard library function *qsort*. You can use it to compare the performance of these two functions:

```cpp
// qs1: Compare speed of two quicksort implementations
//      (to be linked with qsorta.cpp).
#include <iostream.h>
#include <stdlib.h>
#include <time.h>
#include "qsorta.h"

int cmp1(const void *p, const void *q)
{  return *(double *)p < *(double *)q ? -1 :
      (*(double *)p > *(double *)q);
}

int main()
{  double *b, *c;
   int n, ntimes, limit, i, k;
   clock_t t1, t2;
   cout << "Enter n, ntimes, limit: ";
   cin >> n >> ntimes >> limit;
   b = new double[n];
   c = new double[n];
   if (!b || !c) exit(1);
   srand(1);
   for (i=0; i<100; i++) rand();
   t1 = clock();
   for (k=0; k<ntimes; k++)
   {  for (i=0; i<n; i++) b[i] = double(rand() % limit);
      qsort(b, n, sizeof(double), cmp1);
   }
   t2 = clock();
   cout << "qsort: " << double(t2 - t1)/CLK_TCK << endl;
   for (i=0; i<n; i++) c[i] = b[i];
   srand(1);
   for (i=0; i<100; i++) rand();
   t1 = clock();
   for (k=0; k<ntimes; k++)
   {  for (i=0; i<n; i++) b[i] = double(rand() % limit);
      qsorta(b, n, sizeof(double), cmp1);
   }
   t2 = clock();
   cout << "qsorta: " << double(t2 - t1)/CLK_TCK << endl;
   for (i=0; i<n; i++) if (b[i] != c[i])
   {  cout << "Sort wrong!\n"; break;
   }
   return 0;
}
```

In a comparison with array size 100, sorting 5000 times and using nonnegative random array elements less than (*limit* =) 1000, the above function *qsorta* proved to be slightly faster than the Borland C++ 4.5 *qsort* library function.

3.9 Heapsort

The array a with elements

```
a[0], a[1], ..., a[n-1]
```

is said to satisfy the *heap condition* if

$$a[i] \geq a[2 * i + 1]$$
$$a[i] \geq a[2 * i + 2]$$

as far as these elements belong to the array. For example, if the contents of array a are as shown in the second line of

```
i         0   1   2   3   4   5   6   7   8   9
a[i]     80  50  70  30  40  25  60  28  14  20
```

(with $n = 10$), this array forms a heap, because we have

$a[0] \geq a[1]$ and $a[0] \geq a[2]$
$a[1] \geq a[3]$ and $a[1] \geq a[4]$
$a[2] \geq a[5]$ and $a[2] \geq a[6]$
$a[3] \geq a[7]$ and $a[3] \geq a[8]$
$a[4] \geq a[9]$

This heap concept is the basis for a very efficient sorting algorithm. To see how it works, we must first understand the *sift operation* on a heap. Suppose we have an array whose contents form a heap but for its first element, as in the following example:

```
i         0   1   2   3   4   5   6   7   8   9
a[i]     15  50  70  30  40  25  60  28  14  20
```

Note that $a[0]$ is now 15 instead of 80 and therefore no longer satisfies the heap condition. By contrast, the other array elements are the same as in our previous example, so that only $a[0]$ prevents this array from being a heap. The sift process makes a heap of this array by rearranging some elements. The wrong element 15 is to move to the right in rather large steps, until it finds the position where it belongs. More precisely, we do this in the following way. After copying $a[0]$ in the variable x, we compare x with the larger of the two elements $a[1]$ and $a[2]$. Since x (= 15) is less than $a[2]$ (= 70), we may consider swapping $a[0]$ and $a[2]$, but as we are not sure that $a[2]$ will be the final position of x, we only put 70 in $a[0]$, leaving a hole in $a[2]$ (and 15 saved in x):

```
i         0   1   2   3   4   5   6   7   8   9
a[i]     70  50  ..  30  40  25  60  28  14  20        x = 15
```

We now compare x with the larger of $a[2 * 2 + 1]$ and $a[2 * 2 + 2]$, that is, with $a[6]$ (= 60). Since x is also less than $a[6]$, we move 60 to the hole in position 2, leaving a new hole in position 6:

```
i          0  1  2  3  4  5  6  7  8  9
a[i]      70 50 60 30 40 25 .. 28 14 20        x = 15
```

This process now terminates because the next positions to be used for comparisons with x fall outside the array. Then we place x in the hole $a[6]$, after which the array is a heap. The process of moving to the right could also have terminated by x being not less than the greater of the two elements $a[2 * i + 1]$ and $a[2 * i + 2]$, where i is the position of the current hole. This *sifting* process is performed by the first of the following two functions, which is slightly more general than what we have been discussing in that it can start at any position k of the array. In our above example we have used $k = 0$:

```
template <class T>
static void sift(T *a, int k, int n)
{   int i, j;
    T x;
    i = k; x = a[i];
    while ((j = 2 * i + 1) < n)
    {   if (j < n - 1 && a[j] < a[j+1]) j++;
        if (x >= a[j]) break;
        a[i] = a[j]; i = j;
    }
    a[i] = x;
}

template <class T>
void HeapSort(T *a, int n)
{   T x;
    for (int k=n/2-1; k>=0; k--) sift(a, k, n);
    while (--n > 0)
    {   x = a[0]; a[0] = a[n]; a[n] = x;
        sift(a, 0, n);
    }
}
```

The second function, *HeapSort*, does the actual sorting. It first constructs a heap, starting in the middle. Remember, the elements of the right half of an array always satisfy the heap condition because for each of these elements $a[i]$ the elements $a[2 * i + 1]$ and $a[2 * i + 2]$ fall outside the array. For example, if the array

```
i          0  1  2  3  4  5  6  7  8  9
a[i]      58 26 85 24 10 37 93 25 91 16
```

is given (where underlined elements satisfy the heap condition), we begin by sifting $a[4] = 10$, which means that this element is exchanged with $a[9]$, with the following result:

```
i          0  1  2  3  4  5  6  7  8  9
a[i]      58 26 85 24 16 37 93 25 91 10
```

We then sift $a[3] = 24$, so this is exchanged with 91, the larger of $a[7]$ and $a[8]$:

```
i          0  1  2  3  4  5  6  7  8  9
a[i]      58 26 85 91 16 37 93 25 24 10
```

After applying similar sift operations to $a[2]$, $a[1]$ and $a[0]$, we obtain the following heap:

```
i       0  1  2  3  4  5  6  7  8  9
a[i]   93 91 85 26 16 37 58 25 24 10
```

We have now finished with the for-statement in the *HeapSort* function. Sorting this heap is now done in the subsequent while-statement. This begins by swapping $a[0]$ and $a[9]$, which makes sense because the heap condition guarantees that the first array element $a[0]$ is the largest, which we want at the end of the array. So $a[9]$ now has its definitive value and we only need to sort the subarray $a[0]$, ..., $a[8]$:

```
i       0  1  2  3  4  5  6  7  8
a[i]   10 91 85 26 16 37 58 25 24
```

This is a heap but for $a[0]$, so we sift this element to let this subarray satisfy the heap condition. The result of this sifting is the following heap:

```
i       0  1  2  3  4  5  6  7  8
a[i]   91 26 85 25 16 37 58 10 24
```

We now swap the first and final elements of this subarray, after which $a[8]$ also has its definitive value, and so on.

Heapsort is not a stable sorting method, as the following two situations before and after sorting (with digits as keys) demonstrate:

```
5a 1a 5b 1b 5c 1c 2a 1d 5d 1e 2b 2c
1b 1e 1c 1a 1d 2b 2c 2a 5d 5c 5b 5a
```

3.10 Merging and Mergesort

The process of combining two sorted sequences into one is called *merging*. Here is a function that merges the two arrays a (of length na) and b (of length nb) into array c (of length $na + nb$). The user of this function must provide memory space for array c:

```
template <class T>
void merge(const T *a, int na, const T *b, int nb, T *c)
{  int ia=0, ib=0, ic=0;
   while (ia < na && ib < nb)
      c[ic++] = (a[ia] < b[ib] ? a[ia++] : b[ib++]);
   while (ia < na) c[ic++] = a[ia++];
   while (ib < nb) c[ic++] = b[ib++];
}
```

We can use this function as the basis of a simple and fast sorting algorithm, which has one drawback, however: it does not sort in place but requires additional memory space as large as the array to be sorted:

```
template <class T>
void MergeSort(T *a, int n)
{  if (n < 2) return;
   int nLeft = n/2, nRight = n - nLeft;
   MergeSort(a, nLeft); MergeSort(a + nLeft, nRight);
   T *p = new T[n];
   merge(a, nLeft, a + nLeft, nRight, p);
   for (int i=0; i<n; i++) a[i] = p[i];
   delete[] p;
}
```

Note that the position where we apply the *new* operator is crucial. Had we used this operator prior to the recursive calls to *MergeSort*, the amount of temporarily used memory would have been much more than it is now. Since there is no recursive call between *new* and *delete* in the above version, this amount does not exceed $n * sizeof(T)$ bytes.

We will return to mergesort in Section 4.10: as we will see, this method is a very attractive one when applied to linked lists.

3.11 External Sorting

So far, we have been discussing only internal sorting methods, with array elements as the objects to be sorted. Instead, we can sort *externally*, that is, rearrange items in a *file* instead of in an array. Since on most computer systems files may be much larger than arrays, we need external sorting methods as soon as memory is insufficient for internal sorting. A good many years ago, internal sorting methods could hardly ever be used for data-processing applications, because of memory limitations. Now that we are accustomed to rather large amounts of internal memory, we should not reject internal sorting methods too soon. However, memory may still be insufficient to contain all data to be sorted, so we will also pay some attention to external sorting.

Note that the distinction between internal and external sorting methods is pragmatic rather than fundamental. Since in C we have random access to a disk file, we can adapt the methods of the preceding sections to files. For example, we can apply the quicksort method to a disk file, as is demonstrated in *Programs and Data Structures in C* (see Preface). On the other hand, we can simulate sequential file access by accessing arrays strictly sequentially. However, we should remember:

- Most internal sorting methods sort *in situ*, that is, they use only one array. Both the data to be sorted and the sorted data are in this array and no temporary arrays are required for these methods. External methods, on the other hand, are not normally so economical with space, but will use several files.
- Sequential array access is normally not faster than random array access. This is different with files, since with sequential file access large quantities of data can be buffered. So although random access is possible with a disk file, it might be faster to use sequential access if we sort externally. If we have only tapes instead of a disk, as was quite usual in the early days of computing, we are limited to sequential access, so in this case quicksort is out of the question.

There are many methods for external sorting. The algorithm we will discuss is known as *balanced multiway merging* and is reasonably fast. As usual, we will use a *function template* rather than a function. Instead of an array, we will provide the names of input and output files. In this function template, *BMMSort*, the item types will be denoted by *T*. Then in calls to *BMMSort* we must indicate which type is actually to be used instead of *T*. The situation is different from internal sorting, in that no arrays are used in these calls, and the file names arguments do not give any information about the data types in question. We will therefore supply an additional dummy argument for this purpose. For example, the following program sorts a file of characters, hence the *char* argument *dummy*:

```
// bmmdemo1: Sorting by balanced multiway merging:
//   simple demonstration program sorts characters.
#include <iostream.h>
#include <iomanip.h>
#include "bmmsort.h"

int main()
{  char InpFileName[50], OutFileName[50];
   char dummy;
   cout << "Name of input file:  ";
   cin >> setw(50) >> InpFileName;
   cout << "Name of output file: ";
   cin >> setw(50) >> OutFileName;
   // Third argument specifies item type:
   if (BMMSort(InpFileName, OutFileName, dummy))
      cout << "File problem\n";
   return 0;
}
```

As you can see, this application program is simple and easy to use. If, instead of sorting characters, we wanted to sort items of integers, for example, we would have to replace *char dummy* with *int dummy*. More interestingly, we can also modify this program to sort records, using a sorting key, as we will see later. But let us first deal with the sorting algorithm itself. We will do this by examining the header file *bmmsort.h*, used in the above program and to be discussed in a moment:

```
// bmmsort.h: Balanced multiway merging sort.
#include <assert.h>
#include <fstream.h>
#include <stdio.h>
#include <stdlib.h>

const int N=5;
static int in, out, inbuf[3], iOut, TapesWrittenTo[3];
static long nn, nRead[3];
static fstream t[6];

template <class T>
void WriteTape(int i, const T &x)
{  t[i].write((char *)&x, sizeof(T));
}
```

```
template <class T>
int ReadTape(int i, T &x)
{  t[i].read((char *)&x, sizeof(T));
   return !t[i].fail();
}

template <class T>
int oi(T *a, int i)   // Output and input of one item
{  WriteTape(out+iOut, a[i]);
   TapesWrittenTo[iOut] = 1;
   if (nRead[i] == nn) nRead[i] = inbuf[i] = 0; else
   {  inbuf[i] = ReadTape(in + i, a[i]);
      if (inbuf[i]) nRead[i]++;
   }
   return 1;
}

template <class T>
int oi(T *a, int i, int j)
{  return a[i] <= a[j] && oi(a, i);
}

template <class T>
int oi(T *a, int i, int j, int k)
{  return a[i] <= a[j] && a[i] <= a[k] && oi(a, i);
}

template <class T>
void InsertSort(T *a, int n)
{  int j;
   T x;
   for (int i=0; i<n; i++)
   {  x = a[i];
      for (j=i-1; j>=0; j--)
         if (x < a[j]) a[j+1] = a[j]; else break;
      a[j+1] = x;
   }
}

template <class T>
int BMMSort(const char *InpFileName, const char *OutFileName,
   const T &dummy) // dummy indicates item type for template
{  ifstream InpFile;
   ofstream OutFile;
   T a[N], x;
   InpFile.open(InpFileName, ios::in | ios::nocreate);
   if (!InpFile) return 1; // Cannot open input file
   int i, j, n, count, LastTape;
   char strTmp[6][L_tmpnam];
   for (i=0; i<6; i++)
   {  tmpnam(strTmp[i]);
      t[i].open(strTmp[i], ios::out | ios::trunc | ios::binary);
      // You may have to remove this part:  | ios::binary.
      // It is required with MS-DOS, however.
      // The same applies elsewhere in this program.
```

```
         if (t[i].fail())
         {  cout << "Cannot open temporary files\n"; exit(1);
         }
      }
      i = 0; // Write runs of n items to t0, t1 and t2:
      for (;;)
      {  for (n=0; n<N; n++)
            if (!(InpFile >> a[n])) break;
         InsertSort(a, n);
         for (j=0; j<n; j++) WriteTape(i, a[j]);
         i++; i %= 3;
         if (!InpFile) break;
      }
      nn = N; in = 0; out = 3;
      iOut = 0;
      for (i=0; i<3; i++)
      {  t[j=in+i].close();
         t[j].open(strTmp[j], ios::in | ios::binary);
      }
      for (;;)
      {  nRead[0] = nRead[1] = nRead[2] = 0;
         for (i=0; i<3; i++)
         {  inbuf[i] = ReadTape(in + i, a[i]);
            if (inbuf[i]) nRead[i]++;
         }
         while (inbuf[0] && inbuf[1] && inbuf[2])
            oi(a, 0, 1, 2) || oi(a, 1, 2, 0) || oi(a, 2, 0, 1);
         while (inbuf[0] && inbuf[1]) oi(a, 0, 1) || oi(a, 1, 0);
         while (inbuf[1] && inbuf[2]) oi(a, 1, 2) || oi(a, 2, 1);
         while (inbuf[2] && inbuf[0]) oi(a, 2, 0) || oi(a, 0, 2);
         while (inbuf[0]) oi(a, 0);
         while (inbuf[1]) oi(a, 1);
         while (inbuf[2]) oi(a, 2);
         if (t[in].fail() && t[in+1].fail() && t[in+2].fail())
         {  count = 0;
            for (i=0; i<3; i++)
            {  if (TapesWrittenTo[i]) {LastTape = out+i; count++;}
               TapesWrittenTo[i] = 0;
            }
            if (count <= 1) break;
            in = out; out = 3 - in; nn *= 3; iOut = 0;

            for (i=0; i<3; i++)
            {  t[j=in+i].close();
               t[j].open(strTmp[j], ios::in | ios::binary);
               t[j=out+i].close();
               t[j].open(strTmp[j],
                  ios::out | ios::trunc | ios::binary);
            }
         } else if (++iOut == 3) iOut = 0;
      }
      InpFile.close();
      OutFile.open(OutFileName, ios::out);
      if (!OutFile) return 2; // Cannot open output file
      char *pSepar = (sizeof(T) == 1 ? "" : "\n");
```

```
    if (count)
    {   t[LastTape].close();
        t[LastTape].open(strTmp[LastTape], ios::in | ios::binary);
        while (ReadTape(LastTape, x))
            OutFile << x << pSepar;
    }   // else count == 0: empty input and output files
    OutFile.close();
    InpFile.close();
    for (i=0; i<6; i++) {t[i].close(); remove(strTmp[i]);}
    return 0;
}
```

Suppose the input file contains the following string:

`hereisyourbooktheoneyourthousandsoflettershaveaskedmetopublish`

We are using six temporary files, traditionally called *tapes*. We will conform to this
terminology, using the word *tape* for what will more often be a file on disk these days. At
any time, three of these six tapes are used for input and the other three for output. Instead
of three, we could have used any other number greater than 1. If we had used 4 (= 2 + 2)
instead of six tapes, our program would have been simpler, but also slower. On the other
hand, it would have been more complicated (and probably faster) if the number of tapes
had been 8 or 10, for example.

Repeatedly, we read a block of N items from the input file, sort it internally, and write it
to one of the first three tapes, switching to the next tape for each block. The value of N can
be very small, and these internal sort operations will never be done for blocks larger than N
items. In the above file we have $N = 5$, but a larger value may be chosen, depending on the
available memory and the size of each item. (Choosing a larger value for N does *not* make
the program more complicated.) The blocks of N sorted items are written to the tapes 0, 1,
2, 0, 1, 2, and so on. Let us first show the division into blocks of N items:

`herei syour bookt heone yourt housa ndsof lette rshav easke`
`dmeto publi sh`

After sorting *herei*, the result, *eehir*, is written to tape 0. Then *syour* is sorted, giving *orsuy*,
which is written to tape 1, and so on. Since the number of items need not be a multiple of
N, there may be a block of less than N items at the end, and the tapes may contain different
numbers of blocks. After sorting each block and writing it to a tape, we obtain the
following situation for the tapes 0, 1 and 2 (the remaining tapes 3, 4 and 5 not being used
at this stage):

```
Tape 0:   eehir eehno dfnos aeeks hs
Tape 1:   orsuy ortuy eeltt demot
Tape 2:   bkoot ahosu ahrsv bilpu
```

This sorting of blocks of size N can be done by any of the internal sorting methods we have
been discussing in the preceding sections. Our implementation uses the *InsertSort* function
template for this purpose as follows:

```
InsertSort(a, n);
```

For small *n*, such as 5, this is not slower than other sorting methods and it has the advantage of being a stable sorting method. Since the balanced multiway merge algorithm itself does not alter the relative order of records with equal keys, the *BMMSort* function is then also stable. If, instead of 5, a value greater than, say, 20 is used for *N*, we had better replace insertion sort with a method that is faster for large arrays, replacing this line with

```
QuickSort(a, n);
```

for example, although we sacrifice 'stability' in this way.

Normally we have *n* = *N*, but *n* may be less than *N* for the last block (with *n* = 2, *a*[0] = 's' and *a*[1] = 'h' in our example). Incidentally, ascending maximal subsequences, such as *eehir* in the above contents of tape 0, are called *runs*.

We now repeatedly merge three blocks, read from these tapes, and write them to the tapes 3, 4 and 5. Note that we no longer sort internally, because the blocks may now be too large to fit into memory. Instead, we *merge* the three blocks. For example, we begin by reading *e*, *o* and *b*, the very first items of the tapes 0, 1 and 2, storing them in the first three elements of array *a*, and we will not use the remaining elements of this array any more. Since *b* precedes both *e* and *o* in the alphabet, we write *b* to tape 3 and read the next item, *k*, from tape 2, storing this in *a*[2] to replace *b*. We now again compare the first three elements of array *a*, that is, *e*, *o* and *k*, to select *e* as the item to be written to tape 3. Merging the blocks *eehir*, *orsuy* and *bkoot* in this way produces the following block for tape 3: *beehikooorrstuy*. This obviously consists of 3 × *N* = 15 items. Then, for each of the three tapes 0, 1 and 2, we read the items (*eehno*, *ortuy* and *ahosu*) of its next block and merge these, which gives the next block (*aeehhnooorstuuy*) for tape 4, and so on. After having merged all blocks of the tapes 0, 1 and 2 in this way, we have the following situation:

```
Tape 0:    eehir eehno dfnos aeeks hs
Tape 1:    orsuy ortuy eeltt demot
Tape 2:    bkoot ahosu ahrsv bilpu

Tape 3:    beehikooorrstuy abdeeeiklmopstu
Tape 4:    aeehhnooorstuuy hs
Tape 5:    adeefhlnorssttv
```

We now proceed by letting the input and output tapes change roles: the blocks of the tapes 3, 4 and 5 will now be read, merged and written to the tapes 0, 1 and 2, so that we obtain blocks that are again three times as long as the previous ones; in other words, they will consist of $3^2 \times N = 45$ items (except for the final one). The resulting tapes 0, 1 and 2 are shown below:

```
Tape 0:    aabdeeeeeefhhhhiklnnooooooorrrrsssstttttuuuvyy
Tape 1:    abdeeehiklmopsstu
Tape 2:
```

Merging these contents of the tapes 0 and 1 gives the final result on tape 3:

```
aaabbddeeeeeeeeefhhhhhiikkllmnnooooooooprrrrsssssstttttuuuuvyy
```

The array elements $a[0]$, $a[1]$ and $a[2]$ act as buffers containing the last items read from the three input tapes. The corresponding elements of array *inbuf* indicate whether these buffers still contain data that is to be written to output tapes. Yet another array, *nRead*, keeps track of the number of items read from a block. With *nn* as the current block length (equal to N possibly multiplied by a power of 3), the last item of a block has been read when *nRead* is equal to *nn* (or when the file is exhausted). Finally, the array *TapesWrittenTo* indicates to which of the three output tapes data has been written. As soon as merging ends because we are at the end of all three input tapes, and only one element of array *TapesWrittenTo* is nonzero, the whole sort merging process is ready since all items are on the same tape. This tape is then copied to the output file with the given name. The temporary files called *tapes* in this discussion are then removed.

Sorting records

You may wonder if our sorting template *bmmsort.h* is really general enough to be used for sorting records. To show that this is the case, we will sort the following text file, which could be data for a book index. An author may write this list page by page, so that the page numbers appear in ascending order, while he or she wants the index entries, that is, the words, to be in alphabetical order:

```
disk          1
computer      1
program       2
tape          2
computer      3
block         4
disk          5
computer      5
algorithm     5
```

The sorting process uses the above file as input and produces the following output, with the index entries, used as keys, in alphabetical order:

```
algorithm     5
block         4
computer      1
computer      3
computer      5
disk          1
disk          5
program       2
tape          2
```

Note that this example illustrates the fact that our sorting method is stable: for example, *computer* 1 precedes *computer* 3, since this was also the case in the input file. This would not necessarily have been the case if, as part of the BMM algorithm, we had used quicksort instead of insertion sort. The above output file was actually obtained by the following program, which uses the header file discussed before *without any modification*:

```
// bmmdemo2: Producing the index of a book, using
//     balanced multiway merging for external sorting.
#include <iostream.h>
#include <iomanip.h>
#include <string.h>
#include "bmmsort.h"

class rec {
public:
   char IndexEntry[13];
   int PageNr;
};

int operator>=(const rec &x, const rec &y)
{  return strcmp(x.IndexEntry, y.IndexEntry) >= 0;
}

int operator>(const rec &x, const rec &y)
{  return strcmp(x.IndexEntry, y.IndexEntry) > 0;
}

int operator<=(const rec &x, const rec &y)
{  return strcmp(x.IndexEntry, y.IndexEntry) <= 0;
}

int operator<(const rec &x, const rec &y)
{  return strcmp(x.IndexEntry, y.IndexEntry) < 0;
}

ostream &operator<<(ostream &os, const rec &x)
{  return os << setiosflags(ios::left) << setw(12)
      << x.IndexEntry << resetiosflags(ios::left)
      << setw(3) << x.PageNr;
}

istream &operator>>(istream &is, rec &x)
{  return is >> setw(12) >> x.IndexEntry >> x.PageNr;
}


int main()
{  char InpFileName[50], OutFileName[50];
   rec dummy;
   cout << "Name of input file:  ";
   cin >> setw(50) >> InpFileName;
   cout << "Name of output file: ";
   cin >> setw(50) >> OutFileName;
   // Third argument indicates item type:
   if (BMMSort(InpFileName, OutFileName, dummy))
      cout << "File problem\n";
   return 0;
}
```

The balanced-multiway-merging sorting method has running time $O(n \log n)$, so it is very suitable for large files. In an experiment with yet another demonstration program using the file *bmmsort.h*, it took about 26 s (on a 486 PC) to sort 100 000 integers. Another program for external sorting, *nmsort.c*, discussed in *Programs and Data Structures in C*, took about 42 s to sort the same file. That program is based on *natural mergesort*, which also has running time $O(n \log n)$. It uses only three tapes, but since it is not as fast as balanced multiway mergesort, we will not discuss it here.

3.12 Median and Order Statistics

The subject of this section is related to sorting. With a given array of n numbers, we will discuss an efficient way of finding the number that would be at position k ($0 \le k < n$) if the array elements were sorted. An important application of this is finding the *median*. For example, the array with contents

```
50 10 20 30 40
```

has 30 as its median, since this number would be in the middle if the array were sorted. As the very first array element is at position 0, we would find this value 30 at position 2 in the following array, obtained if the array were sorted:

```
10 20 30 40 50
```

In general, if the array length n is odd and all array elements are distinct, we find the median at position $k = (n - 1)/2$ in the sorted array.

There are two medians if all array elements are distinct and n is even. They are found at the positions $n/2 - 1$ and $n/2$ of the sorted array. For example, both 20 and 30 (at the positions 1 and 2) are medians in this array, where $n = 4$:

```
10 20 30 40
```

Another point to be noted is that any equal values are counted individually. For example, 10 is the median of the array

```
10 10 10 10 10 20 30
```

It follows from the above that our algorithm will compute the smallest array element if $k = 0$ and the largest if $k = n - 1$. Some array elements will be swapped, but the array will not be completely sorted. Suppose we are given the following array a, with $n = 10$, and we use $k = 6$, that is, we want to find the element that would be $a[6]$ if a were sorted:

```
60 60 10 20 30 10 30 50 20 40
```

As in the quicksort algorithm, we begin by partitioning this array, using the element $x = a[4] = 30$, as a pivot. After this, the two partitions are as shown below:

20 30 10 20 10   30 60 50 60 40

The second partition starts at position $i = 5$. Let us regard this as a new array of length $n' = n - i$. Since we have $k (= 6) \geq i$, we can proceed with this new array, but we now want the element that would be at position $k' = k - i = 1$ if it were sorted. If k had been less than i, we would obviously have limited our attention to the first partition (with length $n' = i$ and desired position $k' = k$) instead of the second. Here is a complete demonstration program, based on this idea. In contrast to the very general function template *select*, the *main* function is written only to illustrate the above example, where k need not be 6 but can be arbitrarily chosen:

```cpp
// select: For a given array with n elements, find the element
//         that would be at position k if the array were sorted.
#include <iostream.h>

template <class T>
T select(T *a, int n, int k)  // k < n
// Select element belonging in position k (0 <= k < n)
{  while (n > 1)
   {  // Partition:
      int i = 0, j = n - 1;
      T x = a[j/2], w;
      do
      {  while (a[i] < x) i++;
         while (a[j] > x) j--;
         if (i < j){w = a[i]; a[i] = a[j]; a[j] = w;} else
         {  if (i == j) i++;
            break;
         }
      } while (++i <= --j);
      // Partitions: a[0],...,a[i-1] <= x, a[i],...,a[n-1] >= x
      if (k < i) n = i; else {a += i; n -= i; k -= i;}
   }
   return a[0];
}

int main()
{  int k;
   const int n = 10;
   int a[n] = {60, 60, 10, 20, 30, 10, 30, 50, 20, 40};
   cout << "Initial array contents:\n";
   for (int j=0; j<n; j++) cout << a[j] << " ";
   do
   {  cout << "\nEnter k (nonnegative and less than " << n
           << ")\n";
      cout << "to select the value that would be at\n";
      cout << "position k if the array were sorted: ";
      cin >> k;
   } while (k < 0 || k >= n);
   cout << "Selected value: " << select(a, n, k) << endl;
   return 0;
}
```

The way of partitioning is almost the same as that of function *qsort*1 at the beginning of Section 3.7. In the if-statement just before the break-statement, *j* was decremented in function *qsort*1, while this action is omitted here because *j* is not used after execution of the break-statement. Again, this partitioning process is trickier than it may look at first. For example, if we omit the if-statement just mentioned, the case $n = 2$, $k = 0$ with $a[0] < a[1]$ will result in an endless loop.

Note that, in the outer while-loop of the *select* function, the value *k* is not used until the partitioning process is completed. This function is often presented in a recursive form, with only one recursive call being executed at the end of the function. As we know, such tail recursion can easily be eliminated, as has been done in the above version. Here is a demonstration of this program:

```
Initial array contents:
60 60 10 20 30 10 30 50 20 40
Enter nonnegative k (less than 10)
to select the value that would be at
position k if the array were sorted: 6
Selected value: 40
```

You can verify the correctness of this selected value by noting that $a[6] = 40$ in the sorted array:

```
10 10 20 20 30 30 40 50 60 60
```

As discussed above, the given array is modified, but *not* sorted. For large arrays, function *select* is very fast. If we only want to find a median, sorting an entire array would be wasteful. Surprisingly, the expected computing time used by *select* is $O(n)$, while that for quicksort is $O(n \log n)$. Remember, the two partitions constructed by quicksort are both to be sorted, while only one is to be dealt with in the *select* function. A proof of the expected linear time behavior of *select* is beyond the scope of this book. At first sight, this behavior seems unlikely because there are three nested loops. We will find it less unlikely, however, if we take a look at the following fragment, also consisting of three nested loops:

```
for (i=0; i<1000*n; i+=100)
   for (j=i; j<i+100; j+=20)
      for (k=j; k<j+20; k++)
         cout << k << endl;
```

This fragment displays *k* once for each of the values 0, 1, ..., $1000n - 1$, as if we had written the following simple loop:

```
for (k=0; k<1000*n; k++)
   cout << k << endl;
```

For both fragments, computing time is $O(n)$. This example demonstrates that nested loops can result in linear time behavior.

Exercises

3.1   Apply the sorting methods of this chapter to *large* numbers, which were discussed in Chapter 2.

3.2   Show that sorting methods for arrays can also be applied to a file because we can update a file using random access.

3.3   Write a program that reads the integer n, followed by a sequence of n integers. Sort the integers of this sequence according to the sums of their digits. For example, if the input data is

```
4
11111   39   321   45
```

the output will be

```
11111   321   45   39
```

since these last integers have 5, 6, 9 and 12 as the sums of their digits, respectively.

3.4   Combine the quicksort algorithm and the shakersort algorithms: use quicksort to construct partitions consisting of no more than m array elements and let shakersort sort these partitions. Reasonable values of m will be quite small in comparison with the array length n. Examine the required sorting time for various values of m.

3.5   Write a program that reads the positive integers n and m, followed by a matrix (that is, a table) of n rows and m columns of real numbers. Sort the rows of this matrix according to their sums. For example, with the input

```
3   4
1.2   1.0   6.0   8.0
0.4   9.0   0.0   1.1
5.2   1.0   3.5   1.5
```

the rows have sums 16.2, 10.5, 11.2, so that the desired output is as follows:

```
0.4   9.0   0.0   1.1
5.2   1.0   3.5   1.5
1.2   1.0   6.0   8.0
```

4

Stacks, Queues and Lists

4.1 Array Implementation of Stacks

In computer science *stacks* are useful for many purposes. Such a stack is similar to one in daily life: at any time we can add a new object on top of the stack, and if the stack is not empty, we can remove (only) the object that is on the top. For example, if we have a stack of integers, and have added 10, 20 and 30, in that order, then we can remove 30, and add 40. At this moment, we could not immediately remove 20 from the stack because it is not on the top. If we wanted to do this, we would have to remove 40 first. This example is clarified in Figure 4.1.

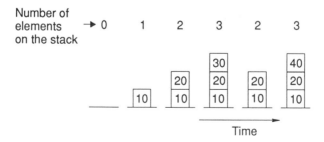

Figure 4.1 Six successive snapshots of a stack

The following program, written in traditional style, demonstrates a very simple application of a stack: after entering some integers followed by a nonnumeric character, the same integers appear as output in reverse order, which is in accordance with the principle Last In First Out (LIFO):

```
// stack0: Program demonstrating a stack.
#include <iostream.h>

int main()
{   const int stacksize = 10;
    int a[stacksize], n = 0, x;
    cout << "Enter at most ten integers, the last one followed\n"
            "by a nonnumeric character:\n";
    while (n < stacksize && (cin >> x)) a[n++] = x;
    while (n > 0) cout << a[--n] << " ";
    cout << endl;
    return 0;
}
```

Here is a demonstration of this program, corresponding to Figure 4.1:

```
Enter at most ten integers, the last one followed
by a nonnumeric character:
10 20 30 a
30 20 10
```

This program is instructive in that it illustrates the following points:

- We add x to the stack by writing $a[n++] = x$; an action such as this is often referred to as *pushing* an object to a stack. The variable n is called a *stack pointer*. It denotes both the first free position and the number of items on the stack. Initially, n is set to zero.
- We remove an item from the stack by using the expression $a[--n]$. This action is called a *pop* operation. We can only pop an item from the stack if n is greater than zero.
- We must be aware of the possibility of *stack overflow*. With a stack implemented as an array of *stacksize* positions, we can only push an item onto the stack if the stackpointer is less than *stacksize*. The exception mechanism discussed in Section 1.6 is used here to deal with stack overflow.

According to the principle of *encapsulation*, we can implement a stack in C++ as a class with member functions *push* and *pop*. By using a *class template*, our stack can be used not only for items of type *int* but also for those of other types. Here is a more interesting demonstration program, based on a class template that we will see in a moment:

```
// stackapp: Application program, demonstrating stacks.

#include <iostream.h>
#include "stack1.h"

int main()
{   int k;
    float x;
    stack1<int, 10> i_st;
    stack1<float, 10> f_st;
    cout << "Enter some integers followed by a "
            "nonnumeric character:\n";
```

```
        try
        {   while (cin >> k) i_st.push(k);
        }
        catch(int i)
        {   cout << "Stack overflow\n";
        }
        f_st.push(1.2);
        f_st.push(3.4);
        cout << "1.2 and 3.4 pushed onto float stack.\n";
        cout << "Items popped from int stack:\n";
        while (i_st.pop(k)) cout << k << " ";
        cout << "\nItems popped from float stack:\n";
        while (f_st.pop(x)) cout << x << " ";
        cout << endl;
        return 0;
    }
```

Note that the class template has not only a type but also an integer as a parameter, the latter denoting the maximum number of elements on the stack. This template is declared in the following header-file:

```
// stack1.h: Template for a stack implemented as an array.
template <class T, int max>
class stack1 {
public:
    stack1() {a = new T[max]; n = 0;}
    ~stack1() {delete[]a;}
    void push(T x)
    {   if (n < max) a[n++] = x;
        else throw 1;
    }
    int pop(T &x)
    {   if (n > 0) {x = a[--n]; return 1;}
        else return 0;
    }
private:
    int n;
    T *a;
};
```

Here is a demonstration of this program:

```
Enter some integers followed by a nonnumeric character:
8 9a
1.2 and 3.4 pushed onto float stack.
Items popped from int stack:
9 8
Items popped from float stack:
3.4 1.2
```

Here is another, to demonstrate stack overflow:

```
Enter some integers followed by a nonnumeric character:
1 2 3 4 5 6 7 8 9
10
11
Stack overflow
1.2 and 3.4 pushed onto float stack.
Items popped from int stack:
10 9 8 7 6 5 4 3 2 1
Items popped from float stack:
3.4 1.2
```

In this program all push operations happen to precede all pop operations. It will be clear from Figure 4.1 that this is not required. Push and pop operations may occur in any order (although we can obviously pop an item only if the stack is not empty).

Stacks and programming languages

In many (old and new) programming languages, such as Algol, PL/1, Pascal, C and C++, we can use *local variables*, with a limited scope and lifetime. The generated code then uses a stack, so that the variables introduced most recently will first disappear. Actually, this stack is used not only for local variables but also for other purposes, such as the address to which a function, after execution, will return. Ignoring these for the moment and focusing on (non-static) local variables, we can easily see that the program fragment below gives rise to successive stack contents that are exactly the same as those shown in Figure 4.1:

```
void g()
{   int i = 30;
    ...  // (4) Stack contents: 10 20 30
}

void h()
{   int i = 40;
    ...  // (6) Stack contents: 10 20 40
}

void f()
{   int i = 20;
    ...  // (3) Stack contents: 10 20
    g();
    ...  // (5) Stack contents: 10 20
    h();
}

int main()
{   ...  // (1) Empty stack
    int i = 10;
    ...  // (2) Stack contents: 10
    f();
    ...
}
```

Note that the *main* function calls *f*, which in turn first calls *g* and then *h*, as illustrated by Figure 4.2.

Figure 4.2 Function calls

It will now be clear that a (recursive) function that calls itself forever will cause *stack overflow*, as this example illustrates:

```
void wrong(int i)    // Infinite recursion: any call to this
{  int j = i + 1;    // function will cause stack overflow.
   wrong(j);
}
```

It is instructive to study the following problem:

> Write a program in which only one variable, of type *char*, is defined. The program is to read a line of text (of arbitrary length) and to write that line backward. For example, if the input is *ABC*, the desired output is *CBA*.

This may seem to be an impossible task, but the solution to this problem is a small and simple program:

```
// reverse: Read a line of text and write it backward.
#include <iostream.h>

void readwrite()
{  char ch;
   cin.get(ch);
   if (ch != '\n'){readwrite(); cout.put(ch);}
}

int main()
{  cout << "Enter a line of text:" << endl;
   readwrite();
   return 0;
}
```

Although there is only one variable definition in the program, there are actually many variables *ch* because function *readwrite* is recursive. Since these variables are located on a built-in stack, this is another program to demonstrate the use of a stack, even though neither arrays nor dynamic data structures occur in the program.

To prepare for the next section, Figure 4.3 shows the final situation of the stack of Figure 4.1 with the stack growing from left to right instead of upward. In other words, the top of the stack is on the right.

Figure 4.3 *Stack with top on the right*

4.2 Array Implementation of Queues

In contrast to a stack (based on the LIFO principle), a *queue* is based on the FIFO (First In First Out) principle. We insert items at one end of the queue, the *rear* or *tail*, and we remove items on the other, the *front* or *head*. If we want to implement a queue as an array, we must remember that arrays are finite. If they were not, we could imagine the front always being the left-hand and the rear the right-hand end of the queue, both moving to the right. In other words, the whole queue would move to the right in this way. In reality, arrays are finite. We will use the integer variables *front* and *rear*, denoting the position of the first item to be removed from the queue and the position where a new item will be placed, respectively. To illustrate this clearly, let us use an array of only ten elements, as shown in Figure 4.4. As with the stack of Figure 4.3, new items are added on the right.

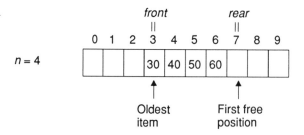

Figure 4.4 *Four items stored in a queue*

You can imagine that initially the items 0, 10, 20, 30, 40, 50, 60, in that order and starting at position 0, were inserted, after which the items 0, 10 and 20 were removed, so that there are now four items stored in the queue. If we now remove three more items, the queue becomes as shown in Figure 4.5.

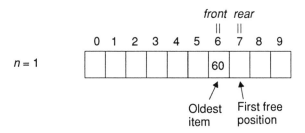

Figure 4.5 *One item stored in a queue*

Removing yet another item, we obtain the empty queue of Figure 4.6. Since removing an item means moving the front one position to the right, the front and the rear now coincide.

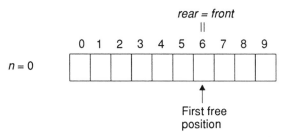

Figure 4.6 *Empty queue*

Now consider the situation of Figure 4.4 once again. If, instead of removing old items, we insert new ones in this situation, we can regard the free position 0 as the successor to position 9. Figure 4.7 shows the queue obtained by adding the items 70, 80, 90, 100 and 110:

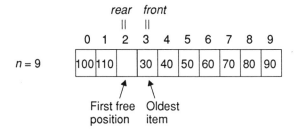

Figure 4.7 *Nine items stored in a queue of length 10*

Adding yet another item, 120, we obtain Figure 4.8. This situation is very curious in that the front coincides with the rear, which is also the case in the empty queue of Figure 4.6. Apparently the positions of the rear and the front do not always uniquely specify how many items there are in the queue.

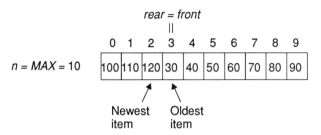

Figure 4.8 Full queue

A simple solution to this problem is using a counter n that specifies how many items are stored. The following class template for a queue works in this way:

```cpp
// queue1.h: Template for a queue implemented as an array.
template <class T, int max>
class queue1 {
public:
    queue1() {a = new T[max]; n = front = rear = 0;}
    ~queue1() {delete[]a;}
    void AddToRear(T x)
    {   if (n == max) throw 2;
        a[rear++] = x; n++;
        rear %= max;
    }
    int GetFromFront(T &x)
    {   if (n > 0)
        {   x = a[front++]; n--;
            front %= max;
            return 1;
        }   else return 0;
    }
private:
    int front, rear, n;
    T *a;
};
```

The following demonstration program shows how to use the *queue*1 member functions:

```cpp
// qapp: Application of queue class.
#include <iostream.h>
#include "queue1.h"

int main()
{   queue1<int, 10> q;
    int i, x;
    try
    {   for (i=0; i<7; i++) q.AddToRear(10 * i);
        q.GetFromFront(x); cout << x << " ";   //  0
        q.GetFromFront(x); cout << x << " ";   // 10
        q.GetFromFront(x); cout << x << endl;  // 20
```

```
              for (i=8; i<13; i++) q.AddToRear(10 * i);
              while (q.GetFromFront(x))
                 cout << x << " ";  // 30 40 50 60 70 80 90 100 110 120
              cout << endl;
              for (i=0; i<1000; i++) q.AddToRear(i);
                 // Only 0, 1, ..., 9 stored, then queue overflow.
          }
          catch(int)
          {   while (q.GetFromFront(x)) ; // Find latest element
              cout << "Queue overflow; latest element stored: "
                   << x << endl;    // 9
          }
          return 0;
      }
```

The output of this program is shown below:

```
0 10 20
30 40 50 60 80 90 100 110 120
Queue overflow; latest element stored: 9
```

4.3 Linked Stacks

Instead of array elements, we can use records containing pointers to other records to represent the items of a stack. Such a list of records is called a *linked list*, and the records are called *nodes* or *elements*. If we insert and remove items only at the beginning of the list, we have another implementation of a stack, which we may call a *linked stack*. Figure 4.9 shows how this works for the example used in Figure 4.2.

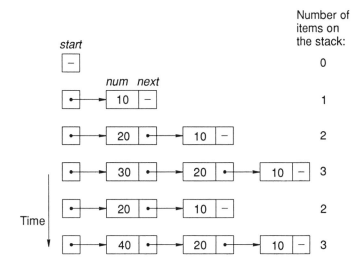

Figure 4.9 Successive snapshots of a linked stack

Note that there is a single pointer, not part of a record, which we will call the *start* of the linked list. If we always had to deal with records with an integer as the only data item, we could write

```
struct elem {int num; elem *next} *start = NULL, *p;
```

Immediately after this declaration the stack is empty, as shown at the top of Figure 4.9. We can then obtain the second situation, with the stack containing only one element with contents 10, as follows:

```
p = start; start = new elem; start->num = 10; start->next = p;
```

We could have done this slightly quicker, without using *p*, but the above line has the advantage that it can be used in almost the same form to obtain the next situation of Figure 4.9, with the stack containing two elements with contents 20 and 10:

```
p = start; start = new elem; start->num = 20; start->next = p;
```

To push yet another value, 30, onto the stack, we use a similar sequence of statements once again:

```
p = start; start = new elem; start->num = 30; start->next = p;
```

In general, to push item *x* onto the stack, we need to execute the statements on this line:

```
p = start; start = new elem; start->num = x; start->next = p;
```

So much for the push operation. Popping an item from the stack and placing this in the variable *x* can be done as follows:

```
x = start->num; p = start; start = start->next; delete p;
```

To make our code reusable, we will use a class template, replacing *int num* with *T data* in type *elem*:

```
// stack.h: Template for a linked stack.
#include <stdlib.h>
template <class T>
struct elem{T data; elem *next;};

template <class T>
class stack {
public:
   stack() {start = NULL;}
   ~stack();
   void push(const T &x)
   {  elem<T> *p = start;
      start = new elem<T>;
      start->data = x; start->next = p;
   }
```

```
    int pop(T &x)
    {   elem<T> *p;
        if (start)
        {   x = start->data;
            p = start;
            start = start->next;
            delete p;
            return 1;
        }   else return 0;
    }
private:
    elem<T> *start;
};

template <class T>
stack<T>::~stack()
{   elem<T> *p;
    while (start){p = start; start = start->next; delete p;}
}
```

This file *stack.h* can be used instead of its array counterpart, *stack1.h*, discussed in Section 4.1. In other words, we can simply replace the lines

```
#include "stack1.h"
stack1<int, 10> i_st;
stack1<float, 10> f_st;
```

in program *stackapp* with the following ones, respectively:

```
#include "stack.h"
stack<int> i_st;
stack<float> f_st;
```

The resulting executable program behaves in the same way as the original version, except that the limitation due to a stack size of 10 no longer applies.

Copying stacks

Although our *stack* class template can be quite useful in practice, we must be careful with operations that require 'deep copies' of *stack* objects. For example, the following code is not allowed:

```
stack<float> s1, s2;
...
s2 = s1; // ???
```

This assignment would not make a deep copy of *s*1, but simply copy its *start* pointer. To make such assignments work properly, we have to write our own assignment operator. It would also be incorrect to use a *stack* object as a function argument (unless we use reference parameters); neither must we let a function return a *stack* object as a value. The following function declaration is incorrect in both respects:

```
stack<float> f(stack<float> s); // ???
```

To make this valid, we should supply class *stack* with a copy constructor, as we will see in Section 4.5.

4.4 Linked Queues

A queue is a suitable candidate to be implemented as a linked list. The header file below can replace its preliminary version *queue1.h*, based on arrays and shown in Section 4.2.

```
// queue.h: Template for a linked queue.
#include <stdlib.h>

template <class T>
struct elem{T data; elem *next;};

template <class T>
class queue {
public:
   queue() {pRear = NULL;} // pRear = NULL means 'empty queue'
   ~queue();
   void AddToRear(const T &x)
   {  elem<T> *p = new elem<T>;
      (pRear ? pRear->next : pFront) = p;
      p->data = x;
      pRear = p;
   }
   int GetFromFront(T &x)
   {  elem<T> *p;
      if (pRear == NULL) return 0;
      p = pFront;
      x = p->data;
      if (p == pRear) pRear = NULL; else pFront = p->next;
      delete p;
      return 1;
   }
private:
   elem<T> *pFront, *pRear;
};

template <class T>
queue<T>::~queue()
{  T x;
   while (GetFromFront(x)) ;
}
```

If we use this header file in program *qapp* (replacing *queue1.h* with *queue.h* and *queue1<int, 10>* with *queue<int>*) we will observe that its output consists of only these two lines:

```
0 10 20
30 40 50 60 80 90 100 110 120
```

The line about queue overflow will not occur because we are now not using a small array, as we did in Section 4.2.

The following program, *simq*, is another application that uses the header file *queue.h*. It simulates a real queue, which you can find, say, in a post office. The user of this program can enter either the name of a new person, who goes to the rear of the queue, or a question mark, to display the name of the person at the front of the queue. This person then disappears from the queue.

```
// simq: Simulation of a queue of persons.
#include <iostream.h>
#include "queue.h"
const int LEN=40;
struct person{char name[LEN];};

int main()
{  person x;
   queue<person> q;
   cout << "Each time, enter either a name to add it to a\n"
        "queue or a question mark to remove it from it.\n"
        "The program terminates when the queue gets empty:\n";
   for (;;)
   {  cout << "Input: "; cin.getline(x.name, LEN);
      if (x.name[0] == '?')
      {  if (q.GetFromFront(x))
         {  cout << "                          Output: "
                 << x.name << endl;
         } else break;
      } else q.AddToRear(x);
   }
   cout << "Empty queue.\n";
   return 0;
}
```

Here is a demonstration of this program:

```
Each time, enter either a name to add it to a
queue or a question mark to remove it from it.
The program terminates when the queue gets empty:
Input: John Smith
Input: Mary Brown
Input: ?
                       Output: John Smith
Input: Henry Gray
Input: ?
                       Output: Mary Brown
Input: ?
                       Output: Henry Gray
Input: ?
Empty queue.
```

Note that the names in the output column on the right are the same as those in the input column on the left and that they are in the same order.

As pointed out at the end of the previous section, we must be aware that we have omitted both an assignment operator and a copy constructor.

4.5 Linked Lists

In our discussion of stacks and queues, the only way to retrieve data from these data
structures was by removing items from them. It will often be desirable to use all the data
stored in a linked list, without necessarily removing items from this list. To demonstrate
how this can be done, we will use a rather simple program, dealing with a linked list that
contains integers. We will discuss the following operations on such a linked list:

-   adding new items at its end, using the function *append*;
-   traversing the list, using the functions *iteratorStart* and *iterator*;
-   searching the list for an item, using the function *find*.

A destructor will delete the entire list when it 'goes out of scope'. All this is realized in the
program listed below. It displays some numbers, found by traversing a linked list. The user
can then enter a number to be searched for in the list. If it is found, this number and all
others that follow in the list are increased by 50.

```
// linklist: Demonstration of linked-list operations.
#include <iostream.h>

struct elem{int num; struct elem *next;};

class LinkedList {
public:
    LinkedList(){pStart = pEnd = NULL;}
    ~LinkedList();
    void append(int i)
    {   pCur = pEnd;
        pEnd = new elem;
        pEnd->num = i;
        pEnd->next = NULL;
        (pCur ? pCur->next : pStart) = pEnd;
    }
    void iteratorStart(elem *p=NULL){pCur = (p ? p : pStart);}
    elem *iterator()
    {   elem *p = pCur;
        if (pCur) pCur = pCur->next;
        return p;
    }
    elem *find(int i);
    void PrintList();
private:
    elem *pStart, *pEnd, *pCur;
};

LinkedList::~LinkedList()
{   while (pStart)
    {   pCur = pStart; pStart = pStart->next; delete pCur;
    }
}
```

```
elem *LinkedList::find(int i)
{  elem *p;
   iteratorStart();
   while ((p = iterator()) != NULL)
      if (p->num == i) return p;
   return NULL;
}

void LinkedList::PrintList()
{  elem *p;
   iteratorStart();
   while ((p = iterator()) != NULL)
      cout << p->num << " ";
   cout << endl;
}

int main()
{  int i;
   LinkedList L;
   elem *p;
   for (i=10; i<18; i++) L.append(i);
   L.PrintList();
   cout << "Enter item to be searched for: ";
   cin >> i;
   p = L.find(i);
   if (p)
   {  cout << "Found. This item and those that follow "
              "are increased by 50:\n";
      L.iteratorStart(p);
      while ((p = L.iterator()) != NULL) p->num += 50;
      L.PrintList();
   } else cout << "Not found.\n";
   return 0;
}
```

Here is a demonstration of this program:

```
10 11 12 13 14 15 16 17
Enter item to be searched for: 14
Found. This item and those that follow are increased by 50:
10 11 12 13 64 65 66 67
```

Copying and assigning linked lists

The class *LinkedList* in program *linklist* contains neither a copy constructor nor an assignment operator. This means that we cannot pass a *LinkedList* object by value as an argument, nor can we perform assignments such as the one in

```
LinkedList l1, l2;
...
l2 = l1;
```

This assignment would be a serious error, because the destructor would try to release both *l*1 and *l*2. Since both objects will contain pointers pointing to the same memory locations, the destructor will apply the *delete* operator twice to this memory, which has undefined effects.

There is no such problem with the class template *LinkList*, listed below, because there is a copy constructor as well as an assignment operator in it:

```cpp
// linklist.h: Template for a linked list that can be copied.
#include <stdlib.h>

template <class T>
struct elem{T info; elem *next;};

template <class T>
class LinkList {
public:
   LinkList() {pStart = pEnd = NULL;}
   LinkList(const LinkList<T> &s)
   {  CopyList(s);
   }
   LinkList<T> &operator=(const LinkList &s)
   {  if (&s != this)
      {  DelList();
         CopyList(s);
      }
      return *this;
   }
   virtual ~LinkList(){DelList();}
   void append(T x)
   {  pCur = pEnd;
      pEnd = new elem<T>;
      pEnd->info = x;
      pEnd->next = NULL;
      (pCur ? pCur->next : pStart) = pEnd;
   }
   void iteratorStart(elem<T> *p=NULL){pCur = (p ? p : pStart);}
   elem<T> *iterator()
   {  elem<T> *p = pCur;
      if (pCur) pCur = pCur->next;
      return p;
   }
   void PrintList();
protected:
   elem<T> *pStart, *pEnd, *pCur;
   void DelList();
   void CopyList(const LinkList<T> &s);
};

template<class T>
void LinkList<T>::DelList()
{  elem<T> *p;
   while (pStart){p = pStart; pStart = pStart->next; delete p;}
}
```

```
template <class T>
void LinkList<T>::CopyList(const LinkList<T> &s)
{  elem<T> *p = s.pStart, *pEnd0;
   pEnd = pStart = new elem<T>;
   for (;;)
   {  *pEnd = *p;
      p = p->next;
      if (p == NULL) break;
      pEnd0 = pEnd;
      pEnd = new elem<T>;
      pEnd0->next = pEnd;
   }
}

template <class T>
void LinkList<T>::PrintList()
{  elem<T> *p;
   iteratorStart();
   while ((p = iterator()) != NULL)
      cout << p->info << " ";
   cout << endl;
}
```

The following demonstration program is based on the above header file. Its function *increase* demonstrates the iterator functions by increasing the *info* member in all list elements by 100:

```
// listapp: Application of the LinkList template,
//          demonstrating list copying and assigning.

#include <iostream.h>
#include "linklist.h"

template <class T>
LinkList<T> increase(LinkList<T> L) // Invokes copy constructor.
{  elem<T> *p;
   L.iteratorStart();
   while ((p = L.iterator()) != NULL)
      p->info += 100;            // Does not affect argument.
   return L;                     // Invokes copy constructor.
}

int main()
{  LinkList<int> l1, l2, l3;
   l1.append(111);
   l1.append(222);
   l2 = l1;
   l2.append(333);
   l3 = increase(l2);
   cout << "l1: "; l1.PrintList();
   cout << "l2: "; l2.PrintList();
   cout << "l3: "; l3.PrintList();
   return 0;
}
```

Its output is as follows:

```
11: 111 222
12: 111 222 333
13: 211 322 433
```

Immediately after the execution of our *operator=* function by

```
12 = 11;
```

the lists *l*1 and *l*2 are equal, but they do not share any elements. This implies that

```
12.append(333);
```

causes 333 to go to *l*2, while *l*1 does not change. Finally, the copy constructor is called twice by the statement

```
13 = increase(12);
```

since function *increase* has a value parameter of type *LinkList* and it returns a value of this type. Because this value is assigned to *l*3, the assignment operator is also used here. If the lists in question were very long, this program would therefore use considerably more computer time than the above two assignment statements suggest.

The orthodox canonical class form

When designing classes that use dynamically allocated memory and should be as reusable as possible, we should provide both a copy constructor and an assignment operator. Some refer to classes that meet these requirements as classes in the *orthodox canonical form* or as *well-formed classes*. Incidentally, such classes should also be provided with both a *default constructor* and a destructor. Remember, a default constructor either has no parameters or has only default parameters. The destructor should be *virtual* if the class in question is used to derive other classes from it, as we will see in the next section. As you can see in the above file *linklist.h*, our class *LinkList* is in accordance with all these requirements, so it is in the orthodox canonical form. In this book, many classes are primarily intended to show the essence of an algorithm; they are usually not presented in the orthodox canonical form because that would make the program listings larger and might distract our attention from the subject under discussion. If you want them to be more generally applicable, you can add a copy constructor, an assignment operator, a default constructor (if not yet present) and a virtual destructor yourself.

4.6 Simple Insertion and Deletion; Inheritance

We may also want to insert and delete list elements at places other than the beginning or the end of the list. Linked lists enable us to do this in an efficient way. Instead of writing an entirely new list class, we will use the principle of *inheritance* to construct a new demonstration program in an easy way. Referring to class template *LinkList* of the previous section, let us abbreviate the class *LinkList<float>* as *fLinkList* by using *typedef*. This class will be a base class for a derived class, *fList*, which will have three functions in addition to those of its base class. For the sake of simplicity, this class is derived in the application program (*listap*1) itself. This program, shown below, shows the three new functions:

- *find*, to search the list for a given *info* value;
- *InsertAfter*, to insert a new node after the one that a given pointer points to;
- *RemoveAfter*, to delete the node (if any) after the one that a given pointer points to.

(Inserting a new node *after* the one that a given pointer points to is simpler than inserting *before* that one, and things are similar with the deletion of a node. This is why the word *simple* occurs in the heading of this section. A more interesting way of inserting and deleting will be a subject of the next section.) Besides a *llist* variable, *L*1, there is also an array *pL* of pointers, so we can demonstrate the use of the *new* operator to generate *llist* objects:

```
// listap1: Class fList derived from LinkList template
//          of Section 4.5.
#include <iostream.h>
#include "linklist.h"

typedef elem<float> Elem;
typedef LinkList<float> fLinkList;

class fList: public fLinkList {
public:
   Elem *find(float x);
   void InsertAfter(Elem *p, float x);
   void RemoveAfter(Elem *p);
};

Elem *fList::find(float x)
{  Elem *p;
   iteratorStart();
   while ((p = iterator()) != NULL)
      if (p->info == x) return p;
   return NULL;
}

void fList::InsertAfter(Elem *p, float x)
{  Elem *q = new Elem;
   q->info = x; q->next = p->next;
   p->next = q;
}

void fList::RemoveAfter(Elem *p)
{  Elem *q = p->next;
   if (q == NULL) return;
   p->next = q->next;
   delete q;
}
```

```
int main()
{   fList L, *pL[2];
    Elem *p;
    L.append(1.1); L.append(3.3); L.append(5.5);
    pL[0] = new fList;
    pL[1] = new fList;
    *pL[0] = *pL[1] = L;
    p = pL[0]->find(3.3);
    if (p) pL[0]->InsertAfter(p, 4.4);
    p = pL[1]->find(1.1);
    if (p) pL[1]->RemoveAfter(p);
    cout << "L:       "; L.PrintList();
    cout << "*pL[0]: "; pL[0]->PrintList();
    cout << "*pL[1]: "; pL[1]->PrintList();
    delete pL[0];
    delete pL[1];
    return 0;
}
```

After the numbers 1.1, 3.3 and 5.5 have been stored in list *L*, this list is assigned to both **pL*[0] and **pL*[1], so that we have three distinct, identical lists. We now search the list **pL*[0] for the value 3.3, to insert 4.4 immediately after this value. Then we search the list **pL*[1] for the number 1.1, to remove the element (3.3) that follows this number. Finally, the three lists are displayed, which gives the following output:

```
L:       1.1 3.3 5.5
*pL[0]: 1.1 3.3 4.4 5.5
*pL[1]: 1.1 5.5
```

In this program many operations applied to *fList* objects are inherited from the base class, *LinkList<float>*. For example, the two assignments in

```
*pL[0] = *pL[1] = L;
```

work correctly thanks to the *operator=* function in file *linklist.h*. Note that the pointers in array *pL* initially have undefined values, so we must not omit the two program lines that immediately precede the above assignments.

Why virtual destructors?

The derived class *fList* has no constructor of its own, nor has it a destructor. Fortunately, the constructor and the destructor of the base class *LinkList* are invoked when an object of the derived class *fList* is created or destroyed. Since the derived class in this example differs from its base class only in function members, not in its data members, this base class constructor works fine also for derived classes and so does its destructor. However, things may be different if the derived class also has some new data members. Let us consider the following example, again based on the *LinkList* template of Section 4.5:

```
// listap2: Virtual destructor in action.

#include <iostream.h>
#include <string.h>
#include "linklist.h"

typedef LinkList<float> fLinkList;

class fList1: public fLinkList {
public:
    fList1(){name = new char[100]; strcpy(name, "Example");}
    ~fList1(){delete[] name;}
private:
    char *name;
};

int main()
{   fLinkList *pList;
    pList = new fList1;
    pList->append(1.1); pList->append(3.3);
    pList->PrintList();   // Output: 1.1 3.3
    delete pList;
    return 0;
}
```

This program creates only one object, which is of type *fList*1. There is a constructor and a destructor for this derived class to allocate and release memory for the character array *name*. In cases such as this the constructor and the destructor of the base class are invoked as well. Altogether, constructors and destructors are invoked in the following order:

1. the constructor for the base class *fLinkList*;
2. the constructor for the derived class *fList*1;
3. the destructor for the derived class *fList*1;
4. the destructor for the base class *fLinkList*.

It is not obvious that step 3 is taken. After all, the statement

```
delete pList;
```

seems to contain no information indicating that an *fList*1 object is to be deleted, since the type of *pList* is 'pointer to *fLinkList*', not 'pointer to *fList*1'. The compiler will not be able to generate code for an explicit call to the *fList*1 destructor. Step 3 is executed only because the *fList*1 destructor has been declared *virtual*. Since it is a virtual function, the actual function that is used is selected according to 'late binding': the object itself contains information about its type, and this information is used at execution time, rather than at compile time. If we had omitted the *virtual* keyword in the file *linklist.h*, step 3 would have been skipped. In that case the memory for the array *name* would not have been released, since the *delete* statement for this is in the *fList*1 destructor.

4.7 Ordered Linked Lists

If an order relation $\leq$ is defined for the items stored in a linked list, we say that a linked list is *ordered* if $A \leq B$ whenever item A precedes item B in the list. We can keep a linked list ordered while we build it. To do this in an efficient way, some tricks not mentioned before will be useful. So far, we had as many nodes in the list as there were items to be stored in them. It is sometimes convenient to have an additional node, called a *sentinel*, at the end of the list. A sentinel is particularly useful with ordered lists, so we will use one here.

List insertion

Suppose that we have an ordered linked list in which the integers 10, 20, 30 and 40 have been stored and that we want to insert a new node to store the value 25. We then search the list until we find a value not less than 25. Figure 4.10 illustrates this, with p pointing to the first node containing a value not less than 25.

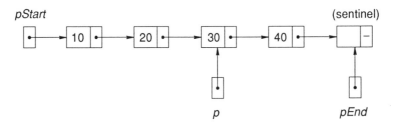

Figure 4.10 A list in which a new node, with contents 25, is to be inserted

It is not obvious how we can insert this new node, since pointer p gives no access to the preceding node (containing 20), and it seems that we have to update the *next* pointer of that node. To solve this problem, we first copy the contents of the node *p to a new one, *q, as shown in Figure 4.11.

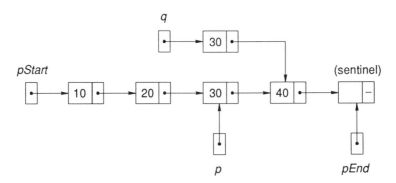

Figure 4.11 Creating a copy of the node pointed to by p

Then all that remains to be done is to update *p: we replace p–>info (= 30) with the new integer, 25, and p–>next with q, which gives the final result, shown in Figure 4.12.

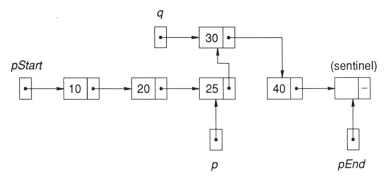

Figure 4.12 Ordered linked list after inserting 25

You can find the program code for this way of inserting nodes in the *olist* member function *InsertBefore* in the following header-file. This file also contains a function *Remove*, to be discussed in a moment, and facilities for copying an entire list, as discussed in the last section.

```
// olist.h: Ordered linked list with sentinel.
#include <stdlib.h>

template <class T>
struct elem{T info; elem *next;};

template <class T>
class olist {
public:
   olist() {pStart = pEnd = new elem<T>; pEnd->next = NULL;}
   olist(const olist& s);
   olist &operator=(const olist &s);
   virtual ~olist();
   void iteratorStart(elem<T> *p=NULL){pCur = (p ? p : pStart);}
   elem<T> *iterator();
   void PrintList();
   elem<T> *FindPosition(T x, int &found);
   void InsertBefore(elem<T> *p, T x);
   void Remove(elem<T> *p);
protected:
   elem<T> *pStart, *pEnd, *pCur;
};

template<class T>
void DelList(elem<T>* &start)
{  elem<T> *p;
   while (start->next != NULL)
   {  p = start; start = start->next; delete p;
   }
}
```

```
template <class T>
olist<T>::~olist()
{  DelList(pStart);   // Leave sentinel
   delete pEnd;       // Delete sentinel, too.
}

template <class T>
void CopyList(elem<T>* pSource, elem<T>* pStart, elem<T>* &pEnd)
{  while (pSource->next != NULL)
   {  *pEnd = *pSource;                    // Copy into sentinel
      pEnd = pEnd->next = new elem<T>;     // New sentinel
      pEnd->next = NULL;
      pSource = pSource->next;
   }
}

template <class T>
olist<T>::olist(const olist<T> &s)
{  pStart = pEnd = new elem<T>; pEnd->next = NULL; // sentinel
   CopyList(s.pStart, pStart, pEnd);
}

template <class T>
olist<T> &olist<T>::operator=(const olist &s)
{  if (&s != this)
   {  DelList(pStart);
      CopyList(s.pStart, pStart, pEnd);
   }
   return *this;
}

template <class T>
elem<T> *olist<T>::iterator()
{  if (pCur == pEnd) return NULL;
   elem<T> *p = pCur;
   pCur = pCur->next;
   return p;
}

template <class T>
void olist<T>::PrintList()
{  elem<T> *p;
   iteratorStart();
   while ((p = iterator()) != NULL) cout << p->info << " ";
   cout << endl;
}

template <class T>
elem<T> *olist<T>::FindPosition(T x, int &found)
{  pEnd->info = x;
   elem<T> *p = pStart;
   while (p->info < x) p = p->next;
   found = (p != pEnd && p->info == x);
   return p;
}
```

```
template <class T>
void olist<T>::InsertBefore(elem<T> *p, T x)
{   elem<T> *q = new elem<T>;
    *q = *p;
    if (p == pEnd) pEnd = q;
    p->info = x;
    p->next = q;
}

template <class T>
void olist<T>::Remove(elem<T> *p)
{   elem<T> *q = p->next;
    *p = *q;
    if (q == pEnd) pEnd = p;
    delete q;
}
```

The following demonstration program inserts and deletes nodes in an ordered linked list. Integers entered on the keyboard must be followed by *I* for insertion or by *D* for deletion. In either case, the *olist* member function *FindPosition* searches the list for the integer entered:

```
// olistap: An ordered list; insertion and deletion.
#include <iostream.h>
#include <ctype.h>
#include "olist.h"
typedef olist<int> Olist;
typedef elem<int> Elem;

int main()
{   Olist L;
    Elem *p;
    int x, found;
    char cmd;
    for (;;)
    {   cout << "Enter an integer, followed by I for insertion\n"
                "or by D for deletion, or enter Q to quit: ";
        if (!(cin >> x >> cmd)) break;
        cmd = toupper(cmd);
        p = L.FindPosition(x, found);
        if (cmd == 'I') L.InsertBefore(p, x); else
        if (cmd == 'D')
        {   if (found) L.Remove(p); else cout << "Not found.\n";
        }
        cout << "Contents: "; L.PrintList(); cout << endl;
    }
    return 0;
}
```

Here is a demonstration of this program:

```
Enter an integer, followed by I for insertion
or by D for deletion, or enter Q to quit: 100 i
Contents: 100
```

```
Enter an integer, followed by I for insertion
or by D for deletion, or enter Q to quit: 200 i
Contents: 100 200

Enter an integer, followed by I for insertion
or by D for deletion, or enter Q to quit: 50 i
Contents: 50 100 200

Enter an integer, followed by I for insertion
or by D for deletion, or enter Q to quit: 100 d
Contents: 50 200

Enter an integer, followed by I for insertion
or by D for deletion, or enter Q to quit: 50 d
Contents: 200

Enter an integer, followed by I for insertion
or by D for deletion, or enter Q to quit: 200 d
Contents:

Enter an integer, followed by I for insertion
or by D for deletion, or enter Q to quit: q
```

Node deletion

To delete a node pointed to by a pointer p, we use a trick similar to the one used for insertion. For example, suppose we want to delete the node containing 20 in Figure 4.13. With q pointing to the node that immediately follows $*p$, we then copy $*q$ into the node $*p$, as Figure 4.14 shows.

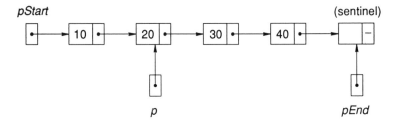

Figure 4.13 *Node *p is to be deleted*

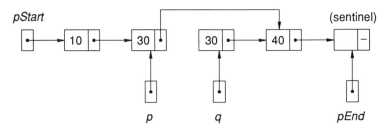

Figure 4.14 *Situation after copying *q to *p*

Deleting *q is now all that remains to be done. You can find the program code for this in the *Remove* member function of class *olist*.

The sentinel at the end of the list makes some operations easier to program and more efficient. For example, the function *FindPosition* begins by placing the given value into the *info* member of the sentinel. Then the simple loop

```
while (p->info < x) p = p->next;
```

will find the desired position. If we had not used a sentinel, an explicit test for 'end of list' would have been required in the loop.

Copying linked lists

Although not demonstrated here, our class *olist* contains both a copy constructor and an assignment operator, so deep copies will be made if we write, for example,

```
olist<int> L1;
...
olist<int> L2 = L1, // Initialization: copy constructor used
  L3;
L3 = L1;             // Assignment operator used
```

4.8 Do-It-Yourself Memory Allocation in an Array

So far, we have been using the operators *new* and *delete* as built-in language facilities, without bothering about the way they are implemented. The more primitive way of allocating memory to be discussed here is instructive in that it gives us an idea how the operators just mentioned (and the C library functions *malloc*, *free* etc.) work. Since computer memory can be regarded as a very large array, we will use an array of fixed length and routines of our own to allocate memory for a linked list in this array. Before languages with memory-allocation facilities became popular, we really had to use this technique if we wanted to work with dynamic data structures such as linked lists. Our example will be similar to the one in the last section, but we will not use templates this time, but rather use type *int* for the *info* member of our list nodes. These nodes will be array elements, and they will contain a *next* member of type *int*, being the index value of the node pointed to. All array elements not used in our linked list (referred to as the *user list*) will be chained together, forming another linked list, known as a *free list*. The two lists are complementary. Initially, all array elements belong to the free list. Allocating a node implies that an array element moves from the free list to the user list. The left half of Figure 4.15 shows an array *a* of (only) ten elements, with *a*[0], *a*[1], *a*[2] and *a*[3] belonging to the user list, while the remaining elements belong to the free list. We use the value −1 (instead of 0) to indicate the end of each list.

This simple situation, with all elements of the user list preceding those of the free list, will not always apply. For example, after releasing the node containing 20 we obtain the right half of Figure 4.15. Since there is a sentinel in the user list, the maximum number of integers that we can store in the *info* fields is $10 - 1 = 9$.

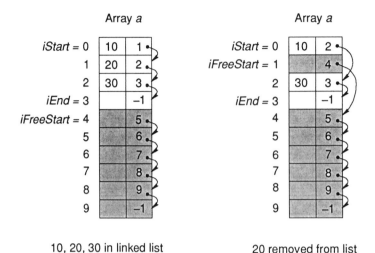

10, 20, 30 in linked list   20 removed from list

Figure 4.15 Linked lists in an array

Instead of pointers *pStart* and *pEnd*, we now use integers *iStart* and *iEnd*; the first node of the user list is *a[iStart]*, and *a[iEnd]* is its sentinel. To traverse a linked list by means of an iterator, there is also *iCur*, replacing *pCur*. The first node of the free list is *a[iFreeStart]*. We store the integer index values just mentioned, as well as array *a* itself, as private data members of the class *alnklist*, as program *alnklist* shows:

```
// alnklist: A linked list implemented in an array.

#include <iostream.h>
#include <stdlib.h>
#include <ctype.h>
struct elem{int info; int next;};

class alnklist {
public:
    alnklist();
    elem *NewNode();             // Instead of new operator
    void DeleteNode(elem *p); // Instead of delete operator
    void iteratorStart(elem *p=NULL)
    {   iCur = (p ? int(p - a) : iStart);
    }
    elem *iterator();
    void PrintList();
    elem *FindPosition(int x, int &found);
    void InsertBefore(elem *p, int x);
    void Remove(elem *p);
private:
    enum {len = 10};
    elem a[len];
    int iFreeStart, iStart, iEnd, iCur;
};
```

```
alnklist::alnklist()
{  iFreeStart = 0;
   for (int i=1; i<len; i++) a[i-1].next = i;
   a[len-1].next = -1;
   iStart = iEnd = int(NewNode() - a);
   a[iEnd].next = -1;
}

elem *alnklist::NewNode()
{  int i = iFreeStart;
   if (i >= 0) iFreeStart = a[iFreeStart].next; else
   {  cout << "Memory problem: array exhausted\n";
      exit(1);
   }
   return a + i;
}

void alnklist::DeleteNode(elem *p)
{  int i = int(p - a);
   a[i].next = iFreeStart;
   iFreeStart = i;
}

elem *alnklist::iterator()
{  if (iCur == iEnd) return NULL;
   int i = iCur;
   iCur = a[iCur].next;
   return a + i;
}

void alnklist::PrintList()
{  elem *p;
   iteratorStart();
   while ((p = iterator()) != NULL)
      cout << p->info << " ";
   cout << endl;
}

elem *alnklist::FindPosition(int x, int &found)
{  a[iEnd].info = x;
   int i = iStart;
   while (a[i].info < x) i = a[i].next;
   found = (i != iEnd && a[i].info == x);
   return a + i;
}

void alnklist::InsertBefore(elem *p, int x)
{  int i = int(p - a), j = int(NewNode() - a);
   a[j] = a[i];
   if (i == iEnd) iEnd = j;
   a[i].info = x;
   a[i].next = j;
}
```

```
void alnklist::Remove(elem *p)
{  int i = int(p - a), j = a[i].next;
   a[i] = a[j];
   if (j == iEnd) iEnd = i;
   DeleteNode(a + j);
}

int main()
{  alnklist L;
   elem *p;
   int x, found;
   char cmd;
   for (;;)
   {  cout << "Enter an integer, followed by I for insertion\n"
              "or by D for deletion, or enter Q to quit: ";
      if (!(cin >> x >> cmd)) break;
      cmd = toupper(cmd);
      p = L.FindPosition(x, found);
      if (cmd == 'I') L.InsertBefore(p, x); else
      if (cmd == 'D')
      {  if (found) L.Remove(p); else cout << "Not found.\n";
      }
      cout << "Contents: "; L.PrintList(); cout << endl;
   }
   return 0;
}
```

For a demonstration of this program, please refer to Section 4.8. When running both programs, the user will find no difference between the programs *olistap* and *alnklist*, with one exception: there is a built-in maximum list length in *alnklist*, while there is no such limitation in *olistap*. In this demonstration program *alnklist*, this maximum length was deliberately given the low value of 10, so we can see how the program behaves if we run out of space. The very simple solution of displaying an error message and terminating program execution was adopted here. Instead, we could have used the C++ exception-handling mechanism, discussed in Section 1.6 and demonstrated in Section 4.1.

The idea of using integer index values instead of pointers, with nodes implemented as array elements, is applicable not only to linked lists but also to trees and other data structures to be discussed in the chapters that follow. An advantage of this way of implementing data structures is that we can easily and efficiently copy them, not only in memory but also to and from files. A disadvantage is their fixed array size: inserting a new node is not possible if the array is full. This problem of array exhaustion can be solved by using the reallocation technique based on chunks and discussed in Section 1.5, but this is rather time consuming and it requires allocating a new, larger array before releasing the old, smaller one, so that we temporarily allocate about twice as much memory as we need.

Copying linked lists; index values vs. pointers

Although class *alnklist* does not contain a copy constructor or an assignment operator, we can nevertheless make deep copies, so we can write program code similar to what we have seen at the end of the previous section:

```
alnklist L1;
...
alnklist L2 = L1, L3;
            // Copy constructor used to initialize L2.
    L3 = L1;    // Assignment operator used.
```

This is possible because

1. the array *a* is contained in the class, not allocated by the *new* operator, and
2. we use integer index values *iStart* etc., not pointers such as *pStart*.

The latter point deserves an explanation. You may have wondered why we use integer index values instead of pointers. After all, we have

$pStart = a + iStart$
$iStart = pStart - a$

so we can compute *iStart* from *pStart* and vice versa, and choosing between them seems irrelevant. Using pointers seems more attractive than using integers, since we need pointers anyway to make the application program (or the *main* function in our example) more similar to what we are used to: note that the *main* function of program *alnklist* is almost identical to that of program *olistap* of the previous section. However, integer index values have the advantage of being related to the beginning of the array, while pointers are absolute addresses. For example, immediately after execution of the assignment statement

```
    L3 = L1;
```

the index value *L3.iStart* is (and should be) equal to *L1.iStart*, but the corresponding pointers would be different since they would point to the elements of the arrays *L3.a* and *L1.a*, respectively. It will now be clear why we have used a hybrid solution: we store index values as private data members so that we need not define a copy constructor and an assignment operator, and we hide this from the user; for example, the function *Remove* has a pointer argument, as if the list consisted of dynamically allocated nodes.

4.9 Circular and Doubly-linked Lists

There are a number of variations of linked list, some of which we will briefly discuss in this section. The programs in this section will focus on the subjects under discussion, so they will be less general than some we have seen before and we will omit facilities for copying and assigning the lists. However, these programs are complete in the sense that you can compile and run them.

Circular linked lists

If we should be able to *insert* nodes at the beginning of the list and to append nodes at its end we do not really need to use two pointers, *pStart* and *pEnd*. We can easily perform both operations mentioned if we make the linked list circular, and use only a pointer *pStart* to the final node, as shown in Figure 4.16.

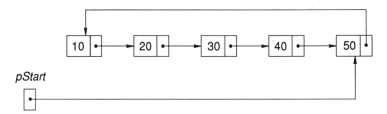

Figure 4.16 *A circular linked list*

The following program shows how this list can be implemented:

```
// cirlist: Circular linked list.

#include <iostream.h>
#include <stdlib.h>

struct elem{int info; elem *next;};

class cirlist {
public:
    cirlist() {pStart = NULL;}
    cirlist(const cirlist& s)
    {   cout << "Copying not allowed.\n"; exit(1);
    }
    cirlist &operator=(const cirlist &s)
    {   cout << "Assignment not allowed.\n"; exit(1);
        return *this;
    }
    ~cirlist();
    void iteratorStart(elem *p=NULL)
    {   pCur = (p ? p : (pStart ? pStart->next : NULL));
    }
    elem *iterator();
    void PrintList();
    void insert(int x)  // Add at the beginning of the list
    {   elem *p = new elem;
        p->info = x;
        if (pStart) p->next = pStart->next; else pStart = p;
        pStart->next = p;
    }
    void append(int x)  // Add at the end of the list
    {   insert(x); pStart = pStart->next;
    }
private:
    elem *pStart, *pCur;
};
```

```
cirlist::~cirlist()
{  elem *p;
   iteratorStart();
   for (;;)
   {  p = iterator();
      if (p) delete p; else break;
   }
}

elem *cirlist::iterator()
{  if (pCur == NULL) return NULL;
   elem *p = pCur;
   pCur = (pCur == pStart ? NULL : pCur->next);
   return p;
}

void cirlist::PrintList()
{  elem *p;
   iteratorStart();
   while ((p = iterator()) != NULL)
      cout << p->info << " ";
   cout << endl;
}

int main()
{  cirlist L;
   cout << "Contents: "; L.PrintList();
   L.append(10);
   cout << "Contents: "; L.PrintList();
   L.append(20); L.append(30);
   L.insert(8); L.insert(5);
   cout << "Contents: "; L.PrintList();
   return 0;
}
```

The *PrintList* function is called three times: first when list *L* is still empty, then after this list contains only the integer value 10, and finally, after appending 20 and 30 and inserting 8 and 5, in that order. This explains the following output:

```
Contents:
Contents: 10
Contents: 5 8 10 20 30
```

Although the operations of copying lists and of assigning them to variables are not allowed, the program contains a copy constructor and an assignment operator, which simply give error messages and terminate program execution. This way, any attempt to use class *cirlist* in program code like

```
cirlist L1;
append(10);
cirlist L2 = L1, L3;
L3 = L1;
```

will result in a clear run-time error message and program termination, which is much better than a crash due to applying a destructor twice to the same object.

It would be a very good exercise if you tried to write the default constructor, the destructor and the member functions *append, insert iteratorStart* and *iterator* for class *cirlist* yourself.

Doubly-linked lists

The lists discussed so far are *singly-linked*: each node contains one link field possibly pointing to the next node, so we can traverse these lists only one way. By contrast, *doubly-linked lists* have two link fields. Figure 4.17 shows an ordered, circular, doubly-linked list, containing a sentinel.

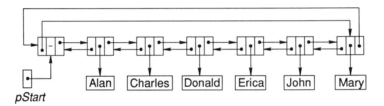

Figure 4.17 Circular, doubly-linked list with sentinel

Instead of integers, the list contains alphabetic data, or rather, pointers to such data, stored elsewhere in memory. We could have stored these data in the nodes themselves, but it would then have been necessary to reserve the same amount of memory for each string. This might have been reasonable for rather short names, such as shown here, but not if the strings had been long and of variable length.

It now makes sense to supply the class with two *iterator* functions, one for forward and the other for backward traversal. Here is a demonstration program in which two such iterators are implemented:

```
// dbllist: Ordered circular doubly-linked list.
#include <iostream.h>
#include <iomanip.h>
#include <stdlib.h>
#include <string.h>

struct elem{char *info; elem *prev, *next;};

class dbllist {
public:
   dbllist()
   {  pStart = new elem;   // Create sentinel
      pStart->prev = pStart->next = pStart;
      pStart->info = 0;
   }
```

```
    ~dbllist();

    void iteratorStart(elem *p=NULL)
    {   pCur = pStart;
    }

    elem *iteratorForward();
    elem *iteratorBackward();

    void PrintList();
    void append(const char *s);
    elem *FindPosition(const char *s);
    void remove(elem *p);

    dbllist(const dbllist& s)
    {   cout << "Copying not allowed.\n"; exit(1);
    }

    dbllist &operator=(const dbllist &s)
    {   cout << "Assignment not allowed.\n"; exit(1);
        return *this;
    }
private:
    elem *pStart, *pCur;
};

dbllist::~dbllist()
{   elem *p;
    iteratorStart();
    for (;;)
    {   p = iteratorForward();
        if (!p) break;
        delete p->info;
    }
    delete pStart; // Sentinel
}

elem *dbllist::iteratorForward()
{   pCur = pCur->next;
    return pCur == pStart ? NULL : pCur;
}

elem *dbllist::iteratorBackward()
{   pCur = pCur->prev;
    return pCur == pStart ? NULL : pCur;
}

void dbllist::PrintList()
{   elem *p;
    iteratorStart();
    while ((p = iteratorForward()) != NULL)
        cout << p->info << " ";
    cout << endl;
}
```

```
void dbllist::append(const char *s)
{   elem *p = new elem;
    int len = strlen(s);
    p->info = new char[len + 1];
    strcpy(p->info, s);
    elem *pEnd = pStart->prev;
    pEnd->next = p;
    p->prev = pEnd;
    p->next = pStart;
    pStart->prev = p;
}

elem *dbllist::FindPosition(const char *s)
{   iteratorStart();
    elem *p;
    do
        p = iteratorForward();
    while (p  &&  strcmp(p->info, s) != 0);
    return p;
}

void dbllist::remove(elem *p)
{   p->prev->next = p->next;
    p->next->prev = p->prev;
    delete p->info;
    delete p;
}

int main()
{   dbllist L;
    char buf[100];
    L.append("Alan"); L.append("Charles");
    L.append("Donald"); L.append("Erica");
    L.append("John"); L.append("Mary");
    cout << "Contents: "; L.PrintList();
    cout << "Name to be deleted: ";
    cin >> setw(100) >> buf;
    elem *p = L.FindPosition(buf);
    if (p)
    {   L.remove(p);
        cout << "Contents: "; L.PrintList();
    } else cout << "Not found.\n";
    return 0;
}
```

The *main* function builds the list shown in Figure 4.17. Then the user is asked for a name to be deleted. Function *FindPosition* searches the list for this name, and if it is found in some node, that node is removed from the list. The contents of the list are displayed before and after this deletion, as the following demonstration illustrates:

```
Contents: Alan Charles Donald Erica John Mary
Name to be deleted: Charles
Contents: Alan Donald Erica John Mary
```

Note that the removal of a node includes the deletion of the allocated memory areas in which the string in question is stored. Such deletions are also performed by the destructor.

Although not demonstrated in this program, the function *iteratorBackward* can be used in the same way as *iteratorForward* is used in functions *PrintList* and *FindPosition*.

4.10 Sorting Linked Lists

It is often desirable to sort a linked list. By rearranging its nodes, we can turn an unsorted list into a sorted one. There are at least two efficient ways of doing this: one is based on quicksort and the other on mergesort, discussed for arrays in Sections 3.7 and 3.10, respectively. Although there are similarities between these two sorting algorithms, there is a fundamental difference:

- quicksort builds two partitions, one with elements not greater and the other with elements not less than a pivot; it then applies itself to both partitions, and finally concatenates the resulting, sorted partitions;
- mergesort splits the entire sequence into two halves; it then applies itself to these two subsequences, and finally merges the resulting, sorted subsequences into one.

When sorting an array, we usually prefer quicksort, because it does not require any temporary array, as mergesort does. However, this drawback of mergesort does not apply to linked lists because these are more flexible than arrays: moving elements from one list to another can be done very efficiently, without any memory-allocation operations. As for the pivot required by quicksort, we cannot find this so efficiently in a linked list as we can in an array. For these reasons we prefer mergesort in this case. Here is a demonstration program to demonstrate this version of mergesort:

```
// lmsort: Merge sort applied to a linked list.
#include <iostream.h>
#include <stdlib.h>
struct elem{int info; struct elem *next;};

class SList {
public:
   SList(){pStart = pEnd = NULL;}
   ~SList();
   void append(int i);
   void AppendFirstNode(SList &L);
   void iteratorStart(elem *p=NULL){pCur = (p ? p : pStart);}
   elem *iterator();
   void MergeSort();
   void PrintList();
   SList(const SList& s)
   {  cout << "Copying not allowed.\n"; exit(1);
   }
   SList &operator=(const SList &s)
   {  cout << "Assignment not allowed.\n"; exit(1);
      return *this;
   }
```

```cpp
private:
   elem *pStart, *pEnd, *pCur;
};

SList::~SList()
{  while (pStart)
   {  pCur = pStart; pStart = pStart->next; delete pCur;
   }
}

void SList::append(int i)
{  pCur = pEnd;
   pEnd = new elem;
   pEnd->info = i;
   pEnd->next = NULL;
   (pCur ? pCur->next : pStart) = pEnd;
}

elem *SList::iterator()
{  elem *p = pCur;
   if (pCur) pCur = pCur->next;
   return p;
}

void SList::PrintList()
{  elem *p;
   iteratorStart();
   while ((p = iterator()) != NULL)
      cout << p->info << " ";
   cout << endl;
}

void SList::AppendFirstNode(SList &L)
// Move first node of list *this to the end of list L
// (L may be empty; *this is not):
{  // Detach first node of list *this:
   elem *p = pStart;
   pStart = pStart->next;
   p->next = NULL;
   // Attach that node (= *p) to list L:
   (L.pStart ? L.pEnd->next : L.pStart) = p;
   L.pEnd = p;
}

void SList::MergeSort()
{  SList L1, L2;
   if (pStart == NULL || pStart->next == NULL) return;
   iteratorStart();
   // Split *this into L1 and L2:
   while (pStart)
   {  AppendFirstNode(L1);
      if (pStart) AppendFirstNode(L2);
   }
   // Sort L1 and L2:
   L1.MergeSort(); L2.MergeSort();
```

```
      // Merge L1 and L2 into *this:
      while (L1.pStart && L2.pStart)
      {   if (L1.pStart->info < L2.pStart->info)
             L1.AppendFirstNode(*this); else
             L2.AppendFirstNode(*this);
      }
      // One of the following loops is empty:
      while (L1.pStart) L1.AppendFirstNode(*this);
      while (L2.pStart) L2.AppendFirstNode(*this);
   }

   int main()
   {   int x;
       SList L;
       cout << "Enter some integers, followed by\n"
               "a nonnumeric character:\n";
       while (cin >> x) L.append(x);
       L.MergeSort();
       cout << "List contents after sorting:\n"; L.PrintList();
       return 0;
   }
```

Much of this program is similar to program *linklist* in Section 4.5. The *Slist* member functions related to mergesort are *AppendFirstNode* and (not surprisingly) *MergeSort*. The first of these is used to move a node from the beginning of one list to the end of another. Note that this is similar to reading data from one file and writing it to another. Some comment in these two functions may be helpful in understanding how they work. Here is a demonstration of this program:

```
Enter some integers, followed by
a nonnumeric character:
23 18 100 7 30 5 20 !
List contents after sorting:
5 7 18 20 23 30 100
```

There is another way of sorting linked lists, radix sort, which is based on the individual bits (or characters) of the keys, as explained in Exercise 4.2 at the end of this chapter.

4.11 Using a Stack for Recursion Removal

As we have seen in Section 4.1, stacks are very important in connection with the implementation of programming languages. In code generated for recursive functions, a stack is normally used to store return addresses, arguments and local variables. If we want to replace a recursive function with an iterative one, a stack will often be helpful, especially in complicated situations. We have seen some simple cases of recursion removal, based on tail recursion, in Section 1.4. We will now deal with some cases other than tail recursion. Since discussions about recursion removal are sometimes hard to follow, we will begin with an extremely simple example:

```
void f(int n)
{  if (n > 0)
   {  f(n - 1);
      cout << n << " ";
   }
}
```

This function prints the numbers 1, 2, ..., *n*, in that order. For example, the call *f*(4) will produce the output

   1 2 3 4

We can easily verify this by analyzing the following tree:

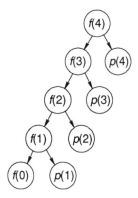

Although we can quickly write a simple iterative function that behaves like function *f*, we will rather use a more general method, which is also applicable in many other situations.

In the above tree, expressions such as *p*(4) denote 'print commands', written in our program as *cout* << ... We will refer to calls as *f*(4) as 'function commands'. Except for the final one, *f*(0), each function command results in another function command, followed by a print command. The print command *p*(4), although placed nearly at the top, is not executed until the function command *f*(3) has been completed. This explains why 4 is printed last.

To write an iterative version of function *f* we observe that we can replace the command *f*(4) with the two commands *f*(3) and *p*(4). Then we can replace *f*(3) with *f*(2) and *p*(3), and so on. This suggests the use of a stack, used to replace single commands with command pairs, as the following successive stack contents illustrate:

Stack	*Comment*
f(4)	Initial situation
p(4), *f*(3)	*f*(4) replaced with *f*(3), *p*(4)
p(4), *p*(3), *f*(2)	*f*(3) replaced with *f*(2), *p*(3)
p(4), *p*(3), *p*(2), *f*(1)	*f*(2) replaced with *f*(1), *p*(2)
p(4), *p*(3), *p*(2), *p*(1), *f*(0)	*f*(1) replaced with *f*(0), *p*(1)

Note that the top of the stack is on the right, as in Figure 4.3. This implies that, for example, in the first replacement, after popping $f(4)$ we have to push $p(4)$ before $f(3)$, because this will cause $f(3)$ to be available before $p(4)$. Remember, the item last pushed onto a stack is the first to be popped. The idea of replacing commands with other commands on a stack is realized in the following demonstration program, which contains an iterative function f that is equivalent to the recursive one listed at the beginning of this section:

```
// rec2itr: From recursion to iteration.
#include <iostream.h>
#include "stack.h"

struct cmnd
{   char code;   // 'f' = function, 'p' = print command
    int val;     // e.g. code = 'f' and val = 4 means f(4)
    cmnd(){}
    cmnd(char c, int v){ code = c; val = v;}
};

void f(int n)
{   cmnd x;
    stack<cmnd> stk;
    stk.push(cmnd('f', n));
    while (stk.pop(x))
    {   if (x.code == 'f')
        {   if (x.val > 0)
            {   stk.push(cmnd('p', x.val));
                stk.push(cmnd('f', x.val - 1));
            }
        }   else cout << x.val << " ";
    }
}

int main(void)
{   f(4);
    cout << endl;
    return 0;
}
```

The header file *stack.h* used here is the one listed in Section 4.3. Function f begins by pushing the command $f(4)$ on the stack. Then, as long as we can pop a command x, we test whether this is a 'function command' or a 'print command'. In the former case we push two new commands on the stack; in the latter we print the value given by the command.

We will now deal in the same way with a slightly more complicated recursive function, which we have also seen at the end of Section 1.4:

```
void h(int n)
{   cout << n << " ";
    for (int j=n-1; j>0; j--) h(j);
}
```

Although this function looks like a simple case of tail recursion, it is more complex because the recursive call is executed in a loop. It is instructive to sketch a tree for, say, $h(4)$, in the same way as we did in our previous example. In this particular case, only 'function commands' need to be pushed on the stack, so we need not distinguish between several command types. Therefore only the header-file *stack.h* is required, not a *cmnd* type as in the previous example, and we can use a stack of *int* values:

```
void h1(int n)
{   int x;
    stack<int> stk;
    stk.push(n);
    while (stk.pop(x))
    {   cout << x << " ";
        // Push function commands in reverse order:
        for (int j=1; j<x; j++) stk.push(j);
    }
}
```

The only tricky point is the reverse order in which the integers j, denoting 'function commands', are pushed on the stack. Both function calls $h(4)$ and $h1(4)$ give the following output:

```
4  3  2  1  1  2  1  1
```

If you have sketched a tree of $h(4)$, as suggested above, you should already have found this result.

Recursive functions that return values

If a recursive function returns a value, writing its iterative equivalent may be more difficult. Let us consider the following function, which calls itself twice if its argument is nonnegative:

```
int fun(int n)
{   return n < 0 ? 0 : 1 + 3 * fun(n - 1) - 2 * fun(n - 2);
}
```

Here are the values that *fun* will return for some argument values:

$$fun(-2) = 0$$
$$fun(-1) = 0$$
$$fun(0) \ = 1$$
$$fun(1) \ = 4$$
$$fun(2) \ = 11$$
$$fun(3) \ = 26$$
$$fun(4) \ = 57$$

In this case, we will construct an equivalent iterative function by using a second stack, just to store intermediate values. We will call it a *value stack*, to be distinguished from the *command stack*. We introduce some commands not occurring in our previous examples:

'*t*': multiply by 3 ('triple') and add 1
'*d*': multiply by 2 ('double')
'*s*': subtract

These commands obtain their operands by popping them from the value stack, and they also return their results on this stack. Command '*t*' pops a value from the value stack, multiplies it by 3, adds 1, and pushes the result again onto the value stack. Analogously, '*d*' doubles the item on the top of the value stack. Command '*s*' pops two values a and b from the value stack and pushes $b - a$ onto this stack. Using these new commands, we can rewrite

```
1 + 3 * fun(2) - 2 * fun(1)
```

as the following command sequence (each written on a separate line and followed by comment):

```
f(2) // Compute fun(2) and leave the result on the value stack
t    // Replace fun(2) (on the stack) with 1 + 3 * fun(2)
f(1) // Put fun(1) on the top of the value stack
d    // Replace fun(1) with 2 * fun(1)
s    // Replace pop both 2 * fun(1) and 1 + 3 * fun(2) and
     // compute (1 + 3 * fun(2)) - (2 * fun(1)
```

As soon as there are no more commands on the command stack, there is only one value on the value stack; returning this value is all that remains to be done. The following demonstration program shows the iterative function *fun*, equivalent to the above function with the same name. Almost at the beginning of the switch-statement, you will find the above command sequence pushed onto the command stack in reverse order (because of the LIFO principle):

```
// rec2ival: From recursion to iteration; value returned.

#include <iostream.h>
#include "stack.h"

struct cmnd
{   char code;
    int val;
    cmnd(){}
    cmnd(char c, int v=0)
    {   code = c;
        val = v;
    }
};
```

```
int fun1(int n)
{   stack<cmnd> cstk; // command stack
    stack<int> vstk;   // value stack
    cmnd x;
    int a, b;
    cstk.push(cmnd('f', n));

    while (cstk.pop(x))
    {   switch (x.code) {
        case 'f':
            a = x.val;
            if (a < 0) vstk.push(0); else
            {   cstk.push('s');    // subtract
                cstk.push('d');    // double
                cstk.push(cmnd('f', a - 2));
                cstk.push('t');    // triple and add 1
                cstk.push(cmnd('f', a - 1));
            }
            break;
        case 'd':
            vstk.pop(a);
            vstk.push(2 * a);
            break;
        case 't':
            vstk.pop(a);
            vstk.push(1 + 3 * a);
            break;
        case 's':
            vstk.pop(a);
            vstk.pop(b);
            vstk.push(b - a);
            break;
        }
    }

    vstk.pop(a);
    return a;
}


int main(void)
{   cout << fun1(4);
    cout << endl;
    return 0;
}
```

Both calls *fun*(4) and *fun*1(4) return the value 57. Incidentally, the recursive function *fun* is very inefficient, and its iterative counterpart *fun*1 is no better. It is far more efficient to use a bottom-up approach, using a table in which we successively store *fun*(i) for increasing values of i. The beginning of this table was shown a short while ago, just after the listing of the recursive function *fun*. Such a table is also the basis of *dynamic programming*, as we will see in Section 10.5.

Quicksort revisited

So far, we have been dealing with rather impractical examples in this section. By contrast, we will now turn to a very useful subject, sorting arrays by means of the quicksort algorithm. The following function template has been copied from Section 3.7.

```
// Quicksort; first version, two recursive calls.
template <class T>
void qsort1(T *a, int n)
{  int i = 0, j = n - 1;
   T x = a[j/2], w;
   do
   {  while (a[i] < x) i++;
      while (a[j] > x) j--;
      if (i < j) {w = a[i]; a[i] = a[j]; a[j] = w;} else
      {  if (i == j){i++; j--;}
         break;
      }
   }  while (++i <= --j);
   if (j > 0) qsort1(a, j+1);      //  a[0], ..., a[j]
   if (i < n-1) qsort1(a+i, n-i);  //  a[i], ..., a[n-1]
}
```

It contains two recursive calls, which we can regard as 'commands', so that we can push them onto a stack. Unlike our previous examples, the order in which we push these commands onto the stack does not affect the end result, since the above function works equally well if we interchange the two if-statements containing the recursive calls. Surprisingly enough, converting this recursive function into an iterative one is easier than our last example. This iterative version is shown in the following demonstration program:

```
// qsort_it: Quicksort, iterative version.

#include <iostream.h>
#include "stack.h"

template <class T>
struct cmnd
{  float *start;
   int len;
   cmnd(float *st=NULL, int n=0)
   {  start = st; len = n;
   }
};

template <class T>
void qsort_it(T *a, int n)
{  stack<cmnd<T> > stk;
   cmnd<T> x;
   stk.push(cmnd<T>(a, n));
   while (stk.pop(x))
   {  a = x.start; n = x.len;
      int i = 0, j = n - 1;
      T x = a[j/2], w;
```

```
        do
        {   while (a[i] < x) i++;
            while (a[j] > x) j--;
            if (i < j) {w = a[i]; a[i] = a[j]; a[j] = w;} else
            {   if (i == j){i++; j--;}
                break;
            }
        } while (++i <= --j);
        if (j > 0) stk.push(cmnd<T>(a, j+1));
        if (i < n-1) stk.push(cmnd<T>(a+i, n-i));
    }
}

int main()
{   float a[] = {19.5, 13, 10, 20.3, 7};
    int n = sizeof(a)/sizeof(*a);
    qsort_it(a, n);
    for (int i=0; i<n; i++) cout << a[i] << " ";
    cout << endl;
    return 0;
}
```

We could have written this program in a slightly simpler form if we had avoided the use of templates. However, once we are used to templates we find them very convenient. At the beginning of function *qsort_it* we find this curious declaration of our command stack *stk*:

```
    stack<cmnd<T> > stk;
```

This nested use of templates is required here because *cmnd* is a parametrized type with *T* as a parameter, and the resulting type *cmnd<T>* is to be used as an argument for the class template *stack*. The blank space between the two occurrences of > is required here because >> would otherwise be regarded as a right-shift operator.

Exercises

4.1   Read a sequence of unsigned integers (terminated by a nonnumeric character) and place them in a linked list. After this, split the list into two: one for all even and the other for all odd numbers of the original list. Remember, the rightmost bit of an even number is 0 and it is 1 for an odd number. Then combine these two lists simply by placing the second after the first. In the resulting list all even numbers come first.

4.2   Implement *radix sort* by extending Exercise 4.1. After splitting a linked list on the basis of the last bit of the key and combining the two resulting lists, you can again split the combined linked list into two, but this time on the basis of the second last bit. The two lists obtained in this way are again combined into one, all numbers that have a second last bit 0 occurring before those with a second last bit 1. The process is then repeated for the third last bit, and so on. After dealing with the leftmost bit, the *unsigned int* keys in the list appear in ascending order. Radix sort, based on the decimal rather than the binary number system, was widely in use until about 1965 to sort decks of punched cards. The cards were first split (into ten portions) using the least significant digit of the key. Then these ten portions were combined into one deck again, with zeros in the least significant digit on top and nines at the bottom. Then the procedure was repeated for the second position from the right, and so on. Since the time for radix sort is $O(n \log n)$, the old-fashioned mechanical sorting machines were faster than computers employing internal $O(n^2)$ sorting methods for large values of n.

4.3   Write a program that reads two positive integers n and k. Build a circular list, in which the numbers 1, 2, ..., n, in that order, are stored. Starting at the node that contains 1, delete each kth node from the list, printing the number stored in that node. Each time continue with the list element just after the deleted one. For example, if $n = 8$ and $k = 3$, we obtain the following output:

  3   6   1   5   2   8   4   7

This process, illustrated by initially having n persons arranged in a circle and by repeatedly eliminating the kth of those who are still present, is known as the *Josephus problem*.

5

Searching and String Processing

5.1 Sequential Search

We introduced the notion of a *sentinel* in Section 4.7, when we were discussing ordered linked lists. A sentinel may also be useful when we sequentially search an array. Suppose we have used the following declaration:

```
int a[N], n, i, x;
```

and only the first *n* array elements are in use, where $n < N$. If we now want to search these elements ($a[0]$, $a[1]$, ..., $a[n-1]$) for *x*, it is a good idea to do this as follows:

```
a[n] = x; i = 0;
while (x != a[i]) i++;
```

After the execution of this fragment, we can use the following code to determine whether or not *x* has been found:

```
if (i == n) ... // Not found
else ...        // x found at position i.
```

The array element $a[n]$ is used as a sentinel. Although there is no explicit test in the loop for *i* being less than *n*, we are sure that the search process will end properly if none of the first *n* array elements is equal to *x*, because it will then be found as the $(n+1)$th element, that is, as $a[n]$. Unless *n* is very small, the above loop will be faster than the following, more natural solution to the above problem:

```
for (i=0; i<n; i++)
    if (x == a[i]) break;
```

If you prefer an equivalent solution without a break-statement, you may instead write

```
i = 0;
while (i < n && x != a[i]) i++;
```

In both cases, the test whether x has been found should be done after the execution of these fragments in the same way as in our first solution. These two more natural solutions will take more time than the one based on a sentinel because of the additional test $i < n$, which is performed in these two loops but omitted in the original one.

Using a sentinel is particularly elegant if searching the array in the above way is done with the purpose of placing the value x in the array immediately after the elements to be searched, if it is not found in the search process. For example, the following fragment reads integers from the keyboard and stores them in the array a if they are different from all integers read in previously. If a newly read number is found among those already stored in the array, it is ignored:

```
int a[N], n=0, i, x;
while (cin >> x)
{  a[n] = x; i = 0;
   while (x != a[i]) i++;
   if (i == n)
   {  n++;
      if (n == N) break; // Array a full
   }
}
```

Storing the value of x in $a[n]$ is done here for two purposes: first, it acts as a sentinel, as we have been discussing, and second, if this value is not found in the sequential search it is already at the position where it belongs, so we need only increase n by one (and test for array exhaustion). To make writing and understanding this algorithm easier, it is wise to begin by thinking of array a as being already partially filled, that is, with $n > 0$; after that, we investigate the situation $n = 0$ to find that it works well also in this case. This way of verifying is also useful for many other, more complicated algorithms.

5.2 Binary Search

This section deals with searching ordered sequences. To keep our discussion simple we will begin with sequences of numbers, keeping in mind that in practice we may have records with keys and satellite data. Those records will have unique keys, so in our case all numbers in the given sequence are different from each other. Besides, the sequence is increasing, so that, with array elements $a[i]$ ($i = 0, 1, ..., n-1$) we have:

$$a[0] < a[1] < ... < a[n-1]$$

Let us declare

```
int a[N], x;
```

where N is greater than or equal to n. The value x is a given integer, for which array a is to be searched. Benefiting from the fact that the sequence is in increasing order, we can search it very efficiently. The method to be discussed is known as *binary search*. We begin with an element in the middle of the sequence, and, if this is not the one we are looking for, we proceed by searching either the left or the right half of the original sequence, depending on whether x is less or greater than the element in the middle, and so on. This description of the method is inaccurate and incomplete, since x may be unequal to all elements $a[i]$, and when writing a function for binary search, we have to provide a means to enable the user of the function to know whether or not x has been found. One solution would be to make the function return either -1 if x is not found, or i if x is found and equal to $a[i]$. We will go a step further and, in case x is not found, provide the user with information about where it logically belongs in the sequence. The function *BinSearch* to be developed will therefore return the integer value i defined as follows:

$$i = \begin{cases} 0 & \text{if } x \le a[0] \\ j & \text{if } a[j-1] < x \le a[j] \text{ for some } j \ (1 \le j < n) \\ n & \text{if } a[n-1] < x \end{cases}$$

In Chapter 7 we will apply binary search to B-trees, and we will then really need such a value i, both if the value x occurs in the array that is searched and if it does not. The first line of *BinSearch* will be

```
int BinSearch(int x, const int *a, int n)
```

Before we proceed with binary search, we observe that we can also obtain the desired value i by using the following function for *linear* search (*not* based on a sentinel as discussed in the previous section):

```
int LinSearch(int x, const int *a, int n)
{   int i=0;
    while (i < n && x > a[i]) i++;
    return i;
}
```

Note that, for all possible values x, function *LinSearch* returns the value of i as defined above. However, linear search is relatively slow, since its running time is $O(n)$. As we are given an ordered array, using linear search here is as inefficient as searching a dictionary for a word without using the fact that the words are listed in alphabetic order. We therefore want to replace the latter function with *BinSearch*, which gives the same result and has the same parameters as *LinSearch*, but runs in $O(\log n)$ time. If the range to be searched is exactly twice as small each time, then we need k steps, where

$$2^k = n$$

so

$$k = \log_2 n$$

which explains the logarithmic time complexity.

Writing a function for binary search is a well-known and instructive programming exercise. We have to be cautious to avoid wrong results and endless loops. If we test for the two cases $x \le a[0]$ and $x > a[n-1]$ in advance, the remaining case to be considered is

$$a[0] < x \le a[n-1]$$

We then have to reduce this condition to

$$a[j-1] < x \le a[j]$$

and we note that both conditions are special cases of

$$a[left] < x \le a[right] \tag{1}$$

so we begin with $left = 0$, $right = n-1$, and all we have to do is to reduce the range $left$, ..., $right$, in such a way that (1) also holds for the reduced range, and to repeat this until we have

$$right - left = 1 \tag{2}$$

When this happens, both (1) and (2) are true, which means that $right$ is the desired value i. The following function *BinSearch* works in this way:

```
/* Function for binary search.
   Array a[0], a[1], ..., a[n-1] is searched for x.
   Returned value:   0 if x <= a[0], or
                     i, where  a[i-1] < x <= a[i], or
                     n if a[n-1] < x.

*/

int BinSearch(int x, const int *a, int n)
{  int middle, left=0, right=n-1;
   if (x <= a[left]) return 0;
   if (x > a[right]) return n;
   while (right - left > 1)
   {  middle = (right + left)/2;
      (x <= a[middle] ? right : left) = middle;
   }
   return right;
}
```

The fourth line from the bottom shows a conditional expression used as an *lvalue*, which is allowed in C++, not in C. We assign the value of *middle* to the variable *right* if

$$x \le a[middle]$$

so that afterwards we have

$$x \le a[right]$$

Similarly, if

$a[middle] < x$

we assign the value of *middle* to *left*, so that

$a[left] < x$

holds after this assignment. Since there are no other assignments to the variables *left* and *right* in the loop, condition (1) will always be satisfied. We also have to verify that the loop terminates. This is rather simple, since, each time, the inner part of the loop is applied to a subrange

left, ..., *right*

of at least three elements, which implies that the computed value of *middle* satisfies

left < *middle* < *right*

It follows that either *left* will increase or *right* will decrease, so it is guaranteed that the length of the subrange under consideration really decreases each time. When discussing condition (2) for loop termination, we implicitly assumed the sequence to consist of at least two elements. However, function *BinSearch* also allows the sequence length 1. In that case, the loop is not entered at all, since then $a[n-1]$ is in fact $a[0]$, so we have either $x \le a[0]$ or $x > a[n-1]$. The return value is 0 in the former case and 1 (that is, *n*) in the latter, as it should be. The case $n = 1$ may seem far-fetched, but it is not. It will actually occur in Section 7.1, and, in general, when dealing with a sequence of length *n*, we ought to know which values for *n* are allowed. For our binary-search algorithm, *n* may be any positive integer, including 1. Binary search is notorious for its pitfalls when programmed sloppily, and it is one of the rare cases in programming in which a correctness proof, such as the above one, is both worthwhile and feasible.

It may not be superfluous to point out how *BinSearch* should be used. If *i* is an *int* variable and, coincidentally, the actual arguments have the same names as the formal parameters of *BinSearch*, we can write

```
i = BinSearch(x, a, n);

if (i < n && x == a[i])
{  // Found.
   //   The given integer x is equal to a[i].
   ...
} else
{  // Not found.
   // Either a[i] is the first element
   // that is greater than x (and i < n),
   // or  x > a[n-1] (and i = n).
   ...
}
```

The test $i < n$ after the call to *BinSearch* is essential, since otherwise the memory location following the final element $a[n-1]$ would be inspected if x happened to be greater than that final element. First, this would be fundamentally incorrect because we may have no access to that memory location. Note that the operator && guarantees that the second operand is not evaluated if the first is zero, so in our function the case that i should be equal to n causes no such problems. Second, that memory location might contain a value equal to x, so if our computer system allows us to inspect it (which is the more probable case), the test $x == a[i]$ may succeed, and our program would behave as if x had been found.

There is also a standard *library function* for binary search. Except for its first parameter, denoting the address of the key to be searched for, it has the same parameters as the *qsort* library function, discussed in Section 3.8. This function, *bsearch*, is declared in the standard header-file *stdlib.h* as follows:

```
void *bsearch(const void *key, const void *base,
              size_t n, size_t width,
              int (*fcmp)(const void*, const void*));
```

Its arguments (including the compare function *fcmp*) are similar to those of the standard library function *qsort*. In contrast to *qsort*, function *bsearch* returns a value, which is either the address of the array element with the given key value or zero if there is no such element. Note that in the latter case *bsearch* does not provide us with any information about the position where that element belongs. There will therefore be applications in which we had better use our own function *BinSearch*, which does give us such information. If the array to be searched has elements of a type other than *int*, we must adapt *BinSearch*, which is a simple task because of the compactness of this function. Better still, we can turn it into a function template, as discussed in Section 1.3.

5.3 Hashing

We will now discuss a well-known technique, called *hashing*, to store and retrieve objects very efficiently. These objects are *records*, containing a unique key used in search operations. It would be nice if we could derive the position of each record from its key. If the keys were natural numbers lying in a range that is small enough, we could indeed store each record in the position given by its key, so that we would know its place when we needed it later. Unfortunately, that is not the case in most practical situations. If the keys are natural numbers, their range is usually much larger than the amount of space available. If the keys are strings, we can associate them with unique natural numbers, but the requirement that unequal strings should give unequal numbers would lead to very large numbers, so again, their range would be too large. However, the idea of associating keys with natural numbers within a reasonable range is useful, both with numbers and with strings as keys. We will assume storage space to be available for at most N records, numbered

$0, 1, ..., N-1$

and we will apply a so-called *hash function* to the keys to obtain a *primary index value*, which is a nonnegative integer i, less than N. Although a one-to-one mapping remains desirable, we will not require this. In other words, we will not require our hashing function to associate any two distinct keys $k1$ and $k2$ with two distinct integers $i1$ and $i2$. This means that, with a hash function h, the situation

$$h(k1) = h(k2) = i$$

called a *collision*, may occur. There are two essentially different ways to deal with collisions, referred to as *chaining* and *open addressing*.

You may think of the records as entries in a phone book. With a given name, we want to find the corresponding number, so the names will be the keys. This *searching* operation is the most important one, but it is obvious that we must be able to *build* the set of records to be searched, so there is another essential operation: *inserting* new records. It may also be desirable to be able to *delete* records, but this is not essential for all applications.

Collision resolution by chaining

The three operations mentioned, searching, insertion and deletion, can easily be realized by means of a collision-resolution method known as *chaining*. The idea is that we build an array of pointers to linked lists, so there are as many linked lists as there are array elements. Applying our hash function to the key provides us with the index to be used in this array to find a start pointer of a linked list. We then simply apply the desired operation (searching, insertion or deletion) to the linked list found in this way. Note that searching these lists is possible only because the keys are part of the records; storing the keys would not be required if there were no collisions because each linked list would contain at most one element in that case. If the array is large enough and we are using a good hash function, these linked lists will be short, which explains why this method of storing and retrieving data is very fast.

Let us use the following table as an example:

```
Nash      9462
Muller    8765
Okada     8888
Earley    2277
Sloane    9281
Rice      1122
Peterson  9999
```

We will discuss a program that accepts the above input, which should be given in the form of a text file, *phone.txt*. Our program uses this data to build a hash table. Although we could have chosen a fixed value, say 1000, as the length N of this table, our program will ask the user to enter this length. Note that N may be less or greater than the number of entries. If we use the above example of seven entries and we choose N less than 7, there will necessarily be collisions. For greater values of N, there *may* be collisions. Here is the hash function that we will use; it is implemented as a public member function of the class *StringHash*:

```
unsigned StringHash::hash(const char *s)const
{   unsigned sum = 0;
    for (int i=0; s[i]; i++)
        sum += (i + 1) * s[i];
    return sum % N;
}
```

Using the very small value $N = 5$ to demonstrate collisions and assuming that we are using ASCII character values, we have

$$hash("Nash") = (1 * 'N' + 2 * 'a' + 3 * 's' + 4 * 'h') \% 5$$
$$= (1 \times 78 + 2 \times 97 + 3 \times 115 + 4 \times 104) \% 5 = 1033 \% 5 = 3$$

Since the hash function returns the value 3 in this example, the record containing the key "Nash" will be stored in the linked list that in our program will be denoted by $a[3]$. In this example, with $N = 5$, the linked lists of our hash table will be as shown in Figure 5.1.

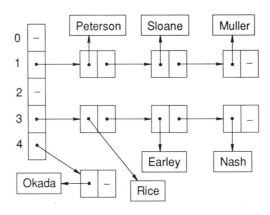

Figure 5.1 Collision resolution by chaining

As you can see, the strings are not stored in the list nodes themselves but elsewhere, as we did in Section 4.9.

The following application file shows that the insert, delete and search operations are available:

```
// hash1ap: Hashing with collision resolution by chaining
//    (application, to be linked with hash1.cpp).

#include <fstream.h>
#include <iomanip.h>
#include "hash1.h"
```

```
int main()
{  ifstream PhoneFile("phone.txt", ios::in);
   if (!PhoneFile)
   {  cout << "Cannot open file phone.txt.\n";
      exit(1);
   }
   char NameBuf[100], answer;
   unsigned num, N;
   cout << "Table length N: "; cin >> N;
   elem *p = 0;
   StringHash PhoneBook(N);
   cout << "Data read from file phone.txt:\n\n";
   while (PhoneFile >> setw(100) >> NameBuf >> num)
   {  cout << setw(30) << setiosflags(ios::left)
           << NameBuf << num << endl;
      PhoneBook.insert(NameBuf, num);
   }
   cout << endl;
   for (;;)
   {  cout << "Enter a name, or ! to quit: ";
      cin >> NameBuf;
      if (*NameBuf == '!') break;
      p = PhoneBook.find(NameBuf);
      if (p)
      {  cout << "Number: " << p->num << endl;
         cout << "Do you want to delete this entry? (Y/N): "
              << flush;
         cin >> answer;
         if (answer == 'Y' || answer == 'y')
            PhoneBook.remove(NameBuf);
      } else cout << "Not found." << endl;
   }
   return 0;
}
```

To understand what this program is supposed to do, the following demonstration, based on the data shown before, will be helpful:

```
Table length N: 5
Data read from file phone.txt:

Nash                          9462
Muller                        8765
Okada                         8888
Earley                        2277
Sloane                        9281
Rice                          1122
Peterson                      9999

Enter a name, or ! to quit: Okada
Number: 8888
Do you want to delete this entry? (Y/N): Y
Enter a name, or ! to quit: Okada
Not found.
```

```
Enter a name, or ! to quit: Sloane
Number: 9281
Do you want to delete this entry? (Y/N): n
Enter a name, or ! to quit: !
```

Immediately after reading the input data, the hash table and the linked lists are as shown in
Figure 5.1. The interface file *hash*1.*h* shows the declaration of the classes *list* and
StringHash. A *StringHash* object is in fact a hash table, with its associated operations
encapsulated in the class, as is usual in C++:

```
// hash1.h: Hashing based on linked lists (chaining)
#include <iostream.h>
#include <stdlib.h>
struct elem{char *name; unsigned num; elem *next;};

class list {
public:
    list(): pStart(NULL){}
    ~list();
    void RemoveNode(const char *s);
    void ListInsert(const char *s, unsigned num);
    elem *FindPosition(const char *s)const;
    void remove(elem *p);

    list(const list& s)
    {  cout << "Copying not allowed.\n"; exit(1);
    }

    list &operator=(const list &s)
    {  cout << "Assignment not allowed.\n"; exit(1);
       return *this;
    }
private:
    elem *pStart;
};

class StringHash {
public:
    StringHash(unsigned len=1021): N(len){a = new list[len];}
    ~StringHash(){delete[] a;}
    void insert(const char *s, unsigned num)
    {  a[hash(s)].ListInsert(s, num);
    }
    elem *find(const char *s)const
    {  return a[hash(s)].FindPosition(s);
    }
    void remove(const char *s)
    {  a[hash(s)].RemoveNode(s);
    }
    unsigned hash(const char *s)const;
private:
    unsigned N;
    list *a;
};
```

For economic reasons, we are not using iterator functions this time, nor are there sentinels at the end of the lists. If we had used the latter, we would have used considerably more memory than we are using now. In practical situations, with N much larger than 5, most lists $a[i]$ would be empty. It would be a waste of memory if there were both a pointer $pCur$ (used by iterator functions) and a sentinel node. In our implementation, each of these empty lists $a[i]$ takes only one pointer, $pStart$ (whose value is zero).

The *StringHash* constructor has a default argument of 1021 for the table length N instead of the very small value 5, used in our demonstration to make collisions happen. Although the round value 1000 would probably have been just as good in the current program, a prime number N, such as 1021, may be better with other hash functions or with other ways of collision handling, as we will see in a moment. Note that the 'array' a, allocated by $a = new$ *list*$[len]$ in this constructor, is implicitly initialized, the *list* constructor being executed for each of the *len* array elements $a[i]$.

Thanks to the *list* class, the *StringHash* class is very simple. Except for the *hash* function, all member functions are defined in the class itself, because each contains only one statement. The implementation file, shown below, is therefore mainly about linked lists, with function *StringHash::hash*, at the end of this file, as the only exception:

```
// hash1.cpp: Hashing based on linked lists (chaining).
//      (Implementation file, to be linked with hash1ap.cpp
//      or any other application file).
#include <string.h>
#include "hash1.h"

list::~list()
{  elem *p = pStart, *q;
   while (p)
   {  q = p; p = p->next;
      delete[] q->name; delete q;
   }
}

void list::RemoveNode(const char *s)
{  elem *p = pStart, *q;
   if (p == NULL) return;
   if (strcmp(p->name, s) == 0)
   {  pStart = p->next;
      delete[] p->name; delete p;
      return;
   }
   for (;;)
   {  q = p->next;
      if (q == NULL) break;
      if (strcmp(q->name, s) == 0)
      {  p->next = q->next;
         delete[] q->name; delete q;
         return;
      }
      p = q;
   }
}
```

```
void list::ListInsert(const char *s, unsigned num)
{   elem *p = new elem;
    int len = strlen(s);
    p->name = new char[len + 1];
    strcpy(p->name, s);
    p->num = num;
    p->next = pStart;
    pStart = p;
}

elem *list::FindPosition(const char *s)const
{   elem *p = pStart;
    while (p && strcmp(p->name, s) != 0) p = p->next;
    return p;
}

unsigned StringHash::hash(const char *s)const
{   unsigned sum = 0;
    for (int i=0; s[i]; i++) sum += (i + 1) * s[i];
    return sum % N;
}
```

Recall that we have listed this *hash* function at the beginning of our discussion. Note the use of type *unsigned* for both the return value and the variable *sum*. If we used type *int* instead, integer overflow in the computation of *sum* might cause this variable to be negative. Then the remainder *sum % N* would also be negative. We avoid this problem by using unsigned integers.

Function *RemoveNode* is more complex than the others. We need it only if we want to delete items, which is not required for all applications of hashing.

Open addressing

There is a fundamentally different way of dealing with collisions. We can use only a table, in which we store all data. This idea has the advantage that no memory space is required for links, but the price to be paid for this is some loss of generality: we have to allocate a fixed amount of memory for the table in advance. Making this table very large reduces the number of collisions and increases the number of entries that we can insert before the table overflows. But this implies that much memory is allocated that is not actually used.

With open addressing, implementation of the deletion operation is possible, but it is very complicated. We will not discuss this aspect, so our class *HashTable* will support only insertion and searching. The following application program is therefore slightly simpler and more restricted than *hash1ap*:

```
// hash2ap: Hashing with open addressing
//      (application, to be linked with hash2.cpp).

#include <fstream.h>
#include <iomanip.h>
#include <stdlib.h>
#include "hash2.h"
```

```
int main()
{  ifstream PhoneFile("phone.txt", ios::in);
   if (!PhoneFile)
   {  cout << "Cannot open file phone.txt.\n";
      exit(1);
   }
   char NameBuf[30];
   unsigned num, N;
   cout << "Table length N (preferably a prime number): ";
   cin >> N;
   elem *p = NULL;
   HashTable PhoneBook(N);
   cout << "Data read from file phone.txt:\n\n";
   while (PhoneFile >> setw(30) >> NameBuf >> num)
   {  cout << setw(30) << setiosflags(ios::left)
           << NameBuf << num << endl;
      PhoneBook.insert(NameBuf, num);
   }
   cout << endl;
   for (;;)
   {  cout << "Enter a name, or ! to quit: ";
      cin >> NameBuf;
      if (*NameBuf == '!') break;
      p = PhoneBook.find(NameBuf);
      if (p)
         cout << "Number: " << p->num << endl;
      else cout << "Not found." << endl;
   }
   return 0;
}
```

As you can see, the table length *N* can again be specified by the user, but this time it is really desirable that *N* should be a prime number because of our way of collision handling, which we will discuss shortly. Here is the interface file for class *HashTable*:

```
// hash2.h: Hashing with open addressing

#include <iostream.h>
struct elem {char name[30]; unsigned num;};

class HashTable {
public:
   HashTable(unsigned len=1021);
   ~HashTable(){delete[] a;}
   void insert(const char *s, unsigned num);
   elem *find(const char *s);
private:
   unsigned hash(const char *s);
   unsigned HashIncr()const{return 1 + sum % (N - 2);}
   int h2(const char *t, unsigned &i)const;
   unsigned N, sum;
   elem *a;
};
```

We could still have stored the strings outside the array, but that would have been against the spirit of open addressing, since no memory outside the array is used for collision resolution either. The strings are therefore stored in the array elements themselves, which implies that we have to make a decision about their maximum length. Since we are dealing with null-terminated strings, the array length of 30 used here means that the maximum string length is 29. To demonstrate the program, let us use the same data as before, with the exception that our table length N will now be 11 (the value of 5 used previously being too small to accommodate all this data):

```
Table length N (preferably a prime number): 11
Data read from file phone.txt:

Nash                          9462
Muller                        8765
Okada                         8888
Earley                        2277
Sloane                        9281
Rice                          1122
Peterson                      9999

Enter a name, or ! to quit: Johnson
Not found.
Enter a name, or ! to quit: Earley
Number: 2277
Enter a name, or ! to quit: !
```

With the names processed in the above order and $N = 11$, our hash function computes the following primary index values:

Name	Primary index value hash(Name)
Nash	10
Muller	1
Okada	6
Earley	2
Sloane	9
Rice	3
Peterson	2

Luckily, the *hash* function assigns unique primary index values to the first six names. With the seventh, however, there is a collision:

```
hash("Peterson") = 2 = hash("Earley")
```

Our program can detect this collision because all strings $a[i].name$ are initially set to contain the empty string. Finding any string other than the empty one ("") in $a[i].name$ therefore indicates that $a[i].name$ is already in use.

Using *double hashing* means that this collision is resolved by applying a secondary hash function to provide us with an increment. It may look more natural to use 1 as this increment and simply try successive array elements (also called *slots*) until a free one is found. However, this idea, known as *linear probing*, leads to clusters of occupied slots. Instead, double hashing searches for a free slot by taking greater steps, with a step size computed by another function, for which we will use this *HashTable* member function *HashIncr*:

```
unsigned HashIncr()const{return 1 + sum % (N - 2);}
```

This function is based on the value *sum*, a private member of class *HashTable* and computed in the *hash* member function:

```
unsigned HashTable::hash(const char *s)
{   sum = 0;
    for (int i=0; s[i]; i++) sum += (i + 1) * s[i];
    return sum % N;
}
```

Applying this function to the name *"Peterson"* gives *sum* = 3951, which explains the above primary index value 3951 % *N* = 2, where *N* = 11. Since a call to *HashIncr* takes place only after a call to *hash*, we can use *sum* in *HashIncr*, finding

$$incr = HashIncr() = 1 + 3951 \% 9 = 1$$

Both functions *insert* and *find* first call the *hash* function to find a primary index. They then call the function *h2*, which, if necessary, calls the secondary hash function *HashIncr* as follows:

```
incr = HashIncr();
```

Then a loop is entered to execute the statement

```
i = (i + incr) % N;
```

as often as is necessary (but less than *N* times). Since we had *hash*(*"Peterson"*) = 2, the next index value *i* will be

$$(2 + 1) \% 11 = 3$$

Unfortunately, *a*[3] has already been used for the name *Rice*, so there is another collision. We now apply the above statement once again, finding the following new value for *i*:

$$(3 + 1) \% 11 = 4$$

Since *a*[4] is still empty, we can use it for *Peterson*. The entries of our 'phone book' are therefore stored as shown in Figure 5.2. In this figure, the rectangles containing the names seem to be chosen much too wide for the rather short names. This was done deliberately because it reflects what happens in memory: although there may be 29 characters in each name, the longest one, *Peterson*, consists only of eight.

0	-	
1	Muller	8765
2	Earley	2277
3	Rice	1122
4	Peterson	9999
5	-	
6	Okada	8888
7	-	
8	-	
9	Sloane	9281
10	Nash	9462

Figure 5.2 Hash table with open addressing

To make the principle of double hashing very clear, we will also look at the subject in a different way, using a different value of *incr*, say 7. Then the step size 7 is actually used, but if the resulting position number is not less than N, it is reduced by N. With $N = 11$ and 2 as a primary hash value, we find

$$2 + 7 = 9 \quad \text{gives position 9}$$
$$9 + 7 = 16 \quad \text{gives position } 16 - 11 = 5$$
$$5 + 7 = 12 \quad \text{gives position } 12 - 11 = 1$$
$$1 + 7 = 8 \quad \text{gives position 8}$$
and so on.

If all slots were occupied, and we went on forever, we would try all positions given in the second of these lines:

2	9	16	23	30	37	44	51	58	65	72	79	...
2	9	5	1	8	4	0	7	3	10	6	2	...

The numbers on this second line are equal to those on the first line modulo 11. For example, we find 2 beneath 79 because 79 % 11 = 2. Starting with 2, we find all eleven values 0, 1, ..., 10, before 2 appears again. This is no coincidence, but rather a consequence of 7 and 11 being *relative prime*, which means that these two numbers have 1 as their greatest common divisor. If N was not a prime number, it might be a multiple of the step size. For example, with 2 as the primary index, 7 as the step size, but N equal to 14, only $a[2]$ and $a[9]$ would be examined for free positions (since $9 + 7 - 14 = 2$). It will now be clear that we had better use a prime number for the table length N. Note that both 11, used above, and 1021, occurring in the file *hash2.h* as the default argument of the *HashTable* constructor, are prime numbers.

To make *N* and *incr* relative prime, we should also pay some attention to the value of *incr*, returned by the secondary hash function, *HashIncr*. Recall that we had $N = 11$ and $incr = 7$ in the above example. Since *incr* is added to *i* before we take the remainder modulo *N*, it seems no problem if *incr* were larger than *N*. However, *incr* must not be a multiple of *N*, because then *incr* and *N* would not be relative prime, in spite of *N* being a prime number. Obviously, it must not be zero either. The expression

```
1 + sum % (N - 2)
```

occurring in function *HashIncr* will now be clearer. We use $N - 2$ instead of $N - 1$ here, because we prefer an odd number as a divisor. With an even number *k*, the value of

```
sum % k
```

is even if *sum* is even and odd if *sum* is odd, while there is no such dependency if *k* is odd. Remember that even in program *hash1ap*, discussed earlier, we used the prime number 1021 as a default value for the table length *N*. In general, to obtain hash values that are 'as random as possible', the modulo operator % should preferably be followed by an integer that has no small divisors such as 2, 3 and 5. Prime numbers, such as 1021, are therefore ideal candidates for *N*. In view of function *HashIncr*, this suggests choosing *N* so that both $N - 2$ and *N* are 'twin primes', such as 101 and 103. You may find it interesting to know that there are as many as 1224 prime numbers *N* less than 100 000 for which $N - 2$ is also a prime number. Here are some examples:

5, 43, 103, 313, 601, 1021, 3001, 7129, 10 009, 30 013, 60 091, 90 019, 99 991

When we apply program *hash2ap* to the input file used throughout this section, we can experimentally verify that using a prime number for *N* is desirable. Since the input file consists of 7 entries, any value of *N* less than 7 will result in an error message *Hash table full*. This message does not occur with $N = 7$, but it is back again with $N = 8$, not because this value is too small but rather because it is not a prime number. Although 10 is no prime number, $N = 10$ works fine in this example, but $N = 12$ does not. By contrast, none of the prime numbers 7, 11, 13, 17, ... will produce this error message.

After this discussion about prime numbers in relation to hash functions, it is now time to consider the implementation file, which is to be linked with the application program *hash2ap*:

```
// hash2.cpp: Implementation file for hashing with open
//            addressing.

#include <iostream.h>
#include <string.h>
#include <stdlib.h>
#include "hash2.h"

HashTable::HashTable(unsigned len)
{  N = (len > 3 ? len : 3); // N >= 3 (see HashIncr)
   a = new elem[N];
   for (unsigned i=0; i<N; i++) a[i].name[0] = '\0';
}
```

```
int HashTable::h2(const char *t, unsigned &i)const
{  unsigned count=0, incr;
   if (strcmp(a[i].name, t))
   {  incr = HashIncr();
      do
      {  if (++count == N) return 0; // Failure
         i = (i + incr) % N;
      }  while (strcmp(a[i].name, t));
   }
   return 1;   // Success
}

void HashTable::insert(const char *s, unsigned num)
{  unsigned i = hash(s);
   if (!h2("", i)){cout << "Hash table full\n"; exit(1);}
   strcpy(a[i].name, s);
   a[i].num = num;
}

elem *HashTable::find(const char *s)
{  unsigned i = hash(s);
   return h2(s, i) ? a + i : NULL;
}

unsigned HashTable::hash(const char *s)
{  sum = 0;
   for (int i=0; s[i]; i++) sum += (i + 1) * s[i];
   return sum % N;
}
```

Note that the files *hash2.h* and *hash2.cpp* for open addressing are simpler than their counterparts, *hash1.h* and *hash1.cpp*, for hashing with chaining. This is an attractive aspect of open addressing. Another positive point is that no memory space is required for pointers. By contrast, hashing by chaining is more complicated because of its intensive use of pointers. But chaining has two important advantages: it does not impose a maximum number of records and it enables us to implement record deletion in a straightforward way.

5.4 Text Searching

Every text processor or editor enables its users to search a text for a given string, also known as a *pattern*. From a practical C or C++ programmer's angle, the simplest way of text searching is by using the standard library function *strstr*, as the following program demonstrates:

```
#include <iostream.h>
#include <string.h>

int main()
{  char *text = "To be or not to be, that is the question",
        *pattern = "that",
        *p = strstr(text, pattern);
   if (p) cout << "Text starting at p:\n" << p;
   return 0;
}
```

This program finds the position of the pattern *"that"* in the given text and prints the text starting at this position. Its output is therefore as follows:

```
Text starting at p:
that is the question
```

In this section we will implement a very sophisticated algorithm for text searching, due to Boyer and Moore. This algorithm requires some initial work to be done, depending only on the pattern, not on the text to be searched. If the same pattern is to be applied to several text strings, it saves time to separate this initial work from the actual searching. We could use two different functions in the traditional way, but we may as well benefit from the C++ class concept. We will therefore declare a class, *search*, and do the initial work in its constructor, while the actual searching is done by a public member function *find*. We can therefore write, for example,

```
search x(pattern);
p = x.find(textA);
q = x.find(textB);
```

to search both strings *textA* and *textB* for the string *pattern*. If *pattern* is to be found only once, we need not use a *search* variable, such as *x* in the above example, but we can also write

```
p = search(pattern).find(text);
```

Using the same pattern several times is useful to find *all* occurrences of that pattern in a given text. Although we have not yet discussed our searching algorithm, let us demonstrate this way of using the class *search* by means of the following application program:

```
// searchap: Searching a textfile for a string
//           (to be linked with search.cpp).
#include <fstream.h>
#include <stdlib.h>
#include <string.h>
#include "search.h"

int main(int argc, char *argv[])
{   if (argc != 3)
    {   cout << "Use file name and pattern as program "
            "arguments.\n"; exit(1);
    }
    ifstream input(argv[1], ios::in);
    if (!input)
    {   cout << "Cannot open file " << argv[1] << endl; exit(1);
    }
    // Find required string length:
    int n=0, i;
    char ch;
    while (input.get(ch), !input.fail()) n++;
    input.clear(); input.seekg(0);
    char *text = new char[n + 1], *p = text, *pattern = argv[2];
```

```
// Read text array from file:
for (i=0; i<n; i++) input.get(text[i]);
text[n] = '\0';
// Specify pattern:
search x(pattern);
// Find all occurrences of pattern in text:
cout << "Text from found pattern to end of line:\n";
while ((p = x.find(p)) != 0)
{   for (i=0; p[i] != '\0' && p[i] != '\n'; i++) cout << p[i];
    cout << endl;
    p++;
}
return 0;
}
```

Let us demonstrate the above program, using this very program file as input text and the string "*argv*" as a pattern to be searched for. The program then prints all occurrences of this string in the text, along with the rest of each program line on which the pattern is found. The first of the following lines is typed as a command; the others are output lines showing that the pattern "*argv*" is found four times:

```
searchap searchap.cpp argv
Text from found pattern to end of line:
argv[])
argv[1]);
argv[1] << endl; exit(1);
argv[2];
```

As we can verify in the above program file, there are four occurrences of "*argv*", and we can tell them apart by printing also the characters that follow on the same program lines.

The following header file, used in the above application program, shows the declaration of class *search*:

```
// search.h: Header file for class search

class search {
public:
    search(const char *pat);
    ~search(){delete[] skip2;}
    char *find(char *text);
private:
    const char *pattern;
    int skip1[256],      // Related to bad character
        *skip2,          // Related to good suffix
        m;               // Pattern length
};
```

It is now time to discuss the Boyer–Moore algorithm on which class *search* is based. Denoting the pattern length by m, let us begin with the pattern "*WELSH*", for which $m = 5$. We will search the text "*PETERSON WELSH*" for this pattern. It will be clear that we have to start on the left, checking whether all characters of the pattern are identical with the corresponding characters of the text:

```
position:     0  1  2  3  4  5  6  7  8  9 10 11 12 13
text:         P  E  T  E  R  S  O  N     W  E  L  S  H
pattern:      W  E  L  S  H
```

As long as the pattern and the text do not match, as in the above situation, it seems obvious that we have to shift the pattern one position to the right and test once again to see whether this shift makes the pattern and the text match, and so on. The strength of the algorithm under discussion is that in most cases we can immediately shift the pattern *more than one position* to the right.

Using a 'bad character' and *skip*1

To find out if there is a match, we begin with the *final* character of the pattern, that is, $pattern[m-1]$. In the above example, this implies that we compare H of the pattern with R of the text. Finding this mismatch, we can do much better than shifting the pattern only one position to the right. It is important to note that R, the text component of the mismatched pair (R, H), does not occur at all in the pattern. This implies that there cannot be a match as long as we are comparing any character of the pattern with this R, that is, with position 4 of the text. We can therefore immediately shift the pattern five positions to the right, leading to the following situation:

```
position:     0  1  2  3  4  5  6  7  8  9 10 11 12 13
text:         P  E  T  E  R  S  O  N     W  E  L  S  H
pattern:                     W  E  L  S  H
```

We now compare W (= $text[9]$) with H (= $pattern[4]$). Again, these characters are different, but this time we find that W does occur in the pattern. This character W is at position 0 in the pattern, while there would be a match for this character if it were at position $m-1=4$. The difference $4-0=4$ between these two positions is the number of positions for the pattern to be shifted to the right. We see that the number of characters that the pattern should shift to the right depends on the mismatched character of the text. For every character of the alphabet, we store the corresponding number of shift positions in the array *skip*1. For example, we have

$skip1['R'] = 5 = m$:   'R' does not occur in pattern (see initial situation above)
$skip1['W'] = 4 = m-1$:   'W' = $pattern[0]$
$skip1['E'] = 3 = m-2$:   'E' = $pattern[1]$
$skip1['L'] = 2 = m-3$:   'L' = $pattern[2]$
$skip1['S'] = 1 = m-4$:   'E' = $pattern[3]$
$skip1['H'] = 0 = m-5$:   'E' = $pattern[4]$

and so on. We see that, for any character *ch*, we have

$skip1[ch] = m - 1 - h$ where either

$ch = pattern[h]$ (and $ch \neq pattern[i]$ for $i = h + 1, ..., m - 1$) or

ch does not occur in the pattern and $h = -1$

If there are several occurrences of character ch in the pattern, we should take the rightmost of them, as the above condition within parentheses indicates. Note that $h = -1$ implies that $m - 1 - h = m$, so that $skip1[ch] = m$ for any ch that does not occur in the pattern.

So far, we have been using the 'bad character' $ch = text[j]$ that aligns with the final pattern character, $pattern[m - 1]$. However, proceeding from right to left, we may find some matching characters before we encounter the first mismatch $text[j] \neq pattern[i]$. Remember, we are using the integer variables i, j, h and m as follows. When finding that the characters $text[j]$ and $pattern[i]$ are different, we have either $h \geq 0$, with $pattern[i] \neq pattern[h] = text[j] = ch$, or $h = -1$ implying that $text[j]$ is different from all characters $pattern[i]$ (where $i = 0, 1, ..., m - 1$). For example, we have $i = j = 4$ and $h = -1$ in:

position:	0	1	2	3	4	5	6	7	8	9	10	11	12
text:	P	E	T	E	R	S	O	N	N	E	S	O	N
pattern:	S	O	N	N	E	S	O	N					

Since 'R' does not occur in the pattern "*SONNESON*" we have $skip1['R'] = m = 8$, but this time we clearly have to shift the pattern 5, not 8, positions to the right. Recall that $skip1['R']$ is based on the final pattern character being compared. We now have to use $skip1['R'] - 3$ because the compared character 'E' occurs 3 positions to the left of the final pattern character 'N'. In general, to find the number of shift positions we have to reduce $skip1[ch]$ by the distance $m - 1 - i$ between the final character $pattern[m - 1]$ and the mismatched character $pattern[i]$. It follows that the required number of shift positions is equal to $skip1[ch] - (m - 1 - i) = (m - 1 - h) - (m - 1 - i) = i - h$. Since $ch = $ 'R' does not occur in the pattern of our last example, we have $i - h = 4 - (-1) = 5$.

Using a 'good suffix' and *skip2*

The above discussion seems to provide us with a general and efficient algorithm, but it does not because there is a flaw. Let us use another example to show the problem and to see how we can solve it:

position:	0	1	2	3	4	5	6	7	8	9	10	11	12
text:	P	E	T	E	S	S	O	N	N	E	S	O	N
pattern:	S	O	N	N	E	S	O	N					

The problem in this example is that the bad character 'S' = $text[4]$ occurs not only as $pattern[0]$ but also as $pattern[5]$, which lies to the right of the mismatch $pattern[4] = $ 'E'. It follows from our discussion above that $skip1['S'] = m - 1 - h = 8 - 1 - 5 = 2$. Reducing this by 3 (the distance between the final character 'N' and the mismatch character 'E' in the pattern) would mean that we shift the pattern -1 positions to the right. This clearly demonstrates that we cannot use *skip1* in this case.

Fortunately, there is a very good solution to this problem. It is based on the portion of the pattern that follows the mismatched character. This portion, *SON* in this example, is called a 'good suffix' because it matches an identical portion of the text. We will now use the fact that *SON* also occurs elsewhere in the pattern. Since this other occurrence lies five positions to the left of the good suffix, we should shift the pattern five positions to the right. Again we should be more precise: if the suffix occurs elsewhere in the pattern not only once but several times, we should take its rightmost occurrence, that is, the one that is nearest to the suffix. In general, if *pattern*[i] is the first mismatched character, that is, if the good suffix starts at *pattern*[$i + 1$] (so that $i = 4$ in the above example), and there are other occurrences of this suffix string in the pattern, the rightmost of which starts at *pattern*[h] (with $h = 0$ in our example), then we can shift the pattern $i + 1 - h$ positions to the right.

We must also know what to do if the good suffix does not occur elsewhere in the pattern. This situation is shown below, where the pattern begins with *SOM* instead of *SON*:

position:	0	1	2	3	4	5	6	7	8	9	10	11	12
text:	P	E	T	E	S̲	S	O	N	N	E	S	O	N
pattern:	S	O	M	N	E̲	S	O	N					

In this case, we can benefit from the knowledge that the suffix *SON* does not occur elsewhere in the pattern. We can immediately see that shifting the pattern only a few positions (1, 2, 3, 4 or 5) to the right would be no good, since then at least one of the three characters of *SON* in positions 5, 6 and 7 of the text would be different from a corresponding character of the pattern. It is therefore not necessary to compare this text substring of length 3 with any other substring of the pattern. We can safely shift the pattern six positions to the right, so that the first character (= *text*[5]) of *SON* in the text falls outside the range used for comparisons. In general, if we find a mismatch at position i of the pattern so that *pattern*[$i + 1$] is the first character of the good suffix, and if the string formed by this suffix does not occur elsewhere in the pattern, we can shift the pattern $i + 2$ positions to the right. Since $i = 4$ in our example, the number of positions for the pattern to be shifted is $4 + 2 = 6$:

position:	0	1	2	3	4	5	6	7	8	9	10	11	12	13
text:	P	E	T	E	S̲	S	O	N	N	E	S	O	N	
pattern:							S	O	M	N	E̲	S	O	N

In this particular case, the end of the pattern now lies to the right of the end of the text, so that the search is completed and the pattern is not found.

Besides the array *skip*1, discussed earlier, we now also introduce the array *skip*2 with subscript values $i = 0, 1, ..., m - 2$. For each of these values of i, we take the string formed by the suffix *pattern*[$i + 1$], ..., *pattern*[$m - 1$], and, if possible, we find the largest value h (not greater than i) that occurs as a start point of another occurrence of this string in the pattern. If there is no such occurrence, we set $h = -1$. We then compute

$$skip2[i] = i + 1 - h$$

Note that $skip2[i] = i + 2$ if $h = -1$. For example, with $pattern = $ "SONNESON", we have

$skip2[0] = 0 + 1 - (-1) = 2$, because "ONNESON" does not occur elsewhere;
$skip2[1] = 1 + 1 - (-1) = 3$, because "NNESON" does not occur elsewhere;
$skip2[2] = 2 + 1 - (-1) = 4$, because "NESON" does not occur elsewhere;
$skip2[3] = 3 + 1 - (-1) = 5$, because "ESON" does not occur elsewhere;
$skip2[4] = 4 + 1 - 0 = 5$, because "SON" also occurs at position 0;
$skip2[5] = 5 + 1 - 1 = 5$, because "ON" also occurs at position 1;
$skip2[6] = 6 + 1 - 3 = 4$, because "N" also occurs at position 3.

As for the last case, "N" also occurs at position 2, but the rightmost occurrence, with the largest start position h (not greater than i) is taken, which explains why $h = 3$ is used here.

Choosing between two alternatives

We have discussed two possible ways of determining how many positions the pattern is to be shifted to the right. If the final character $(= pattern[m - 1])$ of the pattern is different from character $ch = text[j]$ of the text, we simply shift the pattern $skip1[ch]$ positions to the right. If these two characters are equal, but, comparing from right to left, we find that $pattern[i]$ is different from character ch, where $i < m - 1$ and $ch = text[j]$, we choose between the following two numbers of positions that the pattern could be shifted to the right:

$skip1[ch] - (m - 1 - i)$ (which may be less than 1 and therefore unusable), and
$skip2[i]$

The choice to be made is a very easy one: we simply take the larger of these two values. Note that both arrays $skip1$ and $skip2$ are really required: we have to use $skip1$ if the mismatch occurs at the final pattern character; in this case $skip1$ will provide us with a positive value. On the other hand, we have to use $skip2$ if $skip1$ gives a value less than 1. In all other cases we have a free choice but it is wise to take the larger one.

Some comments in the following implementation file may be helpful in addition to the above explanation:

```
// search.cpp: Implementation file

#include <string.h>
#include "search.h"

inline int max(int x, int y){return x > y ? x : y;}

search::search(const char *pat)
{   pattern = pat;
    m = strlen(pattern);
    skip2 = new int[m-1];
    const char *p;
    int ch, i, h, suflen;
```

```
    for (ch=0; ch<256; ch++)
    {   p = strrchr(pattern, ch);
        h = int(p ? p - pattern : -1);
        // If h != -1, pattern[h] == ch
        skip1[ch] = m - 1 - h;
    }
    for (i=m-2; i>=0; i--)
    {   p = pattern + i + 1; // Good suffix p follows position i.
        suflen = m - 1 - i;
        for (h=i; h>=0; h--)
            if (strncmp(pattern + h, p, suflen) == 0) break;
        skip2[i] = i + 1 - h; // h = -1 if not found.
    }
    // Due to the mismatch pattern[i] != text[j] = ch, the
    // pattern will be shifted either skip1[ch]-(m-1-i) or
    // skip2[i] positions to the right, whichever is larger.
}


char *search::find(char *text)
{   int last = m - 1, k = last, j, i;
    // pattern[last] will be compared with text[k]:
    char ch;
    int n = strlen(text);
    while (k < n)
    {   ch = text[k];
        if (pattern[last] != ch) k += skip1[ch]; else
        {   i = last; j = k;
            do
            {   if (--i < 0) return text + k - last; // Match found!
            } while (pattern[i] == text[--j]);
            k += max(skip1[text[j]] - (last - i), skip2[i]);
        }
    }
    return 0;
}
```

In spite of our long discussion of a rather complex algorithm, the function *find* (which does the actual searching) is comparatively simple. More importantly, it is also very fast.

Exercises

5.1   Write a function for binary search, applied to an array of (fixed-length) character strings.

5.2   Write a function for binary search, applied to an array of pointers to character strings stored elsewhere.

5.3   Write a template for binary search.

5.4   Write the function *bsearch*1 that behaves in the same way as the standard library function *bsearch*. Consult Section 3.8, where a similar problem was solved for the standard library function *qsort*.

5.5   The hash functions in Section 5.3 are based on alphabetic keys. Apply hashing to records with numerical keys.

5.6   Apply hashing to a file, using random access.

5.7   What are the contents of the arrays *skip*1 and *skip*2 in Section 5.4 if the pattern to be searched for is *"singing"*?

6

Binary Trees

6.1 Basic Operations on Binary Search Trees

As we saw in Chapter 4, searching a linked list is done by means of linear search, which is slow compared with binary search, discussed in Section 5.2. We now want to apply binary search to dynamic data structures. A *binary tree*, as shown in Figure 6.1, enables us to do this. It consists of a pointer variable, the so-called *root pointer*, and (zero or more) nodes. The tree is said to be *empty* if there are no such nodes; in that case the root pointer has the value *NULL*. Let us use the term *root node* for the node pointed to by the root pointer (in a nonempty tree). Each node has one or more information or data members and two pointer members, each of which acts as a root pointer, either pointing to another node or having the value *NULL*. If a node contains any pointers to other nodes, these latter nodes are said to be the *children* of the former, and we distinguish between a *left* and a *right* child. A node that has children is said to be the *parent* of these children. Unlike a traditional family situation, every child has only one parent; in other words, any two distinct pointers point to distinct nodes. Each pointer stored in a node is the root pointer of a subtree, so each node has a left and a right subtree. This holds even if a pointer member has the value *NULL*, since a subtree may be empty.

A *leaf*, or *terminal node*, is defined as a node that has no children, which means that a leaf has two zero pointer members. With each node we can associate a *level*. The root node is said to be at level 1, and if a node at level i has any children then these are at level $i + 1$. In addition to this, we say that the root pointer of a tree is at level 0. Thus, the level of a node is in fact the number of branches to be traversed if we follow the path from the root pointer of the tree to that node. The highest level that occurs in a binary tree is called the *height* of that tree. For example, the binary tree shown in Figure 6.1 has height 3.

You should be aware that some other books give slightly different definitions. The term *root* is frequently used for either the root node or the root pointer. Some authors define the root node to be at level 0, and, if it is the only node of the tree, they sometimes define the

159

height of that tree to be 0, the empty tree then having height −1. Our definitions, with a clear distinction between a root pointer and a root node and with an empty tree (consisting of a zero root pointer) having height 0, are more convenient from a programmer's point of view.

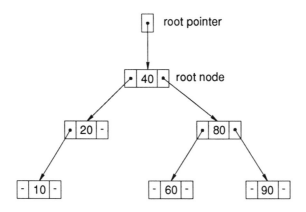

Figure 6.1 Binary tree

One of the data members of a node is frequently regarded as a *key*, to be used for search operations. If there is only one data member in each node, we will refer to these members as keys.

Here is a program that builds a binary tree with keys of type *int* (and no other data members). The actual tree building process is initiated by declaring the *tree* variable *t* in the *main* function:

```
// tree: Introduction to binary trees

#include <iostream.h>

struct node {int info; node *pLeft, *pRight;};

class tree {
public:
    tree();
    void print()const{pr(root);}
private:
    node *root;
    void AddNode(int x, node* &p);
    void pr(const node *p)const;
};

tree::tree()
{   root = NULL;
    int x;
    while (cin >> x, !cin.fail()) AddNode(x, root);
}
```

```
    void tree::AddNode(int x, node* &p)
{   if (p == NULL)
    {   p = new node;
        p->info = x;
        p->pLeft = p->pRight = NULL;
    }
    else AddNode(x, x < p->info ? p->pLeft : p->pRight);
}

    void tree::pr(const node *p)const
{   if (p)
    {   pr(p->pLeft);
        cout << p->info << " ";
        pr(p->pRight);
    }
}

    int main()
{   cout <<
        "Enter some integers to be placed in a binary tree,\n"
        "followed by /:\n";
    tree t;
    cout << "Tree contents (in ascending order):\n";
    t.print();
    cout << endl;
    return 0;
}
```

The trees built by this program, such as the one shown in Figure 6.1, have an important characteristic: the key of each node is both greater than all keys in its left subtree and less than all keys in its right subtree. As this enables us to use the binary search method, we call this type of binary tree a *binary search tree*.

We sometimes call a binary tree a *recursive* data structure, because it can be expressed in terms of smaller binary trees. It is therefore not surprising that recursive functions are extremely useful in this context, as the functions *AddNode* and *pr* illustrate. As for the latter, we can express the task of printing all data stored in a binary tree in terms of printing the data stored in its subtrees (which are also binary trees) and that stored in the root node:

If the tree is empty, nothing is to be printed.
If the tree is not empty, we have to perform the following three tasks, in this order:

- Print all data stored in the left subtree.
- Print the data members in the node pointed to by the given root.
- Print all data stored in the right subtree.

Function *tree::pr* in program *tree* applies this principle recursively. According to the definition of a binary search tree, this procedure leads to an output sequence in ascending order, as the following demonstration of program *tree* shows:

```
Enter some integers to be placed in a binary tree,
followed by /:
40 80 60 20 90 10 /
Tree contents (in ascending order):
10 20 40 60 80 90
```

Although not demonstrated by this output, the binary tree built in memory in this example is the one shown in Figure 6.1.

Instead of *printing* the keys stored in the tree, we could have traversed the tree in the same way for other purposes. Since the root node of each subtree is visited after visiting all nodes of its left subtree and before those of its right subtree, we express this way of visiting all nodes by using the term *inorder traversal*; the ordered triple *Left subtree*, *Visit node*, *Right subtree*, is sometimes abbreviated LVR. Other useful ways of visiting the nodes of binary trees are pre-order traversal (VLR) and postorder traversal (LRV). The subject of traversing binary trees is related to the interpretation of arithmetic expressions, as we will see in Chapter 11.

Tree searching

Let us now develop a useful program, which performs a *frequency count* for words read from a text file. It lists all words in alphabetic order, together with their frequency. After this, we can enter a word to display its frequency once again. This program can be used to analyze text. For example, very frequent use of the same word may indicate bad style.

To be able to search the tree for a given word, the tree will again be a binary search tree. If a word is read more than once, we will store it only once in the tree, but it will be accompanied by a word count, which says how often the word has been encountered. Besides the two pointers to its children, if any, each node will contain both a pointer to a word, stored somewhere else, and the (integer) word count just mentioned. The words will act as keys in string comparisons, for which the terms *greater* and *less* will refer to the usual alphabetic word order. Consider, for example, the following text fragment:

```
"To be or not to be,
that is the question".
William Shakespeare.
```

Since we do not want to distinguish between upper-case and lower-case letters, we will convert any lower-case letters to upper case. Any sequence of nonalphabetic characters, such as blanks, newline characters, punctuation characters and digits, will act as a word separator. In other respects they are ignored, so for our purpose the above fragment is equivalent to

```
TO BE OR NOT TO BE THAT IS THE
QUESTION WILLIAM SHAKESPEARE
```

With either fragment as input, our program will build the tree shown in Figure 6.2.

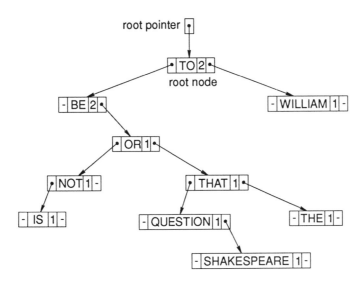

Figure 6.2 Binary search tree with alphabetic keys

Searching a binary search tree can be done either by recursion or by iteration. In a recursive solution, only one recursive call would be executed. As we know, this makes it doubtful whether recursion is really advantageous here. An iterative solution is indeed rather simple. Initially we make pointer *p* equal to the root pointer of the whole tree. Then, in a loop, we perform the following actions:

- If *p* is equal to *NULL*, the key cannot be found, so we return *NULL*.
- If the given key is found in the node pointed to by *p*, we return *p*.
- If the given key is less than the key of the node pointed to by *p*, we assign the root of the left subtree to *p*; otherwise, we assign the root of the right subtree to *p*.

To add new data, including a key, to a binary search tree, we first search the tree for that key. If we find it, we increment the count member (that is, if the application so requires, as in our example). If the key is not found, we create a new node in which we store the given data. The address of the new node, returned by *new*, is then placed in the pointer member (the old value of which is *NULL*) that we have reached during searching, as program *bintree* shows.

```
/* bintree:
    This program builds and searches a binary search
    tree and prints its contents. The program produces
    a frequency distribution of words read from a textfile.
    We can also search the tree for a given word to inquire
    how often that word occurs.
*/
#include <fstream.h>
#include <iomanip.h>
#include <ctype.h>
```

```
#include <string.h>
#include <stdlib.h>

struct node {char *pWord; int count; node *pLeft, *pRight;};

class tree {
public:
   tree(ifstream &input);
   ~tree(){DelTree(root);}
   void print()const{pr(root);}
   node *search()const;
   int ReadWord(istream &input);
private:
   node *root;
   enum {buflen = 50};
   char buf[buflen];
   void AddNode(node* &p);
   void DelTree(node* &p);
   void pr(const node *root)const;
};

int tree::ReadWord(istream &input)
/* This function reads a word from the stream 'input'.
   It skips any leading nonalphabetic characters.
   Then the longest possible string of letters (no longer
   than buflen - 1) is read, converted to upper case and
   placed in 'buf'. Return value: success (1) or failure (0).
*/
{  char ch;
   int i;
   do
   {  input >> ch;
      if (input.fail()) return 0;
   }  while (!isalpha(ch));
   for (i=0; i<buflen-1; )
   {  buf[i++] = toupper(ch);
      input.get(ch);
      if (input.fail() || !isalpha(ch)) break;
   }
   buf[i] = '\0';
   return 1;
}

tree::tree(ifstream &input)
{  root = NULL;
   while (ReadWord(input)) AddNode(root);
}

void tree::DelTree(node* &p)
{  if (p)
   {  DelTree(p->pLeft); DelTree(p->pRight);
      delete[] p->pWord; delete p; p = NULL;
   }
}
```

```
void tree::AddNode(node* &p) // Add word in buf to tree
{  if (p == NULL)
   {  p = new node;
      p->pWord = new char[strlen(buf) + 1];
      strcpy(p->pWord, buf); p->count = 1;
      p->pLeft = p->pRight = NULL;
   } else
   {  int code = strcmp(buf, p->pWord);
      if (code) AddNode(code < 0 ? p->pLeft : p->pRight);
      else p->count++;
   }
}

void tree::pr(const node *p)const
{  if (p)
   {  pr(p->pLeft);
      cout << setw(5) << p->count << " " << p->pWord << endl;
      pr(p->pRight);
   }
}

node *tree::search()const
{  node *p = root;
   for (;;)
   {  if (p == NULL) return NULL;
      int code = strcmp(buf, p->pWord);
      if (code == 0) return p;
      p = (code < 0 ? p->pLeft : p->pRight);
   }
}

int main()
{  ifstream input;
   node *ptr;
   const int NameLen=50;
   char FileName[NameLen];
   cout << "Input file: ";
   cin >> setw(NameLen) >> FileName;
   input.open(FileName, ios::in);
   if (input.fail())
   {  cout << "Cannot open input file.\n"; exit(1);
   }
   tree t(input);
   cout << "Frequency distribution:\n"; t.print();
   for (;;)
   {  cout << "\nEnter a word, or type Ctrl+Z (or Ctrl+D) "
         "to stop: ";
      if (t.ReadWord(cin) == 0) break;
      // Search the tree for the word placed by ReadWord in buf:
      ptr = t.search();
      cout << "Number of occurrences: "
           << (ptr ? ptr->count : 0) << endl;
   }
   return 0;
}
```

The Ctrl+Z key combination acts as end-of-data with MS-DOS and Ctrl+D does the same with UNIX. If you are using another operating system, you may have to use a different key combination. Assuming the above text fragment to be available in the file *shakesp.txt*, we can use program *bintree* as follows:

```
Input file: shakesp.txt
Frequency distribution:
    2 BE
    1 IS
    1 NOT
    1 OR
    1 QUESTION
    1 SHAKESPEARE
    1 THAT
    1 THE
    2 TO
    1 WILLIAM

Enter a word, or type Ctrl+Z (or Ctrl+D) to stop: to
Number of occurrences: 2

Enter a word, or type Ctrl+Z (or Ctrl+D) to stop: something
Number of occurrences: 0

Enter a word, or type Ctrl+Z (or Ctrl+D) to stop: ^Z
```

Program *bintree* does not contain a function for node deletion, which is more difficult than most other operations on trees, as we will see in Section 6.3. It does contain a destructor and an associated function *DelTree* to delete the entire tree. Curiously enough, deleting the whole tree is much easier to program than deleting a single node.

Recall that most classes in this book are not in the 'orthodox canonical form', discussed at the end of Section 4.5. For example, the class *tree* does not contain a copy constructor, an assignment operator or a default constructor. You must therefore not write code like the second, third and fourth of these lines:

```
tree t(input), // OK
     t1,        // Error, no default constructor
     t2 = t;    // Error, no copy constructor
     t1 = t;    // Error, no assignment operator
```

Although the third and the fourth of the above lines are very similar, the third defines and initializes *t2*, while the fourth is an assignment statement. Making deep copies on these lines would require a copy constructor and an assignment operator, respectively, as we discussed in Sections 4.3 and 4.5.

6.2 Perfectly Balanced Binary Trees

It will be clear that we want a binary tree to be reasonably 'balanced'. Even without a definition of this adjective, we feel that the structure shown in Figure 6.3 is hardly worth calling a binary tree, let alone a balanced binary tree. Searching a degenerated tree of this type is no faster than searching a linked list.

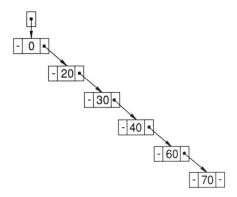

Figure 6.3 A very unbalanced binary tree

However, this really is a binary tree, and with the key values shown in the nodes it is even a binary search tree. A degenerated tree such as this one will be built by program *bintree* or any similar program if the objects given in the input file are in ascending order. As we have developed good sorting algorithms in Chapter 3, files with objects in ascending order are not exceptional, so a warning not to use sorted files as input data for this program is in order here. This example makes it clear that we need some definition about how well or how badly a binary tree is balanced. We will distinguish two such definitions.

We call a binary tree *perfectly balanced*, if each node has a left and a right subtree in which the numbers of nodes differ by at most one. The binary tree in Figure 6.4 is perfectly balanced but the binary tree in Figure 6.5 is not.

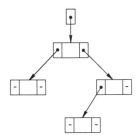

Figure 6.4 A perfectly balanced binary tree

The tree shown in Figure 6.5 is an example of a *height-balanced binary tree* (or simply a *balanced tree*), which is a binary tree with the characteristic that for every node the *heights* of its left and right subtrees differ by at most one. We will discuss height-balanced binary trees, also known as *AVL trees*, in more detail in Section 6.4. Every perfectly balanced binary tree is a height-balanced binary tree, but the converse is not true, as Figure 6.5 shows. Since the *weight* of a tree is defined as its number of nodes, the term *weight-balanced* may be used instead of *perfectly balanced*. The root node in Figure 6.5 has left and right subtrees with weights 1 and 3; as the absolute difference |1 − 3| is greater than 1, this tree is not weight (or perfectly) balanced.

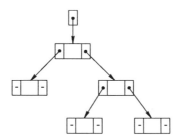

Figure 6.5 *A height-balanced binary tree that is not perfectly balanced*

We usually require these two types of balanced trees to be binary search trees. We then have to face the problem that without special measures the trees will lose their balance property if we insert or delete nodes arbitrarily. As we will see in Section 6.4, there is an efficient algorithm for height-balanced binary trees to maintain their balance property. There is no such algorithm for perfectly balanced binary trees. However, with a simple and elegant algorithm, we can build a perfectly balanced binary tree straightaway, provided that:

(1) The objects to be read are given in ascending order (!)
(2) We know in advance how many objects are to be read.

Program *pbbtree* is a demonstration program for perfectly balanced binary search trees. First, it asks the user how many integers (in ascending order) will follow. It then reads these integers and stores them in a perfectly balanced binary search tree. Finally, the contents of this tree are printed a way that reflects the tree structure, with the tree displayed sideways. The tree is displayed sideways, with its root on the left, as the following demonstration shows:

```
Enter n, followed by n integers in ascending order:
10
11 12 13 14 15 16 17 18 19 20

Here is the resulting perfectly balanced
binary search tree, with its root on the left.
To obtain the usual form, with the root at the top,
turn this output 90 degrees clockwise:
```

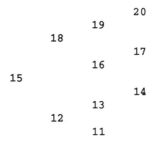

Turning the above tree through 90° clockwise, we obtain the essence of Figure 6.6.

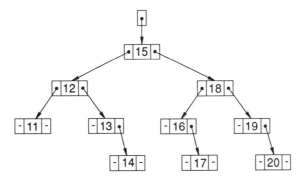

Figure 6.6 Perfectly balanced binary search tree, built by program pbbtree

Program *pbbtree*, which does all this, is surprisingly small:

```
// pbbtree: Building and displaying a perfectly balanced
//          binary tree
#include <iostream.h>
#include <iomanip.h>

struct node {int info; node *pLeft, *pRight;};

class pbbtree {
public:
   pbbtree(int n);
   void print()const{pr(root, 0);}
private:
   node *root;
   void pr(const node *p, int nSpace)const;
};

pbbtree::pbbtree(int n)
{  if (n == 0) root = NULL; else
   {  int nLeft = (n - 1)/2, nRight = n - nLeft - 1;
      root = new node;
      root->pLeft = pbbtree(nLeft).root;
      cin >> root->info;
      root->pRight = pbbtree(nRight).root;
   }
}

void pbbtree::pr(const node *p, int nSpace)const
{  if (p)
   {  pr(p->pRight, nSpace += 6);
      cout << setw(nSpace) << p->info << endl;
      pr(p->pLeft, nSpace);
   }
}
```

```
int main()
{   cout <<
        "Enter n, followed by n integers in ascending order:\n";
    int n;
    cin >> n;
    pbbtree t(n);
    cout << "\nHere is the resulting perfectly balanced\n"
        "binary search tree, with its root on the left.\n"
        "To obtain the usual form, with the root at the top,\n"
        "turn this output 90 degrees clockwise:\n\n";
    t.print();
    return 0;
}
```

The *pbbtree* constructor accepts an *int* argument *n* to build a tree with *n* nodes, read in ascending order from the keyboard. It uses the weight *n* to compute the weights *nLeft* and *nRight* of its subtrees, where

$$n = nLeft + 1 + nRight$$
$$|nLeft - nRight| \leq 1$$

In our example, we have $n = 10$, $nLeft = 4$, $nRight = 5$ (see Figure 6.6). After creating the root node, we postpone reading the data for the *info* member until the left subtree has been built by the recursive constructor call in

```
root->pLeft = pbbtree(nLeft).root;
```

Only now do we read the integer (15 in our example) to be placed in the root node. Then a recursive call for the right subtree completes this constructor.

The private member function *pr* has an argument, *nSpace*, indicating how many positions on a line have been used for the node's parent, if any. When this function is called in the public function *print*, this argument is zero because the root node has no parent. Each integer is printed in six positions, and these are preceded by *nSpace* positions. If we have a node at level *l* and the integer stored in that node is printed by a call to *print*, the argument *nSpace* used in this call is equal to $6(l - 1)$, and the rightmost digit of that integer appears in position $6l$. (Recall that the root node is at level 1.)

An information system based on a perfectly balanced binary search tree

We will now use a perfectly balanced binary tree in a program that we can use to store and retrieve data. The tree will represent a set of items, each consisting of a person's name and a nonnegative number associated with that person, for example a telephone number or a registration number. We will use type *long int* to admit reasonably long numbers, such as 12345678. The names are used as keys, so they must be unique: we do not admit two persons whose names are exactly the same. Our program will be capable of:

(1)   Loading all items from a file and storing them in a perfectly balanced binary search tree.
(2)   Reading names from the keyboard to search the tree for the corresponding numbers.
(3)   Adding new items.
(4)   Deleting items.
(5)   Changing the number of an item.
(6)   Saving all items by writing them to a file at the end of a session.
(7)   Displaying an alphabetically ordered list of all items.

The names of the files mentioned in points (1) and (6) will be entered by the user. We can use the same file for both purposes. The items in this file are ordered, that is, the names are in alphabetic order. However, the file may be empty, which will be the case the very first time we use the program. At this initial stage, we add items to an empty set in the same way as we would add items to a nonempty set, using point (3). We then apply point (6) to obtain an ordered file. Thus, instead of first using a conventional text editor to create a file and then sorting this file by another program, we use the very program we are discussing, starting with an empty tree. Later, we can apply point (1) to build a perfectly balanced binary search tree which will then no longer be empty. To be honest, we must note that the tree may not remain perfectly balanced while we are adding and deleting items. However, as soon as we apply points (6) and (1) again, we start with a fresh, perfectly balanced tree. In practice, the number of updates is likely to be small compared with the total number of items, so it is most unlikely for the tree to degenerate considerably. The latter may occur only if a great many new items, given in (almost) alphabetic order, are entered during a single session. Before we can write a complete program, we have to deal with the *user interface*, that is, we must define how to use it. Since a user may not be familiar with binary trees, we will use the more elementary term *work file* instead. Like a work file used by an editor, our work file is not a permanent file on disk, so its contents are lost at the end of the session, unless they are explicitly saved. We will use the following four commands, each beginning with a period:

.Load   Load the contents of a permanent file into an empty work file.
.Print   Print the contents of the work file.
.Save   Save the work file onto a permanent file.
.Quit   Quit

Actually, only the period and the first letter of the command are used by the program, the remaining letters being ignored, so that we may abbreviate these commands, as *.L, .P, .S* and *.Q* if we like. Also, these commands are not case sensitive, so we may use the lower-case letters *l, p, s, q* (each preceded by a period) instead of the corresponding capital letters. We can add an item by typing a name without any internal spaces, then one or more spaces followed by a number, as, for example,

```
Johnson,P.H.    452319
```

If the name *Johnson,P.H.* already occurs in the work file, the new number overwrites the old one. By typing a slash instead of a number, as in

```
Johnson,P.H.      /
```

we indicate that the item with that name is to be deleted. The question mark in

```
Johnson,P.H.      ?
```

means that we want to know Johnson's number.

This is all the user need to know. As for the implementation of all this, we can borrow some useful material from our last program, *pbbtree*. We will also implement *node deletion*, which is important and interesting enough to devote a new section (6.3) to it. Here we will already add this facility to our program.

Recall that in program *pbbtree* we required the input data to contain the number of input items that followed. Although we could read an input file twice, counting the items in the first scan and using them in the second, there is a more efficient solution. We will count the items when they are entered and, after the command *.S*, write this item count to the file before the items themselves. As a result of command *.L*, we begin by reading this item count, so that we can use our algorithm for a perfectly balanced tree immediately. During the process of updating the tree, we change the variable *ItemCount* accordingly. Since this variable is of type *int*, the size of the tree is limited not only to the available amount of memory, but also to the maximum integer value. Should this be a problem, then using type *long int* for that variable is the obvious solution.

```
// infsys: An information system based on a perfectly balanced
//         binary tree.

#include <fstream.h>
#include <iomanip.h>
#include <ctype.h>
#include <string.h>

const int bufLen = 31;
struct node {char *name; long num; node *pLeft, *pRight;};

class tree {
public:
    tree(){root = NULL; ItemCount = 0;}
    tree(const char *FileName);
    ~tree();
    void print()const{pr(root);}
    node* &search(const char *name);
    void save(const char *FileName)const;
    void AddOrChange(const char *name, long nr);
    int DelNode(const char *name);
private:
    node *root;
    node *BuildTree(ifstream &iFile, int n);
    void pr(const node *p)const;
    void DelTree(node *p);
    void WriteTree(ofstream &oFile, const node *p)const;
    int ItemCount;
};
```

```
node *tree::BuildTree(ifstream &iFile, int n)
{  if (n == 0) return NULL;
   int nLeft = (n - 1)/2, nRight = n - nLeft - 1;
   char buf[bufLen];
   node *p = new node; ItemCount++;
   p->pLeft = BuildTree(iFile, nLeft);
   iFile >> setw(bufLen) >> buf >> p->num;
   p->name = new char[strlen(buf) + 1];
   strcpy(p->name, buf);
   p->pRight = BuildTree(iFile, nRight);
   return p;
}

tree::tree(const char *FileName)
{  ifstream iFile(FileName, ios::in);
   if (iFile.fail())
   {  cout << "Cannot open input file.\n";
      root = NULL; ItemCount = 0;
   } else
   {  int n;
      iFile >> n; ItemCount = 0;
      root = BuildTree(iFile, n);
      iFile.close();
   }
}

void tree::DelTree(node *p)
{  if (p)
   {  DelTree(p->pLeft); DelTree(p->pRight);
      delete[] p->name; delete p;
   }
}

tree::~tree(){DelTree(root);}

void tree::pr(const node *p)const
{  if (p)
   {  pr(p->pLeft);
      cout << setiosflags(ios::left) << setw(bufLen)
           << p->name << resetiosflags(ios::left)
           << setw(8) << p->num << endl;
      pr(p->pRight);
   }
}

node* &tree::search(const char *name)
{  int code;
   node **p = &root; // p is a pointer to a pointer
   for(;;)
   {  if (*p == NULL) return *p;
      code = strcmp(name, (*p)->name);
      if (code < 0) p = &(*p)->pLeft; else
      if (code > 0) p = &(*p)->pRight; else return *p;
   }
}
```

```
void tree::WriteTree(ofstream &oFile, const node *p)const
{ if (p)
   { WriteTree(oFile, p->pLeft);
      oFile << p->name << " " << p->num << endl;
      WriteTree(oFile, p->pRight);
   }
}

void tree::save(const char *FileName)const
{ ofstream oFile(FileName, ios::out);
   if (oFile.fail())
   { cout << "Cannot open output file.\n";
      return;
   }
   oFile << ItemCount << endl;
   WriteTree(oFile, root);
   oFile.close();
}

void tree::AddOrChange(const char *name, long nr)
{ node* &p = search(name);
   if (p == NULL) // Insert new node
   { p = new node;
      p->name = new char[strlen(name) + 1];
      strcpy(p->name, name);
      p->pLeft = p->pRight = NULL;
      ItemCount++;
   }
   p->num = nr;
}

int tree::DelNode(const char *name)
{ node* &p = search(name), *p0 = p, **qq, *q;
   if (p == NULL)
      return 0; // Not found
   delete[] p->name;
   if (p->pRight == NULL){p = p->pLeft; delete p0;} else
   if (p->pLeft == NULL){p = p->pRight; delete p0;} else
   {    // Node *p has a left and a right child
      qq = & p->pLeft;
      while ((*qq)->pRight)
         qq = & (*qq)->pRight;
         // qq contains the address of the pointer field
         // that points to a node without a right child.
      p->name = (*qq)->name; p->num = (*qq)->num;
         // Data copied from **qq to *p
      q = *qq;
      *qq = q->pLeft;
         // *qq replaced with left link field of **qq.
      delete q;
   }
   ItemCount--;
   return 1; // Node deleted
}
```

```
int main()
{  char ch, buf[bufLen];
   long nr;
   node *p;
   ifstream iFile;
   ofstream oFile;
   tree *pTree = new tree;
   cout << "Enter a name and a nonnegative integer, or\n"
           "a name followed either by / or by ?, or\n"
           "one of the commands .Load, .Print, .Save, .Quit.\n"
           "There must be a blank space after a name, not\n"
           "within it.\n";
   int busy = 1;
   while (busy)
   {  cout << ">>";
      cin >> setw(bufLen) >> buf;
      if (buf[0] == '.')
      switch (toupper(buf[1]))
      {
      case 'L':
         cout << "Input file: ";
         cin >> setw(bufLen) >> buf;
         delete pTree;
         pTree = new tree(buf);
         break;
      case 'P':
         cout << "Contents:\n";
         pTree->print();
         break;
      case 'Q':
         busy = 0; delete pTree;
         break;
      case 'S':
         cout << "Output file: ";
         cin >> setw(bufLen) >> buf;
         pTree->save(buf);
         break;
      default:
         cout <<
         "Wrong command, use .Load, .Print, .Save, or .Quit\n";
      } else
      {  cin >> nr;
         if (cin.fail())
         {  cin.clear();
            cin >> ch;
            switch(ch)
            {
            case '?':
               p = pTree->search(buf);
               if (p)
                  cout << setiosflags(ios::left) << setw(bufLen)
                       << p->name << resetiosflags(ios::left)
                       << setw(8) << p->num << endl;
               else cout << "Unknown name.\n";
               break;
```

```
                    case '/':
                        if (!pTree->DelNode(buf))
                            cout << "Unknown name.\n";
                        break;
                    default:
                        cout << "A name must be followed by a number,\n"
                                "a question mark or a slash.\n";
                    }
            }  else pTree->AddOrChange(buf, nr);
        }
        do cin.get(ch); while (ch != '\n');
    }
    return 0;
}
```

Here is our first demonstration of this program to show how entries are entered and how the *.Print*, the *.Save* and the *.Quit* commands can be used:

```
Enter a name and a nonnegative integer, or
a name followed either by / or by ?, or
one of the commands .Load, .Print, .Save, .Quit.
There must be a blank space after a name, not
within it.
>>Wood,E.G. 600123
>>Atkinson,J. 318875
>>Johnson,P.H. 442218
>>Miller,A.A. 181715
>>.P
Contents:
Atkinson,J.                             318875
Johnson,P.H.                            442218
Miller,A.A.                             181715
Wood,E.G.                               600123
>>Johnson,P.H. /
>>.S
Output file: infsys.txt
>>.Q
```

After this session, there is a file *infsys.txt* with the following contents:

```
3
Atkinson,J. 318875
Miller,A.A. 181715
Wood,E.G. 600123
```

Note that the entry for *Johnson,P.H.* is no longer there, and that the number of entries, 3, is present at the beginning of the file. Here is another session, based on this file, to demonstrate the *.Load* command. It also shows that the number associated with the name *Atkinson,J.* is changed:

```
Enter a name and a nonnegative integer, or
a name followed either by / or by ?, or
one of the commands .Load, .Print, .Save, .Quit.
There must be a blank space after a name, not
within it.
>>.L
Input file: infsys.txt
>>Miller,A.A. ?
Miller,A.A.                          181715
>>Atkinson,J. 318800
>>.P
Contents:
Atkinson,J.                          318800
Miller,A.A.                          181715
Wood,E.G.                            600123
>>.Q
```

Besides the aspect of node deletion, to be discussed shortly, there are some other interesting details worth mentioning. Since the *.Load* command may be used several times, it should be possible to delete an entire tree. This is done here by means of both the destructor *~tree* and the recursive function *DelTree*. We should not omit the statement

```
delete[] p->name;
```

in the latter function, bearing in mind that the names are stored outside the nodes of the tree. Each time the user enters the *.Load* command, the old tree is deleted. This implies that there should be such a tree the very first time, even if no data has been entered yet. We therefore let the default constructor

```
tree(){root = NULL; ItemCount = 0;}
```

create an empty tree, when it is called in this statement, occurring in the *main* function:

```
tree *pTree = new tree;
```

An empty tree, with zero *root* pointer, is really a *tree* object. There would not have been such an object if we had written *NULL* instead of *new tree* in this statement.

As you may have noticed, the function *search* in this program does not simply return an address but rather a *reference*. The reason for this will be clear in the next section.

6.3 Deleting Nodes of Binary Search Trees

Deleting an entire binary tree can be done by a simple and elegant recursive function, as shown by the function *DelTree* in program *infsys* of the previous section and in program *bintree* in Section 6.1. Curiously enough, the deletion of a single node is not so simple. We will now see how we can do this for binary search trees. To delete the node with a given key x from a binary search tree t, it will be possible to write

```
if (t.DelNode(x)) ... // Node with key x removed from tree t.
else ...              // There is no node with key x.
```

It follows from this that function *DelNode* should first search the tree for the key *x*. Unlike previous tree searches, we now need not only the address of the node that contains *x*, but rather the address of the pointer that points to that node. If we used the C language, we would need a pointer to a pointer to a node, but in C++ we can benefit from the reference concept. We will use a reference variable *p*; this is not simply a copy of a pointer that belongs to the tree but rather that pointer itself: changing *p* implies that the tree is changed.

If the node to be deleted has at most one child, our task is relatively easy. If there is no left child, the assignment *p = p–>right* does most of the work, as Figure 6.7 illustrates.

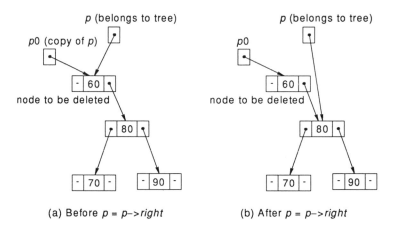

(a) Before *p = p–>right*   (b) After *p = p–>right*

Figure 6.7 *Node to be deleted has only one child*

With a special *search* function, returning a reference, and a reference variable *p*, we can use the following code for the above simple case (where the node to be deleted has at most one child):

```
node* &p = search(x), *p0 = p, ...
...
if (p->pRight == NULL){p = p->pLeft; delete p0;} else
if (p->pLeft == NULL){p = p->pRight; delete p0;} else ...
```

Applying this to Figure 6.7, we have *x* = 60 and *p* is a synonym of the pointer to that node. Since *p–>pLeft == NULL* in our example, that pointer *p* is given the value *p–>pRight*. After this, the node pointed to by *p0* is deleted.

The above fragment also works correctly if there is neither a left nor a right child. In that case, both *p–>left* and *p–>right* are zero, and *p* is also made zero.

If the node in question has two children, we will not really delete the node itself. Instead, we delete one of its descendants, after having copied the data members of the latter node into the former. As we want the tree to remain a binary search tree, we must be very particular about which descendant to choose. We will select the key that would appear as the left neighbor of the key in question, if all keys stored in the tree were written down as an increasing sequence. Starting in the given node (with two children), we first go to its left child and then further downward to the right as far as possible. Thus, of all integers stored in the tree, we find the largest of all those that are less than the one in the given node. This is precisely what we need to maintain a binary search tree. In Figure 6.8, the tree contains the integers

30 40 50 55 60 <u>90</u> 95

The node containing 90 is to be deleted. Out of all the above integers less than 90, we choose the greatest, 60. By first taking the left child, we restrict ourselves to the subsequence to the left of this selected element, 90. All integers in this subsequence are less than 90. Then, as often as possible, we must go to the right-hand child to find the greatest element of that left subsequence. As a result, we arrive at the desired node with integer 60.

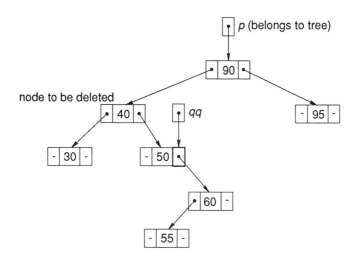

Figure 6.8 Tree with 60 as the greatest of all keys less than 90

We take the left child only once and then the right one as often as possible in the following fragment, which follows the one we have already seen:

```
{   qq = & p->pLeft;
    while ((*qq)->pRight) qq = & (*qq)->pRight;
    ...
```

The variable *qq* is of type *node***, which implies that it points to a pointer, not to a node. Figure 6.8 shows the situation after execution of the above while-loop, with *qq* pointing to the *pRight* pointer member of the node containing 50, so that **qq* is this *pRight* member itself and ***qq* is the node containing 60. In the following code, 90 in node **p* is now replaced with this value 60. Then the address of the node containing 55 is assigned to the pointer **qq*. Finally, the old node containing 60 is deleted.

```
p->info = (*qq)->info;
q = *qq;
*qq = q->pLeft;
delete q;
```

You can find the code we have been discussing in function *DelNode* of the following program:

```
// delnode: Deleting a single node in a binary search tree

#include <iostream.h>
#include <iomanip.h>

struct node {int info; node *pLeft, *pRight;};

class tree {
public:
    tree();
    void print()const{pr(root, 0);}
    node* &search(int x);
    int DelNode(int x);
private:
    node *root;
    void AddNode(int x, node* &p);
    void pr(const node *p, int nSpace)const;
};

tree::tree()
{   root = NULL;
    int x;
    char ch;
    while (cin >> x, !cin.fail())
        AddNode(x, root);
    cin.clear();
    cin.get(ch);
}

void tree::AddNode(int x, node* &p)
{   if (p == NULL)
    {   p = new node;
        p->info = x;
        p->pLeft = p->pRight = NULL;
    } else AddNode(x, x < p->info ? p->pLeft : p->pRight);
}

void tree::pr(const node *p, int nSpace)const
{   if (p)
    {   pr(p->pRight, nSpace += 6);
        cout << setw(nSpace) << p->info << endl;
        pr(p->pLeft, nSpace);
    }
}
```

```
node* &tree::search(int x)
{  node **p = &root;
   for(;;)
   {  if (*p == NULL) return *p;
      if (x < (*p)->info) p = &(*p)->pLeft; else
      if (x > (*p)->info) p = &(*p)->pRight; else return *p;
   }
}

int tree::DelNode(int x)
{  node* &p = search(x), *p0 = p, **qq, *q;
   if (p == NULL) return 0; // Not found
   if (p->pRight == NULL){p = p->pLeft; delete p0;} else
   if (p->pLeft == NULL){p = p->pRight; delete p0;} else
   {  // Node *p has a left and a right child
      qq = & p->pLeft;
      while ((*qq)->pRight) qq = & (*qq)->pRight;
      // qq contains the address of the pointer field
      // that points to a node without a right child.
      p->info = (*qq)->info;
      // Data copied from **qq to *p
      q = *qq;
      *qq = q->pLeft;
      // *qq replaced with left link field of **qq.
      delete q;
   }
   return 1; // Node deleted
}

int main()
{  cout <<
        "Enter some integers to be placed in a binary tree,\n"
        "followed by /:\n";
   tree t;
   cout << "Resulting tree, printed sideways:\n\n";
   t.print();
   cout << "\nEnter the value of the node to be deleted: ";
   int x;
   cin >> x;
   if (t.DelNode(x))
   {  cout << "Tree after deleting " << x << ":\n\n";
      t.print();
   }  else cout << "Node not found.\n";
   return 0;
}
```

Here is a demonstration of this program, showing the tree of Figure 6.8 (with the root on the left) before and after deletion of the node containing 90:

```
Enter some integers to be placed in a binary tree,
followed by /:
90 40 50 95 30 60 55
Resulting tree, printed sideways:
```

```
             95
         90
                          60
                                 55
                    50
              40
                    30
```

```
Enter the value of the node to be deleted: 90
Tree after deleting 90:
```

```
             95
         60
                                 55
                    50
              40
                    30
```

This program prints trees sideways, as discussed in Section 6.2.

Recall that we have also used node deletion in program *infsys* in the previous section. If you understand how node deletion works in program *delnode*, you should be able to understand this aspect of program *infsys* as well.

6.4 AVL Trees

Figure 6.9 shows an *AVL tree* (named after Adelson-Velskii and Landis). As mentioned in Section 6.2, this is a height-balanced tree, so for each node the heights of its left and right subtrees differ by at most one. We will now see how we can insert nodes in such a tree while preserving the AVL characteristic. In order to do this efficiently, we will store a *balance factor*, named *bal* and of type *int*, in each node. It will be equal to the height of the right subtree minus that of the left subtree.

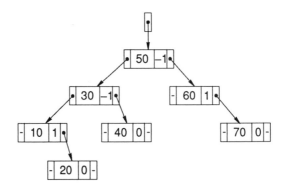

Figure 6.9 AVL tree

and from (1), (3) and (4b) that

$$B' = B + b' - 1 \qquad\qquad \text{if } h(U) < h(T) \qquad\qquad\qquad (6b)$$

You may find the above formula manipulation tedious, but the results (5a), ..., (6b) are simple and easy to use, as the complete *LeftRotate* function shows:

```
void AVLtree::LeftRotate(node* &p)
{   node *q = p;
    p = p->pRight;
    q->pRight = p->pLeft;
    p->pLeft = q;
    q->bal--;                               // b' = b - 1
    if (p->bal > 0) q->bal -= p->bal;  // Correction: b' -= B
    p->bal--;                               // B' = B - 1
    if (q->bal < 0) p->bal += q->bal;  // Correction: B' += b'
}
```

Right rotations

Figure 6.11 shows a right rotation. Again, the balance factor associated with the smaller key (40) is denoted by b or b', the one associated with the larger key (50) by B or B'.

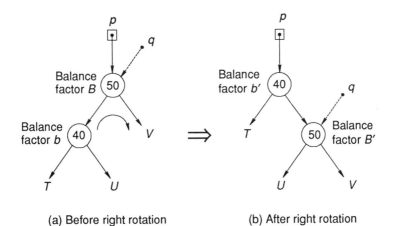

(a) Before right rotation   (b) After right rotation

Figure 6.11 *Right rotation*

We can see in Figure 6.11 that

$$
\begin{aligned}
b &= h(U) - h(T) & & & (7)\\
B &= h(V) - h(U) - 1 & &\text{if } h(U) \ge h(T) & (8a)\\
B &= h(V) - h(T) - 1 & &\text{if } h(U) < h(T) & (8b)\\
B' &= h(V) - h(U) & & & (9)\\
b' &= h(U) - h(T) + 1 & &\text{if } h(U) \ge h(V) & (10a)\\
b' &= h(V) - h(T) + 1 & &\text{if } h(U) < h(V) & (10b)
\end{aligned}
$$

It follows from (8a) and (9) that

$$B' = B + 1 \qquad\qquad \text{if } h(U) \geq h(T) \tag{11a}$$

and from (7), (8b) and (9) that

$$B' = B - b + 1 \qquad\qquad \text{if } h(U) < h(T) \tag{11b}$$

Also, it follows from (7) and (10a) that

$$b' = b + 1 \qquad\qquad \text{if } h(U) \geq h(V) \tag{12a}$$

and from (7), (9) and (10b) that

$$b' = b + B' + 1 \qquad\qquad \text{if } h(U) < h(V) \tag{12b}$$

The results (11a), ..., (12b) are used in the *RightRotate* function:

```
void AVLtree::RightRotate(node* &p)
{   node *q = p;
    p = p->pLeft;
    q->pLeft = p->pRight;
    p->pRight = q;
    q->bal++;                          // B' = B + 1
    if (p->bal < 0) q->bal -= p->bal;  // Correction: B' -= b
    p->bal++;                          // b' = b + 1
    if (q->bal > 0) p->bal += q->bal;  // Correction: b' += B'
}
```

So much for updating balance factors in rotations.

Application of rotations

We will now see in which situations these rotations are required. When inserting nodes with keys in ascending order, we frequently need a left notation, as Figure 6.12 shows. Immediately after inserting 30, the tree is out of balance, as the balance factor 2 in the root node shows. A left rotation will then rebalance the tree. Note that in Figure 6.12 the balance factor (2) in the root node has the same sign as the balance factor (1) in its right child. If they are −2 and −1 instead of 2 and 1, the situation is analogous but we need a right rotation.

The situation is essentially different in Figure 6.13. Here the root node has 2 and its right child −1 as balance factors. In this case we need two rotations. We first apply a right rotation to the right subtree (with keys 30 and 20). Then we have the well-known situation with two positive balance factors, so we can subsequently apply a left rotation to the tree itself, as we have seen in Figure 6.12.

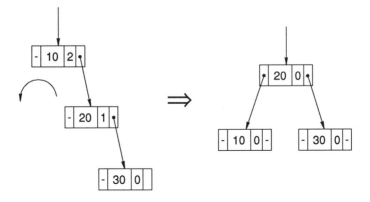

Figure 6.12 Left rotation required

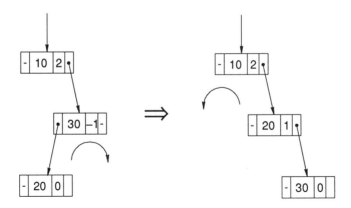

Figure 6.13 Right rotation, to be followed by left rotation

AVL trees and node deletion

So far, we have paid some attention to node insertion. Actually, our demonstration program can also *delete* nodes from an AVL tree in such a way that the tree remains an AVL tree. Node deletion is slightly more complicated than node insertion, so if you want to see how this program works, it is wise to begin with insertion. For deletion not only do we need to rebalance the tree after each tree update but we may also have to select a leaf and to move its contents, as discussed in the previous section and demonstrated there by program *delnode*. Recall that in that program we followed a certain path in the tree if the node to be deleted had two children. Here we use the same method as in that case, but we now exchange the data stored in two nodes. In a recursive call, we can then delete a node that has no right child.

A demonstration program for AVL trees

Program *avl* shows how AVL trees grow and shrink. Repeatedly, the user can enter an integer, either to insert a new node with that integer in it or to delete a node containing that integer (if there is such a node). The integer is followed by I (or i) to indicate insertion and by D (or d) in the case of deletion. Duplicate input values for insertion are ignored, so the tree actually represents a set. After each of these insertion or deletion commands, the updated AVL tree is displayed sideways, as we have already done several times: the usual representation is obtained by rotating the displayed tree 90° clockwise. The letter Q (or any other nonnumeric character) can be entered to quit the program.

```
// avl: Demonstration program for AVL trees;
//       insertion and deletion of nodes
#include <iostream.h>
#include <iomanip.h>
#include <ctype.h>
struct node{int num, bal; struct node *pLeft, *pRight;};

class AVLtree {
public:
   AVLtree():root(NULL){}
   void insert(int x){ins(root, x);}
   void DelNode(int x){del(root, x);}
   void print()const{pr(root, 0);}
private:
   node *root;
   void LeftRotate(node* &p);
   void RightRotate(node* &p);
   int ins(node* &p, int x);
   int del(node* &p, int x);
   void pr(const node *p, int nSpace)const;
};

void AVLtree::LeftRotate(node* &p)
{  node *q = p;
   p = p->pRight;
   q->pRight = p->pLeft;
   p->pLeft = q;
   q->bal--;
   if (p->bal > 0) q->bal -= p->bal;
   p->bal--;
   if (q->bal < 0) p->bal += q->bal;
}

void AVLtree::RightRotate(node* &p)
{  node *q = p;
   p = p->pLeft;
   q->pLeft = p->pRight;
   p->pRight = q;
   q->bal++;
   if (p->bal < 0) q->bal -= p->bal;
   p->bal++;
   if (q->bal > 0) p->bal += q->bal;
}
```

```
int AVLtree::ins(node* &p, int x)
{  // Return value: increase in height (0 or 1) after
   // inserting x in the (sub)tree with root p
   int deltaH=0;
   if (p == NULL)
   {  p = new node;
      p->num = x;
      p->bal = 0;
      p->pLeft = p->pRight = NULL;
      deltaH = 1; // Tree height increased by 1
   }  else
   if (x > p->num)
   {  if (ins(p->pRight, x))
      {  p->bal++; // Height of right subtree increased
         if (p->bal == 1) deltaH = 1; else
         if (p->bal == 2)
         {  if (p->pRight->bal == -1)
               RightRotate(p->pRight);
            LeftRotate(p);
         }
      }
   }  else
   if (x < p->num)
   {  if (ins(p->pLeft, x))
      {  p->bal--; // Height of left subtree increased
         if (p->bal == -1) deltaH = 1; else
         if (p->bal == -2)
         {  if (p->pLeft->bal == 1)
               LeftRotate(p->pLeft);
            RightRotate(p);
         }
      }
   }
   return deltaH;
}

int AVLtree::del(node* &p, int x)
/* Return value: decrease in height (0 or 1) of subtree
   with root p, after deleting the node with key x.
   (If there is no such node, 0 will be returned.)
*/
{  node **qq, *p0;
   int deltaH=0;
   if (p == NULL) return 0;
   if (x < p->num)
   {  if (del(p->pLeft, x))
      {  p->bal++; // Height left subtree decreased
         if (p->bal == 0) deltaH = 1; else
         if (p->bal == 2)
         {  if (p->pRight->bal == -1) RightRotate(p->pRight);
            LeftRotate(p);
            if (p->bal == 0) deltaH = 1;
         }
      }
   }  else
```

```
      if (x > p->num)
      { if (del(p->pRight, x))
        { p->bal--; // Height right subtree decreased
          if (p->bal == 0) deltaH = 1; else
          if (p->bal == -2)
          { if (p->pLeft->bal == 1)
                LeftRotate(p->pLeft);
            RightRotate(p);
            if (p->bal == 0) deltaH = 1;
          }
        }
      } else  // x == p->num
      { if (p->pRight == NULL)
        { p0 = p; p = p->pLeft;
          delete p0; return 1;
        } else
        if (p->pLeft == NULL)
        { p0 = p; p = p->pRight;
          delete p0; return 1;
        } else
        { qq = & p->pLeft;
          while ((*qq)->pRight != NULL)
              qq = & (*qq)->pRight;
          p->num = (*qq)->num;
          (*qq)->num = x;
          if (del(p->pLeft, x))
          { p->bal++; // Height left subtree decreased
            if (p->bal == 0) deltaH = 1; else
            if (p->bal == 2)
            { if (p->pRight->bal == -1) RightRotate(p->pRight);
              LeftRotate(p);
              if (p->bal == 0) deltaH = 1;
            }
          }
        }
      }
      return deltaH;
}

void AVLtree::pr(const node *p, int nSpace)const
{ if (p != NULL)
  { pr(p->pRight, nSpace+=6);
    cout << setw(nSpace) << p->num << " " << p->bal << endl;
    pr(p->pLeft, nSpace);
  }
}

int main()
{ int x;
  char ch;
  AVLtree t;
  cout <<
  "\nEach AVL tree displayed by this program has\n"
  "its root on the left. Turn it 90 degrees\n"
  "clockwise to obtain its usual representation.\n\n";
```

```
    for ( ; ; )
    {  cout <<
       "Enter an integer, followed by I for insertion\n"
       "or by D for deletion, or enter Q to quit: ";
       cin >> x >> ch;
       if (cin.fail()) break;
       ch = toupper(ch);
       if (ch == 'I') t.insert(x); else
       if (ch == 'D') t.DelNode(x);
       t.print();
    }
    return 0;
}
```

Here is a demonstration of this program. As you can see, the integers 4, 5, 7, 2, 1, 3, 6, in that order, are inserted, after which the node containing the integer 4 is deleted. Not only these integers but also the balance factors −1, 0, and 1 are printed. Note that in most cases they are zero. Remember, the roots of these trees are on the left, so you must imagine these trees to be turned 90° clockwise to obtain their usual form:

```
Each AVL tree displayed by this program has
its root on the left. Turn it 90 degrees
clockwise to obtain its usual representation.

Enter an integer, followed by I for insertion
or by D for deletion, or enter Q to quit: 4 i
      4 0
Enter an integer, followed by I for insertion
or by D for deletion, or enter Q to quit: 5 i
        5 0
    4 1
Enter an integer, followed by I for insertion
or by D for deletion, or enter Q to quit: 7 i
        7 0
    5 0
        4 0
Enter an integer, followed by I for insertion
or by D for deletion, or enter Q to quit: 2 i
        7 0
    5 -1
        4 -1
            2 0
Enter an integer, followed by I for insertion
or by D for deletion, or enter Q to quit: 1 i
        7 0
    5 -1
            4 0
        2 0
            1 0
Enter an integer, followed by I for insertion
or by D for deletion, or enter Q to quit: 3 i
```

```
                        7 0
                5 1
        4 0
                        3 0
                2 0
                        1 0
Enter an integer, followed by I for insertion
or by D for deletion, or enter Q to quit: 6 i
                        7 0
                6 0
                        5 0
        4 0
                        3 0
                2 0
                        1 0
Enter an integer, followed by I for insertion
or by D for deletion, or enter Q to quit: 4 d
                        7 0
                6 0
                        5 0
        3 0
                        2 -1
                        1 0
Enter an integer, followed by I for insertion
or by D for deletion, or enter Q to quit: q
```

Exercises

All functions to be developed in the following exercises are to be complemented by program fragments to demonstrate them.

6.1   Write a function which deletes a binary tree and builds a similar one. In the given tree, the information member of each node consists of a pointer to a block of memory, which has been allocated by the operator *new* and contains a (null-terminated) character string. The tree to be built should have the same structure as the original one, but now each node is to contain only an integer as its information member, which denotes the length of the string pointed to in the corresponding node of the original tree. As for the original tree, the memory space used by the tree nodes and that for the character strings should be released by means of the *delete* operator.

In the following exercises, each node in the binary tree in question has an information member which contains only an integer.

6.2   Write a function to transform a given binary search tree into one that is perfectly balanced. The demonstration program should (also) print the heights of the old and the new trees.

Hint: You can do this in two steps. First, transform the given binary tree into a linked list in which the keys are in ascending order. To do this you can use a recursive function similar to our function *printtree*. Each time, instead of using *delete* to delete a node in the tree and *new* to create a node in the list, you can change the pointers (using only one of the two pointer members) and leave the data in the node. While building this linked list, you can count how many keys there are. Then, in the second step, you can use a recursive function similar to *pbtree* to build a perfectly balanced binary search tree. Again, you can leave the data in the nodes and change only the pointer members.

6.3   Write a function to determine whether or not a given binary tree is perfectly balanced.

6.4   Write a function to determine the height of a binary tree (see Section 6.1).

6.5   Write a function to determine whether or not a given binary tree is height-balanced.

6.6   Write a function to determine whether or not a given binary tree is a binary search tree.

6.7   Write a function to print all integers stored in a binary tree, along with the levels of all nodes.

6.8   Write a function to print all integers stored in the *leaves* of a given binary tree (ignoring the integers stored in all other nodes).

6.9   Write a function which, for a given binary search tree, swaps the left and right children of every node, and simultaneously replaces each value i in the tree with $-i$. (The resulting tree is also a binary search tree.)

6.10 Write a function to check whether or not binary trees with balance factors (as discussed in Section 6.4) are AVL trees; in other words, this function will check the correctness of the balance factors.

6.11 Write a program similar to *infsys* of Section 6.2, but based on an AVL tree.

6.12 A *full* (or *strictly*) *binary tree* is defined as one in which every nonleaf node has exactly two children. If all leaves of a full binary tree are on the same level, this binary tree is said to be *complete*. Let N denote the number of nodes and L the number of leaves of a binary tree. Show that, for any (nonempty) full binary tree, we have

$$N = 2L - 1 \tag{1}$$

Hint: Begin by showing that $N = 2^h - 1$ and $L = 2^{h-1}$ in a (nonempty) complete binary tree, where h is the height of the tree. The proof of (1) is then trivial for a complete binary tree. To extend this result to any full binary tree, examine what happens to N and L if two leaf children of the same parent are removed from a binary tree.

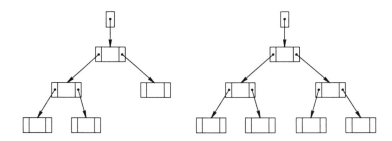

Figure 6.14 Two full binary trees, the one on the right also being a complete binary tree

7

B-trees

7.1 Building and Searching a B-tree

So far, we have been using only binary trees that existed in main memory. We also want to store trees in *secondary storage*, that is, on disk, and load data from them into main memory only when we need it. There are two reasons for this. First, data in main memory exists only temporarily, whereas on disk it is permanent, and, second, the amount of available main memory will probably be less than the amount of secondary storage. However, disk access is slower than memory access. In order to reduce the number of I/O operations, we will no longer use binary trees, which, as we know, have as many nodes as there are keys. Instead, we want to use larger blocks of data, grouping together several items, each including a key, into one node. We will therefore use multiway trees of a certain type, called *B-trees*.

Instead of only one, we store a variable number of data items in each node. If a nonleaf (or *interior*) node contains n data items, it has exactly $n + 1$ children. The maximum number of children a node can have is a fixed positive integer M, the order of the B-tree. In other words, n must be less than M for any node. There is also a lower bound for the number of links in a node, where the term *link* is used for those $n + 1$ pointer members of a node which actually point to other nodes (and are therefore not equal to *NULL*):

$$2 \leq \text{number of links} \leq M \qquad \text{for the root node}$$
$$\frac{M}{2} \leq \text{number of links} \leq M \qquad \text{for all other nodes}$$

Except for leaves (which do not contain any links) the number of keys in a node is one less than the number of links. It follows that any interior node other than the root node has at least $M/2$ links if M is even and at least $(M + 1)/2$ links if M is odd, where M, the order of the B-tree, is the maximum number of links for any node. Leaves have no links at all, and a root node may have any number of links ranging from 2 to M.

The above description of a B-tree is by no means complete. Consider the B-tree of order 4 shown in Figure 7.1.

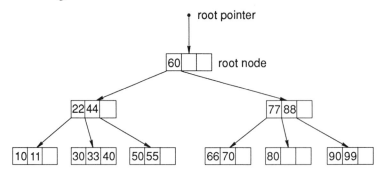

Figure 7.1 A B-tree of order 4

Each square in a node can contain a data item, so we have $n \leq 3$ in this example. B-trees of order 4 are sometimes call *2-3-4-trees*, because all their non-terminal nodes have 2, 3 or 4 links to child nodes. Besides data items and pointers, the value n, denoting the number of data items stored in a node, will also be stored in that node. For example, there is a value $n = 1$ stored in the root node of Figure 7.1 because it currently contains exactly one data item.

Figure 7.1 illustrates some important characteristics applying to any B-tree. As you can see, the keys (k) and links (p) in non-terminal nodes are logically arranged as follows:

$p_0, k_0, p_1, k_1, ..., p_{n-1}, k_{n-1}, p_n$

If we think of each pointer p_i as representing the keys in the node it points to, we can regard the above list as a sequence of keys. These keys are in *ascending order*. We can express this more precisely in the form of the following rules, applying to every node of a B-tree:

- The keys $k_0, k_1, ..., k_{n-1}$, stored in the node, are in ascending order:

    $k_0 < k_1 < ... < k_{n-1}$

- If the node is a leaf, its pointers $p_0, p_1, ..., p_n$ are all *NULL*.
- If the node is not a leaf, each of the $n + 1$ pointers p_i points to a child node. For $i = 1, ..., n$, all keys in the child pointed to by p_i are greater than k_{i-1}. Also, for $i = 0, ..., n - 1$, all keys in the child pointed to by p_i are less than k_i.

Remember, if an interior node contains exactly n keys, it contains exactly $n + 1$ links (so that exactly $M - n - 1$ pointers in that node are unused). The B-tree of Figure 7.1 is well-balanced, which is characteristic for B-trees:

All leaves of a B-tree are on the same level.

(As discussed in Section 6.1 for binary trees, we define the level of a node as the length of the path from the root to that node.) Recall that this characteristic did not apply to perfectly balanced binary trees, so B-trees seem to be 'better than perfect'. However, in binary trees we have exactly one data item in each node, which in general makes it impossible to meet a similar requirement about equal path lengths. The nice shape of B-trees is not without its price, since memory space is also allocated for unused data and pointer members. Yet B-trees are elegant and efficient in many applications, especially since there are good algorithms available to manipulate them. Not all of these are particularly simple, however. We will first discuss the insertion of new items, using a B-tree of order (M =) 5.

Let us begin with an empty B-tree, in which we insert four numbers, say 60, 20, 80, 10. This gives Figure 7.2(a). There is only a root node, which contains the following data:

$n = 4$
$p_0 = p_1 = p_2 = p_3 = p_4 = 0$
$k_0 = 10, k_1 = 20, k_2 = 60, k_3 = 80$

(a) 60, 20, 80, 10 inserted

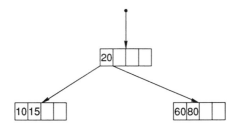

(b) 15 inserted

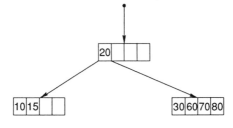

(c) 30, 70 inserted

Figure 7.2 *Growth of a B-tree (continued overleaf)*

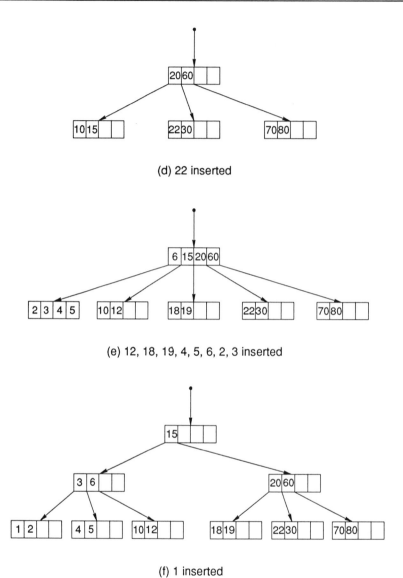

(d) 22 inserted

(e) 12, 18, 19, 4, 5, 6, 2, 3 inserted

(f) 1 inserted

Figure 7.2 Growth of a B-tree

Since n has its maximum value, $M - 1 = 4$, there is no room for the next data item to be inserted, say 15. Ignoring the limitation to four items for one moment, we write down the augmented, ordered sequence

    10, 15, 20, 60, 80

to select the item in the middle, 20. We then remove this item, to store it in another node later, and we move the subsequence [60, 80], found to the right of it, to a newly created node. If the node under consideration had a parent which could accommodate the removed item 20, we would store it in that parent. We will consider that situation shortly. In the present case, there is no parent at all, so we have to create another node to store 20. This will be a new root node, which means that the height of the tree increases. This new root node contains one data item (20), so that two links are required. Fortunately, we have two other nodes to point to, namely both the original one, in which we set the count member to 2, and the one created to store 60 and 80. This leads to Figure 7.2(b). If we now have to insert a new item, say 30, it might be tempting to store it in the root node, since this node has plenty of room. However, this would not be correct because then the root node would have as many data items as it has children. The general rule is that we always try to insert a new item in a leaf node. So 30 is placed in the right child, which makes it necessary to shift 60 and 80 one position to the right. Let us add another item, say 70, which will be placed in the same node because it is also greater than 20. This gives the result shown in Figure 7.2(c). We have now reached the maximum number of data items for that node, so adding another item, say 22, will cause some item to move upward. To find out which, we again forget about the limitation for one moment, and write down the augmented sequence

   22, 30, 60, 70, 80

As we did for the root node, we choose the item (60) in the middle, and split the remaining sequence into

   22, 30   and   70, 80

We now insert the node 60 in the parent node, if this is possible. In our case, this is the case, so we obtain the tree shown in Figure 7.2(d). As a result of splitting a leaf node, there is some new room in the leaves for subsequent items. If we keep inserting new items, we will again reach the situation that a leaf is selected in which already $M - 1$ (= 4) items have been stored. Then again we have to split that leaf and to move some item to its parent, and so on. In this way, we sooner or later have five leaves, which is the maximum number of children for any parent. For example, if we proceed with the tree of Figure 7.2(d), inserting the items

   12, 18, 19, 4, 5, 6, 2, 3

in that order, we obtain the tree shown in Figure 7.2(e). Let us now insert the number 1 in the latter tree. Since 3 is the item in the middle of the sequence 1, 2, 3, 4, 5, obtained by augmenting the bottom-left node, this item 3 is to move upward. We use the remaining items to form the subsequences [1, 2] and [4, 5]. However, the parent node is already full, so this node, too, is to be split. We first write the sequence of five items

   3, 6, 15, 20, 60

and select the element 15, in the middle. Since the parent node in question happens to be the root node, we have to create a new root node to store 15, and at this moment the height of the tree increases again. Figure 7.2(f) shows the resulting tree.

A demonstration program

Now that we understand how B-trees grow, we will discuss a program which realizes all this. It will be clear from what we have discussed that a function to insert an item in a B-tree will be rather complex. We will actually use two functions. At the higher level, in our *main* function, we write

```
t.insert(x);
```

where *t* is a B-tree in which *x* is to be inserted. In this function *insert*, we call the lower-level function *ins* as follows:

```
code = ins(root, x, xNew, tNew);
```

The argument types, in this order, are *node**, *int*, *int&* and *node*&*. Since function *ins* is recursive, there is also a call to *ins* in this function itself:

```
code = ins(r->p[i], x, xNew, pNew);
```

Since *r* is the first parameter of *ins* and *r–>p[i]* is the first argument in a recursive call, we can go from the root to a leaf by executing several of these recursive calls. The final two arguments *xNew* and *tNew* are variables passed by reference so that *ins* can modify them. To understand how *ins* works, we should remember how we inserted new items ourselves in our discussion above. Recall that we first tried to add such an item to a leaf. In our program, we arrive at a leaf by means of several recursive calls to *ins*. We will deal with the third and fourth arguments shortly.

A recursive call to *ins* may or may not be successful. This function therefore returns a *status code*, for which we use the following symbolic constants:

Success:	Insertion successfully completed.
DuplicateKey:	The value *x* has been inserted previously, so the insert request can be ignored.
InsertNotComplete:	See the discussion below.

This last status code occurs when, at the lower level, the insertion has not been a complete success, so that some additional action is required at the current level. The third and fourth arguments then provide us with information about what to do next (and they are not used if *Success* or *DuplicateKey* is returned). If the status code *InsertNotComplete* is returned, there are two possibilities:

(1)   The given subtree is empty. In this case, the third argument *xNew* has been made equal to *x* and the fourth argument *tNew* has been set to *NULL*.

(2)   Although the given subtree is not empty, it has not been able to accommodate *x*. In this case, the root node of this subtree has been split. A new node has been created and its address has been placed in *tNew*. Recall that if a node was full in our examples, we wrote down an increasing sequence of five integers and selected the one in the middle, which was then placed in the parent node. Here that selected integer is placed in *xNew*.

In both cases (1) and (2), the integer in *xNew* is still to be stored in the tree. If *tNew* is *NULL*, the current node is a leaf, so if there is still room left we are free to place the value of *xNew* in the current node without bothering about pointer members in that node. If a real address of a new node has been placed in *tNew*, the values of both *xNew* and *tNew* are to be stored in the current node, if possible. Note that this is in accordance with the rules for B-trees: in a node that is not a leaf, a new data item can only be inserted if we also insert a new pointer. After all, the number of data items must always be exactly one less than the number of pointers to subtrees.

The method we are discussing is similar to an employer who has some work to do and begins by asking his senior employee to do it for him. This employee may have a junior employee working for him. If he has, he in turn delegates the task to this junior employee. In either case, he fulfills his task either completely or incompletely. In the latter case he informs his employer about what still has to be done.

We started the above discussion with the higher-level function *insert*, which is called only in the *main* function. This function is related to the root node. It is wise to study this function first, because it is simpler than the lower-level function *ins*. Function *insert* calls *ins* as a request to insert the given integer *x* in the root node itself. If this call to *ins* returns *InsertNotComplete*, we create a new root node in *insert*, either because this has not yet been done because we are just starting or because the old root node was full. In both cases the height of the B-tree increases by 1.

Let us now turn to the function *ins*, viewed from the inside. Its first line is

```
status Btree::ins(node *r, dtype x, dtype &y, node* &q)
```

where *dtype* is the type of the data items, for which we use *int*. As mentioned above, the task of this function is very simple if *r* is equal to *NULL*. Let us now assume that *r* is the address of a node. We then locate the position where the integer *x* belongs by comparing *x* with the integers stored in the node. In this way, we find the pointer p_i, indicating the subtree in which we now try to insert *x* by means of a recursive call. If this call is not completely successful, we first see if there is room in the current node to store the values of *xNew* and *tNew* returned by the recursive call through the third and fourth arguments. If the current node is full, we split it in the way we did in our examples, using an increasing sequence of *M* keys and selecting the one in the middle. We place this selected item in *y* to return it via the third parameter. The items to the right of the selected one are placed in a newly created node, and the address of this new node is placed in *q* to return it via the fourth parameter. We now return the value *InsertNotComplete* as a status code.

Program *btree* shows further details of B-tree insertion. The program first inserts a given sequence of integers in a B-tree, which initially is empty. In its present form, the program builds a B-tree of order 5, but if a higher order is desired, we have only to alter *M* in a *#define*-line. Once the B-tree has been built, we can enter another integer to search the tree for it. The program prints the complete search path, starting at the root and ending in the node where the integer is stored, or, if we are searching in vain, ending in the leaf where it would have been stored if it had been included in the given input data. This search process is performed in the function *search*. Incidentally, if we replace *M* with a much larger value, we had better also replace function *NodeSearch*, which searches a node for a key, with an equivalent but faster one, based on binary search, as discussed in Section 5.2.

If you like, you can realize this replacement by using the *NodeSearch* function of program *disktree* to be discussed in Section 7.3.

This program also contains some functions (*DelNode* and *del*) for node deletion. This is a new subject, to be discussed in the next section. Facilities for node deletion have already been included in this program to avoid duplication of program text later.

```cpp
// btree: B-tree of order M
//    (with nodes that contain at most M links)
#include <iostream.h>
#include <iomanip.h>
#include <ctype.h>
#define M 5   // Order of B-tree: M link fields in each node
typedef int dtype;

enum status {InsertNotComplete, Success, DuplicateKey,
    Underflow, NotFound};

struct node {
    int n;          // Number of items stored in a node (n < M)
    dtype k[M-1]; // Data items (only the first n in use)
    node *p[M];   // Pointers to other nodes (n+1 in use)
};

// Logical order:
//     p[0], k[0], p[1], k[1], ..., p[n-1], k[n-1], p[n]

class Btree {
public:
    Btree(): root(NULL){}
    void insert(dtype x);
    void print()const{cout << "Contents:\n"; pr(root, 0);}
    void DelNode(dtype x);
    void ShowSearch(dtype x)const;
private:
    node *root;
    status ins(node *r, dtype x, dtype &y, node* &u);
    void pr(const node* r, int nSpace)const;
    int NodeSearch(dtype x, const dtype *a, int n)const;
    status del(node *r, dtype x);
};

void Btree::insert(dtype x)
{   node *pNew;
    dtype xNew;
    status code = ins(root, x, xNew, pNew);
    if (code == DuplicateKey)
        cout << "Duplicate key ignored.\n";
    if (code == InsertNotComplete)
    {   node *root0 = root;
        root = new node;
        root->n = 1; root->k[0] = xNew;
        root->p[0] = root0; root->p[1] = pNew;
    }
}
```

```
status Btree::ins(node *r, dtype x, dtype &y, node* &q)
{ // Insert x in *this. If not completely successful, the
  // integer y and the pointer q remain to be inserted.
  // Return value:
  //    Success, DuplicateKey or InsertNotComplete.
  node *pNew, *pFinal;
  int i, j, n;
  dtype xNew, kFinal;
  status code;
  if (r == NULL){q = NULL; y = x; return InsertNotComplete;}
  n = r->n;
  i = NodeSearch(x, r->k, n);
  if (i < n && x == r->k[i]) return DuplicateKey;
  code = ins(r->p[i], x, xNew, pNew);
  if (code != InsertNotComplete) return code;
  // Insertion in subtree did not completely succeed;
  // try to insert xNew and pNew in the current node:
  if (n < M - 1)
  { i = NodeSearch(xNew, r->k, n);
    for (j=n; j>i; j--)
    { r->k[j] = r->k[j-1]; r->p[j+1] = r->p[j];
    }
    r->k[i] = xNew; r->p[i+1] = pNew; ++r->n;
    return Success;
  }
  // Current node is full (n == M - 1) and will be split.
  // Pass item k[h] in the middle of the augmented
  // sequence back via parameter y, so that it
  // can move upward in the tree. Also, pass a pointer
  // to the newly created node back via parameter q:
  if (i == M - 1) {kFinal = xNew; pFinal = pNew;} else
  { kFinal = r->k[M-2]; pFinal = r->p[M-1];
    for (j=M-2; j>i; j--)
    { r->k[j] = r->k[j-1];
      r->p[j+1] = r->p[j];
    }
    r->k[i] = xNew;
    r->p[i+1] = pNew;
  }
  int h = (M - 1)/2;
  y = r->k[h];              // y and q are passed on to the
  q = new node;            // next higher level in the tree
  // The values p[0],k[0],p[1],...,k[h-1],p[h] belong to
  // the left of k[h] and are kept in *r:
  r->n = h;
  // p[h+1],k[h+1],p[h+2],...,k[M-2],p[M-1],kFinal,pFinal
  // belong to the right of k[h] and are moved to *q:
  q->n = M - 1 - h;
  for (j=0; j < q->n; j++)
  { q->p[j] = r->p[j + h + 1];
    q->k[j] = (j < q->n - 1 ? r->k[j + h + 1] : kFinal);
  }
  q->p[q->n] = pFinal;
  return InsertNotComplete;
}
```

```
void Btree::pr(const node *r, int nSpace)const
{  if (r)
   {  int i;
      cout << setw(nSpace) << "";
      for (i=0; i < r->n; i++)
         cout << setw(3) << r->k[i] << " ";
      cout << endl;
      for (i=0; i <= r->n; i++)
         pr(r->p[i], nSpace+8);
   }
}


int Btree::NodeSearch(dtype x, const dtype *a, int n)const
{  int i=0;
   while (i < n && x > a[i])
      i++;
   return i;
}


void Btree::ShowSearch(dtype x)const
{  cout << "Search path:\n";
   int i, j, n;
   node *r = root;
   while (r)
   {  n = r->n;
      for (j=0; j<r->n; j++)
         cout << " " << r->k[j];
      cout << endl;
      i = NodeSearch(x, r->k, n);
      if (i < n && x == r->k[i])
      {  cout << "Key " << x << " found in position " << i
              << " of last displayed node.\n";
         return;
      }
      r = r->p[i];
   }
   cout << "Key " << x << " not found.\n";
}


void Btree::DelNode(dtype x)
{  node *root0;
   switch (del(root, x))
   {
   case NotFound:
      cout << x << " not found.\n";
      break;
   case Underflow:
      root0 = root;
      root = root->p[0];
      delete root0;
      break;
   }
}
```

```
status Btree::del(node *r, dtype x)
{  if (r == NULL) return NotFound;
   int i, j, pivot, n = r->n;
   dtype *k = r->k;  // k[i] means r->k[i]
   const int nMin = (M - 1)/2;
   status code;
   node **p = r->p, *pL, *pR;       // p[i] means r->p[i]
   i = NodeSearch(x, k, n);
   if (p[0] == NULL) // *r is a leaf
   {  if (i == n || x < k[i])
         return NotFound;
      // x == k[i], and *r is a leaf
      for (j=i+1; j < n; j++)
      {  k[j-1] = k[j]; p[j] = p[j+1];
      }
      return
      --r->n >= (r==root ? 1 : nMin) ? Success : Underflow;
   }
   // *r is an interior node, not a leaf:
   if (i < n && x == k[i])
   {  // x found in an interior node. Go to left child
      // *p[i] and follow a path all the way to a leaf,
      // using rightmost branches:
      node *q = p[i], *q1; int nq;
      for (;;)
      {  nq = q->n;
         q1 = q->p[nq];
         if (q1 == NULL) break;
         q = q1;
      }
      // Exchange k[i] (= x) with rightmost item in leaf:
      k[i] = q->k[nq-1];
      q->k[nq - 1] = x;
   }
   // Delete x in leaf of subtree with root p[i]:
   code = del(p[i], x);
   if (code != Underflow) return code;
   // There is underflow; borrow, and, if necessary, merge:
   // Too few data items in node *p[i]
   if (i > 0 && p[i-1]->n > nMin) // Borrow from left sibling
   {  pivot = i - 1; // k[pivot] between pL and pR:
      pL = p[pivot];
      pR = p[i];
      // Increase contents of *pR, borrowing from *pL:
      pR->p[pR->n + 1] = pR->p[pR->n];
      for (j=pR->n; j>0; j--)
      {  pR->k[j] = pR->k[j-1];
         pR->p[j] = pR->p[j-1];
      }
      pR->n++;
      pR->k[0] = k[pivot];
      pR->p[0] = pL->p[pL->n];
      k[pivot] = pL->k[--pL->n];
      return Success;
   }
```

```
      if (i<n && p[i+1]->n > nMin) // Borrow from right sibling
      {  pivot = i; // k[pivot] between pL and pR:
         pL = p[pivot]; pR = p[pivot+1];
         // Increase contents of *pL, borrowing from *pR:
         pL->k[pL->n] = k[pivot];
         pL->p[pL->n + 1] = pR->p[0];
         k[pivot] = pR->k[0];
         pL->n++; pR->n--;
         for (j=0; j < pR->n; j++)
         {  pR->k[j] = pR->k[j+1];
            pR->p[j] = pR->p[j+1];
         }
         pR->p[pR->n] = pR->p[pR->n + 1];
         return Success;
      }
      // Merge; neither borrow left nor borrow right possible.
      pivot = (i == n ? i - 1 : i);
      pL = p[pivot]; pR = p[pivot+1];
      // Add k[pivot] and *pR to *pL:
      pL->k[pL->n] = k[pivot];
      pL->p[pL->n + 1] = pR->p[0];
      for (j=0; j < pR->n; j++)
      {  pL->k[pL->n + 1 + j] = pR->k[j];
         pL->p[pL->n + 2 + j] = pR->p[j+1];
      }
      pL->n += 1 + pR->n; delete pR;
      for (j=i+1; j < n; j++){k[j-1] = k[j]; p[j] = p[j+1];}
      return
      --r->n >= (r == root ? 1 : nMin) ? Success : Underflow;
}

int main()
{  cout <<
      "B-tree structure shown by indentation. For each\n"
      "node, the number of links to other nodes will not\n"
      "be greater than " << M <<
      ", the order M of the B-tree.\n\n"
      "Enter some integers, followed by a slash (/):\n";
   Btree t;
   dtype x;
   char ch;
   while (cin >> x, !cin.fail()) t.insert(x);
   cout <<
      "\nB-tree representation (indentation similar to the\n"
      "table of contents of a book). The items stored in\n"
      "each node are displayed on a single line.\n";
   t.print();
   cin.clear(); cin >> ch; // Skip terminating character
   for (;;)
   {  cout <<
      "\nEnter an integer, followed by I, D, or S (for\n"
      "Insert, Delete and Search), or enter Q to quit: ";
      cin >> x >> ch;
      if (cin.fail()) break;
      ch = toupper(ch);
```

```
        switch(ch)
        {
        case 'S': t.ShowSearch(x); break;
        case 'I': t.insert(x); break;
        case 'D': t.DelNode(x); break;
        default:
            cout << "Invalid command, use S, I or D\n"; break;
        }
        if (ch == 'I' || ch == 'D') t.print();
    }
    return 0;
}
```

We can use program *btree* to demonstrate how a B-tree is built. The demonstration below first builds the B-tree of Figure 7.2(e). Then the key 1 is inserted, which results in the B-tree of Figure 7.2(f). In the output, the structure of these B-trees is reflected by the way indentation is used. All keys stored in one node are printed on the same line. The children of each node follow that line and are shifted eight positions to the right. To demonstrate our search function, the search path is displayed for each search command. This program can also *delete* items from B-trees, to be discussed in the next section. The following output demonstrates only tree *insertion* and tree *search*:

```
B-tree structure shown by indentation. For each
node, the number of links to other nodes will not
be greater than 5, the order M of the B-tree.

Enter some integers, followed by a slash (/):
60 20 80 10 15 30 70 22
12 18 19 4 5 6 2 3 /

B-tree representation (indentation similar to the
table of contents of a book). The items stored in
each node are displayed on a single line.
Contents:
  6   15   20   60
                 2    3    4    5
               10   12
               18   19
               22   30
               70   80

Enter an integer, followed by I, D, or S (for
Insert, Delete and Search), or enter Q to quit: 1i
Contents:
  15
           3    6
                     1    2
                     4    5
                   10   12
         20   60
                   18   19
                   22   30
                   70   80
```

```
Enter an integer, followed by I, D, or S (for
Insert, Delete and Search), or enter Q to quit: 22s
Search path:
 15
 20 60
 22 30
Key 22 found in position 0 of last displayed node.

Enter an integer, followed by I, D, or S (for
Insert, Delete and Search), or enter Q to quit: q
```

7.2 Deleting Nodes in a B-tree

Given a key, we now want to search our B-tree, and, if we find an item containing this key, we want to remove it from the tree. The basic characteristic concerning the number of items in each node must be maintained during the process of successive deletions. We will use the same type of B-tree as in the previous section, with $M = 5$, so each node will contain at most four data items and five pointers. But, again, our implementation will be more general, so that larger nodes can be obtained by a simple change of the symbolic constant M. In fact, our program *btree* already contains functions for deletion, so there is no need for another demonstration program in this section. Since tree deletion is a rather complex operation, let us not immediately turn to its implementation, but first consider an example.

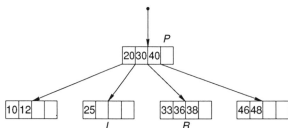

(a) Underflow after deleting item 27 in node *L*

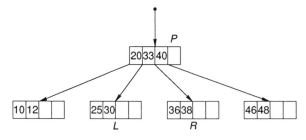

(b) Tree after borrowing an item from node *R*

Figure 7.3 *Underflow resolved by borrowing*

Let us write *nMin* for (the truncated value of) $(M - 1)/2$, the minimum number of data items for any node except the root node. With $M = 5$, we have $nMin = 2$. If we are fortunate enough to find an item with the given key in a leaf that contains more than *nMin* data items, we can simply remove that item, and shift any following items one position to the left. If that leaf contains precisely *nMin* items, we still remove the item in question in the same way, but the function call in which this occurs returns *Underflow*, defined as a symbolic constant. In this case, we try to borrow an item from a neighboring sibling of the child in which underflow has occurred. Figure 7.3(a) shows such a situation. Item 27 has just been deleted in node *L*, and this node now contains only one remaining item, 25, so there is underflow. In the program, we detect this when we are dealing with the parent node *P*, after a recursive call to delete 27 in its child *L*.

Although the parent *P* contains three items, we cannot simply use one of these, 20 or 30, to fill the gap, since then there would remain two data items and four pointers, and, as we know, the number of pointers must be only one more than the number of data items. This is why we need a sibling to borrow an item from. We will first try to borrow an item from a left sibling. This is possible if there is one and if the number of items stored in it exceeds *nMin*. In Figure 7.3(a) there is a left sibling (of node *L*), but this contains only *nMin* (= 2) items, so that we cannot use it to borrow from. We therefore turn to the right sibling, which contains $3 > nMin$ items so we can borrow an item from it. We can then focus on the parent node *P*, the node *L* in which underflow has occurred, and the right sibling *R*. We cannot just move 33 from *R* to *L*, since that would violate the rule that all keys in children to the left of 30 must be less than 30, or, more precisely and in the terminology of the previous section, that all keys in the node pointed to by p_i must be less than k_i. (Here we have $k_0 = 20$, $k_1 = 30$, $k_2 = 40$, and p_1 pointing to node *L*.) So neither item 30 in node *P* nor item 33 in node *R* can help us, that is, by themselves. In combination, however, they can: we move 30 from *P* to *L* and then 33 from *R* to *P*. The resulting tree is shown in Figure 7.3(b).

Unfortunately, this method does not always work. Here it worked fine because node *R* in Figure 7.3(a) contained three items. If *R*, like the leftmost node, had contained only two items (or, in general, $nMin = (M - 1)/2$ items) we would not have been able to borrow one of its items without causing underflow in *R*, which, of course, is just as bad as underflow in *L*. We must also bear in mind that not every node has both a left and a right sibling: node $*p_0$ only has a right one and $*p_n$ only a left one. In these two cases we can try only one sibling. If, in any of the cases mentioned, borrowing an item from a sibling is not possible, we have to merge two nodes *L* and *R* into one. This happens when we delete 30 from node *L*, as Figure 7.4 shows. Since node *P* in Figure 7.4(a) has four links, it seems that we have a problem, for after simply combining the nodes *L* and *R* into one, node *P* would have only three children. To get rid of a link in *P*, we also have to reduce the number of data items in *P* by one, and, fortunately, we can achieve this by moving the item 33, logically belonging between *L* and *R*, to the node resulting from the merge. In the program, we denote this important item 33 of the parent node by *k[pivot]*. Then the following items will appear in the node resulting from the merge operation:

- all items of node *L*, that is, of node **p[pivot]*;
- item *k[pivot]* of node *P*;
- all items of node *R*, that is, of node **p[pivot + 1]*.

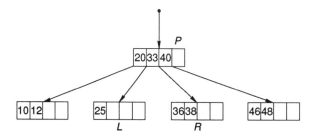

(a) Underflow after deletion of item 30 in node *L*

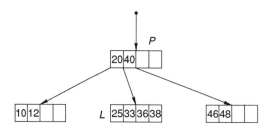

(b) Result after merging *L* and *R* and deleting *R*

Figure 7.4 *Underflow resolved by merging*

As for the actual implementation of this merge operation, we will use node *L* as a host: after moving item *k*[*pivot*] from *P* and all items from node *R* to node *L*, we delete node *R*. Figure 7.4(b) shows the situation after this merge operation.

In the above discussion we have focused on the data items. Besides these, there are also pointer members in the nodes, and it is time to see what happens with them in the borrow and merge operations. It is true that pointers in leaves are not very interesting because they are *NULL*, but even with these we must not be inaccurate. More importantly, the above discussion about borrowing and merging applies not only to leaves but also to interior nodes, provided that the pointer members are dealt with properly. Recall that in each node we have data items k_i and pointers p_i in the following logical order:

$$p_0 \ k_0 \ p_1 \ k_1 \ \dots \ p_{n-1} \ k_{n-1} \ p_n$$

If a node contains its minimum number of items, we have $n = nMin$, and in the case of underflow we have $n = nMin - 1$. Let us now consider Figure 7.4(a) once again, without the assumption that we are dealing with leaves: we imagine that the nodes *L*, *R* (and their two siblings) may have children. In node *L*, we have $k_0 = 25$, and immediately to the right of k_0 we imagine pointer p_1, which, if *L* is an interior node, is the root of a subtree with items lying between 25 and 33. We can express this more briefly by saying that p_1 in node *L* *represents* such items. When borrowing an item from node *R* to obtain the tree of Figure 7.4(b), we assign 33 to k_1 in node *L*, so p_1 in node *L* has the correct pointer value.

Returning to Figure 7.4(a), we see that pointer p_0 in node R represents items lying between 33 and 36, so this is precisely the pointer we need as p_2 in node L of Figure 7.4(b). Summarizing, when we remedy underflow in node L by borrowing an item from the right sibling R, the pointer on the extreme left in R becomes the rightmost pointer in L. If, instead of borrowing an item, we have to merge two nodes, we can again find out what to do with pointers by thinking of the range of items they represent.

In the above discussion, we suggested that borrowing and merging take place not only for leaves, but also for interior nodes. Consider, for example, Figure 7.2(f) in the previous section. The node that contains the items 3 and 6 has exactly $nMin$ items, and so have its three children. If we delete one item in such a child, say 1 in the leftmost leaf, the two leaves on the left are to be merged into one. The item 3 in the parent node also participates in this merge, so after the merge only 6 remains and we have underflow in this interior node. We now proceed in the same way as we did with underflow in leaves. If the interior node in question has a right sibling with more than $nMin$ items, we borrow an item from it. If borrowing is impossible, as is the case in Figure 7.2(f) (where 1 is being deleted), we merge the two nodes, which means that we fetch an item from the parent of the two interior nodes. Again underflow may occur in this parent, in which case we again either borrow or merge, and so on, until we are at the root. Here a special rule applies, namely that a root node is allowed to have less than $nMin$ items, as long as it has at least one. In Figure 7.2(f), the root node has only one item, 15, and when this participates in the merge of its two children, the number of items in the root node becomes zero. This is the moment that there is underflow in the root node. We then remove the entire node, which decreases the height of the tree. This gives the tree of Figure 7.2(e). Note that the reduction from Figure 7.2(f) to Figure 7.2(e) by deleting item 1 is exactly the reverse action from inserting 1 in the tree, which we did in Section 6.1.

So far, everything started with a deletion in a leaf, and we have seen that this may have far-reaching consequences with regard to the whole tree structure. We still have to consider a deletion which starts in an interior node. For example, let us again use Figure 7.2(f) and try to delete the item 15 in the root node. We are now faced with a new problem, since a root node must always have at least one item, and we cannot simply borrow an item from its children. Fortunately, this problem can be reduced to deleting an item in a leaf. Recall that in Section 6.3, when dealing with binary search trees, we solved a similar problem by finding a key that was as great as possible but less than the key in the given node. We first went to the left child of that node and then followed the path all the way to a leaf, each time taking the right child. The same method is useful here. If in an interior node item k_i is to be deleted, we find the greatest item that is less than k_i. All items stored in the subtree with root p_i are less than k_i; to find the largest, we follow a path, starting in the node pointed to by p_i, and each time going to the rightmost child, until we arrive at a leaf. The rightmost data item stored in this leaf is the one we are looking for. We can exchange it with the item k_i in the given node, without violating any rule for B-trees. In Figure 7.2(f) this means that we can exchange the items 15 and 12. Note that it would not have been correct if we had exchanged 15 with item 6 in the left child of the root node, since then in that child the new position of 15 would have been k_1, with p_2 pointing to the smaller items 10 and 12. After the exchange of 15 and 12, we can delete item 15 in the usual way because it now resides in a leaf. Further details can be found in the functions *DelNode* and *del*, which have already been included in program *btree*, listed in Section 6.1. The program is useful to demonstrate how a B-tree grows and shrinks by insertions and deletions. After each operation that changes the tree, we can search the tree for given items. Such a search causes a complete search path to be shown, which enables us to examine the structure of the tree. The best way to learn how B-trees work is to build and modify them on paper or on a blackboard, inserting and deleting items ourselves; program *btree* then enables us to check our results step by step.

The following demonstration displays three B-trees. The first shows the one of Figure 7.3(a), except that, in the output below, underflow due to deleting item 27 has not yet occurred. The second corresponds with Figure 7.3(b), after deleting item 27 and borrowing an item from a right sibling to deal with underflow. Then item 30 is deleted, which leads to underflow as shown in Figure 7.4(a), resolved by merging two nodes and resulting in the B-tree of Figure 7.4(b), displayed as the final B-tree representation below:

```
B-tree structure shown by indentation. For each
node, the number of links to other nodes will not
be greater than 5, the order M of the B-tree.

Enter some integers, followed by a slash (/):
10 12 20 25 27 30
33 36 40 46 48 38 /


B-tree representation (indentation similar to the
table of contents of a book). The items stored in
each node are displayed on a single line.
Contents:
  20   30   40
            10   12
            25   27
            33   36   38
            46   48


Enter an integer, followed by I, D, or S (for
Insert, Delete and Search), or enter Q to quit: 27d
Contents:
  20   33   40
            10   12
            25   30
            36   38
            46   48


Enter an integer, followed by I, D, or S (for
Insert, Delete and Search), or enter Q to quit: 30d
Contents:
  20   40
            10   12
            25   33   36   38
            46   48


Enter an integer, followed by I, D, or S (for
Insert, Delete and Search), or enter Q to quit: q
```

7.3 B-trees on Disk

In this section we will implement a B-tree as a random-access file (on disk). For most computer systems, this means that the tree can grow much larger than a tree in main memory. At any moment, only a few nodes of the tree will be in memory, but these may represent a considerable amount of data because M, the number of pointer members in each node, can be as large as we wish. The greater we choose M, the more memory will be used, but the faster the program will be likely to run because of less frequent disk access. The program to be developed in this section will enable us to investigate its efficiency experimentally. Though essentially an adaptation of program *btree* in Section 7.2, it will deal with one or two files. One file is essential because it represents the B-tree itself; the other is an optional input file which contains integers to be stored in the B-tree. In this way, we need no longer supply all input data interactively, but we can also prepare a text file containing integers, as required by the standard C++ input operator >>. To create such a file, any text-editor will do, but instead we can use program *gennum*, listed below, to generate a random number sequence:

```
// gennum: Generation of a textfile with integers,
//         to be read by program disktree.

#include <fstream.h>
#include <iomanip.h>
#include <stdlib.h>
#include <time.h>

class intfile {  // Creating a file with integers
public:
   intfile()
   {  char fname[50];
      cout << "Name of output file: ";
      cin >> setw(50) >> fname;
      out.open(fname, ios::out);
      if (out.fail())
      {  cout << "Cannot open output file.\n";
         exit(1);
      }
   }

   ~intfile(){out.close();}

   void write(int x)
   {  int cnt = 0;
      out << x;
      if (++cnt == 10)
      {  out << '\n'; cnt = 0;
      }
      else out << ' ';
   }
private:
   ofstream out;
};
```

```
int main()
{   long i, n;
    srand(int(time(NULL)));
    cout << "How many integers are to be generated? ";
    cin >> n;
    intfile output;
    for (i=0; i<n; i++) output.write(rand());
    return 0;
}
```

With this program we can easily generate a file of, say, 10 000 integers, and our program *disktree*, which we are developing, will be able to read these and insert them in the B-tree, in the same way as it does with integers entered one by one on the keyboard, which, incidentally, will still be possible. Program *disktree* will ask for the names of the two files. The first is the name of the tree file. If it already exists, the B-tree stored in it will be updated, otherwise a new tree file with the given name will be created. The second is the input file discussed above; if it exists, the integers read from it are inserted in the tree, which before this insertion may or may not be empty depending on whether or not a new tree file had to be created. To avoid confusion, it is wise to use different file-name extensions, such as *.bin* for the (binary) tree file and *.txt* for the optional text file that contains input data. Integers to be inserted can also be entered on the keyboard: at the beginning we can enter a whole sequence of integers, terminated by a nonnumeric character, such as /. Later, we can enter individual integers, followed by one of the characters *I*, *D*, and *S*, for insertion, deletion and search, respectively. Recall that we used similar interactive commands in program *btree* in Section 7.2. However, after we enter the quit command, *Q*, the B-tree will not get lost this time, but remain safely in the tree file for subsequent use. Thus the program will be somewhat similar to a text-editor, where we can also either begin with a new file or use an existing file. However, most editors perform a special save operation at the end of a normal edit session, to store the work file onto a permanent file; by contrast, program *disktree* will be dealing with a permanent file all the time.

We now turn to the internal aspects of the program. It will be clear that in a file we cannot use normal pointers, since these have memory addresses as their values, and on disk we use positions, which are (long) integers denoting byte numbers. Recall that in C++ we can write

```
file.seekp(pos, ios::beg);
file.write((char*)&buf, sizeof(buf));
```

where *pos* is a *long int* value denoting the desired position relative to the beginning of the file. We have

$pos = 0$ for the first byte
$pos = 1$ for the second byte

and so on. In the above call *file.write*, the object *file* is of type *fstream*; the first argument *&buf* is the start address in memory from which data is to be written to the file specified in a previous call *file.open*. The number of bytes to be transmitted is given by *sizeof(buf)*. We will now use *pos*, the first argument of *seekp*, like a pointer. Instead of

```
struct node {int n; dtype k[M-1]; node *p[M];};
node *root, ...
```

we can now use

```
struct node {int n; dtype k[M-1]; long p[M];};
long root, ...
```

Each element of array p can contain a file position, and so can the variable *root*. We have now solved the problem of data representation, but there is still a more difficult question to be answered, namely how to find alternatives for the standard operators *new* and *delete*. If new nodes are to be created, where shall we place them on disk, and if nodes are to be deleted, will there be portions of unused space in the file? To begin with the latter question, we will consider such gaps acceptable, provided that they are reused as soon as any new nodes are to be inserted again. We will therefore insert new nodes in such gaps, if any; otherwise we simply append these nodes to the file. We will *not* allocate a certain amount of space in advance, and, in principle, there is no limit to the number of nodes in the tree. We want the file to be a complete representation of the tree, which implies that, given only the file, we must be able to find the position of the root node. We will therefore store the root itself, that is, the position of the root node, before all other data in the file. Also, some information about any gaps as a result of deleted nodes must be stored in the file, in order that we can start program execution with an existing file and fill the gaps when nodes are inserted. We will therefore form a *linked list* of these gaps, using pointer member $p[0]$ to point to a next gap, if any. Note that we are now using the term *pointer* for long integers which denote positions, or, in other words, byte numbers. Let us use $-1L$, and write this as *NIL*, instead of *NULL* used for real pointers in memory.

The technique used here is similar to what we did in Section 4.8, where we used an array to implement a linked list. Here we use disk storage instead, but there will again be a free list of 'deleted' nodes. We will use the *long int* variable *FreeList* as a 'pointer' to the first element of this list. If the list is empty, *FreeList* will have the value *NIL*. As long as the program is running, *root* and *FreeList* are internal variables, but we reserve room for them at the beginning of the file. At the end of program execution, just before the file is closed in our *Btree* destructor, we write the values of *root* and *FreeList* in the file. Figure 7.5 shows the file contents for the B-tree of Figure 7.2(b). The position numbers shown here are based on 32-bit *int* (and *long*) values, that is, *sizeof(int)* = *sizeof(long)* = 4. Note, however, that our program will not be based on this assumption: you can also use it if your compiler uses 16-bit integers. As you can see, with 32-bit integers, each node takes 10×4 = 40 bytes.

We are again using $M = 5$; as we know, this means that, except for the root node, there are at least two and at most four data items in each node. As in Figure 7.2(b), there are two links in the root node. Here they are represented by the long integers 8 and 48, which are the position numbers of this root node's left and right children. The root pointer *root* is equal to 88, which is the position number of the root node. In this representation, no nodes have been deleted, so the free list of deleted nodes is empty. At the end of this section there is a simple program to display the contents of a B-tree on disk in the format that we are using. This program, *showfile*, came in handy when I had to draw Figure 7.5.

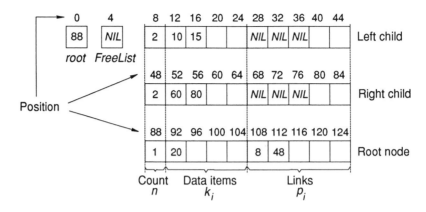

Figure 7.5 *B-tree on disk*

Actually, we will write one extra byte at the very end of the file. This byte will contain the value of *sizeof(int)*, that is 2 or 4, to be used as a *signature*, so that, in a later session, we can immediately reject the file if this value is not found there. This drastically reduces the risk of undefined actions due to the user supplying an existing file in a wrong format. For example, with *sizeof(int)* = 2 and *sizeof(long)* = 4, a hexadecimal dump of an empty B-tree (containing two *NIL* values at its beginning) will look like

```
FF FF FF FF    FF FF FF FF    02
```

while the value at the end will be 04 if *sizeof(int)* = 4.

For a B-tree on disk, a small value such as 5 for *M* may not lead to a very fast program, but, with only integer data items, the program will probably not be useful for real applications anyway; we will use it only for demonstration purposes, and it is instructive to see how fast or slow it is with *M* = 5. After all, we can then speed it up considerably in a very simple way, namely by choosing larger values for the constant *M*, such as *M* = 1000. As Figure 7.5 shows, the root node may not be the first node in the file. In fact the situation shown here with the root node at the end of the file will occur more frequently, which follows from the way B-trees grow. As this root node will be needed quite often, it will be worthwhile to have a copy of it available in main memory, although it must be said that this requirement makes the program slightly more complicated. We will use the function *ReadNode*, which normally reads a node from the file, but, instead, it uses the internal variable *RootNode* if the given pointer to the desired node happens to be equal to the variable *root*. Function *ReadNode* should not be confused with *GetNode*; the latter is to return the position of a newly created node, so it plays the role of the *new* operator in program *btree*. It first tries to obtain an element of the free list of gaps, mentioned above. If this free list is empty, there are no such gaps, so we go to the end of the file and write a node there with no well-defined contents; this may seem odd, but we need it to reserve room, so that any subsequent call to *GetNode* should not return the same location. Further details can be found in the program text itself. Complex as it is, the program is easy to use, and it may be instructive to run it on various machines to see how it behaves. As mentioned above, it will probably run faster if we increase the value of *M*. The function *NodeSearch* (to search a node for a given key) in this program is based on binary search, so it will be much faster than the one in program *btree* of Section 7.1 for large values of *M*. Except for their speed, these two versions of *NodeSearch* are completely equivalent, and apart from their first lines they are copies of the functions *LinSearch* and *BinSearch* in Section 5.2.

```
/* disktree:
   Demonstration program for a B-tree on disk. After
   building the B-tree by entering integers on the
   keyboard or by supplying them as a text file, we can
   insert and delete items via the keyboard. We can also
   search the B-tree for a given item. Each time, the tree
   or a search path is displayed. In contrast to program
   btree, program disktree writes, reads and updates nodes
   on disk, using a binary file. The name of this file is
   to be entered on the keyboard. If a B-tree with that
   name exists, that B-tree is used; otherwise such a file
   is created.
   Caution:
      Do not confuse the (binary) file for the B-tree with
      the optional textfile for input data. Use different
      file-name extensions, such as .bin and .txt.
*/

#include <fstream.h>
#include <iomanip.h>
#include <stdlib.h>
#include <ctype.h>

#define M 5   // Order of B-tree: M link fields in each node

enum status {InsertNotComplete, Success, DuplicateKey,
      Underflow, NotFound};

typedef int dtype;

struct node {
   int n;         // Number of items stored in a node (n < M)
   dtype k[M-1]; // Data items (only the first n in use)
   long p[M];     // 'Pointers' to other nodes (n+1 in use)
};

// Logical order:
//    p[0], k[0], p[1], k[1], ..., p[n-1], k[n-1], p[n]

class Btree {
public:
   Btree(const char *TreeFileName);
   ~Btree();
   void insert(dtype x);
   void insert(const char *InpFileName);
   void print(){cout << "Contents:\n"; pr(root, 0);}
   void DelNode(dtype x);
   void ShowSearch(dtype x);
```

```
private:
   enum {NIL=-1};
   long root, FreeList;
   node RootNode;
   fstream file;
   status ins(long r, dtype x, dtype &y, long &u);
   void pr(long r, int nSpace);
   int NodeSearch(dtype x, const dtype *a, int n)const;
   status del(long r, dtype x);
   void ReadNode(long r, node &Node);
   void WriteNode(long r, const node &Node);
   void ReadStart();
   long GetNode();
   void FreeNode(long r);
};

Btree::Btree(const char *TreeFileName)
{  ifstream test(TreeFileName, ios::in | ios::nocreate);
   int NewFile = test.fail();
   test.clear(); test.close();
   if (NewFile)
   {  file.open(TreeFileName, ios::out | ios::in |
         ios::trunc | ios::binary);
         // ios::binary required with MSDOS, but possibly
         // not accepted with other environments.
      root = FreeList = NIL;
      long start[2] = {NIL, NIL};
      file.write((char*)start, 2 * sizeof(long));
   } else
   {  long start[2];
      file.open(TreeFileName, ios::out | ios::in |
         ios::nocreate | ios::binary); // See above note.
      file.seekg(-1L, ios::end);
      char ch;
      file.read(&ch, 1); // Read signature.
      file.seekg(0L, ios::beg);
      file.read((char *)start, 2 * sizeof(long));
      if (ch != sizeof(int))
      {  cout << "Wrong file format.\n"; exit(1);
      }
      root = start[0]; FreeList = start[1];
      RootNode.n = 0;    // Signal for function ReadNode
      ReadNode(root, RootNode);
      print();
   }
}

Btree::~Btree()
{  long start[2];
   file.seekp(0L, ios::beg);
   start[0] = root; start[1] = FreeList;
   file.write((char*)start, 2 * sizeof(long));
   char ch = sizeof(int), ch1; // Signature
   file.seekg(-1L, ios::end); file.read(&ch1, 1);
```

```
      if (ch1 != ch)
      { file.seekp(0L, ios::end);
        file.write(&ch, 1);
      } // else signature already present.
      file.close();
   }

   void Btree::insert(dtype x)
   { long pNew;
     dtype xNew;
     status code = ins(root, x, xNew, pNew);
     if (code == DuplicateKey)
        cout << "Duplicate key ignored.\n";
     if (code == InsertNotComplete)
     { long root0 = root;
       root = GetNode();
       RootNode.n = 1; RootNode.k[0] = xNew;
       RootNode.p[0] = root0; RootNode.p[1] = pNew;
       WriteNode(root, RootNode);
     }
   }


   void Btree::insert(const char *InpFileName)
   { ifstream InpFile(InpFileName, ios::in | ios::nocreate);
     if (InpFile.fail())
     { cout << "Cannot open input file "
               << InpFileName
               << endl;
       return;
     }
     dtype x;
     while(InpFile >> x) insert(x);
     InpFile.clear(); InpFile.close();
   }


   status Btree::ins(long r, dtype x, dtype &y, long &q)
   { // Insert x in *this. If not completely successful, the
     // integer y and the pointer q remain to be inserted.
     // Return value:
     //    Success, DuplicateKey or InsertNotComplete.
     long pNew, pFinal;
     int i, j, n;
     dtype xNew, kFinal;
     status code;
     if (r == NIL){q = NIL; y = x; return InsertNotComplete;}
     node Node, NewNode;
     ReadNode(r, Node);
     n = Node.n;
     i = NodeSearch(x, Node.k, n);
     if (i < n && x == Node.k[i]) return DuplicateKey;
     code = ins(Node.p[i], x, xNew, pNew);
     if (code != InsertNotComplete) return code;
     // Insertion in subtree did not completely succeed;
     // try to insert xNew and pNew in the current node:
```

```
     if (n < M - 1)
     {  i = NodeSearch(xNew, Node.k, n);
        for (j=n; j>i; j--)
        {  Node.k[j] = Node.k[j-1]; Node.p[j+1] = Node.p[j];
        }
        Node.k[i] = xNew; Node.p[i+1] = pNew; ++Node.n;
        WriteNode(r, Node); return Success;
     }
     // Current node is full (n == M - 1) and will be split.
     // Pass item k[h] in the middle of the augmented
     // sequence back via parameter y, so that it
     // can move upward in the tree. Also, pass a pointer
     // to the newly created node back via parameter q:
     if (i == M - 1) {kFinal = xNew; pFinal = pNew;} else
     {  kFinal = Node.k[M-2]; pFinal = Node.p[M-1];
        for (j=M-2; j>i; j--)
        {  Node.k[j] = Node.k[j-1]; Node.p[j+1] = Node.p[j];
        }
        Node.k[i] = xNew; Node.p[i+1] = pNew;
     }
     int h = (M - 1)/2;
     y = Node.k[h];          // y and q are passed on to the
     q = GetNode();          // next higher level in the tree
     // The values p[0],k[0],p[1],...,k[h-1],p[h] belong to
     // the left of k[h] and are kept in *r:
     Node.n = h;
     // p[h+1],k[h+1],p[h+2],...,k[M-2],p[M-1],kFinal,pFinal
     // belong to the right of k[h] and are moved to *q:
     NewNode.n = M - 1 - h;
     for (j=0; j < NewNode.n; j++)
     {  NewNode.p[j] = Node.p[j + h + 1];
        NewNode.k[j] =
           (j < NewNode.n - 1 ? Node.k[j + h + 1] : kFinal);
     }
     NewNode.p[NewNode.n] = pFinal;
     WriteNode(r, Node); WriteNode(q, NewNode);
     return InsertNotComplete;
  }


  void Btree::pr(long r, int nSpace)
  {  if (r != NIL)
     {  int i;
        cout << setw(nSpace) << "";
        node Node; ReadNode(r, Node);
        for (i=0; i < Node.n; i++) cout << Node.k[i] << " ";
        cout << endl;
        for (i=0; i <= Node.n; i++) pr(Node.p[i], nSpace+8);
     }
  }


  int Btree::NodeSearch(dtype x, const dtype *a, int n)const
  {  int middle, left=0, right = n - 1;
     if (x <= a[left]) return 0;
     if (x > a[right]) return n;
```

```
      while (right - left > 1)
      {  middle = (right + left)/2;
         (x <= a[middle] ? right : left) = middle;
      }
      return right;
}


void Btree::ShowSearch(dtype x)
{  cout << "Search path:\n";
   int i, j, n;
   long r = root;
   node Node;
   while (r != NIL)
   {  ReadNode(r, Node);
      n = Node.n;
      for (j=0; j<Node.n; j++) cout << " " << Node.k[j];
      cout << endl;
      i = NodeSearch(x, Node.k, n);
      if (i < n && x == Node.k[i])
      {  cout << "Key " << x << " found in position " << i
            << " of last displayed node.\n";
         return;
      }
      r = Node.p[i];
   }
   cout << "Key " << x << " not found.\n";
}


void Btree::DelNode(dtype x)
{  long root0;
   switch (del(root, x))
   {
   case NotFound:
      cout << x << " not found.\n";
      break;
   case Underflow:
      root0 = root;
      root = RootNode.p[0]; FreeNode(root0);
      if (root != NIL) ReadNode(root, RootNode);
      break;
   }
}


status Btree::del(long r, dtype x)
{  if (r == NIL) return NotFound;
   node Node;
   ReadNode(r, Node);
   int i, j, pivot, n = Node.n;
   dtype *k = Node.k;   // k[i] means Node.k[i]
   const int nMin = (M - 1)/2;
   status code;
   long *p = Node.p, pL, pR;          // p[i] means Node.p[i]
   i = NodeSearch(x, k, n);
```

```
if (p[0] == NIL)  // Are we dealing with a leaf?
{  if (i == n || x < k[i]) return NotFound;
   // x == k[i]
   for (j=i+1; j < n; j++)
   {  k[j-1] = k[j]; p[j] = p[j+1];
   }
   Node.n--;
   WriteNode(r, Node);
   return Node.n >= (r==root ? 1 : nMin) ?
      Success : Underflow;
}
// *r is an interior node, not a leaf:
if (i < n && x == k[i])
{  // x found in an interior node. Go to left child
   // and follow a path all the way to a leaf,
   // using rightmost branches:
   long q = p[i], q1; int nq; node Node1;
   for (;;)
   {  ReadNode(q, Node1);
      nq = Node1.n; q1 = Node1.p[nq];
      if (q1 == NIL) break;
      q = q1;
   }
   // Exchange k[i] (= x) with rightmost item in leaf:
   k[i] = Node1.k[nq-1];
   Node1.k[nq - 1] = x;
   WriteNode(r, Node); WriteNode(q, Node1);
}
// Delete x in leaf of subtree with root p[i]:
code = del(p[i], x);
if (code != Underflow) return code;
// There is underflow; borrow, and, if necessary, merge:
// Too few data items in node *p[i]
node NodeL, NodeR;
if (i > 0)
{  pivot = i - 1; pL = p[pivot]; ReadNode(pL, NodeL);
   if (NodeL.n > nMin) // Borrow from left sibling
   {  // k[pivot] between pL and pR:
      pR = p[i];
      // Increase contents of *pR, borrowing from *pL:
      ReadNode(pR, NodeR);
      NodeR.p[NodeR.n + 1] = NodeR.p[NodeR.n];
      for (j=NodeR.n; j>0; j--)
      {  NodeR.k[j] = NodeR.k[j-1];
         NodeR.p[j] = NodeR.p[j-1];
      }
      NodeR.n++;
      NodeR.k[0] = k[pivot];
      NodeR.p[0] = NodeL.p[NodeL.n];
      k[pivot] = NodeL.k[--NodeL.n];
      WriteNode(pL, NodeL); WriteNode(pR, NodeR);
      WriteNode(r, Node);
      return Success;
   }
}
```

```
      pivot = i;
      if (i < n)
      { pR = p[pivot+1]; ReadNode(pR, NodeR);
         if (NodeR.n > nMin) // Borrow from right sibling
         { // k[pivot] between pL and pR:
            pL = p[pivot]; ReadNode(pL, NodeL);
            // Increase contents of *pL, borrowing from *pR:
            NodeL.k[NodeL.n] = k[pivot];
            NodeL.p[NodeL.n + 1] = NodeR.p[0];
            k[pivot] = NodeR.k[0];
            NodeL.n++; NodeR.n--;
            for (j=0; j < NodeR.n; j++)
            { NodeR.k[j] = NodeR.k[j+1];
               NodeR.p[j] = NodeR.p[j+1];
            }
            NodeR.p[NodeR.n] = NodeR.p[NodeR.n + 1];
            WriteNode(pL, NodeL); WriteNode(pR, NodeR);
            WriteNode(r, Node);
            return Success;
         }
      }
      // Merge; neither borrow left nor borrow right possible.
      pivot = (i == n ? i - 1 : i);
      pL = p[pivot]; pR = p[pivot+1];
      // Add k[pivot] and *pR to *pL:
      ReadNode(pL, NodeL); ReadNode(pR, NodeR);
      NodeL.k[NodeL.n] = k[pivot];
      NodeL.p[NodeL.n + 1] = NodeR.p[0];
      for (j=0; j < NodeR.n; j++)
      { NodeL.k[NodeL.n + 1 + j] = NodeR.k[j];
         NodeL.p[NodeL.n + 2 + j] = NodeR.p[j+1];
      }
      NodeL.n += 1 + NodeR.n;
      FreeNode(pR);
      for (j=i+1; j < n; j++)
      { k[j-1] = k[j]; p[j] = p[j+1];
      }
      Node.n--;
      WriteNode(pL, NodeL); WriteNode(r, Node);
      return
      Node.n >= (r == root ? 1 : nMin) ? Success : Underflow;
   }

void Btree::ReadNode(long r, node &Node)
{ if (r == NIL) return;
   if (r == root && RootNode.n > 0) Node = RootNode; else
   { file.seekg(r, ios::beg);
      file.read((char*)&Node, sizeof(node));
   }
}

void Btree::WriteNode(long r, const node &Node)
{ if (r == root) RootNode = Node;
   file.seekp(r, ios::beg);
   file.write((char*)&Node, sizeof(node));
}
```

```
void Btree::ReadStart()
{  long start[2];
   file.seekg(0L, ios::beg);
   file.read((char *)start, 2 * sizeof(long));
   root = start[0]; FreeList = start[1];
   ReadNode(root, RootNode);
}

long Btree::GetNode()
{  long r;
   node Node;
   if (FreeList == NIL)
   {  file.seekp(0L, ios::end);
      r = file.tellp();
      WriteNode(r, Node);     // Allocate space on disk
   } else
   {  r = FreeList;
      ReadNode(r, Node);      // To update FreeList:
      FreeList = Node.p[0]; // Reduce the free list by 1
   }
   return r;
}

void Btree::FreeNode(long r)
{  node Node;
   ReadNode(r, Node);
   Node.p[0] = FreeList;
   FreeList = r;
   WriteNode(r, Node);
}

int main()
{  cout <<
       "Demonstration program for a B-tree on disk. The\n"
       "structure of the B-tree is shown by indentation.\n"
       "For each node, the number of links to other nodes\n"
       "will not be greater than " << M <<
       ", the order M of the B-tree.\n" <<
       "The B-tree representation is similar to the\n"
       "table of contents of a book. The items stored in\n"
       "each node are displayed on a single line.\n\n";
   char TreeFileName[50];
   cout <<
       "Enter name of (possibly nonexistent) BINARY file for\n"
       "the B-tree: ";
   cin >> setw(50) >> TreeFileName;
   Btree t(TreeFileName);
   cout <<
       "\nEnter a (possibly empty) sequence of integers,\n"
       "followed by a slash (/):\n";
   dtype x;
   char ch = 0;
   while (cin >> x, !cin.fail())
   {  t.insert(x); ch = 1;
   }
```

```
    if (ch) t.print();
    cin.clear(); cin >> ch; // Skip terminating character
    cout <<   "\nDo you want data to be read from a text"
        "file? (Y/N): ";
    cin >> ch;
    if (toupper(ch) == 'Y')
    {   char InpFileName[50];
        cout << "Name of this textfile: ";
        cin >> setw(50) >> InpFileName;
        t.insert(InpFileName);
        t.print();
    }
    for (;;)
    {   cout <<
        "\nEnter an integer, followed by I, D, or S (for\n"
        "Insert, Delete and Search), or enter Q to quit: ";
        cin >> x >> ch;
        if (cin.fail()) break;
        ch = toupper(ch);
        switch(ch)
        {
        case 'S': t.ShowSearch(x); break;
        case 'I': t.insert(x); break;
        case 'D': t.DelNode(x); break;
        default:
            cout << "Invalid command, use S, I or D\n"; break;
        }
        if (ch == 'I' || ch == 'D') t.print();
    }
    return 0;
}
```

To see how this program can be used, let us use a very simple example. Suppose we have a text file with input data, possibly produced by program *gennum*. When this program was executed with the (very small) number 3 as input, it generated the sequence

```
2037 13756 5842
```

in a file named *gennum.txt*. This file is used in the following demonstration of program *disktree*:

```
Demonstration program for a B-tree on disk. The
structure of the B-tree is shown by indentation.
For each node, the number of links to other nodes
will not be greater than 5, the order M of the B-tree.
The B-tree representation is similar to the
table of contents of a book. The items stored in
each node are displayed on a single line.

Enter name of (possibly nonexistent) BINARY file for
the B-tree: demo.bin

Enter a (possibly empty) sequence of integers,
followed by a slash (/):
```

```
1 2 3 4 5 6/
Contents:
3
        1 2
        4 5 6


Do you want data to be read from a textfile? (Y/N): y
Name of this textfile: gennum.txt
Contents:
3 6
        1 2
        4 5
        2037 5842 13756


Enter an integer, followed by I, D, or S (for
Insert, Delete and Search), or enter Q to quit: 20 i
Contents:
3 6
        1 2
        4 5
        20 2037 5842 13756


Enter an integer, followed by I, D, or S (for
Insert, Delete and Search), or enter Q to quit: 2 d
Contents:
6
        1 3 4 5
        20 2037 5842 13756


Enter an integer, followed by I, D, or S (for
Insert, Delete and Search), or enter Q to quit: q
```

Finally, you may find the following program useful if you want to experiment with program *disktree* and to see how your B-trees are stored on disk, especially if you want to draw illustrations such as Figure 7.5. It is essential that *int* values take as many bytes in this program, *showfile*, as they do in program *disktree*. Therefore, you had better use the same C++ compiler for these two programs:

```
// showfile: Show contents of B-tree file

#include <fstream.h>
#include <iomanip.h>
#include <stdlib.h>

typedef int dtype;
#define M 5   // Order of B-tree: M link fields in each node

int main()
{   char fname[50];
    cout << "B-tree file name: ";
    cin >> setw(50) >> fname;
    ifstream file(fname, ios::in | ios::binary | ios::nocreate);
          // ios::binary required with MSDOS, but possibly
          // not accepted with other environments.
```

```
        if (file.fail())
        {  cout << "Cannot open file " << fname << endl;
           exit(1);
        }
        int i;
        long start[2], pos;
        struct node {
           int n;        // Number of items stored in a node (n < M)
           dtype k[M-1]; // Data items (only the first n in use)
           long p[M];    // 'Pointers' to other nodes (n+1 in use)
        } Node;
        file.seekg(-1L, ios::end);
        char ch;
        file.read(&ch, 1); // Read signature.
        if (ch != sizeof(int))
        {  cout << "Wrong file format.\n"; exit(1);
        }
        file.seekg(0L, ios::beg);
        file.read((char *)start, 2 * sizeof(long));
        cout << "root: " << start[0] <<
             "     Freelist: " << start[1] << endl;
        for (;;)
        {  pos = file.tellg();
           file.read((char*)&Node, sizeof(node));
           if (file.fail()) break;
           cout << "\nPosition " << setw(8) << pos << ": ";
           cout << "n = " << Node.n << "\nData : ";
           for (i=0; i<Node.n; i++)
              cout << setw(6) << Node.k[i];
           cout << "\nLinks: ";
           for (i=0; i<=Node.n; i++)
              cout << setw(8) << Node.p[i];
           cout << endl;
        }
        return 0;
     }
```

Exercises

7.1   Write a function to count how many data items have been stored in a given B-tree.

7.2   Write a function to determine the height of a B-tree.

7.3   Write a function to delete an entire B-tree.

7.4   Write and demonstrate both a copy constructor and an assignment operator for class *Btree* of Section 7.1.

7.5   Write a program, based on *btree* in Section 7.1, in which each data item consists of both a fixed-length string, used as a key, and an integer.

7.6   As Exercise 7.5, except that your program is based on *disktree* of Section 7.3.

8

Tries, Priority Queues and File Compression

8.1 Tries

This chapter is about three distinct subjects. Tries and priority queues have little in common, but we will need some knowledge of both when discussing the third subject, file compression.

In the trees of Chapters 6 and 7, each node contained one or more data items, including a key, and we have seen that this principle may require special measures to prevent those trees from becoming very unbalanced. Obviously, if a tree is to be searched efficiently, the nodes must contain certain values that enable us to decide which branch to take, and, up to now, we have taken it for granted that those values must be complete keys, identifying the data items. However, this is not absolutely necessary. Instead of using a complete key in each comparison, we can compare only a certain portion of it. This idea is the basis of a special type of tree, called a *trie*. This peculiar word is derived from the two words *tree* and *retrieval*, and, in spite of this derivation, *trie* is often pronounced as *try*, to distinguish it from *tree* in spoken language. To understand what a trie is about, let us consider an example. Our keys will be words, consisting of capital letters only, for example:

```
A
ALE
ALLOW
AN
ANY
ANYTHING
SOME
```

We will use the individual characters of the string to determine how to branch. All nonleaf nodes, called *branch nodes*, will have 27 pointer members and an integer member to be discussed later. The leaves, also called *data nodes*, will contain the information to be stored. As we have already done many times in this book, we will actually store the strings not in the data nodes themselves but rather elsewhere, which is more economical because of their variable length. An integer, n, in the data nodes will indicate how often the word has occurred in the input data. In the branch nodes, there is a pointer member for each of the letters A, ..., Z. The main rule is that branching on the mth level in the trie is determined by the mth character of the key. Figure 8.1 shows the trie for the above seven words, regardless of the order in which these words are inserted.

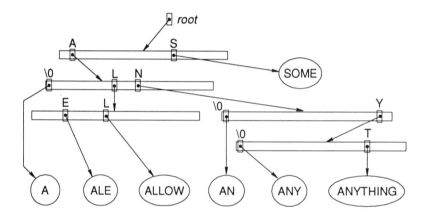

Figure 8.1 A trie

If, for example, we search the trie for the word *ALE*, we take the branch that corresponds to the letter A in the root node, then the branch corresponding to L, and, finally, the one corresponding to E. We find the word *ALLOW* similarly, but here we need only the first three letters, since there is no other word beginning with those letters to be found. We say that *ALL* is a *prefix* of the word *ALLOW* which, in contrast to the prefix *AL*, determines this word uniquely. Similarly, *ANYT* is a prefix that uniquely determines the word *ANYTHING*. At first sight, the complete word *ANY* seems to be a prefix of longer words that begin with these three letters, such as *ANYTHING*. However, the word *ANY* is actually stored in four bytes, the last one containing the null character, '\0', and we regard this also as a 'character', similar to the 26 capital letters. Our words should therefore be read as

```
A\0
ALE\0
ALLOW\0
AN\0
ANY\0
ANYTHING\0
```

In every branch node, a pointer member for '\0' precedes those for $A, B, ..., Z$. In Figure 8.1 these pointer members are marked with the corresponding character as far as they are in use. In our example, the words A, AN, ANY are at the end of arrows that start with '\0' because these words also occur at the beginning of other words (ALE, $ALLOW$ and $ANYTHING$). All pointer members that are not in use are $NULL$.

An empty trie consist only of a root pointer, called $root$ both in Figure 8.1 and in the program. This root pointer is then $NULL$. After insertion of the first word, this root pointer points directly to the data node for that word, so a trie containing only one word has no branch nodes. Suppose this first word is ANY, and the second word, $SOME$, is being inserted. A branch node, used as a root node, is now required. This node will contain two nonzero pointers, one corresponding with A and the other with S, and pointing to the data nodes for the two words in question. When more words beginning with A are inserted, branch nodes are inserted between the root node and the data node for ANY, as Figure 8.1 illustrates.

This illustration is simplified with regard to the data nodes. Actually, every data node contains two members: a character pointer, s, pointing to a null-terminated string stored elsewhere, and a word count n, indicating how often the word in question has occurred. This is illustrated more clearly in Figures 8.2 and 8.3. There is an unusual aspect in Figure 8.1: the pointers we are using can point to either a branch node or a data node. If we follow a path from the root to a leaf, we must be able to tell branch nodes from data nodes. We will therefore include an integer member $n = 0$ in every branch node. As we know, every data node also contains an integer n, which is a word count and therefore at least equal to 1. By placing n at the very beginning of the two node types, we can use this member to tell these node types apart:

$n = 0$ in a branch node;
$n > 0$ in a data node.

Since branch nodes and data nodes are of different types, it is not immediately clear which pointer types there should be in branch nodes. Fortunately, one pointer type can be converted to another by means of a cast. Consider the following fragment, which will actually occur in our program:

```
const int nBranches = 'Z' - 'A' + 2; // = 27 with ASCII
struct dnode{int n;   char *s;};
typedef dnode *ptr;
struct bnode{int n; ptr p[nBranches];};
typedef bnode *bPtr;
```

The pointer type ptr that we will normally use is actually declared as if it were used only to point to data nodes, of type $dnode$. If r is of type ptr, we cannot write

```
r->p[i]
```

since p is a member of our branch node type $bnode$. Before using the –> operator, we have to convert r from type ptr to type $bPtr$ (defined above), and this can easily be done in C++ as follows:

```
bPtr(r)->p[i]
```

With ASCII values for characters, a branch node has these members:

n:	0 (indicating that the node is a branch node)
p[0]:	a pointer corresponding to '\0'
p[1]:	a pointer corresponding to '*A*'
	. . .
p[26]:	a pointer corresponding to '*Z*'

With character values other than ASCII, the characters '*A*' to '*Z*' may not be consecutive, so that array *p* will have more than 27 elements. Although our discussion is based on ASCII values, our program will also be correct if these do not apply.

A demonstration program

We will now discuss program *trie*, which builds, prints, and searches a trie of the type we are discussing. The program will read words from a file and store them in a trie. Each data node will contain a word and a count member, the latter indicating how many occurrences of the word have been read and also being used to distinguish data nodes from branch nodes. Internally, all names will consist of capital letters only: we will convert any small letters to the corresponding capital letters. The words are separated by sequences of any characters other than letters. For example, the text file

```
a[index] = temp;
index = 0;
```

is perfectly valid as input for our program, and it is equivalent to the following file for our purposes:

```
A Index
TEMP INDEX
```

After the trie has been built, we will print all words (in capital letters) in alphabetical order, each preceded by its word count. With the above example, this part of the output would be as follows:

```
1 A
2 INDEX
1 TEMP
```

Our program also demonstrates searching the trie for words entered on the keyboard. As in Section 6.1, we assume that some key combination, such as Ctrl+Z or Ctrl+D, is interpreted as 'end of data'.

```
// trie: Demonstration program for tries
#include <stdlib.h>
#include <fstream.h>
#include <iomanip.h>
#include <string.h>
#include <ctype.h>

const int MaxWordLength = 80;
const int nBranches = 'Z' - 'A' + 2; // = 27 with ASCII
struct dnode{int n;  char *s;};
typedef dnode *ptr;
struct bnode{int n; ptr p[nBranches];};
typedef bnode *bPtr;

class trie {
public:
    trie(const char *fname);
    void insert(const char *s);
    void print()
    {  if (root){cout << "Contents of trie:\n"; pr(root);}
        else cout << "Empty trie.\n";
    }
    ptr search(const char *s);
private:
    void pr(const ptr r);
    ptr NewNode(const char *s = NULL);
    int position(char ch){return ch ? ch - 'A' + 1 : 0;}
    ptr root;
};

int GetWord(istream &f, char *s)
{  char ch;
    int i;
    do
    {  f >> ch; ch = toupper(ch);
        if (f.fail()) return 0;
    }  while (ch < 'A' || ch > 'Z');
    for (i=0; i<MaxWordLength-1; )
    {  s[i++] = ch;
        f.get(ch); ch = toupper(ch);
        if (f.fail() || ch < 'A' || ch > 'Z') break;
    }
    s[i] = '\0';
    return i;
}

trie::trie(const char *fname)
{  char s[MaxWordLength + 1];
    ifstream file(fname, ios::in | ios::nocreate);
    if (file.fail())
    {  cout << "Cannot open input file.\n"; exit(1);
    }
    root = NULL;
    while (GetWord(file, s) > 0) insert(s);
}
```

```
void trie::insert(const char *s)
{   int m = 0;
    ptr *pp = &root, q;
      // pp contains the address of the current pointer
      // q will be a copy of this current pointer
    for (;;)
    {   q = *pp;
        if (q == NULL){*pp = NewNode(s); return;}
        if (q->n > 0)   // Data node:
        {   if (strcmp(s, q->s) == 0)
            {   q->n++;
                return;
            }
            // Prefix s[0], ..., s[m-1] of new word identical
            // with that of existing word q->s.
            // Insert a new branch node between pointer
            // *pp and data node *q, and continue at next level:
            ptr q0 = q;
            *pp = q = NewNode();
            int j = position(q0->s[m]);
            bPtr(q)->p[j] = q0;
        }
        int i = position(s[m++]);
        pp = & bPtr(q)->p[i];   // Go to next level to insert s
    }
}


void trie::pr(const ptr r)
{   if (r->n)     // n > 0: r points to data node
        cout << setw(5) << r->n << " " << r->s << endl;
    else          // n = 0: r points to a branch node
    for (int i=0; i<nBranches; i++)
    {   ptr q = bPtr(r)->p[i];
        if (q)
            pr(q);
    }
}


ptr trie::NewNode(const char *s)
{   ptr q;
    if (s) // New data node:
    {   q = new dnode;
        q->n = 1;
        q->s = new char[strlen(s) + 1];
        strcpy(q->s, s);
    } else // New branch node:
    {   bPtr qb = new bnode;
        qb->n = 0;
        for (int i=0; i<nBranches; i++)
            qb->p[i] = NULL;
        q = ptr(qb);
    }
    return q;
}
```

```
ptr trie::search(const char *s)
{  ptr r = root;
   char ch;
   int m=0, i;
   while (r && r->n == 0) // While r points to branch node
   {  ch = s[m++];
      i = position(ch);
      if (i < 0 || i >= nBranches) return NULL;
      r = bPtr(r)->p[i];
   }
   return r && strcmp(s, r->s) == 0 ? r : NULL;
}

int main()
{  char fname[50], s[MaxWordLength + 1];
   ptr q;
   cout <<
      "This program can read any text file. Then for any\n"
      "word (consisting of at most " << MaxWordLength
      << " letters), you can\n"
      "ask how often that word occurs in this file.\n"
      "Input file: ";
   cin >> setw(50) >> fname;
   trie t(fname); // Create entire trie
   t.print();
   for (;;)
   {  cout << "\nEnter a word, or type Ctrl+Z (or Ctrl+D) "
         "to stop: ";
      if (GetWord(cin, s) == 0) break;
      q = t.search(s);
      if (q) cout << "Word found, count = " << q->n << endl;
      else cout << "Word not found.\n";
   }
   return 0;
}
```

It is a good idea to study the member functions *trie*, *print*, *pr*, and *search* of class *trie* as a preparation for the more difficult function *insert*. This function is the most interesting one of the program. Note that *pp* is a pointer to a pointer; its value is the address of a pointer pointing to a node, unless it is *NULL*. If you still find pointers to pointers hard to understand, Figure 8.2 may be helpful.

You can easily see what happens the very first time *insert* is called. The root pointer *root* is then *NULL*, so in this case the *insert* function does little more than executing the statement

```
*pp = NewNode(s);
```

which creates a new data node, stores the word *s*, and places the address of this data node in the root pointer, the address of which is the value of *pp*. In the for-loop, starting with

```
for(;;)
```

we follow a path starting at the root node and following branch nodes, for which $q{-}{>}n$ is zero. If we end with $q == NULL$, we can simply create a new data node for word s and place the address of that node in $*pp$. Except for the very first time as just discussed, $*pp$ is in fact an element $p[i]$, previously equal to $NULL$, in a branch node. We have another simple case if word s turns out to have already been stored in the tree. If this happens, and $*q$ is the data node in question, increasing the count member by

```
q->n++
```

is all we need to do.

What remains is the situation where $*q$ is a data node in which we find a word different from s, but with the same m initial letters as s. We then use the fragment

```
ptr q0 = q;
*pp = q = NewNode();
int j = position(q0->s[m]);
bPtr(q)->p[j] = q0;
```

to insert a new branch node. Figure 8.2 shows the situation just after the execution of the first of the above four statements. While trying to insert the new word $s = PROGRAM$, we encounter the word $q{-}{>}s = PROBLEM$, stored previously, exactly at the position that we want to use for the new word. This happens because we have $s[2] = q{-}{>}s[2] = 'O'$, and only the first three letters of $PROBLEM$ have been used to determine the position of this word in the trie. It will be clear that we also have to use its fourth letter, B, so we have to insert a new branch node. This is what the above fragment does, giving the result shown in Figure 8.3. Since we have $m = 3$, the third of the above four statements finds the position of pointer $p[j]$, with $q0{-}{>}m = 'B'$ and $j = 2$. Recall that the values $j = 0, 1, 2, ..., 26$ correspond with the characters $\backslash 0, A, B, ..., Z$. You may be disappointed that the new word, $PROGRAM$, has not yet been stored, but that will be taken care of in the next step of the for-loop, after increasing m. Some comments in the function $insert$ will also be helpful in understanding this function.

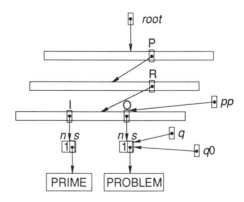

Figure 8.2 Situation when word PROGRAM is about to be inserted

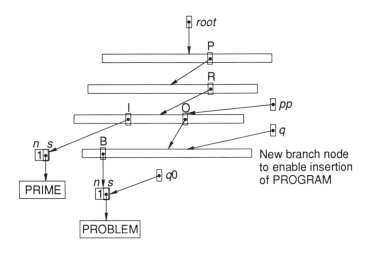

Figure 8.3 *New branch node inserted to prepare for new word PROGRAM*

Function *GetWord* in program *trie* skips all non-alphabetic characters and converts lower case letters to capital. Thanks to this function, we can use any text file as input for this program. To illustrate this, here is a demonstration in which the program is supplied with its own source code (that is, file *trie*) as input data. Since there are a great many distinct words in this file, the middle part of the alphabetic list of words is omitted to save space in this book:

```
This program can read any text file. Then for any
word (consisting of at most 80 letters), you can
ask how often that word occurs in this file.
Input file: trie.cpp
Contents of trie:
     8 A
     1 ADDRESS
     2 AND

   ...    (middle part of output omitted)

     7 WORD
     1 YOU
     4 Z

Enter a word, or type Ctrl+Z (or Ctrl+D) to stop: this
Word found, count = 3

Enter a word, or type Ctrl+Z (or Ctrl+D) to stop: ^Z
```

Not only words in the input file but also those entered on the keyboard are converted to capital letters, so the word *this* to be search for is actually converted into *THIS*.

From a user's point of view, program *trie* is very similar to program *bintree* of Section 6.1. If the words in an input file happen to occur in alphabetic order, the binary tree constructed by *bintree* will be degenerated, while there is no such problem with our *trie* program. On the other hand, tries are not particularly economical with memory space, especially because there are 27 pointers in each of our branch nodes. Instead of using arrays with 27 elements, we could use linked lists, with nodes only for the elements that are in use, but this would require additional space for the links of such lists. Besides, searching such linked lists would take more time than selecting elements in our arrays. However, the type of trie we have been discussing is very efficient with respect to time. Tries are suitable data structures for spell-checking programs. The data nodes would then contain the words of a dictionary.

We could use only branch nodes and no data nodes at all, provided that, instead of a unique prefix, all letters of each word are used in the branching process. But, unfortunately, we would then need many additional branch nodes, which may cost more than we would gain by omitting the data nodes. To use the best of both worlds, we can save space in the data nodes by omitting the characters of the prefix used in the search process. For example, in Figure 8.3, we could have stored only *LEM* instead of *PROBLEM*, omitting the first four characters *P*, *R*, *O* and *B* since these have been used to arrive at the data node, so they are already known.

We have not discussed how trie nodes can be deleted. This can be done, and is considerably simpler than deleting nodes in a B-tree, as we discussed in Section 7.2. If the option of deleting nodes is available, we could use it in a spell checker. We have just suggested that the trie should contain all words of a dictionary, so that we can search the trie for each word in the text that is to be checked. Alternatively, we can proceed the other way round, storing each word of the text in question (only once) in a trie and then searching the trie for each word in the dictionary. Each time a word is found, we delete it from the trie, so that the trie gradually shrinks. When all words of the dictionary have been searched for, any remaining words in the trie are just those which do not occur in the dictionary. Obviously, this method is feasible only if the dictionary is very limited in size. A curious point is that in this way we do not benefit from the alphabetic order of the dictionary. This observation suggests yet another method, namely *traversing* the trie (rather than searching it), so that we encounter all words of our text in alphabetic order, and at the same time scan the dictionary sequentially, each time comparing a word in the trie with a word in the dictionary.

There is another aspect of tries that deserves our attention, namely that a trie is a very suitable means to search for all words with a given prefix. For example, we may want to enter *COM* to obtain a list of words beginning with this prefix, such as

COMMAND, COMPILER, COMPUTE, COMPUTER, COMPUTING

As a final remark, it should be mentioned that we can implement a trie on disk rather than in memory, as we did for B-trees in Section 7.3. This will slow down the search process considerably, but, provided that it is still fast enough for our application, we may benefit from this method because of the large capacity of disks. Another favorable point is the permanent nature of disk files, compared with data in main memory.

8.2 A Priority Queue Implemented as a Heap

We have often been dealing with collections of items, each of which contains a unique key. Instead, we will now consider items that contain a special member called its *priority*, which need not be unique. A *priority queue* is such a set for which two operations are defined:

1. Adding an item.
2. Extracting the item that has the highest priority.

You can think of a priority queue as a set of tasks with priorities. At any time a new task can be added. Also, a task can be removed from the priority queue, but this can only be the one with the highest priority. If this highest priority is shared by more than one task, we do not care which one is taken.

As we have often done in this book, we will simplify this subject by omitting any 'satellite data' in the items: the priority will be the sole member of each item. Unlike sets, such simple priority queues can contain several copies of the same item. Instead of integers, let us use characters as items, with their values as priorities. For example, beginning with an empty priority queue, we may successively add the items

p, b, r, h, p, a, h

If we now remove all items one by one, we will obtain these in the reverse alphabetic order:

r, p, p, h, h, b, a

It follows from the above description that a priority queue is an abstract concept, not a concrete data structure. Since we want to focus on programming, we will now see how to implement priority queues. A very efficient data structure for priority queues is a *heap*, which we have also encountered in Section 3.9, when dealing with heapsort. As discussed there, a heap is an array, of which we use the first n elements

```
a[0], a[1], ..., a[n-1]
```

satisfying the *heap condition*

$$a[i] \geq a[2 * i + 1]$$
$$a[i] \geq a[2 * i + 2]$$

Since the first element, $a[0]$, is the largest, no searching is required if we want to remove the largest value of the heap. Yet the remove operation is not trivial, because the gap at position 0 must be filled. We can do this by moving the final item, $a[n-1]$, to this position and then 'sifting' it to the right, as we did in Section 3.9:

```
char PrQ::remove()
{   char ch = a[0];
    a[0] = a[--n];
    sift0();
    return ch;
}
```

Recall that sifting an element means that if necessary, starting with $i = 0$, we repeatedly replace $a[i]$ with the larger of its two 'children' $a[2 * i + 1]$ and $a[2 * i + 2]$, until the 'parent' $a[i]$ is no longer less than these children. (We will see in a moment why we use the words 'children' and 'parent' here.) The gap at the position of the latest moved child is then filled up with the original value of $a[0]$:

```
void PrQ::sift0()
{   int i = 0, j;
    char x;
    x = a[0];
    while ((j = 2 * i + 1) < n)
    {   if (j < n - 1 && a[j] < a[j+1]) j++;
        if (x >= a[j]) break;
        a[i] = a[j]; i = j;
    }
    a[i] = x;
}
```

Using the above example, we can see how this works by demonstrating program *prqchar*, which we will see in a moment. The seven letters p, b, r, h, p, a, h are entered one by one, and the heap is shown after each insertion. Then three times the character at position 0 is removed. Note that at any time the removed item is the 'greatest' of all elements that are still present in the heap:

```
A priority queue implemented as a heap.
Enter letters to insert, - to remove, or / to quit.

Enter a letter or a command (- or /): p
        i ->:  0
     a[i] ->:  p

Enter a letter or a command (- or /): b
        i ->:  0  1
     a[i] ->:  p  b

Enter a letter or a command (- or /): r
        i ->:  0  1  2
     a[i] ->:  r  b  p

Enter a letter or a command (- or /): h
        i ->:  0  1  2  3
     a[i] ->:  r  h  p  b

Enter a letter or a command (- or /): p
        i ->:  0  1  2  3  4
     a[i] ->:  r  p  p  b  h
```

```
Enter a letter or a command (- or /): a
      i  ->:  0   1   2   3   4   5
   a[i] ->:   r   p   p   b   h   a

Enter a letter or a command (- or /): h
      i  ->:  0   1   2   3   4   5   6
   a[i] ->:   r   p   p   b   h   a   h

Enter a letter or a command (- or /): -
      i  ->:  0   1   2   3   4   5
   a[i] ->:   p   h   p   b   h   a

Enter a letter or a command (- or /): -
      i  ->:  0   1   2   3   4
   a[i] ->:   p   h   a   b   h

Enter a letter or a command (- or /): -
      i  ->:  0   1   2   3
   a[i] ->:   h   h   a   b

Enter a letter or a command (- or /): /
```

The terms 'child' and 'parent' will be clear if we realize that a heap is in fact an array representation of a special type of binary tree. This is illustrated by Figure 8.4, which shows the binary tree that corresponds with our heap just after insertion of all seven items.

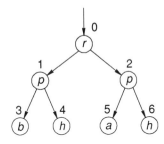

Figure 8.4 Heap illustrated by a binary tree

The numbers above the circles are position numbers *i*. For example, there is a 3 above the circle containing *b* because $a[3]$ = '*b*'. Note that this tree is *not* a binary search tree. The difference between the two tree types is as follows:

Binary search tree: left descendants ≤ parent ≤ right descendants
Heap: left descendants ≤ parent *and* right descendants ≤ parent

We now see that in the sifting process we follow a path from the root to a leaf, or at least part of it. The opposite direction, from leaf to root, is taken in insert operations. You can find the *insert* function in the following class template:

```
// priorq.h: Template for priority queue
#define nil (-1)

template <class T>
class PrQ {
public:
    PrQ(int size, int increment=10)
    {   N = size; a = new T[N];
        n = 0; ChunkSize = increment;
    }
    ~PrQ(){delete[]a;}
    void insert(T x);
    T remove();
    int empty(){return n == 0;}
protected:
    T *a;
    int N, n, ChunkSize;
    int parent(int i){return (i-1)/2;}
    int left(int i){return 2 * i + 1;}
    int right(int i){return 2 * i + 2;}
    void sift0();
};

template <class T>
void PrQ<T>::insert(T x)
{   int i, j;
    if (n == N)
    {   T *aOld = a;
        a = new T[N += ChunkSize];
        for (i=0; i<n; i++) a[i] = aOld[i];
        delete[] aOld;
    }
    i = n++;
    while (i > 0 && x > a[j = parent(i)])
    {   a[i] = a[j]; i = j;
    }
    a[i] = x;
}

template <class T>
T PrQ<T>::remove()
{   T x = a[0];
    a[0] = a[--n]; sift0(); return x;
}

template <class T>
void PrQ<T>::sift0()
{   int i = 0, j;
    T x;
    x = a[0];
    while ((j = 2 * i + 1) < n)
    {   if (j < n - 1 && a[j+1] > a[j]) j++;
        if (a[j] > x){a[i] = a[j]; i = j;} else break;
    }
    a[i] = x;
}
```

To understand how this works, we want to display successive heap contents. Since a display function for this is normally not required, it is not included in the above *PrQ* template. Fortunately, C++ enables us to define such a function in a class derived from a class such as *PrQ<char>*. In the following program, this derived class is named *CharPrQ*. In addition to the member functions of its base class, this derived class also has a member function *display*, which produces the output in the demonstration that we saw a short while ago.

```
// prqchar: A priority queue for characters

#include <iostream.h>
#include <iomanip.h>
#include <string.h>

#include "priorq.h"

class CharPrQ: public PrQ<char> {
public:
    CharPrQ(int size, int increment): PrQ<char>(size,
increment){}
    void display();
};

void CharPrQ::display()
{   int i;
    cout << "       i  ->:";
    for (i=0; i<n; i++) cout << setw(3) << i;
    cout << endl;
    cout << "    a[i] ->:";
    for (i=0; i<n; i++) cout << setw(3) << a[i];
    cout << endl;
}

int main()
{   CharPrQ Q(10, 5); // Initial N = 10, ChunkSize = 5
    char ch;
    cout << "A priority queue implemented as a heap.\n";
    cout << "Enter letters to insert, - to remove, or "
            "/ to quit.\n";
    for (;;)
    {   cout << "\nEnter a letter or a command (- or /): ";
        cin >> ch;
        if (ch == '/') break;
        if (ch == '-')
        {   if (Q.empty())
                cout << "Cannot remove from empty queue.\n";
            else ch = Q.remove(); // ch not used here
        } else Q.insert(ch);
        Q.display();
    }
    return 0;
}
```

You may wonder why we should use a heap to implement a priority queue, rather than, say, a sorted array. The remove operation would then simply consist of taking the final array element and decreasing the logical array length n. However, the insert operation would then take more time than it does with a heap. Since on average half the number of elements would have to be shifted to the right, the time required for insertion with a sorted array implementation would be $O(n)$, while it is only $O(\log n)$ with a heap.

8.3 The Huffman Algorithm for File Compression

We will now discuss an application of priority queues which is also related to tries. The subject to be dealt with is an algorithm for file compression, based on a well-known method due to Huffman. Although we will not restrict ourselves to textfiles, let us begin with a file in which only a very small vocabulary is used, say, the nine letters A, B, ..., I. For each of these characters, when occurring in a textfile, we normally use eight bits. Since there are only nine characters in our example, and $9 \leq 2^4$, a code with only four instead of eight bits would be sufficient. For example, using $A = 0000$, $B = 0001$, $C = 0010$, ..., $I = 1000$, we could represent the string

   AAABBBCCDEFGGGGGHHII

by a sequence of $20 \times 4 = 80$ bits instead of 20×8 bits with the traditional coding of one character per byte. However, we can do even better, provided we use a code of *variable length*. The idea is that we want to use very few bits for characters that occur often, such as G in our example. We accept that a price has to be paid for this: characters with low frequency, D and E in the example, may take considerably more bits. To avoid ambiguity in the decoding process, the code of one character must not be a prefix of another. Codes meeting this requirement are referred to as *prefix codes*. For example, 101 and 1010 cannot both appear as codes. The following *code table* for the above nine characters has no such problems:

$A =$	101	$D =$	11010	$G =$	01
$B =$	111	$E =$	11011	$H =$	001
$C =$	100	$F =$	1100	$I =$	000

The lengths of these codes are based on the frequency of the characters A, ..., I in the above 20-character string: this length is 5 for the letters D and E (occurring only once) and only 2 for G (which occurs as many as five times). This code table has been constructed by means of the *Huffman algorithm*. This is based on a binary tree, known as a *Huffman tree* and shown in Figure 8.5.

The code length of each character is equal to the number of arrows between the root node and the leaf containing that character. Also, starting at the root node, a left link corresponds with 0, a right one with 1. For example, starting at the root node, we find $D = 11010$ (with length 5) by taking five steps, in this order: right, right, left, right, left. If we are given a Huffman tree and a code for an unknown character, we can follow the path that corresponds to this code to find that character in a leaf. In other words, we can use this tree straightforwardly for *decompression*.

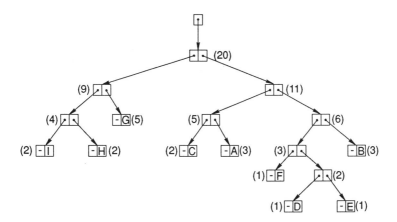

Figure 8.5 *Huffman tree for text AAABBBCCDEFGGGGGHHII*

Since branching is based on the individual positions of a code, we see that a Huffman tree is very similar to a *trie*, with codes acting as words. Unlike normal tries, a Huffman tree is a binary tree because the 'words' are binary numbers. Another difference is that the actual data stored in each data node is the character that belongs to the code in question, not that code itself.

Since a Huffman tree is constructed on the basis of character frequencies, these are given in Figure 8.5 between parentheses. The parenthesized numbers for each nonleaf node indicate the sum of the frequencies of its two children, which is equal to the sum of all its leaf descendants. For example, for the subtree on the left we have $9 = 4 + 5 = 2 + 2 + 5$. The frequencies appear in Figure 8.5 outside the nodes because they are not stored in the tree. Every nonleaf node of a Huffman tree has exactly two children; trees with this characteristic are said to be *full* (or *strictly*) *binary trees* (see Exercise 6.12).

Although this is by no means essential, we can represent this tree efficiently in an array. Each element $A[i]$ of this array is a record consisting of two integers, *left* and *RightOrCh*. Our 'characters' will be integers ranging from 0 to 255, and our link fields will be subscript values. Since data is stored only in leaves, each node contains either two such link fields or only a 'character'. This 'character' and the right-hand link field can share the same record member, and we can tell leaves from nonleaf nodes by testing their *left* members: these are *nil* only for leaves. The following header file shows how we can realize this.

```
// huffman.h
#include <fstream.h>
#include <string.h>
#include <iomanip.h>
#include <stdlib.h>
#define nil (-1)
typedef unsigned char uchar;
typedef unsigned short ushort;
typedef unsigned long ulong;

void GetStreams(ifstream &ifile, ofstream &ofile);
```

```
inline void error(const char *s)
{   cout << "Error: " << s << endl; exit(1);
}

struct node {int left, RightOrCh;};

class HuffmanTree {
public:
   HuffmanTree(const ulong *freq);
   ~HuffmanTree(){delete[]A;}
   int NewNode(int left, int x)
   {   A[n].left = left; A[n++].RightOrCh = x;
       return n - 1;
   }
   node *A;
   int n, root;
};
```

As the constructor of class *HuffmanTree* suggests, we base a Huffman tree on the frequency distribution of the 'characters' in the input file. The actual Huffman algorithm uses a priority queue, with the character with the lowest (not, as usual, the highest) frequency returned by the *remove* operation. Since our program will accept any file, all possible 256 byte contents will be regarded as 'characters'. After we have made a frequency distribution for the input file, we insert an item in our priority queue for every character with nonzero frequency. Figure 8.6 illustrates this. At this stage, each item in the priority queue consists of both the frequency count of a character and a link *ptr* referring to a node that eventually will be a leaf of the Huffman tree and that contains that character. The two *freq* values shown in Figure 8.6 are equal to 1 because both *D* and *E* occur only once in the input string.

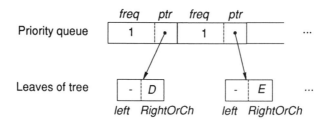

Figure 8.6 *Priority queue before any nodes are removed*

In a loop, the items for the two characters with the lowest frequencies are extracted and the sum of their frequencies is computed. Then a single item is inserted, containing both this sum and a link to a newly created node, which in turn refer to the nodes that the two extracted items pointed to. Figure 8.7 illustrates the situation when this has happened the first time. The *freq* value shown here is 2 = 1 + 1.

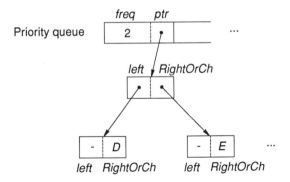

Figure 8.7 *Situation after creation of the first nonleaf node*

The tree is constructed bottom-up in this way, with the priority queue shrinking while the tree grows. Since at any time we take the lowest frequencies first, leaves for characters with low frequencies will be farther away from the root than those for characters with high frequencies. For example, the lowest-frequency characters D and E are found at the very bottom of the final tree, so that their Huffman codes are longest.

The following module is to be used by both the compression and the decompression programs. You can find the loop just mentioned in the *HuffmanTree* constructor.

```
// huffman.cpp: To be linked with huffman1 or huffman2
#include "huffman.h"
#include "priorq.h"

void GetStreams(ifstream &ifile, ofstream &ofile)
{   char iname[50], oname[50];
    cout << "Name of input file:   ";
    cin >> setw(50) >> iname;
    ifile.open(iname, ios::in | ios::nocreate | ios::binary);
        // ios::binary required with MSDOS, but possibly
        // not accepted with other environments.
    if (ifile.fail()) error("Cannot open input file.");
    cout << "Name of output file: ";
    cin >> setw(50) >> oname;
    ofile.open(oname, ios::out | ios::trunc | ios::binary);
        // See above note.
    if (ofile.fail()) error("Cannot open output file.");
}

struct item
{   ulong freq;
    int ptr;
    item(){}
    item(ulong f, int p): freq(f), ptr(p){}
    int operator>(item &x){return freq < x.freq;}
    // u > v defined as u.freq < v.freq because we want
    // the items to appear in ascending (not in descending)
    // order of frequency.
};
```

```
HuffmanTree::HuffmanTree(const ulong *freq)
{  A = new node[511];
      // At most 256 leaves and 511 = 2 * 256 - 1 nodes,
      // see Exercise 6.12.
   n = 0;
   PrQ<item> Q(256);  // Size of priority queue
   for (int j=0; j<256; j++)
      if (freq[j]) Q.insert(item(freq[j], NewNode(nil, j)));
   item t1, t2;
   if (Q.empty()) error("Empty input file."); else
   {  for (;;)
      {  t1 = Q.remove();
         if (Q.empty()) break;
         t2 = Q.remove();
         Q.insert(item(t1.freq + t2.freq,
            NewNode(t1.ptr, t2.ptr)));
      }
      root = t1.ptr;
   }
}
```

The process of file compression consists of these five steps:

1. Setting up a frequency table for all 'characters' that occur in the input file.
2. Building a Huffman tree.
3. Constructing a code table t, each entry $t[ch]$ of which contains both the Huffman code of 'character' ch and the length, that is, the number of bits, of this code.
4. Writing the frequency table in a compact form to the output file.
5. Reading the input file once again, and, for each 'character', writing the corresponding code to the output file.

We implement step 3 by recursively traversing the tree, keeping track of the path we follow from the root node to a leaf. In each recursive step, we place a 0-bit at the end of the current code if we take the left branch and a 1-bit if we take the right branch. At the same time we increase the code length by 1.

Step 4 will enable us to reconstruct the Huffman tree in the decompression program. Instead of the frequency table, we could have written this tree itself to the output file, since we have implemented it in an array. Unfortunately, that would make the output file larger, and we want it to be as small as possible. We could perform step 4 in this single statement:

```
ofile.write((char *)freq, sizeof(freq));
```

This would result in writing $256 \times 4 = 1024$ bytes to the compressed file (that is, if *sizeof(long)* = 4). It is worthwhile to use a more compact format. We do this by first determining the smallest possible range *jLower*, ..., *jUpper* of values *j* which includes all nonzero array elements *freq[j]*. For this range we deal with consecutive subranges of frequencies that fit into the same format. Using the data types *unsigned char*, *unsigned short* and *unsigned long* for these formats, we avoid, for example, using four bytes for very low frequencies. Each such subsequence of frequencies in the same format is preceded by a control byte, indicating both which format applies and how long the sequence is. For a consecutive sequence of zero frequencies we write only the control bytes. Thus, altogether we have four formats: zero, one byte, unsigned short and unsigned long, and we code these as two bits 00, 01, 10 and 11, respectively in the control byte, using the remaining six bits of the control byte for the length of the sequence. (If such a sequence happens to be longer than 63, we split it so each sequence length fits into six bits.)

The very last code written in step 5 may end anywhere in the middle of a byte, so it may be followed by some (zero) bits to round the number of bits up to a multiple of 8. To enable the decompression program to determine how many bits are relevant in the last byte written in step 5, we write that number, ranging from 1 to 8, as an additional byte at the very end of the file.

The following program takes the five steps above. It uses the header file *huffman.h* and the *huffman.cpp* module we have already seen:

```
// huffman1: File compression (to be linked with huffman.cpp)

#include <limits.h>
#include "huffman.h"

struct TableItem {unsigned code, len;}; // For code table

void traverse(HuffmanTree &Tr, TableItem *t, int p,
   unsigned code, int len)
{  if (Tr.A[p].left == nil)
   {  uchar ch = Tr.A[p].RightOrCh;
      t[ch].code = code;
      t[ch].len = len;
   }  else
   {  code <<= 1; len++;
      traverse(Tr, t, Tr.A[p].left, code, len);
      traverse(Tr, t, Tr.A[p].RightOrCh, code | 1, len);
   }
}

uchar FindLenCode(ulong f)
{  return f > USHRT_MAX ? 3 :
          f > UCHAR_MAX ? 2 : (f != 0);
// Code for number of bytes that each frequency takes:
// 00 -> zero, 01 -> one, 10 -> two, 11 -> four
}

void WriteFreqTable(ofstream &ofile, const ulong *freq)
{  /* Frequencies will now be written to ofile in a compact
      form. We deal with the smallest possible range
      freq[jLower], ..., freq[jUpper] that includes all
      nonzero elements of array freq. We divide this sequence
      into consecutive subsequences, each with elements of a
      fixed length. Each of these subsequences is preceded
      by a control byte, consisting of a 2-bit length code
      followed by six bits indicating how many of such
      frequencies follow in that sequence.
   */
```

```
        int jLower = 0, jUpper = 255, j, j0, LenCode;
        ulong f;
        ushort u;
        while (jLower < 256 && freq[jLower] == 0) jLower++;
        while (freq[jUpper] == 0) jUpper--;
        ofile.put((uchar) jLower);
        ofile.put((uchar) jUpper);
        for (j0 = jLower; j0 <= jUpper; )
        {   LenCode = FindLenCode(freq[j0]);
            j = j0 + 1;
            while (j<=jUpper && j - j0 < 0x3F &&
                FindLenCode(freq[j]) == LenCode) j++;
            ofile.put(uchar((LenCode << 6) | (j - j0)));
            while (j0 < j)
            {   f = freq[j0++];
                switch(LenCode){
                case 1: ofile.put(uchar(f)); break;
                case 2: u = ushort(f);
                        ofile.write((char*)&u, sizeof(ushort)); break;
                case 3: ofile.write((char*)&f, sizeof(ulong)); break;
                }
            }
        }
    }

int main()
{   ifstream ifile;
    ofstream ofile;
    cout << "Huffman file compression.\n";
    GetStreams(ifile, ofile);
    ulong freq[256];
    uchar ch;
    int j, k, b;
    for (j=0; j<256; j++) freq[j] = 0;
    while (ifile.get(ch), !ifile.fail()) freq[ch]++;
    ifile.clear(); ifile.seekg(0, ios::beg);
    HuffmanTree Tr(freq);
    TableItem t[256]; // t is the code table
    for (int i=0; i<256; i++) t[i].code = t[i].len = 0;
    traverse(Tr, t, Tr.root, 0, 0);
    WriteFreqTable(ofile, freq);
    uchar buf = 0;
    k = 0;
    while (ifile.get(ch), !ifile.fail())
    {   for (int i=t[ch].len-1; i>=0; i--)
        {   b = (t[ch].code >> i) & 1;
            if (k < 8){buf = (buf << 1) | b; k++;} else
            {   ofile.put(buf); buf = b; k = 1;
            }
        }
    }
    ofile.put(char(buf << (8 - k)));
    ofile.put(char(k)); // k relevant bits in last byte
    return 0;
}
```

After paying so much attention to data compression, implemented in the above program *huffman*1, the opposite operation of *data decompression* will be comparatively simple. It is realized by program *huffman*2, listed below. If we use the output of *huffman*1 as input for *huffman*2, we obtain an exact copy of the original file, used as input for *huffman*1. After reading (and decoding) the frequency table, we construct the Huffman tree in the same way as we did in program *huffman*1. Thanks to the separate module *huffman.cpp* and the header file *huffman.h*, this requires very little code in program *huffman*2.

When reading the actual codes, we use three variables, *buf*1, *buf*2 and *buf*3, normally containing the values of three successive bytes of the input file. When we are dealing with *buf*1, we want to know whether *buf*3 has successfully been read. If this is not the case, we know that *buf*2 contains the very last byte of the file, so that it is equal to the number of relevant bits in *buf*1.

```
// huffman2: File decompression (to be linked with
//           huffman.cpp)
#include "huffman.h"

void ReadFreqTable(ifstream &ifile, ulong *freq)
{  uchar jLower, jUpper, ch, ControlByte, LenCode;
   ushort u;
   ulong f;
   int j, j0;
   for (j=0; j<256; j++) freq[j] = 0;
   ifile.get(jLower);
   ifile.get(jUpper);
   for (j = jLower; j <= jUpper; )
   {  j0 = j;
      ifile.get(ControlByte);
      LenCode = ControlByte >> 6;
      j = j0 + (ControlByte & 0x3F);
      while (j0 < j)
      {  switch(LenCode) {
         case 0: f = 0; break;
         case 1: ifile.get(ch); f = ch; break;
         case 2: ifile.read((char*)&u, sizeof(ushort));
                 f = u; break;
         case 3: ifile.read((char*)&f, sizeof(ulong)); break;
         }
         freq[j0++] = f;
      }
   }
}

int main()
{  ifstream ifile;
   ofstream ofile;
   cout << "Huffman file decompression.\n";
   GetStreams(ifile, ofile);
   ulong freq[256];
   ReadFreqTable(ifile, freq);
   HuffmanTree Tr(freq);
   int root = Tr.n - 1, p = root, b, nBits;
   unsigned char buf1, buf2, buf3;
```

```
      ifile.get(buf1); ifile.get(buf2);
      for (;;)
      {  ifile.get(buf3);
         nBits = (ifile.fail() ? buf2 : 8);
         for (int i=0; i<nBits; i++)
         {  b = (buf1 >> 7) & 1;
            buf1 <<= 1;
            p = (b ? Tr.A[p].RightOrCh : Tr.A[p].left);
            if (Tr.A[p].left == nil)
            {  ofile.put(char(Tr.A[p].RightOrCh));
               p = root;
            }
         }
         if (ifile.fail()) break;
         buf1 = buf2; buf2 = buf3;
      }
      return 0;
   }
```

The following demonstration shows how we can compress the source file *disktree.cpp*, using the program *huffman*1:

```
Huffman file compression.
Name of input file:  disktree.cpp
Name of output file: disktree.bin
```

The compressed file *disktree.bin* is now decompressed by program *huffman*2, resulting in the file *disktree.out*, which is an exact copy of the original file, *disktree.cpp*:

```
Huffman file decompression.
Name of input file:  disktree.bin
Name of output file: disktree.out
```

The sizes of the three files in question, obtained by using the command *dir disktree.**, are listed below:

```
DISKTREE CPP        14,296
DISKTREE BIN         8,803
DISKTREE OUT        14,296
```

Exercises

8.1   In the tries in this chapter, we used arrays of 27 pointer members because we distinguished only the 26 capital letters. If, instead, we have to distinguish all printable ASCII characters, we had better use linked lists instead of those arrays. Write a demonstration program for such a trie.

8.2   Write a demonstration program which manipulates a trie on disk.

8.3   Write an extension to program *trie* in Section 8.2, to delete words of a trie.

8.4 Change the print function in program *trie* to print tries in a form that reflects their structure.

8.5 Investigate the various ways of constructing a spell checker by means of a trie, as suggested near the end of this chapter. Examine analytically how running time will depend on:

(a) the size of the text to be checked,
(b) the number of distinct words in this text,
(c) the size of the dictionary.

Choose the method that seems best for your purposes and write a program for it.

8.6 Write a program to find all words in a trie which have a given prefix.

8.7 An eccentric doctor visits his patients in order of decreasing age. Patients entering the waiting list specify not only their names but also their ages. Each time the doctor wants to visit a patient, the oldest is selected and removed from the list (so children may have to wait a very long time). Write a program, based on a priority queue, which this doctor can use for this purpose.

8.8 Huffman's algorithm is based on the frequency of single bytes. Can you devise an algorithm based on the frequencies of contiguous groups of bytes? For example, if the word *the* appears very frequently in a textfile, it seems a good idea to use a code for it that is much shorter than three bytes.

9

Graphs

9.1 Directed and Undirected Graphs

The term *graph* is used for a set of *vertices* (or *nodes*), along with a set of *edges*, each of which connects a pair of vertices. We may consider each edge between two vertices i and j to be the ordered pair (i, j), and we then say that we have a *directed* graph. Alternatively, we can use only unordered pairs (i, j), in which case we are dealing with an *undirected* graph. We have in fact been dealing with directed graphs for a long time, since linked lists and trees are special cases of them. In a directed graph, we represent each edge $\langle i, j \rangle$ by an arrow, pointing from i to j. Obviously, for two distinct vertices i and j, the two pairs $\langle i, j \rangle$ and $\langle j, i \rangle$ represent distinct edges. In an undirected graph, the pairs (i, j) and (j, i) are two different notations for the same edge. Incidentally, we can regard an undirected graph as a directed graph in which each edge $\langle i, j \rangle$ is accompanied by an edge $\langle j, i \rangle$; the notation (i, j) then represents this pair of edges. In Figure 9.1(a) we have a directed graph, with vertices labeled 1, 2, 3, 4, 5 and edges $\langle 1, 3 \rangle$, $\langle 1, 4 \rangle$, $\langle 3, 5 \rangle$, $\langle 5, 2 \rangle$, $\langle 2, 3 \rangle$, $\langle 2, 1 \rangle$. Figure 9.1(b) shows an undirected graph. A network of pipes through which water can flow in one direction is an example of a directed graph; the pipes are then drawn as arrows and the points of connection as vertices. If in each pipe the water can flow in both directions, we have an undirected graph.

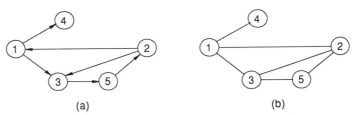

(a)   (b)

Figure 9.1 (a) Directed graph; (b) undirected graph

Graph theory is an extensive branch of mathematics with many interesting theorems and useful applications. Since we are focusing on programming in the C++ language, not on graph theory, we will select two applications of graphs, and work these out in complete, efficient and possibly useful programs. The first is about *project planning* by means of a directed graph, also called an *activity network*, the second about finding the shortest path in a directed or an undirected graph. But let us first see how we can represent directed graphs internally. From now on, we will use the term *graph* for what actually is a directed graph.

9.2 Graph Representations

Since the vertices of a graph are nodes and the edges refer to other nodes, it seems at first logical to implement these vertices as records that contain pointers to other records, in the same way as we did with binary trees, for example. After all, a binary tree is a special case of a graph. However, unlike binary trees, the number of pointer members in each such record would, in principle, be unlimited. Also, copying an entire graph would be very complicated with this representation.

An elegant but rather expensive alternative means of representing a graph is a so-called *adjacency matrix*. For a graph with n vertices, numbered 1, 2, ..., n, the corresponding adjacency matrix has n rows and n columns. If $\langle i, j \rangle$ is an edge in the graph, the matrix element on the ith row and the jth column is 1, otherwise it is 0. For example, the adjacency matrix for the graph of Figure 9.1(a) is

$$\begin{pmatrix} 0 & 0 & 1 & 1 & 0 \\ 1 & 0 & 1 & 0 & 0 \\ 0 & 0 & 0 & 0 & 1 \\ 0 & 0 & 0 & 0 & 0 \\ 0 & 1 & 0 & 0 & 0 \end{pmatrix}$$

Since the given graph contains an edge from vertex 1 to vertex 3, the third element in the first row of the matrix is 1, and so on. Adjacency matrices in the form of two-dimensional arrays are not frequently used in practice, because for large graphs they use too much memory space, and with many algorithms they lead to quadratic computing time. Matrices such as those under consideration, with a large proportion of zero elements, are called *sparse*. If they are large, it may be advantageous to use dynamic data structures instead of two-dimensional arrays to represent them.

Adjacency lists

The dynamic data structures we will be using are linked lists, called *adjacency lists*. For a given graph, each row of its adjacency matrix (as discussed above) will correspond to such a list. We will place the start pointers of these lists in an array. Each list corresponds to a row of the adjacency matrix and therefore to a vertex of the graph. Each list element contains at least a vertex number (which is the same as a column number of an adjacency matrix) and a pointer to the next list element. Figure 9.2 shows such adjacency lists for the graph of Figure 9.1(a).

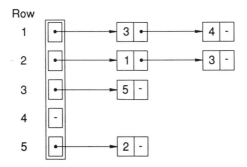

Figure 9.2 Adjacency lists for the graph of Figure 9.1(a)

Each element in an adjacency list represents in fact an edge. Since there are two edges ($\langle 1, 3 \rangle$ and $\langle 1, 4 \rangle$) that start at vertex 1, the adjacency list for row 1 has two nodes, with 3 and 4 as their contents. In general, for each edge $\langle i, j \rangle$ of the graph, there is a list node containing the value j, and this node occurs in the linked list with start pointer indicated in Figure 9.2 as row i. In other words, each 'row number' corresponds with a vertex number i of an edge $\langle i, j \rangle$ and vertex number j can be found in the linked list for i.

Adjacency lists such as those shown in Figure 9.2 are an excellent means to find all immediate *successors* of a given vertex. For example, we find the edges $\langle 1, 3 \rangle$ and $\langle 1, 4 \rangle$ by traversing the first linked list. However, these lists do not provide an efficient way of finding all immediate *predecessors* of a given vertex. If, for example, we want to find all immediate predecessors of vertex 2, we would have to scan all linked lists, to find the number 2 in the final one, as the only immediate successor of vertex 5. To find predecessors, we had better use *inverted* adjacency lists. These contain the vertex numbers of immediate predecessors instead of immediate successors; all immediate predecessors of vertex 1 are in the first list, and so on. We will use inverted adjacency lists in Section 9.4.

9.3 Topological Sorting; Detecting Cycles

In Figure 9.1(a), the edges $\langle 2, 3 \rangle$, $\langle 3, 5 \rangle$, $\langle 5, 2 \rangle$ form a *cycle*: if we start at vertex 2 and we follow these three edges, we arrive at vertex 2 again. In many applications we have to deal only with so-called *acyclic graphs*, which have no cycles. With an acyclic graph, we can write all its vertex numbers in a sequence, in such a way that for any edge $\langle i, j \rangle$ vertex number i precedes vertex number j in this sequence. Such a sequence is called a *topological order*. Note that there may be several topological orders for the same graph. For example, each of the sequences

    1, 2, 3, 4

and

    1, 3, 2, 4

is a topological order for the graph shown in Figure 9.3 (and there are no others for this graph). A cyclic graph has no topological orders.

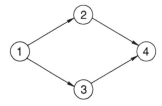

Figure 9.3 *An acyclic graph that has two topological orders*

It is sometimes required to find a topological order of an acyclic graph. There may be many of them, but we normally need only one: any will do. As a preparation for the next sections, we will now develop a program which may be applied to any (directed) graph; it will detect the occurrence of cycles, if any, and it will produce a topological order of the vertex numbers if the graph is acyclic. We will use adjacency lists similar to Figure 9.2, with one extension. The array a, appearing there as a column on the left, will have structures rather than pointers as its elements. Each of these array elements contains not only a pointer $a[i].link$, pointing to an adjacency list, but also an integer $a[i].count$. The latter is intended primarily to indicate how many immediate predecessors the vertex corresponding to that array element has. That integer is called the *in-degree* of the vertex in question. Figure 9.4 shows array a and the adjacency lists for the graph of Figure 9.3. The integers that denote in-degrees are surrounded by parentheses, to distinguish them from vertex numbers.

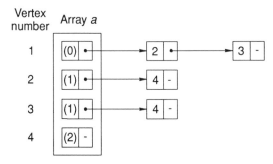

Figure 9.4 *Adjacency lists for the graph of Figure 9.3*

So far, we have hardly paid any attention to the way our vertices are numbered. If, for each edge $\langle i, j \rangle$, we required number i to be less than number j, our task of finding a topological order would be very simple. First, this condition would exclude the possibility of cycles, and second, we would obtain a topological order simply by sorting all vertex numbers. For example, this would lead to the topological order

1, 2, 3, 4

for the graph of Figure 9.3. However, we will not impose that requirement on our vertex numbering, because in practical applications alterations may be necessary, and the requirement $i < j$ might force us to renumber a great many vertices if we had to insert one somewhere in the middle of the graph. Our vertex numbering will be almost completely free, the only restriction being that the range of numbers used should not be too large for the amount of memory that is available. After all, the range of these numbers will be the range of our subscripts and, depending on our computer system, we have to reckon with certain limitations with respect to the maximum array size.

Instead of a normal array, we will use a pointer, pointing to some allocated area of memory which is just as large as we need. Although we think in terms of array a, the variable a is actually a pointer, declared in:

```
struct edge{int num; edge *next;};
...
struct vertex{int count; edge *link;} *a;
```

Let us denote the user's vertex numbers by capital letters I and J. We will read them from a file, which enables us to scan them more than once. We first determine the smallest and the greatest values (*min* and *max*) of all given vertex numbers. After this first scan, we compute

$$n = max - min + 1$$

which is the number of array elements that we will allocate. Internally, we then use vertex numbers i, j, related to I, J as follows:

$$i = I - min$$
$$j = J - min$$

The smallest and the greatest internal vertex numbers are now 0 and $n - 1$, respectively. (Of course, in the output we reconstruct the user's vertex numbers I and J again by adding *min* to i and j.) For example, for the graph of Figure 9.5 we have:

$$min = 100$$
$$max = 130$$
$$n = 31$$

so the internal vertex numbers are 0, 10, 20, 30, and we allocate memory for $a[0]$, $a[1]$, ..., $a[30]$.

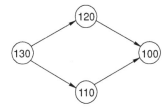

Figure 9.5 Graph with large vertex numbers

Since a subset of the reserved array elements $a[0]$, ..., $a[n-1]$ may not be used, we will mark those elements by a code. Each count member

```
a[i].count
```

is primarily intended for the in-degree of vertex i, as mentioned above, and, as such, can have only a nonnegative value. This opens the possibility of storing a negative value in these members as a code indicating the absence of vertex i in the graph. Let us use the symbolic constant *absent* = -2 for this code (-1 having a different meaning, as we will see shortly). Thus, in the above example, all count members except those of $a[0]$, $a[10]$, $a[20]$ and $a[30]$ are equal to *absent*.

As for the topological order we want, we begin with all vertices that have zero count members. This means that these vertices have zero in-degree, that is, they have no predecessors, so they are to come first in a topological order. Our algorithm works as follows. We begin by replacing these zero count members with subscript values, in such a way that the array elements for all vertices without predecessors form a linked list (to be distinguished from the adjacency lists). This linked list does not require any additional memory space allocated by *new*, but, instead, we use elements of array a as nodes. The subscript values stored in their count members act as 'pointers'. An integer variable *start* is the start pointer of the list. At the end of the list we use the value *nil* = -1 instead of 0. For example, if we have

```
start = 34
a[34].count = 87
a[87].count = 22
a[22].count = NIL
```

then the vertices 34, 87, 22 have no predecessors. Note that our algorithm is destructive, since we actually alter the count members. We even go a step further and gradually reduce the graph, each time deleting vertices that have no predecessors, until, in an acyclic graph, there are no vertices left. If, in this way, we do not get rid of all vertices, that is, if at some moment there are still vertices in the graph but each of them has at least one predecessor, then the graph has a cycle. The list of vertices that have no predecessors will be used as a linked stack: insertions and deletions occur only at the head of the list. This stack will grow and shrink all the time; when we are deleting a vertex, we place all its immediate successors on the stack, since these successors will be vertices without a predecessor after that deletion. Our program, *topol*, reads a file containing number pairs $\langle I, J \rangle$ for each edge of the graph. Its output consists of either all vertex numbers in a topological order or a message saying that there is a cycle.

```
// topol: Topological sorting; any cycles will be detected.

#include <fstream.h>
#include <iomanip.h>
#include <stdlib.h>

struct edge{int num; edge *next;};
```

```
class graph {
public:
   int min, n; // Minimum vertex number and n = max - min + 1
   void SetRange(const char *fname);
   void build(const char *fname);
   void StartNodes();
   void topol();
private:
   struct vertex{int count; edge *link;} *a;
   enum {nil=-1, absent=-2};
   int start; // Start of simulated linked list
              // for nodes without a predecessor
};

void graph::SetRange(const char *fname)
{  ifstream file(fname, ios::in | ios::nocreate);
   if (file.fail())
   {  cout << "Cannot open input file.\n";
      exit(1);
   }
   int max, x, first=1;
   for (;;)
   {  file >> x;
      if (file.fail()) break;
      if (first){min = max = x; first = 0;} else
      if (x < min) min = x; else
      if (x > max) max = x;
   }
   file.close();
   n = max - min + 1;
}

void graph::build(const char *fname)
{  int i, j, I, J;
   edge *p;
   a = new vertex[n];
   for (i=0; i<n; i++)
   {  a[i].count = absent;
      a[i].link = 0;
   }
   ifstream file(fname, ios::in | ios::nocreate);
   for (;;)
   {  file >> I >> J;
      if (file.fail()) break;
      i = I - min; j = J - min;
      if (a[i].count == absent) a[i].count = 0;
      if (a[j].count == absent) a[j].count = 0;
      p = new edge;
      p->num = j;
      p->next = a[i].link;
      a[i].link = p;
      a[j].count++;
   }
   file.close();
}
```

```cpp
void graph::StartNodes()
{ int i;
   // Set up simulated linked list of start nodes:
   start = nil;
   for (i=0; i<n; i++)
      if (a[i].count == 0){a[i].count = start; start = i;}
}

void graph::topol()
{ int i, j, J, k;
   edge *p;
   cout << "Topological order:\n";
   for (i=0; i<n; i++)
   { while (a[i].count == absent) i++;
      if (start == nil)
      { cout << "There is a cycle.\n"; return;
      }
      /* Take a vertex from the stack, print it, and
         decrease the in-degree of all its immediate
         successors by 1. As soon as the updated
         in-degree of a successor is zero, place it
         on the stack and dispose of the (edge) node
         in the adjacency list.
      */
      j = start; start = a[j].count;
      J = min + j;
      cout << J << " ";
      for (;;)
      {  p = a[j].link;
         if (p == 0) break;
         k = p->num;
         a[k].count--;
         if (a[k].count == 0)
         { a[k].count = start; start = k;
         }
         a[j].link = p->next;
         delete p;
         // In the adjacency list we have disposed of a node
         // that we don't need any longer.
      }
   }
   cout << endl;
}

int main()
{ graph g;
   char fname[50];
   cout << "Input file: ";
   cin >> setw(50) >> fname;
   g.SetRange(fname); // Find range of vertex numbers
   g.build(fname);    // Build adjacency lists for graph
   g.StartNodes();    // Form linked list of start nodes
   g.topol();         // Print topological order
   return 0;
}
```

Note the following fragment in the *topol* function, which you may find tricky because there is a while-loop that changes the running variable i of the surrounding for-loop:

```
cout << "Topological order:\n";
for (i=0; i<n; i++)
{   while (a[i].count == absent) i++;
    if (start == nil)
    {   cout << "There is a cycle.\n"; return;
    }
```

As a result of the while-loop, the variable i will have only real vertex numbers as values in the program fragment that follows. However, the vertices are not dealt with in the order of these i-values. Instead, we always use *start*, the top of the linked stack containing all vertices that have no predecessor. Each time, we pop the vertex that is to be deleted from this stack, but, at the same time, we push its immediate successors on it if these, as a consequence of this deletion, no longer have any predecessors. If the linked stack is empty while i is still less than n, we have a situation where there are still vertices left each of which has a predecessor, which means that there is a cycle. If our input file contains the four lines

```
120   100
130   110
110   100
130   120
```

which correspond to the graph of Figure 9.5, we obtain the following topological order as output:

```
130 110 120 100
```

Instead of this extremely simple example, we could have used a very large graph without any problems as to computing time, because the algorithm that we have been using is very efficient. If the graph contains n vertices and e edges, running time is $O(n + e)$, in other words, it is *linear* in the size of the problem. This is worth mentioning, since there are many graph problems where we can do no better than 'try all possibilities', which normally leads to exponential growth rate.

9.4 Activity Networks; Critical Path Method

An important application of graphs is project planning and scheduling. Some well-known techniques in this area are *CPM* (Critical Path Method) and *PERT* (Performance Evaluation and Review Technique). A project consists of a number of activities, some of which are related to others. For example, when we are building a house, it is obvious that the construction of its roof cannot take place until its walls are ready. There are two possible ways of placing activities in a graph: we can use either the vertices or the edges for them. Let us choose the edges for this purpose. Besides the vertex pair $\langle i, j \rangle$ each activity also has a given *duration*, which is an estimate of the time that activity will take, and a *description*, which, technically speaking, is a string of, say, at most 80 characters. In the framework of project planning, we use the terms *activities* and *events* instead of *edges* and *vertices*, respectively. Figure 9.6 shows an *activity network*, for a simple project.

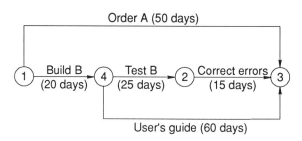

Figure 9.6 *An activity network for a project*

Two components A and B are involved in manufacturing a certain product; we have only to place an order to obtain component A, but it is estimated that the article will be delivered as many as 50 days after the order has gone out. Things are more complex for component B. We have to build it ourselves, which takes 20 days. Then we have to test it (25 days) and to correct the errors (15 days). Also, we have to write a user's guide (60 days), but for some reason the person who is to do this can start writing only after B has been built. Events 1 and 3 denote the start and the completion of the entire project, respectively.

Note that this network includes two activities $\langle i, j \rangle$ for which i is greater than j. A long time ago, there were real CPM programs that admitted only activities $\langle i, j \rangle$ for which i is less than j. This restriction would exclude any cycles; it would make the task of obtaining a topological order extremely easy and would therefore simplify our program considerably. Instead, we will allow vertices to be numbered freely, but it is nevertheless a good idea from the planner's point of view to begin with a network with $i < j$ for all activities $\langle i, j \rangle$, so the network shown in Figure 9.6 is not a good example for project managers. However, when activities are to be inserted in a complex network, any user of a more tolerant program like ours will appreciate that he or she need not worry about vertex numbers. Incidentally, the danger of introducing cycles should not be exaggerated: they can also be avoided simply by drawing all activities as arrows pointing more or less from left to right, as is usual in practice. If, in spite of this good advice, cycles should occur, then our program will detect them. (It would not be fair if we, as programmers, imposed the restriction $i < j$ on all activities $\langle i, j \rangle$, using the argument about cycles as a pretext for our inability to solve an interesting programming problem!)

Instead of numbers, we may want to use *names* to identify vertices. We will see how this can be done in Sections 9.5 and 9.6.

If all activities start as soon as possible, each event i occurs at its *earliest event* time, $ee(i)$. In our example, we have:

$ee(1) = 0$
$ee(2) = 45$
$ee(3) = 80$
$ee(4) = 20$

Note that even for this very simple project we have to be careful. We cannot take just any path from event 1 to event 3, but we have to find the longest path, or, as we say, the *critical path*, which consists of the activities $\langle 1, 4 \rangle$ and $\langle 4, 3 \rangle$.

In general, we have $ee(j) = 0$ for all events j that have no predecessors. If event j has one or more predecessors, its earliest event time $ee(j)$ is the maximum value of

$ee(i) +$ duration of $\langle i, j \rangle$

where all immediate predecessors i of event j are to be considered. To compute these values efficiently, we traverse all events in a topological order (1, 4, 2, 3 in the example), using an algorithm similar to the one on which program *topol* in Section 9.3 was based. We also use similar data structures, that is, array a for the events and adjacency lists with a node for each activity, as Figure 9.7 shows.

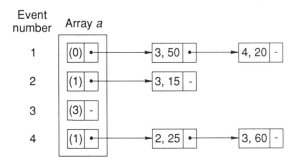

Figure 9.7 *Adjacency lists for the project of Figure 9.6*

For each activity, its duration is stored in its node. (Remember that each activity, that is, each edge in the activity network, uniquely corresponds to a node of an adjacency list.) Again, the parenthesized integers in the array elements $a[i]$ denote the in-degree of vertex i, and are called $a[i].count$ in the program. Though not included in Figure 9.7, each element $a[i]$ also contains two integer members $a[i].ee$ (earliest event) and $a[i].le$ (latest event, to be discussed shortly). Initially, all members ee are set to zero. We now traverse the events in a topological order, using a linked stack and each time deleting events that have no predecessors. However, we do not destroy the members ee and le as we are deleting events. When dealing with event i, we update the earliest event times of all its successors j. Using the notation $ee(i)$ as an abbreviation for $a[i].ee$, we test, for each of these successors, to see if the sum

$ee(i) +$ duration of $\langle i, j \rangle$

is greater than the current value of $ee(j)$, and, if so, we assign that greater value to $ee(j)$. The greatest value of all earliest event times thus computed is the time needed for the entire project.

In the example of Figure 9.6, we see that the activities $\langle 1, 3\rangle$, $\langle 4, 2\rangle$, $\langle 2, 3\rangle$ do not lie on the critical path (1, 4, 3). It is not absolutely necessary for them to begin as early as possible. For example, the activity $\langle 2, 3\rangle$ may begin as late as 15 days before the completion time (80) of the entire project, so instead of at time $ee(2) = 45$, we may start at time 65, without any danger of delaying the project (provided that all duration times are exact values instead of estimates). Again focusing on the events, rather than on the activities, we can compute their latest event times $le(i)$. The value of $le(i)$ is the minimum value of

$$le(j) - \text{duration of } \langle i, j\rangle$$

where all immediate successors j of event i are to be considered. We compute the latest event times in a backward scan, which is analogous to the forward scan in which we computed the earliest event times. We therefore need *inverted adjacency lists*, as shown in Figure 9.8.

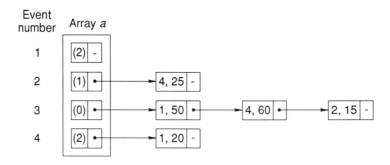

Figure 9.8 *Inverted adjacency lists for the project of Figure 9.6*

We will use the same array a as before. The nodes of the old adjacency lists were deleted when we were computing the earliest event times. (Recall that the earliest event times themselves are stored in array a, so we did not destroy them when we were deleting the adjacency lists.) We now build the inverted adjacency lists. In the new situation, each array element $a[j]$ contains the start pointer of a linked list in which the numbers of all predecessors i of event j are stored. Each node of the list starting at $a[j].link$ corresponds to an activity $\langle i, j\rangle$. A parenthesized integer $a[j].count$ denotes the *out-degree* of vertex j, that is, the number of immediate successors of vertex j. Initially, we set all members le to the time needed for the entire project, and we form a linked stack of all events that have no successor. Working with this stack in the same way as in the forward scan, we deal with all events in a reverse topological order, and, when dealing with event j, we update the latest event time of all its predecessors i as follows. If the difference

$$le(j) - \text{duration of } \langle i, j\rangle$$

is less than the current value of $le(i)$ we assign that difference to $le(i)$. After this backward scan, we have computed both the earliest event times and the latest event times of all events, and we can find them in array a. However, in the program output there is a line for each activity, not for each event. For every activity $\langle i, j \rangle$, with duration d, we therefore define its *earliest start time* $EST(i, j)$, its *earliest completion time* $ECT(i, j)$, its *latest start time* $LST(i, j)$, and its *latest completion time* $LCT(i, j)$ as follows:

$$EST(i, j) = ee(i)$$
$$ECT(i, j) = ee(i) + d$$
$$LST(i, j) = le(j) - d$$
$$LCT(i, j) = le(j)$$

The meanings of these quantities are as their names indicate. For example, *LST* denotes the latest time the activity may start without delaying the completion time of the entire project. If, for some activity, the earliest start time is equal to the latest start time, then that activity is said to lie on a *critical path*. We also define the *(free) slack* as

$$SLACK(i, j) = LST(i, j) - EST(i, j)$$

Thus, any activity on a critical path has zero slack. Note that we may instead define

$$SLACK(i, j) = LCT(i, j) - ECT(i, j)$$

since we have

$$LST(i, j) - EST(i, j) = \{le(j) - d\} - ee(i)$$
$$LCT(i, j) - ECT(i, j) = le(j) - \{ee(i) + d\}$$

so both expressions for $SLACK(i, j)$ are equivalent.

We now want to write a program to compute all these quantities for a given project. For each activity of a project, we will read the two relevant event numbers, the duration and a description, from a file. For example, this file, say *project.txt*, may have the following contents for the network shown in Figure 9.6:

```
1   3      50 Order A
1   4      20 Build B
4   2      25 Test B
2   3      15 Correct errors
4   3      60 User's guide
```

If this file *project.txt* is available, we will be able to run our program by entering its name on the keyboard, as the following demonstration shows:

```
Input file: project.txt
Output:
```

I	J	DUR	EST	LST	ECT	LCT	SLACK		DESCRIPTION
1	3	50	0	30	50	80	30		Order A
1	4	20	0	0	20	20	0	<--	Build B
4	2	25	20	40	45	65	20		Test B
2	3	15	45	65	60	80	20		Correct errors
4	3	60	20	20	80	80	0	<--	User's guide

Lines with an arrow pointing to a slack value 0 denote activities lying on a critical path.
The order in which the activities are listed is based on the input file. We read this file in a
third scan (after the two scans for the computation of *ee* and *le*), and we copy each line,
together with the computed items found in array *a*. In this way, we need not store all
descriptions in main memory: in the first and the second scans we simply skip them, and in
the third scan we print each description immediately after reading it, which in the case of a
large project saves a good deal of memory space. In real critical path programs we can
usually specify the order in which the output lines are to be printed. For example, we may
want them to appear with the slack in ascending order. After our discussion of sorting
methods in Chapter 3, this should not be a difficult problem. Program *cpm*, demonstrated
above, is listed below:

```
/* cpm: Critical path method
   The program asks for an input file, containing
   a line for each activity with two (integer)
   event numbers, a duration (integer), and an
   optional description. The range of the event
   numbers influences the amount of memory needed.
   Apart from this, there are no limitations
   imposed on the number of events or on the way
   they are numbered, nor are there any restrictions
   on the number of activities or on their order in
   the input file, except for memory limitations of
   the machine on which the program runs.
*/

#include <fstream.h>
#include <iomanip.h>
#include <stdlib.h>

struct activity{int num, dur; activity *next;};

class project {
public:
   project(){tMax = 0;}
   int min, n; // Minimum event number and n = max - min + 1
   void SetRange(const char *fname);
   void build(const char *fname);
   void StartNodes();
   void EarliestEventTime();
   void inverted(const char *fname);
   void EndNodes();
   void LatestEventTime();
   void output(const char *fname);
```

```
private:
   struct event{int count, ee, le; activity *link;} *a;
   int tMax;
   enum {nil=-1, absent=-2};
   int start; // Start of simulated linked list
              // for nodes without a predecessor
   void SkipRestLine(ifstream &file);
};

void project::SkipRestLine(ifstream &file)
{  char ch;
   do file.get(ch); while (!file.fail() && ch != '\n');
}

void project::SetRange(const char *fname)
{  ifstream file(fname, ios::in | ios::nocreate);
   if (file.fail())
   {  cout << "Cannot open input file.\n"; exit(1);
   }
   int max, x, first=1, jRead = 1;
   for (;;)
   {  file >> x;
      jRead = !jRead; // x is either i or j of <i, j>
      if (jRead) SkipRestLine(file);
      if (file.fail()) break;
      if (first){min = max = x; first = 0;} else
      if (x < min) min = x; else
      if (x > max) max = x;
   }
   file.close();
   n = max - min + 1;
}

void project::build(const char *fname)
{  int i, j, I, J, d;
   activity *p;
   a = new event[n];
   for (i=0; i<n; i++)
   {  a[i].count = absent; a[i].ee = 0; a[i].link = 0;
   }
   ifstream file(fname, ios::in | ios::nocreate);
   for (;;)
   {  file >> I >> J >> d;
      SkipRestLine(file);
      if (file.fail()) break;
      i = I - min; j = J - min;
      if (a[i].count == absent) a[i].count = 0;
      if (a[j].count == absent) a[j].count = 0;
      p = new activity;
      p->num = j; p->dur = d;
      p->next = a[i].link;
      a[i].link = p; a[j].count++;
   }
   file.close();
}
```

```
void project::StartNodes()
{  int i;
   // Set up simulated linked list of start nodes:
   start = nil;
   for (i=0; i<n; i++)
      if (a[i].count == 0){a[i].count = start; start = i;}
}

void project::EarliestEventTime()
{  int i, j, k, t1;
   activity *p;
   for (i=0; i<n; i++)
   {  while (a[i].count == absent) i++;
      if (start == nil)
      {  cout << "There is a cycle.\n"; return;
      }
      /*  Take an event from the stack, and decrease
          the in-degree of all its immediate
          successors by 1. As soon as the updated
          in-degree of a successor is zero, place it
          on the stack and dispose of the (activity)
          node in the adjacency list.
      */
      j = start; start = a[j].count;
      for (;;)
      {  p = a[j].link;
         if (p == 0) break;
         k = p->num;
         a[k].count--;
         t1 = a[j].ee + p->dur;
         if (t1 > a[k].ee)
            a[k].ee = t1;
         if (t1 > tMax) tMax = t1;
         if (a[k].count == 0)
         {  a[k].count = start;
            start = k;
         }
         a[j].link = p->next;
         delete p;
         // In the adjacency list we have disposed of a node
         // that we don't need any longer.
      }
   }
}

void project::inverted(const char *fname)
{  int i, j, I, J, d;
   activity *p;
   for (j=0; j<n; j++)
      if (a[j].count != absent)
      {  a[j].le = tMax;
         a[j].count = 0;
         a[j].link = 0;
      }
   ifstream file(fname, ios::in | ios::nocreate);
```

```
      for (;;)
      {   file >> I >> J >> d;
          SkipRestLine(file);
          if (file.fail()) break;
          i = I - min; j = J - min;
          p = new activity;
          p->num = i; p->dur = d;
          p->next = a[j].link;
          a[j].link = p;
          a[i].count++;
      }
      file.close();
}


void project::EndNodes()
{   start = nil;
    for (int j=0; j<n; j++)
        if (a[j].count == 0){a[j].count = start; start = j;}
}


void project::LatestEventTime()
{   int i, j, k, t1;
    activity *p;
    for (j=0; j<n; j++)
    {   while (a[j].count == absent) j++;
        i = start; start = a[i].count;
        for (;;)
        {   p = a[i].link;
            if (p == 0) break;
            k = p->num;
            a[k].count--;
            t1 = a[i].le - p->dur;
            if (t1 < a[k].le) a[k].le = t1;
            if (a[k].count == 0)
            {   a[k].count = start; start = k;
            }
            a[i].link = p->next;
            delete p;
        }
    }
}


void project::output(const char *fname)
{   char descript[80];
    int i, j, I, J, d, est, lct, ect, lst, slack;
    cout << "Output:\n\n";
    cout << "  I    J   DUR   EST   LST   ECT   LCT   "
            "SLACK    DESCRIPTION\n\n";
    ifstream file(fname, ios::in | ios::nocreate);
    for (;;)
    {   file >> I >> J >> d;
        if (file.fail()) break;
        file.getline(descript, 80);
```

```
        i = I - min; j = J - min;
        est = a[i].ee; // Earliest start time
        lct = a[j].le; // Latest completion time
        ect = est + d; // Earliest completion time
        lst = lct - d; // Latest start time
        slack = lst - est;
        cout << setw(3) << I << " "
             << setw(3) << J << " "
             << setw(4) << d << " "
             << setw(5) << est << " "
             << setw(4) << lst << " "
             << setw(5) << ect << " "
             << setw(4) << lct << " "
             << setw(6) << slack << " "
             << (slack ? "    " : "<--")
             << descript << endl;
    }
    file.close();
}


int main()
{ project g;
    char fname[50];
    cout << "Input file: ";
    cin >> setw(50) >> fname;
    g.SetRange(fname);          // Find range of event numbers
    g.build(fname);             // Build adjacency lists
    g.StartNodes();             // Form linked list of start nodes
    g.EarliestEventTime();      // Find ee for each node
    g.inverted(fname);          // Build inverted adjacency lists
    g.EndNodes();               // Form linked stack of end nodes
    g.LatestEventTime();        // Find le for each node
    g.output(fname);            // Produce resulting table
    return 0;
}
```

9.5 Associating Strings with Integers

In Sections 9.3 and 9.4 we have used integers to identify vertices. It was not necessary for these integers to be consecutive, so that we could use, for example 100, 105, 107 and 110 as vertex numbers. Since the range of these numbers determined the size of 'array' *a*, it would not have been very economical if we had used, say, 1, 1000, 20 000, 30 000 instead. With many applications of graphs, we prefer vertex names to vertex numbers. For example, if the vertices represent cities, it would be very awkward if we had to assign a number to each city name. We will now discuss a class *strings* to do this task for us. As usual, there are two files to be used in addition to our application programs: a header file *strings.h* and an implementation file *strings.cpp*. For example, consider the following very simple application program (postponing a more interesting application until Section 9.6):

```
// strap: An application of class 'strings'
//         (to be linked with strings.cpp).
#include <iostream.h>
#include "strings.h"

int main()
{  strings T;
   char *a = "Lincoln", *b = "Washington";
   int ia = T.add(a), ib = T.add(b), ic;
   cout << "Enter a name: "; ic = T.read(cin);
   cout << "code    string\n";
   cout << "  " << ia << "    " << T[ia] << endl;
   cout << "  " << ib << "    " << T[ib] << endl;
   cout << "  " << ic << "    " << T[ic] << endl;
   cout << "Object T contains " << T.size() << " strings.\n";
   return 0;
}
```

The *strings* object *T* is used to store strings. The member function *add* adds a string to this object, unless this string is already present in it. In either case it returns an integer (0, 1, 2, ...) that is unique for the string. The function *read* works similarly, but it reads the string in question from the specified input stream. Later, we can use these integers to obtain the associated strings. Although a normal member function could be used for this purpose, this is done here by overloading the subscripting operator [ ]. Here is a demonstration of this program:

```
Enter a name: Eisenhower
code    string
   0    Lincoln
   1    Washington
   2    Eisenhower
Object T contains 3 strings.
```

Since there are three distinct strings, the three integers 0, 1 and 2 are assigned to them. This is different in the following case, where a name is read from the keyboard that has already been stored previously:

```
Enter a name: Washington
code    string
   0    Lincoln
   1    Washington
   1    Washington
Object T contains 2 strings.
```

This table shows two identical lines because program *strap* contains three explicit output statements for the contents of this table. There would have been no such duplication if we had written

```
for (int i=0; i<T.size(); i++)
   cout << "  " << i << "    " << T[i] << endl;
```

instead of the three output lines ending with << *endl;* in program *strap*. The header file
strings.h used in program *strap* is listed below:

```
// strings.h: Strings stored and represented
//            by ints 0, 1, 2, ...
#include <fstream.h>
#include <iomanip.h>
#include <string.h>
#include <stdlib.h>

class strings {
public:
    strings(){p = NULL; N = n = 0;}
    ~strings();
    int add(const char *s);
    char *operator[](int i)const{return p[i];}
    int read(istream &f);
    int size()const{return n;}
private:
    enum {ChunkSize = 64};
    char **p;
    int n, N;
};
```

The strings in question are stored in dynamically allocated memory, and their start
addresses in a dynamic array *p*. Since the elements of this 'array' are pointers to characters,
the type of *p* is pointer-to-pointer-to-*char*. Not knowing in advance how many strings are
to be stored, we reallocate memory for this array when this is required, and we do this in
chunks of length *ChunkSize* rather than one array element at a time, as discussed in Section
1.5. The implementation file to be linked with applications such as *strap* is shown below:

```
// strings.cpp: See header file strings.h
#include "strings.h"
typedef char *charptr;

strings::~strings()
{   for (int i=0; i<n; i++) delete[](p[i]);
    delete[]p;
}

int strings::add(const char *s)
{   int i;
    for (i=0; i<n; i++) if (strcmp(p[i], s) == 0) return i;
    if (n == N)
    {   char **pOld = p;
        p = new charptr[N += ChunkSize];
        for (i=0; i<n; i++) p[i] = pOld[i];
        delete[]pOld;
    }
    p[n] = new char[strlen(s) + 1];
    strcpy(p[n++], s);
    return n - 1;
}
```

```
int strings::read(istream &f)
{   char buf[100];
    f >> setw(100) >> buf;
    return f.fail() ? -1 : add(buf);
}
```

The *read* member function skips any leading white-space characters; on the other hand, after reading characters other than white space, any white-space character signals the end of the string. For example, if we tried to use a single call to this function to read the string

```
Abraham Lincoln
```

we would obtain only the name *Abraham*. On the positive side, we can use *strings::read* in a loop to read a great many names, some of which are placed on the same line, such as in

```
London   Exeter   Edinburgh  Glasgow
Newcastle  Bristol  Chichester
```

9.6 The Shortest Path Between Two Vertices

Let us again consider a directed graph with a value attached to each edge. We may regard these values as the time required to move from one vertex to another, or, as we will do, as *lengths*. Although there are also other useful applications, we will view vertices as towns and edges as (one-way) roads. Since most real roads allow two-way traffic, it seems more logical to use undirected graphs here. However, as pointed out in Section 9.1, we can simply use two edges with opposite directions and equal lengths for such roads, as Figure 9.9 shows for AB and AD.

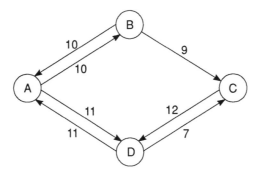

Figure 9.9 A directed graph

By using directed graphs, we admit one-way roads, such as BC in Figure 9.9. As for DC, we may regard the unequal lengths accounting for some asymmetry, say, due to a difference in level, the cost of moving from C to D being 12 and that of moving from D to C only 7. One-way and asymmetric roads such as BC and DC are possible with directed graphs, not with undirected ones. On the other hand, we can regard undirected graphs as a special case of directed graphs, with all edge pairs similar to the connections AB and AD in Figure 9.9.

Using A as a start and C as a finish vertex, the *shortest path* is ADC, with length $11 + 7 = 18$, since the other path, ABC, has length $10 + 9 = 19$. Strictly speaking, there are more paths from A to C, such as ABCDABC and ABABABADC, but these are ignored because we are interested in the shortest path. Incidentally, it does not always make sense to speak about *the* shortest path. For example, with B as a start and D as a finish vertex, both paths BAD and BCD have length 21. Conforming to common usage, we often speak of *the* shortest path, when we actually mean *a* shortest path.

We will now implement an algorithm to determine, for any directed graph, if there is a path leading from a given start to a given finish vertex, and, if so, to find the shortest one. This algorithm, published by E. W. Dijkstra in 1959, is based on a set S of vertices. As with normal program variables, S changes during program execution. Initially, S consists of only one element, the start vertex, which we will denote by v_0. Repeatedly, we add a vertex to S, until S consists of all vertices of the graph. At any time during this growing process of S, for each vertex v in S, the shortest path from start vertex v_0 to v in S lies wholly in S. Also, for any vertex v, we denote the length of a path from v_0 to v by D_v, and v's predecessor by *connect*$_v$. If v belongs to S, D_v is the length of the *shortest* path from v_0 to v. For any two distinct vertices v and w of the graph, $\langle v, w \rangle$ may or may not be an edge. Depending on this, we define

$$
\begin{aligned}
length(v, w) \;&=\; \text{the length of } \langle v, w \rangle, \text{ if this is an edge;} \\
&=\; \text{the large value } inf = INT\_MAX / 2, \text{ if } \langle v, w \rangle \text{ is not an edge.}
\end{aligned}
$$

(In the last line, only half the value *INT_MAX* is used for *inf* so we can compute *inf* + *inf* without *int* overflow.) We can now express Dijkstra's algorithm as follows:

```
for (each vertex v of the graph)
{   if (v == v0) Dv ← 0 else Dv ← length(v0, v)
    connectv ← v0
}

S ← {v0}

while (not all vertices belong to S)
{   Among all vertices that are not in S, choose w, such that Dw is as small as possible.
    Add w to S.

    for (each vertex v not belonging to S)
    {   if (Dw + Length(w, v) < Dv)
        {   Dv ← Dw + Length(w, v)
            connectv ← w
        }
    }
}
```

After execution of this algorithm, for any vertex v, the length of the shortest path from v_0 to any vertex v is equal to D_v and the immediate predecessor of v on this path is $connect_v$. We are actually interested only in one shortest path, from *start* to *finish*, where $start = v_0$. To find this path, we have to trace all the way back from *finish* to *start*, using $w = connect_{finish}$, $x = connect_w$, and so on, until we arrive at *start* (= v_0). If D_{finish} is still equal to the large value *inf*, this indicates that there is no path from *start* to *finish*.

You can find a proof of this algorithm in more theoretical books, such as the one by Aho, Hopcroft and Ullman, listed in the Bibliography. The algorithm requires $O(n^2)$ time, where n is the number of vertices. This time behavior is very reasonable. Remember, the number of all possible paths grows exponentially with n, so that any algorithm based on comparing all paths would require computing time $O(c^n)$, which would make such an algorithm extremely slow compared with the one discussed here.

We will now implement it in a program that you may find useful as a *route planner*. Let us first see how this works in practice, using the following input file, *roads.txt*, based on 25 English and Welsh towns (omitting Scotland to keep Figure 9.10 within reasonable limits):

```
Birmingham Bristol 91 Manchester 86 Northampton 56
        Nottingham 50 Oxford 63
Brighton Dover 84 London 53 Portsmouth 48 Southampton 61
Bristol Exeter 84 Oxford 73 Southampton 79 Cardiff 46
Cardiff Swansea 40
Cambridge Harwich 78 London 55 Northampton 54 Norwich 61
        Nottingham 88
Dover London 76
Exeter Plymouth 46
Fishguard Swansea 76
Harwich London 79 Norwich 67
Hull Leeds 61 Middlesbrough 89 Nottingham 94
Leeds Liverpool 75 Manchester 43 Middlesbrough 66
        Newcastle 95 Nottingham 74
Liverpool Manchester 35
London Northampton 69 Oxford 59 Portsmouth 78 Southampton 87
Manchester Nottingham 72
Middlesbrough Newcastle 41
Northampton Nottingham 70 Oxford 42
Nottingham Oxford 98
Oxford Portsmouth 85 Southampton 64
Penzance Plymouth 78
Portsmouth Southampton 21
```

For example, the first two lines of this file specify that our graph contains edges connecting the vertex Birmingham with each of the five vertices Bristol, Manchester, Northampton, Nottingham and Oxford, with corresponding edge lengths 91, 86, 56, 50 and 63. Each indented line is interpreted as a continuation of the preceding one. These distances (in miles) were found in the distance table of the 1991 edition of *Michelin Touring Atlas Britain*. All English and Welsh towns listed in this table were used, but only distances less than 100 miles were included as edges. It would be inconvenient if we had to specify every edge twice because we are dealing with directed graphs and two-way roads. It will therefore be possible for the user to choose between *Directed* and *Undirected*, the latter implying that each (directed) edge is automatically to be accompanied by its counterpart in the opposite direction. Obviously the above input file could be expanded and improved. Any strange results with this route planner will almost certainly be due to its input data, not to the program itself. You are encouraged to improve this file, or replace it with one of the country you are interested in. With suitable input files, you can use this program for transport not only by road, but also by rail, air, sea and canals. In the following demonstration, only the text printed in *italics* has been entered by the user:

```
Input file: roads.txt
Is the graph Directed or Undirected? (D/U) u
Vertices:
Birmingham Bristol Manchester Northampton Nottingham
Oxford Brighton Dover London Portsmouth
Southampton Exeter Cardiff Swansea Cambridge
Harwich Norwich Plymouth Fishguard Hull
Leeds Middlesbrough Liverpool Newcastle Penzance
Enter start and finish:
Penzance Newcastle
Shortest path:

          Vertex                 Distance
start   = Penzance                     0
          Plymouth                    78
          Exeter                     124
          Bristol                    208
          Birmingham                 299
          Nottingham                 349
          Leeds                      423
finish = Newcastle                   518
Do you want another path? (Y/N) y
Enter start and finish:
Liverpool Harwich
Shortest path:

          Vertex                 Distance
start   = Liverpool                    0
          Manchester                  35
          Nottingham                 107
          Cambridge                  195
finish = Harwich                     273
Do you want another path? (Y/N) n
```

The complete distance table in the atlas mentioned above specifies 490 instead of 518 miles as the distance between Penzance and Newcastle. This is possible because we have omitted all road lengths of 100 miles and more in the input file. Curiously enough, the computed distance of 273 miles between Liverpool and Harwich is shorter than the distance of 280 miles specified in the distance table of the atlas. Apparently the following small print in the atlas applies:

> The distances quoted are not necessarily the shortest but have been based on the roads which afford the best driving conditions and are therefore the most practical.

The graph corresponding with the above input file *roads.txt* is shown in Figure 9.10.

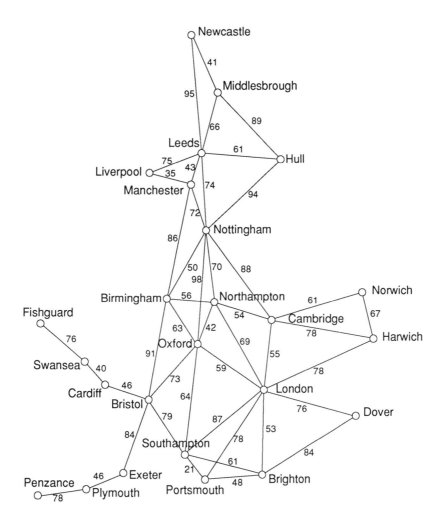

Figure 9.10 Graph used in the shortest-path demonstration

In the above sketch of the algorithm, we have not discussed the data structures to be used in the program. The class *strings*, discussed in the previous section, is very useful here to store and retrieve the names of the towns. As in Sections 9.2–9.4, we will use adjacency lists for the graphs. Thanks to the class *strings*, the vertex numbers are consecutive this time: 0, 1, 2, ..., without any gaps.

At first it seems that we obtain the desired path in the wrong direction because we only have the predecessor, not the successor, of each vertex. Fortunately, tracing the shortest path back from finish to start, we can replace each predecessor of a vertex with the desired successor, as the *graph::output* function shows in this program:

```
// shpath: Finding the shortest path: Dijkstra's algorithm
//    (to be linked with strings.cpp, see Section 9.5).

#include <stdlib.h>
#include <limits.h>
#include <ctype.h>
#include "strings.h"

struct edge{int num, len; edge *next;};

class graph {
public:
   int n, N, start, finish, nInS, undirected;
   void build(strings &T, ifstream &file);
   void output(const strings &T)const;
   int length(int i, int j)const;
   void prepare();
   void ExpandSetS();
private:
   struct NodeType{int count, D, connect, inS; edge *link;}
      *list;
   enum {nil=-1, inf=INT_MAX/2};
   int ReadName(strings &T, istream &file, char &PrevChar);
};

void error(const char *s)
{  cout << s << endl; exit(1);
}

int graph::ReadName(strings &T, istream &file, char &PrevChar)
{  char s[100];
   s[0] = '\n';
   do
   {  PrevChar = s[0];
      file.get(s[0]);
   }  while (!file.fail() && !isalpha(s[0]));
   if (file.fail()) return -1;
   file >> setw(99) >> &s[1];
   return T.add(s);
}

void graph::build(strings &T, ifstream &file)
{  int i, j, len;
   edge *p;
   char PrevChar;
   const int ChunkSize = 64;
   N = n = 0;
   list = NULL;
   for (;;)
   {  j = ReadName(T, file, PrevChar);
      if (j < 0) break;
      if (PrevChar == '\n')
      {  i = j;
         j = ReadName(T, file, PrevChar);
      }
```

```
                file >> len;
                if (file.eof()) break;
                if (file.fail())
                    error("Incorrect input file.");
                int max = i > j ? i : j;
                if (max >= N)
                {   NodeType *listOld = list;
                    list = new NodeType[N += ChunkSize];
                    for (int v=0; v<N; v++)
                        if (v < n)
                            list[v] = listOld[v];
                        else
                        {   list[v].count = 0;
                            list[v].link = NULL;
                        }
                    delete[]listOld;
                }
                if (max >= n) n = max + 1;
                p = new edge;
                p->num = j; p->len = len;
                p->next = list[i].link;
                list[i].link = p;
                list[j].count++;
                        // Undirected graph: add <j, i> besides <i, j> :
                if (undirected)
                {   p = new edge;
                    p->num = i;
                    p->len = len;
                    p->next = list[j].link;
                    list[j].link = p;
                    list[i].count++;
                }
            }
        file.close();
    }

int graph::length(int i, int j)const
{   edge *p = list[i].link;
    while (p)
    {   if (p->num == j)
            return p->len;
        p = p->next;
    }
    return inf;
}

void graph::prepare()
{   for (int v=0; v<n; v++)
    {   list[v].D = (v == start ? 0 : length(start, v));
        list[v].inS = 0;
        list[v].connect = start;
    }
    list[start].inS = 1;
    nInS = 1;
}
```

```cpp
void graph::ExpandSetS()
{ int v, w = inf, min = INT_MAX;
  // Choose a vertex w in V such that list[w].D
  // is a minimum:
  for (v=0; v<n; v++)
  if (list[v].inS == 0)
  { if (list[v].D < min)
    { min = list[v].D;
      w = v;
    }
  } // w != inf
  // Move w from V to S:
  list[w].inS = 1;  nInS++;
  // Update distances list[v].D and predecessors
  // list[v].connect for all vertices v in V:
  for (v=0; v<n; v++)
  if (list[v].inS == 0)
  { int sum = list[w].D + length(w, v);
    if (sum < list[v].D)
    { list[v].D = sum;
      list[v].connect = w;
    }
  }
}


void graph::output(const strings &T)const
{ if (list[finish].D == inf)
  { cout << "No path from start to finish.\n";
    return;
  }
  // Replace predecessors with successors:
  int j = finish, i, jnext = 0;
  for (;;)
  { i = list[j].connect;
    list[j].connect = jnext;
    if (j == start) break;
    jnext = j;
    j = i;
  }
  cout << "Shortest path:\n\n";
  i = start;
  cout << "          Vertex             Distance\n";
  for (;;)
  { cout << (i == finish ? "finish = " :
             i == start  ? "start   = " :
                           "        ")
       << setw(20) << setiosflags(ios::left) << T[i] << "  "
       << setw(6) << resetiosflags(ios::left) << list[i].D
       << endl;
    if (i == finish)
      break;
    i = list[i].connect;
  }
}
```

```
int main()
{  graph g;
   strings T;
   char fname[50], ch;
   cout << "Input file: ";
   cin >> setw(50) >> fname;
   ifstream file(fname, ios::in | ios::nocreate);
   if (file.fail())
      error("Cannot open input file.");
   cout << "Is the graph Directed or Undirected? (D/U) ";
   cin >> ch;
   g.undirected = (ch == 'u' || ch == 'U');
   g.build(T, file);      // Build adjacency lists
   cout << "Vertices:";
   int n = T.size();
   for (int i=0; i<n; i++)
   {  if (i % 5 == 0)
         cout << endl;
      cout << T[i] << " ";
   }
   do
   {  cout << "\nEnter start and finish:\n";
      g.start = T.read(cin);
      g.finish = T.read(cin);
      if (g.start >= g.n || g.finish >= g.n)
         cout << "Incorrect start or finish.\n";
      else
      {  g.prepare();
         while (g.nInS < g.n)
            g.ExpandSetS();
         g.output(T);
      }
      cout << "Do you want another path? (Y/N) ";
      cin >> ch;
   }  while (ch == 'y' || ch == 'Y');
   return 0;
}
```

The status of each vertex is given by *list*[*v*].*inS*, which is equal to 1 if vertex *v* belongs to *S* and to 0 if it does not. The *graph* member *nInS* is equal to the number of vertices in *S*, while *n* is the total number of vertices. The set *S* is expanded as long as *nInS* is less than *n*, as you can see in the *main* function.

If there is no path at all between the start and finish vertices, the program will detect this. It will also display an error message if the user enters unknown vertex names. Linear search, used in the class *strings*, requires $O(n^2)$ time for string handling, where *n* is the number of vertices. For example, if we increase *n* by a factor of 10, not only the number of vertex names to be searched for but also the length of the list to be searched will increase by a factor of 10, so computing time increases by a factor of 10^2. We may find this acceptable, bearing in mind that the time required for Dijkstra's algorithm itself is also $O(n^2)$.

Exercises

9.1   If we require i to be less than j for all edges $\langle i, j \rangle$ in a directed graph, then the graph will have no cycles and we can easily find a topological order of all vertices. Write a program to demonstrate this. Do not use adjacency lists or an adjacency matrix.

9.2   Write a simple CPM program in the spirit of Exercise 9.1, but allowing only activities $\langle i, j \rangle$ with $i < j$.

9.3   Replace the tabular output of program *cpm* with graphical output in the form of line segments for the activities, each having a length proportional to its duration, and placed in its proper position based on a horizontal time axis.

9.4   Extend program *cpm*, so that, in case of a cycle, the vertex numbers of the cycle are printed.

9.5   Write a program which, for any directed graph, lists all vertices that are (not necessarily immediate) successors of a given vertex. The input data for this program consists of a file with a pair $\langle i, j \rangle$ for each edge, as shown at the end of Section 9.3, along with a number entered on the keyboard, denoting the vertex whose successors are desired.

9.6   Use the *strings* module of Section 9.5 for a CPM program similar to that of Section 9.4, so that the smallest possible range of vertex numbers is internally used. Note that class *strings* can handle any strings, not just names consisting of letters. It will therefore still be possible to use vertex numbers, but their range is irrelevant. This will give the user the freedom to use event labels such as 10000, 72000, 23A and *START*.

10

Some Combinatorial Algorithms

10.1 A Variable Number of Nested Loops

Suppose that we have an integer array r, say, of length 3, and that we want some action, such as printing the contents of r, to be performed for all possible values of $r[0]$, $r[1]$, $r[2]$, where each $r[i]$ ranges from a given lower bound $lower[i]$ to a given upper bound $upper[i]$. For example, suppose we have

i	0	1	2
$lower[i]$	5	2	8
$upper[i]$	7	2	9

Then we want array r initially to be given the values 5, 2, 8, followed by 5, 2, 9, and so on, until 7, 2, 9, as the following table shows:

i	0	1	2
	5	2	8
Successive	5	2	9
values of	6	2	8
$r[i]$	6	2	9
	7	2	8
	7	2	9

Obviously, we can achieve this by means of three nested loops:

```
for (r[0] = lower[0]; r[0] <= upper[0]; r[0]++)
for (r[1] = lower[1]; r[1] <= upper[1]; r[1]++)
for (r[2] = lower[2]; r[2] <= upper[2]; r[2]++)
    PrintArray();
```

Although in function *PrintArray* the contents of array *r* can be used for any purpose, let us simply display a line with the integer values $r[0]$, $r[1]$, $r[2]$, in that order:

```
void PrintArray()
{   int i;
    for (i=0; i<n; i++) cout << setw(6) << r[i];
    cout << endl;
}
```

Note that there will be no call to *PrintArray* at all if for some value of *i* the value *lower*[i] is greater than *upper*[i].

So far, everything is extremely simple. We now wish to generalize these three nested loops to *n* nested loops, where *n* is variable. It is our task to achieve the effect that we can write in pseudo-code as follows:

```
for (r[0] = lower[0]; r[0] <= upper[0]; r[0]++)
for (r[1] = lower[1]; r[1] <= upper[1]; r[1]++)

                    . . .

for (r[n-1] = lower[n-1]; r[n-1] <= upper[n-1]; r[n-1]++)
    PrintArray();
```

The problem is that we cannot write down a variable number of nested for-loops. However, recursion provides a simple and elegant solution to this problem. Let us use a function *f*, with one integer argument, *k*. With $0 \leq k < n$, the effect of $f(k)$ will be the execution of

```
for (r[k] = lower[k]; r[k] <= upper[k]; r[k]++)
for (r[k+1] = lower[k+1]; r[k+1] <= upper[k+1]; r[k+1]++)

                    . . .

for (r[n-1] = lower[n-1]; r[n-1] <= upper[n-1]; r[n-1]++)
    PrintArray();
```

Here we have $n - k$ nested loops. With $k = 0$, we have our original *n* nested loops. Making the call $f(n)$ equivalent to *PrintArray*( ), we can describe the effect of $f(k)$ for *k* less than *n* as follows:

```
for (r[k] = lower[k]; r[k] <= upper[k]; r[k]++)
    f(k+1);
```

The following program is based on this idea:

```
// nested: A variable number of nested loops
#include <iostream.h>
#include <iomanip.h>

class loops {
public:
   loops();
   ~loops()
   {  delete[]lower; delete[]upper; delete[]r;
   }
   void print();
private:
   int *lower, *upper, *r, n;
   void f(int k);
   void PrintArray();
};

loops::loops()
{  cout << "Enter n: "; cin >> n;
   lower = new int[n];
   upper = new int[n];
   r = new int[n];
   cout << "Enter " << n << " pairs (lower, upper):\n";
   for (int i=0; i<n; i++)
      cin >> lower[i] >> upper[i];
}

void loops::print()
{  cout << "Output:\n\n ";
   for (int i=0; i<n; i++)
      cout << "  r[" << i << "]";
   cout << endl;
   f(0);  // This call initiates the whole process.
}

void loops::f(int k)
{  if (k == n) PrintArray(); else
   for (r[k] = lower[k]; r[k] <= upper[k]; r[k]++)
      f(k + 1);
}

void loops::PrintArray()
{  for (int i=0; i<n; i++)
      cout << setw(6) << r[i];
   cout << endl;
}

int main()
{  loops L;
   L.print();
   return 0;
}
```

Here is a demonstration of this program:

```
Enter n: 3
Enter 3 pairs (lower, upper):
5   7
2   2
8   9
Output:
    r[0]   r[1]   r[2]
      5      2      8
      5      2      9
      6      2      8
      6      2      9
      7      2      8
      7      2      9
```

Although there is only one occurrence of a recursive call in function f, this call will normally be executed more than once, so dynamically there are several recursive calls. We can analyze the effect of $f(0)$ by means of a tree, as shown in Figure 10.1 for the above example.

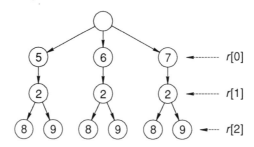

Figure 10.1 Nested loops represented by a tree

There is a node in this tree for each call to f. For example, the root node corresponds with the call $f(0)$, in the function *loops::print*. This call leads to successively storing the values 5, 6 and 7 in array element $r[0]$ and performing a call $f(1)$ for each of these values, and so on. As for the *leaves* of the tree, showing the values of $r[2]$, each corresponding call $f(3)$ results in a call *PrintArray( )*, which prints the values stored in $r[0]$, $r[1]$ and $r[2]$. In many recursive programming problems it will be helpful to imagine a tree similar to this one.

It is instructive to compare our recursive function f with an iterative one. The argument k is necessary in function f because there are so many calls to this function which we must be able to tell apart. With a nonrecursive version there is only one function call, say *fIterative( )*, and no argument is required. We begin by copying the values of *lower*[0], ..., *lower*[$n-1$] into $r[0]$, ..., $r[n-1]$. At the same time we check to see if each of these values is less than or equal to the corresponding element of array *upper*, since otherwise no further actions are to be performed. After copying *lower* into r, we enter a loop in which we immediately perform the call *PrintArray( )*. In the same loop, we then update array r. Since the final element, $r[n-1]$, changes most frequently, it is this element that is incremented. Only when it is equal to *upper*[$n-1$] do we have both to reset it to the value of *lower*[$n-1$] and to go back to $r[n-2]$. If this is less than *upper*[$n-2$] we increment it, otherwise we reset it to the value *lower*[$n-2$] and go back to $r[n-3]$, and so on:

```
void loops::fIterative()
{   int i, n1 = n - 1;
    for (i=0; i<n; i++)
        if (lower[i] > upper[i]) return;
        else r[i] = lower[i];
    for (;;)
    {   PrintArray();
        i = n1;
        for (;;)
        {   if (r[i] < upper[i]){r[i]++; break;}
            r[i] = lower[i];
            if (--i < 0) return;
        }
    }
}
```

If we replace function *loops::f* with the above function *loops::fIterative* in program *nested*, we must also replace

```
void f(int k);
```

with

```
void fIterative();
```

in the declaration of class *loops*. Similarly, we have to replace the call

```
f(0);
```

in function *loops::print*.with this one:

```
fIterative();
```

Function *fIterative* is longer and may be harder to understand than its elegant recursive counterpart *f*, but it will be somewhat faster. In *f*, a recursive call takes place each time $r[n-1]$ is incremented, which happens quite frequently. In the same situation, *fIterative* executes the break-statement, which has the effect of jumping back to the call to *PrintArray*. However, with our function *PrintArray*, which takes a comparatively long time, the difference in speed between *fIterative* and *f* will be negligible.

There is, however, another argument in favor of an iterative solution. On the basis of the iterative function *fIterative*, we can easily write a function, say, *NextSequence*, which generates the next sequence $r[0]$, ..., $r[n-1]$. In our example, with {5, 2, 8} as initial contents of *r*, the first call to *NextSequence* would replace these contents with {5, 2, 9}, and after the second call the contents of *r* would be {6, 2, 8}, and so on. This way of generating sequences is required if we want to generate these sequences on the basis of certain decisions, made elsewhere in our program and possibly initiated by the user. A recursive function, such as *f*, can only generate these sequences 'under its own control', which is not always what we want. We will discuss this point in more detail at the end of the next section.

10.2 Permutations

With n (distinct) objects, we can form

$$n! = 1 \times 2 \times ... \times n$$

distinct sequences. We verify this as follows. We can choose n objects as the first element of the sequence. Then for the second element, we have to choose out of the $n-1$ remaining objects. Since such a choice of $n-1$ elements can be made after each of the n previous choices for the first element, we have

$$n \times (n-1)$$

possible choices for the first two elements of the sequence. Now there are only $n-2$ objects left, out of which we choose the third element, so for the first three elements we have

$$n \times (n-1) \times (n-2)$$

possible choices, and so on. Continuing in this way until there is only one object left, we find that altogether the number of choices (that is, the number of possible sequences) is equal to

$$n \times (n-1) \times (n-2) \times ... \times 2 \times 1 = n!$$

As each of these sequences is called a *permutation*, there are $n!$ permutations of n distinct objects. Without loss of generality, we will use the numbers

$$1, 2, ..., n$$

for these objects. In case of other objects, we can use their positions in an array to identify them. In this and the next section, we will simplify our discussion by also using array subscript values 1, 2, ..., n, instead of 0, 1, ..., $n-1$. We can realize this by simply increasing the array length by 1, writing, for example, $r = new\ int\ [n + 1]$, and accepting that $r[0]$ is never used. (The following, more complicated method would avoid allocating memory space for an unused array element: int $*u = new\ int[n]$, $*r = u-1$; we would then be able to use $r[1]$, ..., $r[n]$ (not $r[0]$) and to release this array later by writing $delete[\,]u;$. This method might be useful for arrays with very large elements, but it would be silly to use it here.)

We now want to write a program which, after reading n, generates all permutations of those n numbers. Each of these permutations can be regarded as a (long) integer in the number system with base m, where m can be any number greater than n. Quite simply, if n is less than 10, we can associate each sequence with an integer written as n decimal digits. For example, with $n = 6$, the permutation

3 6 1 5 4 2

corresponds with the integer 361542. With this association of permutations and integers, we can order the permutations according to the *less than* relation for integers. For example, if $n = 3$, our program is to generate the following six permutations, in this order:

```
1   2   3
1   3   2
2   1   3
2   3   1
3   1   2
3   2   1
```

We will write function *permut*, which in the array elements $r[1]$, ..., $r[n]$, generates all permutations of the integers 1, ..., n, as shown above for $n = 3$. This function is based on induction. Using its parameter k, we divide the relevant elements of array r into a left and a right partition, the latter starting at position k:

$$r[1] \quad ... \quad r[k-1] \qquad \qquad r[k] \quad ... \quad r[n]$$
$$(k - 1 \text{ elements}) \qquad \qquad (n - k + 1 \text{ elements})$$

Instead of demanding that all n array elements be used in our permutation-generating process, we keep those in the left partition constant. In other words,

$permut(k)$ prints all permutations of $r[k]$, ..., $r[n]$

where each of these permutations is preceded by the same $k - 1$ elements. It follows that in the *main* function we can write $permut(1)$ to print all $n!$ permutations of the given array elements, because $k = 1$ implies that the left partition is empty and that the right one has length n. As you may expect, function *permut* is recursive, and any call $permut(k)$ gives rise to recursive calls $permut(k+1)$, that is, if $k \leq n$. Remember, the higher k is, the simpler the problem. In particular, we simply print the current values of $r[1]$, ..., $r[n]$ if $k = n + 1$. We now assume that $permut(k+1)$ works properly, and we use this to construct the actions required for the call $permut(k)$. In other words, we assume that we know how to generate all permutations of the final $n - k$ elements, and we use this to generate all permutations of the final $n - k + 1$ elements (of the right-hand partition). Each of the elements $r[i]$ ($i = k$, ..., n) of this partition must in turn appear in position k. For example, with $n = 6$ and $k = 3$, there are $6 - 3 + 1 = 4$ elements in the right partition, which gives $4! = 24$ permutations of this partition. These can be divided into four groups of six permutations. The first of these groups, generated by $permut(4)$, is

```
1   2   3   4   5   6                                      (P₃)
1   2   3   4   6   5
1   2   3   5   4   6
1   2   3   5   6   4
1   2   3   6   4   5
1   2   3   6   5   4
```

The six integers on each line are the current values of $r[1]$, ..., $r[6]$. After this first group of six permutations, based on (P$_3$), there follows a similar one, also generated by *permut*(4), but this time based on (P$_4$), shown below:

$$1 \quad 2 \quad \mathbf{4} \quad 3 \quad 5 \quad 6 \qquad\qquad\qquad\qquad (P_4)$$

After this second group, two more such groups of six permutations appear, each generated by a call *permut*(4). The third one is based on

$$1 \quad 2 \quad \mathbf{5} \quad 3 \quad 4 \quad 6 \qquad\qquad\qquad\qquad (P_5)$$

and the fourth one on

$$1 \quad 2 \quad \mathbf{6} \quad 3 \quad 4 \quad 5 \qquad\qquad\qquad\qquad (P_6)$$

Each of these four groups is characterized by its kth position, printed here in boldface. For each group, we use its first permutation to construct the others by means of recursive calls *permut*(k+1). The first permutation (P$_3$) of the first group is given. The only remaining problem is how to derive the first permutations (P$_4$), (P$_5$), (P$_6$) of the other three groups from it. We do this by means of *rotations*. For example, we find (P$_5$) as follows. Starting with (P$_3$), we shift the contents of $r[3]$ and $r[4]$ one position to the right and place the old contents of $r[5]$ into $r[3]$. In general, with a given initial permutation (P$_k$) (such as (P$_3$) in our example), we find (P$_i$) ($i = k$+1, ..., n) as follows:

```
tmp = r[i];
for (j=i; j>k; j--) r[j] = r[j-1];
r[k] = tmp;
```

Here is a complete demonstration program, including function *permut*, in which all this is realized:

```
// perm: Generation of permutations in natural order
#include <iostream.h>

class permutations {
public:
    permutations();
    ~permutations(){delete[]r;}
    void print(){cout << "Permutations:\n"; permut(1);}
private:
    int *r, n;
    void permut(int k);
};

permutations::permutations()
{   cout << "Enter n: "; cin >> n;
    r = new int[n + 1];
    for (int i=1; i<=n; i++)
        r[i] = i;
}
```

```
void permutations::permut(int k)
/* The call permut(k) prints a group of (n-k+1)! lines, each
   with the n integers r[1], ..., r[k-1], r[k], ..., r[n] in
   which r[1], ..., r[k-1] do not change but in which
   r[k], ..., r[n] assume all permutations of these n-k+1
   elements on the right. It follows that the call permut(1)
   prints all n! permutations of r[1], ..., r[n]. The
   permutations are printed in ascending order.
*/
{  int i, j, tmp;
   if (k <= n)
   for (i=k; i<=n; i++)
   {  /* For each i, element r[i] is moved to
         position k and the (old) elements
         r[k], ..., r[i-1] are shifted one
         position to the right:
      */
      tmp = r[i];
      for (j=i; j>k; j--) r[j] = r[j - 1];
      r[k] = tmp;
      // Without altering r[k], a recursive call
      // is applied to r[k+1], ..., r[n]:
      permut(k+1);
      // Restore old situation:
      for (j=k; j<i; j++) r[j] = r[j+1];
      r[i] = tmp;
   } else
   {  // If k == n, the group consists of only one
      // permutation, which is now printed:
      for (i=1; i<=n; i++) cout << r[i] << " ";
      cout << endl;
   }
}

int main()
{  permutations P;
   P.print();
   return 0;
}
```

Here is a demonstration of this program:

```
Enter n: 3
Permutations:
1 2 3
1 3 2
2 1 3
2 3 1
3 1 2
3 2 1
```

As in the previous section, a tree may be helpful in understanding how program *perm* works. For $n = 3$, this tree is shown in Figure 10.2.

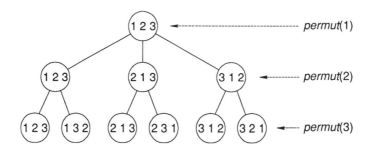

Figure 10.2 Tree illustrating the generation of permutations

Each node shows the contents of array r just before a call to *permut* indicated by a dotted arrow on the right. For example, the node in the center of the tree indicates that we have $r[1] = 2$, $r[2] = 1$, $r[3] = 3$ immediately before a call *permut*(2). The argument 2 of this call expresses that only the partition $\{r[2], r[3]\}$ is permuted in the two child nodes, shown in the middle at the bottom, with contents 2, 1, 3 and 2, 3, 1.

Generating one permutation at a time

In program *perm* the generation process is controlled by the recursive function *permut*. This is undesirable or even unacceptable if our program, with a flow of control dictated by our application, simply contains a loop in which repeatedly the next permutation of the sequence 1, 2, ..., n is required. We could of course generate all permutations beforehand, store them in a file, and read them one by one later. However, it is more elegant and more efficient not to generate a new permutation until we need it. The idea of generating permutations in ascending order is now very helpful. Initially we fill array r in the same way as before, that is, with 1 in $r[1]$, 2 in $r[2]$, ..., n in $r[n]$. Then we can derive each new permutation from the previous one. For example, suppose that $n = 4$ and that, at some moment, the current permutation is

$$2 \quad 3 \quad 1 \quad 4 \tag{1}$$

Since $1 < 4$, the next permutation is obtained by exchanging 1 and 4, which gives

$$2 \quad 3 \quad 4 \quad 1 \tag{2}$$

Now that the two final elements 4 and 1 are in decreasing order, finding the next permutation is somewhat trickier. We cannot simply use (2) to swap 3 and 4, because that would *not* lead to the result

$$2 \quad 4 \quad 1 \quad 3 \tag{3}$$

we need. We can obtain this desired result (3), however, by exchanging 3 and 4 in (1). If we use some more concrete examples, we soon find that we should proceed as follows:

1. Find the longest decreasing subsequence (possibly of length 1) at the end of the current permutation. Suppose this sequence starts immediately after position k. The process terminates if $k = 0$, for then all elements of r are in decreasing order and all permutations have been generated.
2. Convert this subsequence into an increasing one.
3. There is at least one element in this subsequence that is greater than $r[k]$. Out of these elements greater than $r[k]$, select the smallest one, say, $r[i]$.
4. Exchange $r[k]$ and $r[i]$.

This algorithm is remarkably simple. It is implemented as function *NextPerm* in the following program. This function is called each time the user enters 1 on the keyboard.

```cpp
// nextperm: Find the next permutation

#include <iostream.h>

class perm {
public:
    perm();
    ~perm()
    {  delete[]r;
    }
    void demo();
private:
    int *r, n;
    void NextPerm(void);
};

perm::perm()
{  cout << "Iterative permutation generator"
        << " for 1, 2, ..., n.\n"
        << "Enter n: "; cin >> n;
   r = new int[n + 1];
   for (int i=1; i<=n; i++)
      r[i] = i;
}

void perm::demo()
{  int code, i, j=0;
   for (;;)
   {  cout << "Enter 1 to display the next permutation"
           << " or 0 to stop: ";
      cin >> code;
      if (code == 0)
         return;
      cout << "Permutation " << ++j << ": ";
      for (i=1; i<=n; i++)
         cout << r[i] << " ";
      cout << endl;
      NextPerm();
   }
}
```

```
void perm::NextPerm()
{  /* This function replaces r[1], ..., r[n],
      containing a permutation of 1, ..., n,
      with the next permutation.
   */
   int i, k, tmp, left, right;
   // Find longest decreasing subsequence
   // r[k+1], ..., r[n] on the right:
   k = n - 1;
   while (k > 0 && r[k] > r[k+1])
      k--;
   left = k + 1; right = n;
   // Convert that subsequence into an
   // increasing one:
   while (left < right)
   {  tmp = r[left];
      r[left++] = r[right];
      r[right--] = tmp;
   }
   if (k == 0) return; // No element to the left of r[k+1]
   /* The subsequence mentioned above is increasing.
      Out of this subsequence, select the smallest
      element r[i] that is greater than r[k]. Swap r[i] and
      r[k]:
   */
   i = k+1;
   while (r[i] < r[k]) i++;
   tmp = r[i];
   r[i] = r[k];
   r[k] = tmp;
}

int main()
{  perm P;
   P.demo();
   return 0;
}
```

Here is a demonstration of this program. Only three of the 4! = 24 permutations are shown:

```
Iterative permutation generator for 1, 2, ..., n.
Enter n: 4

Enter 1 to display the next permutation or 0 to stop: 1
Permutation 1: 1 2 3 4

Enter 1 to display the next permutation or 0 to stop: 1
Permutation 2: 1 2 4 3

Enter 1 to display the next permutation or 0 to stop: 1
Permutation 3: 1 3 2 4

Enter 1 to display the next permutation or 0 to stop: 0
```

10.3 Combinations

If we are given both a set of n distinct objects, say, the numbers 1, 2, ..., n, and an integer k $(0 \le k \le n)$, we may be interested in all possible subsets that contain exactly k of these objects. There are

$$\binom{n}{k} = \frac{n(n-1)(n-2) \ldots (n-k+1)}{k!} = \frac{n!}{k!(n-k)!}$$

such subsets, each of which is called a *combination*. For example, if $n = 5$ and $k = 3$, we have the following 10 combinations:

```
1 2 3
1 2 4
1 2 5
1 3 4
1 3 5
1 4 5
2 3 4
2 3 5
2 4 5
3 4 5
```

Since each combination is a subset, the order of the elements in it is irrelevant, as the order of the elements in any set is irrelevant. For example, the triple

```
3 2 1
```

is not included in these ten lines, since it would represent the same combination as

```
1 2 3
```

Let us write each combination as an increasing sequence. We now want to write a program to generate all combinations of k elements out of n objects, where n and k are given. Besides representing each combination by an increasing sequence, we also want these representations to appear in ascending order, in the same way as the permutations were ordered in the previous section. Note that the ten combinations listed above are in this order. This time, we begin with a tree for the above example with $n = 5$ and $k = 3$, as Figure 10.3 shows.

Each node corresponds with a call to a recursive function, *combin*, with an argument equal to the node level (1 for the root node and 4 for the leaves). The numbers in the nodes are the values placed in $r[1]$, $r[2]$ or $r[3]$, as indicated in the column on the right. Each path from the root to a leaf represents a combination. For the first element, $r[1]$, we can choose 1, 2 or 3 as its possible values, but not 4 or 5, for then not enough greater numbers would be available to follow $r[1]$.

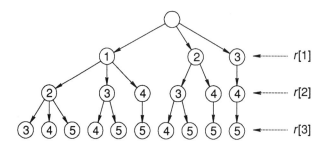

Figure 10.3 Tree illustrating the generation of combinations (n = 5, k = 3)

In general, $r[1]$ ranges from 1 to $n - k + 1$. Depending on $r[1]$, we can make one or more choices for $r[2]$. More precisely, $r[2]$ ranges from $r[1] + 1$ to $n - k + 2$. In the same way, $r[3]$ ranges from $r[2] + 1$ to $n - k + 3$, and so on. So conceptually we need the following nested for-statement:

```
for (r[1] = 1; r[1] <= n - k + 1; r[1]++)
for (r[2] = r[1] + 1; r[2] <= n - k + 2; r[2]++)
                        . . .
for (r[k] = r[k-1] + 1; r[k] <= n; r[k]++)
   print r[1], r[2], ..., r[n]
```

This problem is similar to the subject of Section 10.1. Again we can implement this variable number of loops by means of a recursive function. The above nested loops can be given a more homogeneous appearance if we define $r[0] = 0$, since this enables us to replace the first line with

```
for (r[1] = r[0] + 1; r[1] <= n - k + 1; r[1]++)
```

which makes it more similar to the others. The complete program for the rather complex task is surprisingly small:

```
// comb: Generation of combinations in natural order
#include <iostream.h>

class combinations {
public:
    combinations();
    ~combinations()
    { delete[]r;
    }
    void print()
    { cout << "Combinations:\n"; combin(1);
    }
private:
    int *r, n, k;
    void combin(int m);
};
```

```
combinations::combinations()
{  do
   {  cout << "Enter n and k (k not greater than n): ";
      cin >> n >> k;
   }  while (n < 0 || k < 0 || k > n);
   r = new int[k + 1]; r[0] = 0;
}

void combinations::combin(int m)
{  if (m <= k)
   {  for (r[m] = r[m-1] + 1; r[m] <= n-k+m; r[m]++)
         combin(m + 1);
   }  else
   {  for (int i=1; i<=k; i++) cout << r[i] << " ";
      cout << endl;
   }
}

int main()
{  combinations P;
   P.print();
   return 0;
}
```

The following demonstration generates all combinations with $n = 4$ and $k = 2$:

```
Enter n and k (k not greater than n): 4 2
Combinations:
1 2
1 3
1 4
2 3
2 4
3 4
```

Generating one combination at a time

Like permutations, combinations may be required one by one. We can therefore also write an iterative function *comb*::*NextComb*, which manipulates the array elements $r[1]$, ..., $r[k]$ containing a combination of 1, 2, ..., n:

```
// nextcomb: Find the next combination
#include <iostream.h>

class comb {
public:
   comb();
   ~comb(){delete[]r;}
   void demo();
private:
   int *r, n, k;
   int NextComb(void);
};
```

```
comb::comb()
{  cout << "Iterative combination generator for k elements\n"
        << "out of 1, 2, ..., n.\n";
   do
   {  cout << "Enter n and k (k not greater than n): ";
      cin >> n >> k;
   }  while (n < 0 || k < 0 || k > n);
   r = new int[k + 1];
   for (int i=1; i<=k; i++)
      r[i] = i;
}

void comb::demo()
{  int code, i, j=0;
   do
   {  cout << "\nEnter 1 to display the next combination "
           << "or 0 to stop: ";
      cin >> code;
      if (code == 0)
         return;
      cout << "Combination " << ++j << ": ";
      for (i=1; i<=k; i++)
         cout << r[i] << " ";
      cout << endl;
   }  while (NextComb());
}

int comb::NextComb()
{  // If another combination can be generated, this is
   // placed in r[1], ..., r[k] and the value 1 is returned.
   // Otherwise, the return value is 0.
   int i = k, j;
   // Find the greatest i for which r[i] can be increased:
   while (i > 0 && r[i] == n - k + i)
      i--;
   if (i == 0)
      return 0;   // No new combination
   // Increase r[i] and reset r[i+1], ..., r[k] to their
   // lowest possible values (with r in ascending order).
   r[i]++;
   for (j=i+1; j<=k; j++)
      r[j] = r[j-1] + 1;
   return 1;
}

int main()
{  comb P;
   P.demo();
   return 0;
}
```

Function *NextComb* simply replaces the contents of array *r* with the next combination (according to the way we have ordered them). In addition to some comments in program *nextcomb*, the following demonstration may also be helpful in understanding it:

```
Iterative combination generator for k elements
out of 1, 2, ..., n.
Enter n and k (k not greater than n): 4 2

Enter 1 to display the next combination or 0 to stop: 1
Combination 1: 1 2

Enter 1 to display the next combination or 0 to stop: 1
Combination 2: 1 3

Enter 1 to display the next combination or 0 to stop: 1
Combination 3: 1 4

Enter 1 to display the next combination or 0 to stop: 1
Combination 4: 2 3

Enter 1 to display the next combination or 0 to stop: 0
```

10.4 The Knapsack Problem

The combination problem in the last section was essentially about finding subsets of a given set. This is also the case in the classic *knapsack problem*. Suppose we have to choose some out of several items, to be carried on our back. Each item has both a weight and a utility value, and a choice must be made such that the total weight of the selected items does not exceed some limit (the maximum load that can be carried). At the same time, the total utility of the chosen items should be maximized. We will simplify this problem in two respects. First, we will require the total weight to be exactly equal to the given limit, and, second, we will assume the utility values of the items to be proportional to their weights. This means that, if possible, we have to find a subset consisting of items with a total weight equal to the maximum weight that can be carried. It will be clear that we can think of many similar problems, for example how to choose a subset of the coins and banknotes that are in our purse, to pay some amount of money. In general, we are given both a sum s and n positive integers

$$d_0, d_1, ..., d_{n-1}$$

and we are to find a subset of these integers (each occurring at most once) whose sum is s. To solve this problem, we will develop a function *ExactSum*, called in the main program as follows:

```
if (ExactSum(s, 0)) ... // Solution found
   else cout << "No solution.\n";
```

In general, the call *ExactSum(t, i)* is to examine if the target t can be formed as the sum of some integers chosen out of the sequence

$$d_i, d_{i+1}, ..., d_{n-1}$$

If this is possible, the chosen integers are to be printed and the value to be returned is 1; if not, the value 0 is to be returned. Function *ExactSum* is recursive; as usual with recursion, we have an 'escape clause' to prevent the function from calling itself forever. If $t = 0$, the problem is solved by using an empty subset, and the problem cannot be solved if $t < 0$ or $i = n$. If t is positive and i is less than n, *ExactSum* (with arguments t and i) finds out if the target $t - d_i$ can be formed as the sum of some integers chosen out of the sequence

$d_{i+1}, d_{i+2}, ..., d_{n-1}$

For this, we use the recursive call

```
ExactSum(t - d[i], i + 1)
```

If its value is 1, we know that there is a solution, and we print the value of d_i, which is included in the solution. If it returns 0, we perform the call

```
ExactSum(t, i + 1)
```

to examine if there is a solution that does not include d_i. If this is not the case either, there is no solution. Program *knapsack* shows both the definition of function *ExactSum* and the way this function can be used.

```
/* knapsack:
      This program solves the (simplified) knapsack problem:
      given a sum s and a set of positive integers, it finds
      a subset whose elements have sum s, if this is possible.
*/
#include <iostream.h>

class knapsack {
public:
   knapsack();
   ~knapsack()
   { delete[]d;
   }
   void solve();
private:
   int s, *d, n;
   int ExactSum(int t, int i);
};

knapsack::knapsack()
{ cout << "Knapsack problem; enter the desired sum: ";
   cin >> s;
   cout << "Enter n, followed by n integers:\n";
   cin >> n;
   d = new int[n];
   for (int i=0; i<n; i++)
      cin >> d[i];
}
```

```
void knapsack::solve()
{  cout << "Output:\n";
   if (ExactSum(s, 0)) cout << "(sum = " << s << ")\n";
   else cout << "No solution.\n";
}

int knapsack::ExactSum(int t, int i)
{  // Is t equal to the sum of some elements
   // of the sequence d[i], d[i+1], ..., d[n-1]?
   // If so, display these elements and return 1.
   // Otherwise, return 0.
   if (t < 0) return 0;         // No solution
   if (t == 0) return 1;        // Trivial solution
   // For each available d[j], check if it can be
   // part of the solution:
   for (int j=i; j<n; j++)
       if (ExactSum(t - d[j], j+1))
       {  cout << d[j] << " "; return 1;
       }
   return 0;
}

int main()
{  knapsack K;
   K.solve();
   return 0;
}
```

Here is a demonstration of this program:

```
Knapsack problem; enter the desired sum: 18
Enter n, followed by n integers:
7
2 2 2 5 5 9 11
Output:
9 5 2 2 (sum = 18)
```

We see that program *knapsack* simply gives the first solution it finds. Instead, we may want to select the best, or *optimal*, solution in some particular sense. In our example, we may require the sum s to consist of as few terms as is possible. We see that besides the computed solution

$$18 = 9 + 5 + 2 + 2$$

there is also the solution

$$18 = 11 + 5 + 2$$

which, according to the above requirement, would be required instead, because this sum consists of only three terms instead of four. Program *knapsack* would actually have found the latter solution if we had entered the numbers d_i in the reverse order, that is, as

```
11 9 5 5 2 2 2
```

We could, of course, sort the numbers d_i in the program itself, and use them in decreasing order, regardless of the order in which they are entered. However, a decreasing sequence does not guarantee finding the 'shortest' solution either, as the following demonstration shows:

```
Knapsack problem; enter the desired sum: 18
Enter n, followed by n integers:
7
7 7 6 6 6 2 2
Output:
2 2 7 7 (sum = 18)
```

Unfortunately, the shorter solution

$$18 = 6 + 6 + 6$$

is not found. Although in most cases it is a good strategy to use the largest number available, there are exceptions. An algorithm based on the strategy of selecting what 'looks best' is said to be *greedy*. (For some problems, there are greedy algorithms that always lead to an optimal solution, so 'greedy' is not necessarily a bad qualification, as far as algorithms are concerned.) In the next section, we will find an optimal solution for a problem for which we cannot use a greedy algorithm.

10.5 Dynamic Programming

We will now deal with a problem that is more interesting than the previous one. Again, an integer sum s is given, along with n positive integers

$$d_0, d_1, ..., d_{n-1}$$

In contrast to the knapsack problem, solved in Section 10.4, each integer d_i may now occur more than once as a term in the solution. A more interesting new point is that we will now insist on using as few terms as possible in forming sum s. For example, if we have

$$s = 18$$
$$n = 3$$
$$d_0 = 2, d_1 = 6, d_2 = 7$$

then we want the sum s to be formed as

$$18 = 6 + 6 + 6$$

but not as, for example,

$$18 = 7 + 7 + 2 + 2$$

or as

$$18 = 6 + 2 + 2 + 2 + 2 + 2 + 2$$

Recall that there was no such requirement with the knapsack problem in the previous section. As you can see, 6 occurs three times in the above correct solution, although it is given only once in the input data. This, too, was different in our discussion of the knapsack problem. An application of this is making change in a shop, assuming that we have plenty of coins and banknotes. For example, suppose that, in some currency, we had plenty of coins with values of 1c, 5c, 10c and 25c, and we have to pay 42c. We would then immediately compute

$$42 = 25 + 10 + 5 + 1 + 1$$

if we wanted to use as few coins as possible. With the coin values mentioned, we always obtain the optimal solution by using a *greedy* algorithm. As mentioned in Section 10.4, this means that, each time, we simply use the largest coin that does not exceed the remaining amount to be paid. However, we will use a more general algorithm, which gives an optimal solution even in cases where a greedy algorithm does not. We really need such an algorithm if there are no coins of 5c available. With

$$s = 42,$$
$$n = 3,$$
$$d_0 = 1, d_1 = 10, d_2 = 25,$$

a greedy algorithm would yield

$$42 = 25 + 10 + 1 + 1 + 1 + 1 + 1 + 1 + 1$$

with a sum of nine terms, instead of the optimal solution of only six terms:

$$42 = 10 + 10 + 10 + 10 + 1 + 1$$

In cases like this (and many others) we can use a tabular technique, called *dynamic programming*. Explaining this important technique in full generality would be beyond the scope of this book, so we will discuss it only in connection with our problem. We define function $F(x)$ as the minimum number of terms (or coins) needed to form the sum x. It follows that F is defined only for those values x for which there is a solution. Since we will be storing the function values $F(x)$ as array elements $F[x]$, we will from now on use the latter notation. If the smallest value d_i is greater than 1, $F[1]$ is undefined because we cannot form the sum 1 using only such d_i values. Dynamic programming, applied to our application, is based on the equation

$$F[x] = 1 + \min_{0 \le i < n} F[x-d_i]$$

for certain positive integers x (see below) and on

$$F[0] = 0$$

If, with the given range of i, some values $F[x - d_i]$ exist, we select the minimum of them, and add 1 to this minimum to obtain the value $F[x]$. If no such values $F[x - d_i]$ exist, then $F[x]$ does not exist either. Although the above formula suggests recursion, we had better take the 'bottom-up' approach this time (see also Section 4.11, where we analyzed a simple recursive function in a similar way). Thus, we will not begin with the given sum s, but rather try to compute $F[1]$, $F[2]$, ..., $F[s]$, in that order. The resulting program would be very simple if only the value $F[s]$ were needed, since then we would only have to use an array of integers to store the computed values $F[x]$. As we are also interested in the selected values d_i, we have to store these as well. We will see in a moment how this can be done, after we have seen the program in action.

The following demonstration shows that the program is not restricted to such small numbers as we have been using in our previous examples:

```
Enter the desired sum: 5000
Enter n, followed by n integers:
3
9 132 1234
Solution:
5000 = 32 x 9 + 17 x 132 + 2 x 1234
```

As you can see, long lists of equal terms are written as products in the usual way. Obviously, the original terms are still counted individually; in other words, we regard the last output line as 5000 expressed as a sum of $32 + 17 + 2 = 51$ terms. This example demonstrates that the algorithm is not greedy: although both 3×1234 and 4×1234 are less than the desired sum 5000, it is not possible to combine these with multiples of 9 and 132 to obtain this sum.

If there is no solution at all, the program will tell this, as the following example shows:

```
Enter the desired sum: 11
Enter n, followed by n integers:
3
9 7 5
No solution.
```

Let us use the following example in our discussion of the algorithm:

```
Enter the desired sum: 18
Enter n, followed by n integers:
3
7 6 2
Solution:
18 = 6 + 6 + 6
```

It may be instructive to see what is actually computed in a simple case, such as the last example:

x	$F[x]$	Selected integers
0	0	
1	-	
2	1	2
3	-	
4	2	$2 + 2$
5	-	
6	1	6
7	1	7
8	2	$6 + 2$
9	2	$7 + 2$
10	3	$6 + 2 + 2$
11	3	$7 + 2 + 2$
12	2	$6 + 6$
13	2	$7 + 6$
14	2	$7 + 7$
15	3	$7 + 6 + 2$
16	3	$7 + 7 + 2$
17	4	$7 + 6 + 2 + 2$
18	3	$6 + 6 + 6$

To find the final value, $F[18]$, the minimum of the three values

$$F[18 - 7] = F[11] = 3$$
$$F[18 - 6] = F[12] = 2$$
$$F[18 - 2] = F[16] = 3$$

is chosen and increased by 1, so we have

$$F[18] = F[18 - 6] + 1 = 3$$

The program *dynpro* is listed below; it will be followed by a discussion of some implementation details:

```
/* dynpro: An application of dynamic programming.
      With a given integer s and a set of positive integers,
      we try to write s as a sum of as few terms as
      possible, each term belonging to the given set.
*/
#include <iostream.h>
#include <limits.h>
#include <stdlib.h>

class dynpro {
public:
   dynpro();
   ~dynpro(){delete[]d; delete[]F; delete[]ref; delete[]val;}
   void solve(), print();
```

```cpp
private:
   int s, n, *d, *F, *ref, *val;
   void product(int m, int v)
   { if (m > 1) cout << m << " x ";
     cout << v;
   }
};

dynpro::dynpro()
{  cout << "Enter the desired sum: ";
   long sLong;
   cin >> sLong;
   if (sLong < 0 || sLong > INT_MAX)
   {  cout << "Invalid value\n"; exit(1);
   }
   s = int(sLong);
   F = new int[s + 1];
   ref = new int[s + 1];
   val = new int[s + 1];
   cout << "Enter n, followed by n integers:\n";
   cin >> n;
   d = new int[n];
   for (int i=0; i<n; i++) cin >> d[i];
}

void dynpro::solve()
{  int x, u, u1, i, i1, F1;
   F[0] = 0;
   for (x=1; x<=s; x++)
   {  F1 = INT_MAX;
      for (i=0; i<n; i++)
      {  u = x - d[i];
         if (u >= 0 && F[u] < F1){F1 = F[u]; i1 = i; u1 = u;}
      }
      if (F1 < INT_MAX)
      {  F[x] = F1 + 1; ref[x] = u1; val[x] = d[i1];
      } else F[x] = INT_MAX;
   }
}

void dynpro::print()
{  if (F[s] == INT_MAX) cout << "No solution.\n"; else
   {  cout << "Solution:\n";
      cout << s << " = ";
      int k = s, v = val[s], m = 1;
      for (int j=2; j<=F[s]; j++)
      {  k = ref[k];
         if (val[k] == v) m++; else
         {  product(m, v); cout << " + ";
            v = val[k]; m = 1;
         }
      }
      product(m, v); cout << endl;
   }
}
```

```
int main()
{   dynpro DP;
    DP.solve();
    DP.print();
    return 0;
}
```

Some implementation details

Program *dynpro*, listed above, shows an implementation of the algorithm we have been discussing. A class, also called *dynpro*, enables us to do all work by these three statements in the *main* function:

```
dynpro DP; DP.solve(); DP.print();
```

The program has no limitations other than those imposed by the environment. For example, memory for the table is allocated dynamically after it is known how much is actually required. The selected terms that belong to $F[x]$ (and which add up to x) are stored in an economic way. Recall that each value $F[x]$, except $F[0]$, is based on some selected value $F[u]$, where u is less than x and $F[x] = F[u] + 1$. The terms that together form x are the same as those that form u, except that one new term is added. Instead of storing all these terms for $F[x]$, we need to store only a reference to u along with the new term used for x. Since the information at position u may in turn be based on a previous position in the table, we have to follow a *chain of table entries* to find all terms required for x. As for the table in question, we might consider using a dynamically allocated array of structures, as in

```
struct table{int F, ref, val} *t;
...
t = new table[s + 1];
```

However, in view of possibly very large values of s, it may be wise to replace this single 'array' t with three separate ones:

```
int *F, *ref, *val, ...;
...
F = new int[s + 1];
ref = new int[s + 1];
val = new int[s + 1];
```

This also works if three separate memory blocks, of $(s + 1) * sizeof(int)$ bytes each, are available, while one contiguous block for t, three times as large, is not.

As will be clear from our previous discussion, $F[x]$ is equal to the number of terms that add up to x. These terms are found as the following elements of array *val*:

```
val[x]
val[u1] where u1 = ref[x]
val[u2] where u2 = ref[u1]
val[u3] where u3 = ref[u2]
```

and so on, until we have found $F[x]$ terms.

Exercises

10.1   Write a program to generate 'words'. The program is to read the word length n and, for each of the n positions, the letters that are allowed in that position. For example, with $n = 3$, the following letters may be given:

Position 1: B, L, N, R
Position 2: A, E, O, U
Position 3: L, M, N, S, T

This should lead to $4 \times 4 \times 5 = 80$ words:

```
BAL
BAM
 . . .
RUS
RUT
```

(It may disappoint you that only a few of such generated 'words' have a meaning. It shows that if we need an unused letter combination for a new word, there are plenty, even if we want the word to be very short!)

10.2   In Section 10.2, we were generating permutations in a certain order. To achieve this, each recursive call was preceded by a rotation to the right. If the order in which the permutations appear is irrelevant, it is faster to exchange two elements instead. The inverse operation is to be performed after the recursive call. Write a program that uses this faster method.

10.3   Write a program which reads a positive integer n, followed by n distinct capital letters. The program is to generate all words that are permutations of the given n letters, except for words with more than two successive vowels and words with more than two successive consonants. The five letters A, E, I, O, U are vowels, the 21 others are to be regarded as consonants.

10.4   Write a program which reads the positive integers n and k ($k \leq n$), followed by n names. Generate all combinations of k names out of the given n names. This program may be useful if for some game we want a list of all possible teams of k persons, to be formed out of a population of n persons.

Hint: You can use class *strings* of Section 9.5.

11

Fundamentals of Interpreters and Compilers

11.1 Syntax Diagrams for a Very Simple Language

This chapter deals with a well-defined infinite set of character strings that represent arithmetic expressions. In formal language theory such a set of strings (not necessarily consisting of arithmetic expressions) is called a *language*, so this word has a special technical meaning, to be distinguished from what we call a 'language' in everyday life. Whether or not a given string belongs to the language in question is determined by certain formation rules, also called *grammar* or *syntax rules*. For example, the C++ language can be defined as the set of all possible C++ programs. In this case, and for programming languages in general, there are also *semantic rules*, which define the actions to be performed when the programs are executed. We will define the Very Simple Language VSL. This is not just a language in the sense of formal language theory, but each element of the language is a simple arithmetic expression with a very clear meaning, namely a computation in accordance with elementary arithmetic and resulting in an integer. Although it may be a bit pretentious, we will speak about VSL *programs*. Our goal will be to *implement* this new language, or, as we may say, we are interested in VSL *implementations*. As may be expected in this book, we will present such implementations in the form of C++ programs. Depending on how they work, we call these C++ programs either *interpreters* or *compilers*.

The present chapter is included in this book for two reasons. First, as we use real interpreters and compilers quite often, it is good to have some idea about how they work, and basic principles are always best explained by simple examples, hence our Very Simple Language. Second, we may want to write programs that allow the user to enter some arithmetic expression, so that the program can read this and either interpret it or convert it to some internal format. This chapter will enable us to write such programs.

The language that we will be dealing with consists of VSL programs. Here are three examples:

```
{3 - 5}
{1 - 2 * ((9 - 5 + 1 - 2 * 3) - 2)}
{8}
```

A VSL program is written as an *expression*, as defined below, surrounded by a pair of braces { }. These redundant braces make it easy to check the correctness of the very beginning and the very end of the 'program'. An expression consists of one or more *terms* separated by addition and subtraction operators (+ and −). Similarly, each term consists of one or more *factors*, separated by multiplication operators (*). Finally, each factor consists of either a one-digit integer or an expression surrounded by parentheses. A verbal description like this would do for VSL, but not for a real programming language. We therefore normally use a more formal means for syntactic definitions, such as a set of *syntax diagrams*. Figure 11.1 shows syntax diagrams for VSL. (It will be clear that in the last diagram the three dots denote the remaining seven digits 2, 3, 4, 5, 6, 7, 8.) The first diagram says that a program consists of three components, namely an open brace ({), an expression, and a close brace (}), in that order. In these syntax diagrams, symbols in circles, such as { in

are *primitive* or *terminal symbols*: they may occur literally in a program, whereas names such as *expression* in

Expression

denote *syntactic categories*, also known as *nonterminal symbols*. In a complete set of syntax diagrams (such as Figure 11.1), there is a syntax diagram for every nonterminal symbol that is used.

A VSL program can be quite complex, as the following example, consisting of two lines, shows:

```
{((1 + 8 * (9 - 1) * 5 - (2 + (3 * 4))) *
(7 - (3 - 1)) + 1) * 2}
```

In spite of this, the syntactic description of VSL is very simple. This is because our syntax diagrams are *recursive*; indirectly, we define an expression in terms of itself, since an expression contains a term, a term contains a factor, and a factor may again contain an expression. It is therefore quite natural to use recursive functions when we are writing a program to process expressions, as the next section will show.

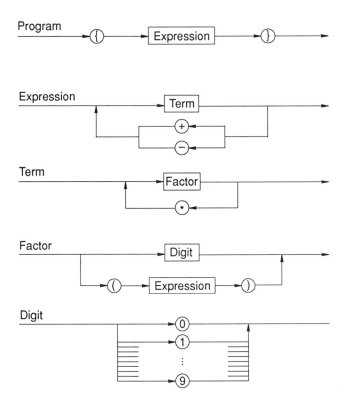

Figure 11.1 *Syntax diagrams for VSL*

We have not explicitly discussed any precedence rules for the three operators +, −, *, but the above syntactic descriptions, both in words and in syntax diagrams, clearly suggest that * has higher precedence than + and −. After all, a term is composed of factors, not the other way round. For example, since each of two lines

```
2 * 4 * 1
7 * 5
```

denotes a term and because terms are separated by + and −, the line

```
2 * 4 * 1 + 7 * 5
```

represents an expression consisting of two terms separated by +. This makes it clear that this expression is to be read as

```
(2 * 4 * 1) + (7 * 5)
```

and not, for example, as

```
(2 * 4 * 1 + 7) * 5
```

Incidentally, the latter form would be the correct interpretation if * and + had equal precedence.

We can represent our expressions as binary trees, as Figure 11.2 shows.

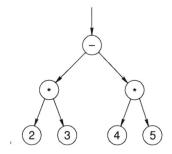

*Figure 11.2 Binary tree for 2 * 3 – 4 * 5*

This tree clearly shows that the minus operator is to be applied to the terms 2 * 3 and 4 * 5. Note that we are using only *binary* operators, so

```
{2 * 3 - 4 * 5}
```

must not be written

```
{-4 * 5 + 2 * 3}
```

because we do not implement the *unary* operator –, used in the last line. Another point worth observing is that our operators are *left-associative*. This is relevant for operators with the same precedence, as + and – in our language VSL. For example, the expression

```
9 - 3 + 1
```

means

```
(9 - 3) + 1
```

and not

```
9 - (3 + 1)
```

We can see the difference between the second and the third of these three expressions very clearly by examining their binary trees. Since 9 − 3 + 1 and (9 − 3) + 1 have exactly the same meaning, they correspond with the same binary tree, shown in Figure 11.3(a). The tree for the expression 9 − (3 + 1) is different, as Figure 11.3(b) shows.

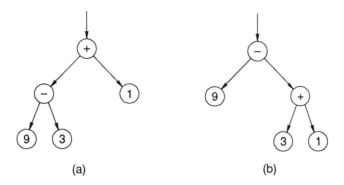

Figure 11.3 Binary trees for: (a) 9 – 3 + 1; (b) 9 – (3 + 1)

11.2 A Source-text Interpreter

When designing a programming language, we have to define it not only *syntactically*, but also *semantically*, that is, each valid language construct must be given a *meaning* in terms of the operations to be performed. In our case, the language is so simple that the meaning of VSL programs can be expressed in few words. We want the given expression to be evaluated according to the usual arithmetic rules and the resulting integer to be printed. For example, the program

```
{9 - 2 * 4}
```

means that the product of 2 and 4 is to be subtracted from 9 and that the resulting value, 1, is to be printed.

In this section, we will write a C++ program which accepts any VSL program and performs the actions prescribed by it, so with the VSL program {9 – 2 * 4} as input, the output of our C++ program will be 1. We will call this C++ program an *interpreter*, and, more specifically, a *source-text* interpreter. The term *source text* is used here for VSL programs to distinguish them from any code derived from them, as we will discuss after this section.

Our method of analyzing source text is known as *recursive descent*, because it is based on a hierarchy of recursive functions. In principle, there is a function for each syntactic category, such as *factor*. Each of these functions has a well-defined task, which can be expressed in terms of its input data and its return value. For example, each time the function *factor* is called, it reads one factor, which may be a simple or a more complex one, such as these two examples:

```
5
(3 - 4 * 5 - (3 + 6 * 2))
```

(Note that, according to Section 11.1, there would not be a factor on the last line if the outer pair of parentheses were omitted.) Not only does this function *read* a factor; it also *evaluates* it and returns its (integer) value. For example, if function *factor* reads the factor consisting of only the character '5', it will return the integer 5, which we compute in the interpreter as

```
'5' - '0'
```

If the function *factor* reads and processes the more complex factor $(3 - 4 * 5 - (3 + 6 * 2))$, it will also return the correct value, which is -32 in this case.

Although each integer in VSL consists of only one character, the output can be any integer, such as -32 in the last example. If the input is incorrect, we will print an error message and stop program execution. Blanks and newline characters will be allowed in the input, which enables us to write VSL programs on more than one line. When reading characters, we may sometimes find it convenient to look one character ahead, or, equivalently, to push one character back into the input stream. In C we normally do this by using *ungetc*, in C++ by *putback*. Our approach will be slightly different because each time we read a character we will also display it; if a character were pushed back (by *ungetc* or *putback*) and read later again, it would be displayed once again. To prevent this, we will rather use a variable *buf* as a character buffer of our own. The advantage of this is that we can initially set it to zero (that is, the null character) to indicate that it is 'empty'. When a new character is desired we first test to see if there is one available in *buf*. If so, we use it and make *buf* zero; if no character is found in *buf* because it is empty, we read one from the input file and display it on the screen. Pushing a character back in the input stream now simply means assigning this character to *buf*.

The actual reading from the input file and writing onto the screen is done in the function *next*. There is also function *NextIs*, which we use to examine whether a given character can be read from the input stream. If this is the case, *NextIs* reads this character and returns 1; if not, it returns 0. This is implemented by reading a character and placing it back into *buf* if it is not identical with the given character. This way of reading characters conditionally is very convenient in programs that analyze their input character by character. For example, a VSL term consists of one or more factors separated by *, so to read a term we begin by reading a factor; if this is followed by *, another factor must follow, and so on. Our function *term* can therefore be extremely simple:

```
int interpreter::term()
{   int x;
    x = factor();
    while (NextIs('*'))
       x *= factor();
    return x;
}
```

Program *interprt* shows further details; it should be studied in connection with the syntax diagrams of Section 11.1.

```
// interprt: A source-text interpreter for vsl
#include <fstream.h>
#include <iomanip.h>
#include <stdlib.h>
#include <ctype.h>
class interpreter {
public:
    void prepare();
    void interpret();
    void output()
    { cout << "\n\nComputed value: " << result << endl;
    }
private:
    int factor();
    int term();
    int expression();
    void error(const char *s)
    { cout << "\nError: " << s << endl; exit(1);
    }
    char next();
    int NextIs(char chGiven);
    int isnum(char ch){return ch == '-' || isdigit(ch);}
    int result;
    char buf;
    ifstream file;
};

void interpreter::prepare()
{ char fname[51];
    cout << "This program reads an input file, containing\n";
    cout << "a VSL program, such as, for example, {3-2*5}\n";
    cout << "\nName of input file: "; cin >> setw(51) >> fname;
    file.open(fname, ios::in | ios::nocreate);
    if (file.fail()) error("Cannot open input file.");
    cout << "VSL program read from file:\n\n";
    buf = '\0';
}

void interpreter::interpret()
{ if (!NextIs('{')) error("Open brace ({) expected.\n");
    result = expression();
    if (!NextIs('}')) error("Close brace (}) expected.\n");
}

char interpreter::next()
{ char ch;
    do
    { if (buf) {ch = buf; buf = 0;} else
        { file.get(ch);
            if (file.fail()) error("Premature end of file?");
            cout << ch;
        }
    } while (isspace(ch));
    return ch;
}
```

```
int interpreter::NextIs(char chGiven)
{  char ch = next();
   if (ch != chGiven) buf = ch;
   return ch == chGiven;
}

int interpreter::factor()
{  int x;
   char ch=next();
   if (isdigit(ch)) x = ch - '0'; else
   if (ch == '(')
   {  x = expression();
      if (!NextIs(')')) error("')' expected");
   }  else error("Digit or '(' expected");
   return x;
}

int interpreter::term()
{  int x;
   x = factor();
   while (NextIs('*')) x *= factor();
   return x;
}

int interpreter::expression()
{  int x = term();
   for ( ; ; )
   {  if (NextIs('+')) x += term(); else
      if (NextIs('-')) x -= term(); else break;
   }
   return x;
}

int main()
{  interpreter I;
   I.prepare();
   I.interpret();
   I.output();
   return 0;
}
```

Program *interprt* reads a VSL program from a file prepared by the user, and it also displays each character read from this file, so in the following demonstration we need not list the contents of file *test.txt* separately:

```
This program reads an input file, containing
a VSL program, such as, for example, {3-2*5}

Name of input file: test.txt
VSL program read from file:

{ 2
  + 3 * 4 * (7 - 2 - 1)
  - (1 + 2)
}

Computed value: 47
```

11.3 Conversion from Infix to Postfix

We usually place a binary operator *between* its two operands, as in 8 − 3, for example, and we call this *infix* notation. Instead, we may place the same operator either before or after its operands, and we use the terms *prefix* and *postfix* for these notations. Thus we have:

        − 8 3 prefix
        8 − 3 infix
        8 3 − postfix

The usual notation of functions with arguments is essentially prefix notation; for example, if we define the function *subtract* and write

        subtract(8, 3)

to represent the difference 8 − 3 = 5, we can regard the function name *subtract* as an operator, written before its operands 8 and 3. However, in the framework of compiler construction, we are more interested in postfix notation, which, incidentally, is also known as *reverse Polish*. Postfix expressions can be evaluated very straightforwardly, as Section 11.4 will show. For the time being, let us assume that they are useful, so that it makes sense to perform automatic conversion from infix to postfix. If an infix expression is represented by a binary tree, as shown by Figures 11.2 and 11.3, we can find the corresponding postfix expression by traversing this tree (and its subtrees) as follows:

1. Traverse the left subtree.
2. Traverse the right subtree.
3. Use the root node of the (sub-)tree.

Applying this to the left and the right subtrees in Figure 11.2, we obtain 2 3 * and 4 5 *, respectively. For the entire tree, we find the postfix expression

        2   3   *   4   5   *   −

Note that we do not need any parentheses in postfix notation. For example, Figures 11.3(a) and 11.3(b) lead to:

        Infix   *Postfix*
        9 − 3 − 1   9 3 − 1 −
        9 − (3 − 1)   9 3 1 − −

Fortunately, it will not be necessary to build a real binary tree because we do not need all information in the tree at the same time. However, we will use recursion, which is closely related to trees, as we have seen in Section 1.5. The basic idea of our method is quite simple. Let us focus on a term, which has infix form

$$f_1 * f_2 * f_3 * \ldots * f_n$$

where $f_1, ..., f_n$ are factors. To transform this into postfix, all we need is a function (to be called *term*) which reads this from an input file and writes the desired postfix form

$$f_1 \ f_2 \ * \ f_3 \ * \ ... \ f_n \ *$$

to an output file. So first we have to copy factor f_1, which is always present. If an asterisk follows, we read it, but we postpone writing it until we have copied f_2; in other words, we read * f_2 and write f_2 *. Similarly, if an asterisk follows, both * and f_3 are read in that order and written in the reverse order, and so on. Using function *NextIs* in the same way as in program *interpret* (see Section 11.2) and stream *ofile* for the output file, we can write this function *term* as follows:

```
void InfixToPostfix::term()
{  factor();
   while (NextIs('*'))
   {  factor();
      ofile << '*';
   }
}
```

This function really does what we have said above, provided that function *factor*, used here, performs its copying task properly. If the factor to be copied is a only a digit, it is to be copied literally. For example, if the input is

    3 * 8

then the digit 3 is copied by the first call of *factor*, before the while-loop is entered. In the inner part of the loop, there is another call of *factor*, which copies 8. The important point to be noticed is that the asterisk is read before copying 8, but is written after it, so that the output is

    3 8 *

In the case of more complex factors, they must not be copied literally, but instead must in turn be converted from infix to postfix. For example, if one of these factors is read as

    (9 - 5)

it is to be written as

    9 5 -

So we do not write the parentheses in the output, and we deal with the remaining infix expression $9 - 5$ in a way that is similar to the way we would deal with $9 * 5$. Program *postfix* shows further details.

```
/* postfix: Conversion from infix to postfix; the input
      consists of a VSL program, which has the form

          { expression }

      The given expression is converted to postfix, and
      written to another file. The names of both files
      are to be supplied by the user.
*/

#include <fstream.h>
#include <iomanip.h>
#include <stdlib.h>
#include <ctype.h>

class InfixToPostfix {
public:
    void prepare();
    void convert();
    void show();
private:
    void factor();
    void term();
    void expression();
    void error(const char* s)
    {   cout << "\nError: " << s << endl; exit(1);
    }
    char next();
    int NextIs(char chGiven);
    int isnum(char ch){return ch == '-' || isdigit(ch);}
    int result;
    char buf;
    ifstream ifile;
    fstream ofile;
};

void InfixToPostfix::prepare()
{   char fname[51];
    cout << "This program reads an input file, containing\n";
    cout << "a VSL program, such as, for example, {3-2*5}\n";

    cout << "\nName of input file: ";
    cin >> setw(51) >> fname;
    ifile.open(fname, ios::in | ios::nocreate);
    if (ifile.fail()) error("Cannot open input file.");

    cout << "\nName of output file: ";
    cin >> setw(51) >> fname;
    ofile.open(fname, ios::out | ios::in | ios::trunc);
    if (ofile.fail()) error("Cannot open output file.");

    cout << "VSL program read from file:\n\n";
    buf = '\0';
}
```

```cpp
void InfixToPostfix::convert()
{  if (!NextIs('{'))
      error("Open brace ({) expected.\n");
   expression();
   if (!NextIs('}'))
      error("Close brace (}) expected.\n");
}

void InfixToPostfix::show() // Copy output file to screen:
{  char ch;
   cout << "\n\nContents of output file (postfix):\n";
   ofile.seekg(0, ios::beg);
   for (;;)
   {  ofile >> ch;
      if (ofile.fail()) break;
      cout << ch;
   }
}

char InfixToPostfix::next()
{  char ch;
   do
   {  if (buf) {ch = buf; buf = 0;} else
      {  ifile.get(ch);
         if (ifile.fail())
            error("Premature end of file?");
         cout << ch;
      }
   }  while (isspace(ch));
   return ch;
}

int InfixToPostfix::NextIs(char chGiven)
{  char ch = next();
   if (ch != chGiven) buf = ch;
   return ch == chGiven;
}

void InfixToPostfix::factor()
{  char ch = next();
   if (isdigit(ch)) ofile << ch; else
   if (ch == '(')
   {  expression();
      if (!NextIs(')'))
         error("')' expected");
   }  else error("Digit or '(' expected");
}

void InfixToPostfix::term()
{  factor();
   while (NextIs('*'))
   {  factor();
      ofile << '*';
   }
}
```

```
void InfixToPostfix::expression()
{  term();
   for ( ; ; )
   {  if (NextIs('+')) {term(); ofile << '+';} else
      if (NextIs('-')) {term(); ofile << '-';} else
         break;
   }
}

int main()
{  InfixToPostfix IP;
   IP.prepare();
   IP.convert();
   IP.show();
   return 0;
}
```

The results are first placed in an output file, which we will use in Section 11.4. Then they are copied to the screen, so that we can immediately see what the result is. There are only digits and operators in the output file, no white-space characters. This causes no ambiguity at all because all integers in VSL consist of only one digit. Thus, in the following demonstration, 34 stands for the two integers 3 and 4:

```
This program reads an input file, containing
a VSL program, such as, for example, {3-2*5}

Name of input file: infix.txt
Name of output file: postfix.txt
VSL program read from file:

{ 3 * 4 - 5 * 6
  - 7 * (4 + 2 + 2)
}

Contents of output file (postfix):
34*56*-742+2+*-
```

11.4 A Postfix Interpreter

It is now time to see why postfix expressions are useful. In Section 11.3, we did not compute the integer values associated with the given infix expressions. Instead, we produced postfix expressions, and these might seem to be of little use if we want the integer values, as computed in Section 11.2. We will now discuss how to evaluate postfix expressions, and we will see that this can be done extremely simply. The main tool to be used is a *stack*. Scanning a given postfix expression from left to right, we place each operand on this stack, so that each time the stack height increases by 1. Whenever, during this scan, we encounter an operator, we apply the corresponding operation to the two most recent operands on the stack, and the result of that operation will replace these two operands, so that the stack height decreases by 1. For example, with the VSL program

```
{5 - 3 - 4 - 7 * 3}
```

as input, program *postfix* gives the postfix expression

```
53-4-73*-
```

as output, and this gives rise to the successive stack contents shown in Figure 11.4.

							3	
	3		4			7	7	21
5	5	2	2	-2	-2	-2	-2	-23

Figure 11.4 Successive stack contents, when evaluating 5 3 – 4 – 7 3 * –

In each column, we find the stack elements $s[0]$, $s[1]$, ..., from bottom to top. We begin with $s[0] = 5$, as shown in the first column. Then 3, the second character of the postfix expression, is placed in $s[1]$, as the second column shows. We now encounter the minus operator (–) in the postfix expression, so we compute

$$5 - 3 = 2$$

and place the result in $s[0]$ (see the third column) so that it replaces the values 5 and 3. The important thing is that if we proceed in this way, we end with $s[0] = -23$, which is just the value we want as the result of the given VSL program. Thus, if $s[t]$ is the next free stack location, each integer i in the postfix expression will be pushed on the stack as follows:

```
s[t++] = i;
```

Also, the operator + performs the operation

```
t--; s[t-1] += s[t];
```

and the two other operators – and * work similarly. In every (infix or postfix) expression with only binary operators, the number of operators is one less than the number of operands. For example, in the above expression we have five operands and four operators. Each operand causes the stack pointer t to be increased by one and each operator causes it to be decreased by one. Altogether, this means that the final value of t is one higher than its initial value. So if initially we have $t = 0$, then we end with $t = 1$. The latter implies that $s[1]$ is the next free location, so the result is $s[0]$. We will assume that there is a file with a correct postfix expression, produced by program *postfix*. Then program *postint* is a postfix interpreter, which reads the given file and computes the desired integer result.

```
// postint:
//    A postfix interpreter, which interprets the
//    postfix expression produced by program 'postfix'.
#include <fstream.h>
#include <iomanip.h>
#include <ctype.h>
#include <stdlib.h>
```

```
class PostfixInterpreter {
public:
   void prepare();
   void evaluate();
   void output()
   {  cout << "\nComputed result: " << s[0] << endl;
   }
private:
   enum {StackSize = 30};
   int t, s[StackSize];
   ifstream file;
   void push(int i)
   {  if (t == StackSize) error("StackSize too small");
      s[t++] = i;
   }
   void add(){t--; s[t-1] += s[t];}
   void subtract(){t--; s[t-1] -= s[t];}
   void multiply(){t--; s[t-1] *= s[t];}
   void error(const char *str)
   {  cout << "\nError: " << str << endl; exit(1);
   }
};

void PostfixInterpreter::prepare()
{  char fname[51];
   cout << "Name of input file (postfix): ";
   cin >> setw(51) >> fname;
   file.open(fname, ios::in | ios::nocreate);
   if (file.fail()) error("Cannot open input file.");
   t = 0;
}

void PostfixInterpreter::evaluate()
{  char ch;
   cout << "The given postfix expression is\n";
   for (;;)
   {  file >> ch;
      if (file.fail()) break;
      cout << ch;
      if (isdigit(ch)) push(ch - '0'); else
      if (ch == '+') add(); else
      if (ch == '-') subtract(); else
      if (ch == '*') multiply(); else break;
   }
   if (t != 1) error("incorrect postfix expression.");
}

int main()
{  PostfixInterpreter P;
   P.prepare();
   P.evaluate();
   P.output();
   return 0;
}
```

Let us use the last example of Section 11.3 to demonstrate this program. Recall that our VSL program was

{3 * 4 - 5 * 6 - 7 * (4 + 2 + 2)}

so we eventually have to compute:

$12 - 30 - 7 * 8 = -74$

Executing program *postint*, and supplying the file *postfix.txt*, produced by program *postfix* on the basis of this example, we obtain this desired result:

```
Name of input file (postfix): postfix.txt
The given postfix expression is
34*56*-742+2+*-
Computed result: -74
```

It will be clear that we can combine the programs *postfix* and *postint*, and it is then not difficult to develop a program that we can use in the same way as *interprt* in Section 11.2. Program *interprt* interprets the source code immediately, whereas the combined new program uses a postfix expression as intermediate code. For a real programming language, the latter method is more efficient. Real interpreters usually first produce some intermediate code, which is subsequently interpreted. This has the advantage that in loops, where the same type of computation is done repeatedly, the relatively time-consuming task of processing the original source text, and performing all kinds of syntactic checks, is done only once; after this stage, we have intermediate code available, which can be interpreted more rapidly than the source text. However, if we are not dealing with a complete programming language, but have instead only to interpret arithmetic expressions, even though these may be more realistic than those in VSL, it is not particularly advantageous to use postfix expressions as intermediate code, so direct interpretation of the source text, in the spirit of Section 11.2, should be seriously considered.

11.5 Object Program and Run-time System

In the previous section we saw that there may be good reasons to separate the actual computation from the syntactic analysis, and to interpret intermediate code rather than the given source code. We can go a significant step further in this direction. Instead of generating intermediate code that has to be interpreted, we can generate executable code, consisting of real program text. Traditionally, a real compiler translates a program from source text into machine code. This can be done by first producing assembly language, and subsequently transforming this to machine code. Automatically generated assembly-language code is not the same as machine code, but its purpose is similar, and it is fundamentally different from intermediate code as used in Section 11.4. Although the task of producing machine code is delegated to an assembler (which relieves the task of the compiler), the final result will be an autonomous program, which has full control over the machine. Note that this is not the case when we are using an interpreter; the intermediate code then acts merely as input data; we do not transfer control to it. Thus, the distinction between an interpreter and a (code-generating) compiler can be summarized as follows. An interpreter keeps control over the machine, and performs actions prescribed by its input data, which is either source text or intermediate code. A compiler, on the other hand, produces code that will eventually result in an independent program. Let us use the term *object program* for such code, even though it does not yet have the form of machine code. Before writing a compiler to produce object programs, we have to think about the structure of these object programs themselves. To keep our discussion machine-independent, we will not use real assembly language (let alone machine code). Instead, our object programs will consist of C text (also conforming to the C++ language rules). Unlike everywhere else in this book, we prefer C to C++ here, deliberately restricting ourselves to low-level language elements because we want to mimic machine or assembly code. We prefer C++ for programs that we write ourselves, C for automatically generated programs. For example, consider the following VSL program:

```
{9 - 2 * 4 + 5}
```

Rewriting this in postfix would give

```
9 2 4 * - 5 +
```

Instead, the VSL compiler (to be discussed in Section 11.6) will translate $\{9 - 2 * 4 + 5\}$ into the object program that starts after the following comment:

```
/* object.c: Sample object program, generated by the
              'compiler' to be discussed in Section 11.6
              (to be linked with rts.c).
*/

int main(void)
{   void push(int i), add(void), subtract(void),
         multiply(void), PrintResult(void);

    push(9);
    push(2);
    push(4);
    multiply();
    subtract();
    push(5);
    add();
    PrintResult();
    return 0;
}
```

Note the resemblance between this and the above postfix expression: we find *push*(9) instead of 9, *multiply*() instead of *, and so on. This object program is a syntactically correct C module, which can be compiled by any (ANSI) C or C++ compiler. Instead of producing assembly language, to be processed by an assembler, our VSL compiler will produce C code such as the above example. Such 'object modules' have the same structure as assembly-language modules that consist only of subroutine calls. With some imagination we may therefore consider our object programs to be expressed in a machine-independent assembly language, which in turn is only a means to present machine code in a reasonably readable form. Our object modules, though expressed in C for reasons of readability, are essentially no different from object modules in machine code. (The modules *object.c* and *rts.c* are at the same time valid C++ modules, but we give them *.c* file-name extensions because they only contain 'low-level' code, similar to assembly language.)

To form a ready-to-run program, we have to supply an additional program module, which we call a *run-time system*. We will express this also in C, but again we will be using only very simple and low-level C-language concepts, so that run-time system *rts.c* may be regarded as being expressed in a very readable machine code:

```
/* rts.c: A run-time system for VSL; after compilation,
         this module is to be linked with object.c or
         with another file generated by the 'compiler'
         of Section 11.6.
*/

#include <stdio.h>
#include <stdlib.h>

#define STACKSIZE 20
int t, s[STACKSIZE]; /*  Initially, t = 0  */

void error(char *str)
{  printf("\n\nError: %s\n", str); exit(1);
}

void push(int i)
{  if (t == STACKSIZE)
     error(
     "STACKSIZE too small for this postfix expression");
     s[t++] = i;
}

void add(void)
{  t--; s[t-1] += s[t];
}

void subtract(void)
{  t--; s[t-1] -= s[t];
}

void multiply(void)
{  t--; s[t-1] *= s[t];
}

void PrintResult(void)
{  if (t != 1) error("Incorrect object program");
     printf("Result: %d\n", s[0]);
}
```

If we compile object program *object.c* and we link it together with the compiled version of *rts*, we obtain an executable program, which, when executed, gives the output

```
Result: 6
```

Recall that we used

```
{9 - 2 * 4 + 5}
```

as input for our compiler, so the above result is what we expect.

It should be noted that our run-time system does not depend on the particular VSL program that we are dealing with. It need therefore be compiled only once, so its compiled version, say, *rts.obj*, is a constant component, whereas, for each VSL program that we want to deal with, we have to generate a program *object.c*, the variable component. The name we chose for the latter reflects that it is an object program generated by our VSL compiler, to be discussed in Section 11.6. Curiously enough, the 'object program' *object.c* is a source program for the standard C (or C++) compiler. This might seem confusing, but we should not forget that we are expressing our 'object programs' in C merely for reasons of readability. If we had expressed them immediately in machine language, we would have avoided any confusion of this kind.

11.6 A VSL Compiler

There is only one thing that remains to be done, namely translating a given VSL program, such as

```
{9 - 2 * 4 + 5}
```

into the corresponding object program, such as *object.c* in Section 11.5. Since this object program is essentially a postfix expression, such as

```
9 2 4 * - 5 +
```

in a different notation, and since in Section 11.3 we have already written program *postfix* to produce postfix, our remaining task is extremely simple. All we have to do is to alter the code-generating parts of *postfix*. After doing this we obtain the following program:

```
/* compiler:
    This program has been derived from postfix, discussed
    in Section 11.3. It reads a VSL program, and translates
    it into the VSL object program object.c. The latter is
    a C program with the structure of an assembly-language
    program. After compiling object.c by a standard C
    compiler, it is to be linked together with the compiled
    version of rts, see Section 11.5.
*/
```

```cpp
#include <fstream.h>
#include <iomanip.h>
#include <stdlib.h>
#include <ctype.h>

class compiler {
public:
    void prepare();
    void compile();
    void show();
private:
    void factor();
    void term();
    void expression();
    void error(const char* s)
    {   cout << "\nError: " << s << endl; exit(1);
    }
    char next();
    int NextIs(char chGiven);
    int isnum(char ch){return ch == '-' || isdigit(ch);}
    int result;
    char buf;
    ifstream ifile;
    fstream ofile;
};

void compiler::prepare()
{   char fname[51];
    cout << "This program reads an input file, containing\n";
    cout << "a VSL program, such as, for example, {3-2*5}\n";
    cout << "The resulting object module will be written\n"
            "to the file object.c.\n";
    cout << "\nName of input file: ";
    cin >> setw(51) >> fname;
    ifile.open(fname, ios::in | ios::nocreate);
    if (ifile.fail())
        error("Cannot open input file.");
    ofile.open("object.c", ios::out | ios::in | ios::trunc);
    if (ofile.fail())
        error("Cannot open output file.");
    cout << "VSL program read from file:\n\n";
    buf = '\0';
}

void compiler::compile()
{   if (!NextIs('{')) error("Open brace ({) expected.\n");
    ofile <<
    "int main(void)\n"
    "{   void push(int i), add(void), subtract(void),\n"
    "         multiply(void), PrintResult(void);\n";
    expression();
    ofile << "    PrintResult();\n"
             "    return 0;\n}\n";
    if (!NextIs('}')) error("Close brace (}) expected.\n");
}
```

```
void compiler::show() // Copy output file to screen:
{   char ch;
    cout << "\n\nContents of output file object.c:\n\n";
    ofile.seekg(0, ios::beg);
    for (;;)
    {   ofile.get(ch);
        if (ofile.fail()) break;
        cout << ch;
    }
}

char compiler::next()
{   char ch;
    do
    {   if (buf) {ch = buf; buf = 0;} else
        {   ifile.get(ch);
            if (ifile.fail()) error("Premature end of file?");
            cout << ch;
        }
    } while (isspace(ch));
    return ch;
}

int compiler::NextIs(char chGiven)
{   char ch = next();
    if (ch != chGiven) buf = ch;
    return ch == chGiven;
}

void compiler::factor()
{   char ch = next();
    if (isdigit(ch))
        ofile << "   push(" << ch << ");\n"; else
    if (ch == '(')
    {   expression();
        if (!NextIs(')')) error("')' expected");
    } else error("Digit or '(' expected");
}

void compiler::term()
{   factor();
    while (NextIs('*'))
    {   factor(); ofile << "   multiply();\n";
    }
}

void compiler::expression()
{   term();
    for ( ; ; )
    {   if (NextIs('+'))
        {   term(); ofile << "   add();\n";
        } else
        if (NextIs('-'))
        {   term(); ofile << "   subtract();\n";
        } else break;
    }
}
```

```
int main()
{  compiler C;
   C.prepare();
   C.compile();
   C.show();
   return 0;
}
```

For a demonstration, let us use the same file *infix.txt* as in Sections 11.3 and 11.4, where we used the programs *postfix* and *postint* to compute the value −74. Here, too, we need two steps. We first run the above compiler, to obtain:

```
This program reads an input file, containing
a VSL program, such as, for example, {3-2*5}
The resulting object module will be written
to the file object.c.

Name of input file: infix.txt
VSL program read from file:

{ 3 * 4 - 5 * 6
  - 7 * (4 + 2 + 2)
}

Contents of output file object.c:

int main(void)
{  void push(int i), add(void), subtract(void),
        multiply(void), PrintResult(void);
   push(3);
   push(4);
   multiply();
   push(5);
   push(6);
   multiply();
   subtract();
   push(7);
   push(4);
   push(2);
   add();
   push(2);
   add();
   multiply();
   subtract();
   PrintResult();
   return 0;
}
```

After compiling this and linking the result together with (the compiled version *rts.obj* of) *rts.c* (see Section 11.5), we obtain an executable program which when executed gives the expected output:

```
Result: -74
```

Exercises

Each of the exercises 11.1–11.4 can be implemented in three ways:

(1)   By a source-text interpreter: see Section 11.2.
(2)   By both a conversion from infix to postfix and a postfix interpreter: see Sections 11.3 and 11.4.
(3)   By both a compiler producing an object program and a run-time system: see Sections 11.5 and 11.6.

11.1   Extend the language VSL to admit also integers of more than one decimal digit, and implement the extended language.

11.2   Extend VSL to admit the binary operators / and %, which, respectively, yield the quotient and the remainder of an integer division. Implement the extended language.

11.3   Extend VSL to admit the unary minus operator. Since we have

```
(-a) * b  =  -(a * b)
```

you may regard the expression

```
- a * b
```

either as the product of $-a$ and b or as the negated product of a and b (where a and b stand for decimal digits). This means that you must make a choice: you can apply the new minus operator either to a factor or to a term, whichever you prefer. If you apply it to a factor (and define the result to be a factor as well), you will admit constructions such as

```
3 * - - -(4 * 5)
```

Such constructions are not valid if the unary minus operator is applied to a term, since then − cannot immediately follow *. It is instructive to notice the difference between C(++) and Pascal in this regard. In any postfix output a unary minus operator must be represented by a different character, say $, to distinguish it from a binary minus operator; it is placed after its operand. For example, depending on the choice mentioned above, the postfix equivalent of $- a * b$ is either

```
a $ b *
```

or

```
a b * $
```

Implement the extended language.

11.4   Define and implement the 'Very Logical Language' VLL. Expressions in VLL may contain:

- the characters 0 and 1 (to be regarded as false and true, respectively),
- the operators !, &, |, listed here with decreasing precedence and meaning NOT, AND and OR,
- parentheses, with their usual meaning.

11.5   Write a calculator program, similar to the source-text interpreter of Section 11.2. An (infix) expression is to be read from the keyboard rather than from a file. Use class *large* (see Section 2.7 and Appendix A) to admit very large integers. Define a language with constants, parentheses and the operators +, −, *, / and % as its components. An equals sign signals the end of the input. For example, it must be possible for the user to enter the following input:

```
1 + 12345678901234567890 * 123456789012345 / (9876543 +
1122 + 3344) =
```

This will result in the following output:

```
1542512384437535597789218283
```

A Class for Large Integers

The first part of the following header-file also occurs in Section 2.7:

```
// large.h: Multi-precision integer arithmetic.
#include <iostream.h>
typedef unsigned int uint;

class large {
public:
    large(const char *str);
    large(int i);
    large(uint i=0);
    large(long i);
    large(const large &v);
    ~large(){delete[]p;}
    friend large operator+(large x, const large &y);
    friend large operator-(large x, const large &y);
    friend large operator*(large x, const large &y);
    friend large operator/(large x, const large &y);
    friend large operator%(large x, const large &y);
    friend large operator<<(large u, uint k);
    friend large operator>>(large u, uint k);
    large operator-()const;
    large &operator=(const large &y);
    large &operator+=(const large &y);
    large &operator-=(const large &y);
    large &operator*=(int y);
    large &operator*=(uint y);
    large &operator*=(large y);
    large &operator/=(const large &divisor);
    large &operator%=(const large &divisor);
    large &operator<<=(uint k);
    large &operator>>=(uint k);
    friend int operator==(const large &x, const large &y)
        {return x.compare(y)==0;}
    friend int operator!=(const large &x, const large &y)
        {return x.compare(y)!=0;}
```

```
    friend int operator<(const large &x, const large &y)
        {return x.compare(y) < 0;}
    friend int operator>(const large &x, const large &y)
        {return x.compare(y) > 0;}
    friend int operator<=(const large &x, const large &y)
        {return x.compare(y)<=0;}
    friend int operator>=(const large &x, const large &y)
        {return x.compare(y)>=0;}
    friend ostream &operator<<(ostream &os, const large &v);
    friend istream &operator>>(istream &os, large &v);
    friend large power(large x, uint n);
    friend large sqrt(const large &x);
    friend large abs(const large &x);
private:
    uint *p;
    int len, Len, neg; // len in use, Len allocated
    void IncrLen(int lenNew);
    int RoundUp(int i)const;
    void SetLen(uint n);
    void reduce();
    void MakeLarge(uint i);
    int compare(const large &y)const;
    void DDproduct(uint A, uint B, uint &Hi, uint &Lo)const;
    uint DDquotient(uint A, uint B, uint d)const;
    void subtractmul(uint *a, uint *b, int n, uint &q)const;
    int normalize(large &denom, large &num, int &x)const;
    void unnormalize(large &rem, int x, int SecondDone)const;
    void divide(large denom,
        large &quot, large &rem, int RemDesired)const;
    friend class numstring;
};
```

The implementation file is listed below. It is not based on any assumption about the word length, and it has been tested with Microsoft Visual C++ and Linux/GNU C++ (both 32-bit) and also Borland C++ 4.5 (16-bit). Each *large* object has four data members:

p, a pointer used as an array of unsigned int elements,
len, the logical length of this array,
Len, the physical length of this array ($Len \geq len$), and
neg, equal to 0 if the large number in question is positive or 1 if it is negative.

A large number x is stored in array p as a number with radix B, where B is equal to $UINT\_MAX + 1$, that is, B is 2^{16} or 2^{32} for 16- and 32-bit integers, respectively (see also Section 2.6). If x is zero, so is *len*; otherwise $p_i > 0$ for $i = 0, 1, ..., len - 1$, and

$$|x| = p_{len-1} B^{len-1} + p_{len-2} B^{len-2} + ... + p_1 B + p_0$$

Useful references are Knuth (1969) for general background information, Kaliski (1992) for a set of multiple-precision functions in C, and Mifsud (1970) for fast multiple-precision division. Mifsud's algorithm is the basis of the function *large::divide*, which is the most difficult one of this class.

```cpp
// large.cpp: Multi-precision integer arithmetic.
#include <strstrea.h>
// This filename strstrea.h is in accordance
// with the draft C++ standard. If your compiler
// does not accept it, use strstream.h instead.

#include <iomanip.h>
#include <stdlib.h>
#include <limits.h>
#include <string.h>
#include <ctype.h>
#include "large.h"
#define max(x, y) ((x) > (y) ? (x) : (y))
const uint uintmax = UINT_MAX;
const int MemUnit=64; // Use multiples of MemUnit words
const int wLen = sizeof(uint) * 8;  // Number of bits
const int hLen = wLen/2;
const uint rMask = (1 << hLen) - 1;
const uint lMask = uintmax - rMask;
const uint lBit = uintmax - (uintmax >> 1);

void large::IncrLen(int lenNew)
{  int lenOld = len, i;
   len = lenNew;  // len > lenOld
   if (len > Len)
   {  Len = RoundUp(len);
      uint *pOld = p;
      p = new uint[Len];
      for (i=0; i<lenOld; i++) p[i] = pOld[i];
      delete[]pOld;
   }
   for (i=lenOld; i<len; i++) p[i] = 0;
}

int large::RoundUp(int i)const // Find suitable new block size
{  return ((i + i/3) / MemUnit + 1) * MemUnit;
}

void large::SetLen(uint n)
{  len = n;
   if (len > Len)
   {  Len = RoundUp(len);
      delete[]p; p = new uint[Len];
   }
}

void large::reduce()
{  for (int i=len-1; i>=0; i--)
      if (p[i] == 0) len--; else break;
   if (len == 0) neg = 0;
}

void large::MakeLarge(uint i)
{  Len = MemUnit;
   p = new uint[Len]; *p = i;
   len = i != 0;
}
```

```
large::large(const char *str)
{   if (*str == '-'){neg = 1; str++;} else neg = 0;
    int n = strlen(str), i;
    large v=0;
    for (i=0; i<n; i++)
        v = v * 10 + (str[i] - '0');
    len = v.len; Len = RoundUp(len);
    p = new uint[Len];
    for (i=0; i<len; i++) p[i] = v.p[i];
    reduce();
}


large::large(int i)
{   neg = i < 0;
    if (neg) i = -i;
    MakeLarge(uint(i));
}


large::large(long L)
{   neg = L < 0;
    unsigned long UL = neg ? -L : L;
    MakeLarge(uint(UL));
#if LONG_MAX != INT_MAX
    len = 0;
    while (UL != 0)
    {   p[len++] = uint(UL & UINT_MAX);
        UL >>= wLen;
    }
#endif
}


large::large(uint i)
{   neg = 0; MakeLarge(i);
}


large::large(const large &v)
{   len = v.len; Len = v.Len; neg = v.neg;
    p = new uint[Len];
    for (int i=0; i<len; i++) p[i] = v.p[i];
}


large operator+(large x, const large &y){return x+=y;}
large operator-(large x, const large &y){return x-=y;}
large operator*(large x, const large &y){return x*=y;}
large operator/(large x, const large &y){return x/=y;}
large operator%(large x, const large &y){return x%=y;}
large operator<<(large u, uint k){return u <<= k;}
large operator>>(large u, uint k){return u >>= k;}


large large::operator-()const
{   large v = *this; v.neg = !v.neg; return v;
}
```

```
large &large::operator=(const large &y)
{  if (this != &y)
   {  SetLen(y.len); neg = y.neg;
      for (int i=0; i<len; i++) p[i] = y.p[i];
   }
   return *this;
}

large &large::operator+=(const large &y)
{  if (neg != y.neg) return *this -= -y;
   int i;
   uint d, carry = 0;
   IncrLen(max(y.len, len) + 1);
   for (i=0; i<len; i++)
   {  if (i >= y.len && carry == 0) break;
      d = p[i] + carry;
      carry = d < carry;
      if (i < y.len)
      {  p[i] = d + y.p[i];
         if (p[i] < d) carry = 1;
      } else p[i] = d;
   }
   reduce();
   return *this;
}

large &large::operator-=(const large &y)
{  if (neg != y.neg) return *this += -y;
   if (!neg && y > *this || neg && y < *this)
      return *this = -(y - *this);
   int i, borrow = 0;
   uint d;
   for (i=0; i<len; i++)
   {  if (i >= y.len && borrow == 0) break;
      d = p[i] - borrow;
      borrow = d > p[i];
      if (i < y.len)
      {  p[i] = d - y.p[i];
         if (p[i] > d) borrow = 1;
      } else p[i] = d;
   }
   reduce();
   return *this;
}

large &large::operator*=(int y)
{  *this *= uint(y < 0 ? -y : y);
   if (y < 0) neg = !neg;
   return *this;
}

large &large::operator*=(uint y)
{  int len0 = len, i;
   uint Hi, Lo, dig = p[0], carry = 0;
   IncrLen(len + 1);
```

```
      for (i=0; i<len0; i++)
      {  DDproduct(dig, y, Hi, Lo);
         p[i] = Lo + carry;
         dig = p[i+1];
         carry = Hi + (p[i] < Lo);
      }
      p[i] = carry;
      reduce();
      return *this;
   }

   large &large::operator*=(large y)
   {  if (len == 0 || y.len == 0) return *this = 0;
      int DifSigns = neg != y.neg;
      if (len + y.len == 2) // len = y.len = 1
      {  uint a = p[0], b = y.p[0];
         p[0] = a * b;
         if (p[0] / a != b)
         {  len = 2;
            DDproduct(a, b, p[1], p[0]);
         }
         neg = DifSigns;
         return *this;
      }
      if (len == 1)   //  && y.len > 1
      {  uint digit = p[0]; *this = y;
         *this *= digit;
      } else
      if (y.len == 1) *this *= y.p[0]; else
      {  int lenProd = len + y.len, i, jA, jB;
         uint sumHi = 0, sumLo, Hi, Lo,
         sumLoOld, sumHiOld, carry=0;
         large x = *this;
         SetLen(lenProd); // Give *this length lenProd
         for (i=0; i<lenProd; i++)
         {  sumLo = sumHi; sumHi = carry; carry = 0;
            for (jA=0; jA<x.len; jA++)
            {  jB = i - jA;
               if (jB >= 0 && jB < y.len)
               {  DDproduct(x.p[jA], y.p[jB], Hi, Lo);
                  sumLoOld = sumLo; sumHiOld = sumHi;
                  sumLo += Lo;
                  if (sumLo < sumLoOld) sumHi++;
                  sumHi += Hi;
                  carry += (sumHi < sumHiOld);
               }
            }
            p[i] = sumLo;
         }
      }
      reduce();
      neg = DifSigns;
      return *this;
   }
```

```cpp
large &large::operator/=(const large &divisor)
{  large r;
   divide(divisor, *this, r, 0);
   return *this;
}

large &large::operator%=(const large &divisor)
{  large q;
   divide(divisor, q, *this, 1);
   return *this;
}

large &large::operator<<=(uint k)
{  int q = k / wLen;
   if (q) // Increase len by q:
   {  int i;
      IncrLen(len + q);
      for (i=len-1; i>=0; i--)
         p[i] = (i < q ? 0 : p[i - q]);
      k %= wLen;
   }
   if (k)   // 0 < k < wLen:
   {  int k1 = wLen - k;
      uint mask = (1 << k) - 1;
      IncrLen(len + 1);
      for (int i=len-1; i>=0; i--)
      {  p[i] <<= k;
         if (i > 0)
            p[i] |= (p[i-1] >> k1) & mask;
      }
   }
   reduce();
   return *this;
}

large &large::operator>>=(uint k)
{  int q = k / wLen;
   if (q >= len){len = 0; return *this;}
   if (q)
   {  for (int i=q; i<len; i++) p[i-q] = p[i];
      len -= q;
      k %= wLen;
      if (k == 0){reduce(); return *this;}
   }
   int n = len - 1, k1 = wLen - k;
   uint mask = (1 << k) - 1;
   for (int i=0; i<=n; i++)
   {  p[i] >>= k;
      if (i < n)
         p[i] |= ((p[i+1] & mask) << k1);
   }
   reduce();
   return *this;
}
```

```
int large::compare(const large &y)const
{   if (neg != y.neg) return y.neg - neg;
    int code = 0;
    if (len == 0 || y.len == 0) code = len - y.len; else
    if (len < y.len) code = -1; else
    if (len > y.len) code = +1; else
    for (int i = len - 1; i >= 0; i--)
    {   if (p[i] > y.p[i]) {code = 1; break;} else
        if (p[i] < y.p[i]) {code = -1; break;}
    }
    return neg ? -code : code;
}


void large::DDproduct(uint A, uint B,
                        uint &Hi, uint &Lo)const
// Multiplying two digits: (Hi, Lo) = A * B
{   uint hiA = A >> hLen, loA = A & rMask,
         hiB = B >> hLen, loB = B & rMask,
         mid1, mid2, old;
    Lo = loA * loB; Hi = hiA * hiB;
    mid1 = loA * hiB; mid2 = hiA * loB;
    old = Lo;
    Lo += mid1 << hLen; Hi += (Lo < old) + (mid1 >> hLen);
    old = Lo;
    Lo += mid2 << hLen; Hi += (Lo < old) + (mid2 >> hLen);
}


uint large::DDquotient(uint A, uint B, uint d)const
// Divide double word (A, B) by d. Quotient = (qHi, qLo)
{   uint left, middle, right, qHi, qLo, x, dLo1,
         dHi = d >> hLen, dLo = d & rMask;
    qHi = A/(dHi + 1);
    // This initial guess of qHi may be too small.
    middle = qHi * dLo;
    left = qHi * dHi;
    x = B - (middle << hLen);
    A -= (middle >> hLen) + left + (x > B); B = x;
    dLo1 = dLo << hLen;
    // Increase qHi if necessary:
    while (A > dHi || (A == dHi && B >= dLo1))
    {   x = B - dLo1; A -= dHi + (x > B); B = x; qHi++;
    }
    qLo = ((A << hLen) | (B >> hLen))/(dHi + 1);
    // This initial guess of qLo may be too small.
    right = qLo * dLo; middle = qLo * dHi;
    x = B - right; A -= (x > B); B = x;
    x = B - (middle << hLen); A -= (middle >> hLen) + (x > B);
    B = x;
    // Increase qLo if necessary:
    while (A || B >= d)
    {   x = B - d; A -= (x > B); B = x; qLo++;
    }
    return (qHi << hLen) + qLo;
}
```

```
void large::subtractmul(uint *a, uint *b, int n,
   uint &q)const
// a -= q * b: b in n positions; correct q if necessary
{  uint Hi, Lo, d, carry = 0;
   int i;
   for (i=0; i<n; i++)
   {  DDproduct(b[i], q, Hi, Lo);
      d = a[i];
      a[i] -= Lo;
      if (a[i] > d) carry++;
      d = a[i + 1];
      a[i + 1] -= Hi + carry;
      carry = a[i + 1] > d;
   }
   if (carry) // q was too large
   {  q--; carry = 0;
      for (i=0; i<n; i++)
      {  d = a[i] + carry;
         carry = d < carry;
         a[i] = d + b[i];
         if (a[i] < d) carry = 1;
      }
      a[n] = 0;
   }
}


int large::normalize(large &denom, large &num, int &x)const
{  int r = denom.len - 1;
   uint y = denom.p[r]; x = 0;
   while ((y & 1Bit) == 0){y <<= 1; x++;}
   denom <<= x; num <<= x;
   if (r > 0 && denom.p[r] < denom.p[r-1])
   {  denom *= uintmax; num *= uintmax;
      return 1;
   }
   return 0;
}


void large::unnormalize(large &rem, int x, int SecondDone)const
{  if (SecondDone) rem /= uintmax;
   if (x > 0) rem >>= x; else rem.reduce();
}


void large::divide(large denom,
   large &quot, large &rem, int RemDesired)const
{  if (denom.len == 0) {cout << "Zero divide.\n"; return;}
   int QuotNeg = neg ^ denom.neg, RemNeg = neg,
      i, r, SecondDone, x = 0, n;
   uint q, d;
   large num = *this;
   num.neg = denom.neg = 0;
   if (num < denom)
   {  quot = 0; rem = num; rem.neg = RemNeg; return;
   }
```

```
      if (denom.len == 1 && num.len == 1)
      {  quot = uint(num.p[0]/denom.p[0]);
         rem = uint(num.p[0]%denom.p[0]);
         quot.neg = QuotNeg; rem.neg = RemNeg;
         return;
      }  else
      if (denom.len == 1 && (denom.p[0] & lMask) == 0)
      {  // Denominator fits into a half word
         uint divisor = denom.p[0], dHi = 0,
            q1, r, q2, dividend;
         quot.SetLen(len);
         for (int i=len-1; i>=0; i--)
         {  dividend = (dHi << hLen) | (p[i] >> hLen);
            q1 = dividend/divisor; r = dividend % divisor;
            dividend = (r << hLen) | (p[i] & rMask);
            q2 = dividend/divisor; dHi = dividend % divisor;
            quot.p[i] = (q1 << hLen) | q2;
         }
         quot.reduce(); rem = dHi;
         quot.neg = QuotNeg; rem.neg = RemNeg;
         return;
      }
      large num0 = num, denom0 = denom;
      SecondDone = normalize(denom, num, x);
      r = denom.len - 1; n = num.len - 1;
      quot.SetLen(n - r);
      for (i=quot.len-1; i>=0; i--) quot.p[i] = 0;
      rem = num;
      if (rem.p[n] >= denom.p[r])
      {  rem.IncrLen(rem.len + 1); n++;
         quot.IncrLen(quot.len + 1);
      }
      d = denom.p[r];
      for (int k=n; k>r; k--)
      {  q = DDquotient(rem.p[k], rem.p[k-1], d);
         subtractmul(rem.p + k - r - 1, denom.p, r + 1, q);
         quot.p[k - r - 1] = q;
      }
      quot.reduce(); quot.neg = QuotNeg;
      if (RemDesired)
      {  unnormalize(rem, x, SecondDone);
         rem.neg = RemNeg;
      }
   }

large power(large x, uint n)
{  large y=1;
   while (n)
   {  if (n & 1) y *= x;
      x *= x;
      n >>= 1;
   }
   return y;
}
```

```
class numstring {
public:
   numstring(large v);
   ~numstring(){delete[]pStr;}
   char *pStr;
};

numstring::numstring(large v)
{  int len = int(long(v.len) * wLen / 3) + 1, n = len, i = 0;
                                   // 1/3 > ln(2)/ln(10)
   static uint p10 = 1, ip10 = 0;
   pStr = new char[len];
   if (v.len == 0) {*pStr = '0'; i = 1;} else
   {  uint r;
      if (p10 == 1)
      {  while (p10 <= UINT_MAX/10)
         {  p10 *= 10;
            ip10++;
         }
      }                           // p10 is max uint power of 10
      large R, LP10 = p10;   // LP10 = p10 = pow(10, ip10)
      if (v.neg) {*pStr = '-'; i = 1;}
      do
      {  v.divide(LP10, v, R, 1);
         r = (R.len ? R.p[0] : 0);
         for (uint j=0; j<ip10; j++)
         {  pStr[--n] = char(r % 10 + '0');
            r /= 10;
            if (r + v.len == 0) break;
         }
      }  while (v.len);
      while (n < len)
         pStr[i++] = pStr[n++];
   }
   pStr[i] = '\0';
}


ostream &operator<<(ostream &os, const large &v)
{  numstring numstr(v);
   int i=0;
   char ch;
   while ((ch = numstr.pStr[i]) != '\0')
   {  os << ch;
      i++;
   }
   return os;
}


istream &operator>>(istream &is, large &v)
{  char ch;
   v = 0;
   int neg = 0;
   is >> ch;
   if (ch == '-'){neg = 1; is.get(ch);}
```

```
      while (isdigit(ch))
      {   v = v * 10 + (ch - '0');
          is.get(ch);
      }
      if (v.len && neg) v.neg = 1;
      is.putback(ch);
      return is;
}

large sqrt(const large &a)
{   large x = a, b = a, q;
    b <<= 1;
    while (b >>= 2, b > 0)
        x >>= 1;
    while (x > (q = a/x) + 1 || x < q - 1)
    {   x += q;
        x >>= 1;
    }
    return x < q ? x : q;
}

large abs(const large &a)
{   if (a.neg) {large b = a; b.neg = 0; return b;}
    return a;
}
```

Bibliography

Aho, A. V., J. E. Hopcroft, and J. D. Ullman (1983) *Data Structures and Algorithms*, Reading, MA: Addison-Wesley.

Ammeraal, L. (1992) *Programs and Data Structures in C*, 2nd Edition, Chichester: John Wiley.

Ammeraal, L. (1995) *C++ for Programmers*, 2nd Edition, Chichester: John Wiley.

Bellman, R. E. (1957) *Dynamic Programming*, Princeton, NJ: Princeton University Press.

Borwein, J. M., and P. B. Borwein (1987) *Pi and the AGM*, New York, NY: John Wiley.

Cormen, T. H., C. E. Leiserson, and R. L. Rivest (1991) *Introduction to Algorithms*, 5th Edition, Cambridge, MA: MIT Press.

Dijkstra, E. W. (1959) *A note on two problems in connexion with graphs*, Numerische Mathematik, Vol. 1, 269-271.

Flamig, B. (1995) *Practical Algorithms in C++*, New York, NY: John Wiley.

Horowitz, E., and S. Sahni (1977) *Fundamentals of Data Structures*, Bath: Pitman.

Horowitz, E., and S. Sahni (1978) *Fundamentals of Computer Algorithms*, Rockville: Computer Science Press.

Kaliski, B. S. (1992) *Multiple-precision arithmetic in C*, Dr. Dobb's Journal, August 1992.

Knuth, D. E. (1968) *The Art of Computer Programming, Vol. I: Fundamental Algorithms*, Reading, MA: Addison-Wesley.

Knuth, D. E. (1969) *The Art of Computer Programming, Vol. II: Seminumerical Algorithms*, Reading, MA: Addison-Wesley.

Knuth, D. E. (1973) *The Art of Computer Programming, Vol. III: Sorting and Searching*, Reading, MA: Addison-Wesley.

Mifsud, C. J. (1970) *A multiple-precision division algorithm*, Comm. ACM, Vol. 13, Number 11 (November 1970), 666-668.

Sedgewick, R. (1992) *Algorithms in C++*, Reading, MA: Addison-Wesley.

Stroustrup, B. (1986) *The C++ Programming Language*, Reading, MA: Addison-Wesley.

Wirth, N. (1986) *Algorithms and Data Structures*, Englewood Cliffs, NJ: Prentice-Hall.

Index